"One of the most important books in decades defending capitalism. Well researched and well written, it not only makes the case for free markets but also demolishes Thomas Piketty's much publicized tract trashing capitalism. Adam Smith would have been impressed—and proud."

STEVE FORBES, CHAIRMAN AND EDITOR-IN-CHIEF OF FORBES MEDIA

"Supporters of capitalism should keep a copy of *In Defense of Capitalism* close at hand wherever they are. Historian Rainer Zitelmann's new book is full of interesting and convincing arguments that will not only make the reader understand that capitalism is the greatest invention in human history, but also equip them to counter the negative arguments against it. The many myths critical of capitalism are refuted with a wealth of facts and cogent arguments that the critics will not be able to effectively answer. Anyone who wants to know the truth about capitalism should read this book."

JOHN MACKEY, WHOLE FOODS MARKETS FOUNDER

"Capitalism has long been defined by its enemies. They mischaracterize it as cronyism, when the true logic of capitalism brings an end to unearned privileges and offers opportunities for all. This new book by Rainer Zitelmann answers a critical need, especially as illiberal politicians now blame capitalism for the misery they themselves created through interventionist economic policies. People all over the world need to stand up for capitalism as an engine of innovation and of rising living standards for all. Let us be grateful that *In Defense of Capitalism* provides a thorough review of the facts that make our case."

BRAD LIPS, CEO ATLAS NETWORK

"There are dozens of fashionable anti-capitalist platitudes which have reached the status of conventional wisdoms. Even though these are all profoundly wrong and ill-informed, some of them can be amazingly hard to counter in a debate, because anti-capitalists have a tendency to talk in clichés, soundbites, abstractions and assertions, which are difficult to engage with in a rational way. As a result, they all too often go unchallenged, which further cements the anti-capitalist intellectual hegemony. In this book, Zitelmann provides the perfect antidote."

KRISTIAN NIEMIETZ, HEAD OF POLITICAL ECONOMY, INSTITUTE FOR ECONOMIC AFFAIRS LONDON

"For well over 100 years people have been emigrating away from socialism to countries where there is more economic freedom and entrepreneurial opportunity. To capitalism, in other words. Even the Berlin Wall was not an airtight Venus flytrap for the East German socialists. Chances are, however, that you were taught the opposite in school—that capitalism is the source of virtually all human misery including poverty, pollution, war, and even fascism. In his book *In Defense of Capitalism* Rainer Zitelmann exposes the myths and superstitions that you were taught in school and provides you with a scholarly yet eminently readable explanation of economic reality. It is socialism that is the real ideological opiate of the masses that has caused the greatest miseries the world has known, as generations of immigrants have demonstrated by 'voting with their feet' (for capitalism and against socialism)."

PROFESSOR THOMAS DILORENZO, SENIOR FELLOW, LUDWIG VON MISES INSTITUTE, AND AUTHOR OF *HOW CAPITALISM SAVED AMERICA* AND *THE PROBLEM WITH SOCIALISM*

"Rainer Zitelmann is already well known for his well-informed defence of capitalism and wealth accumulation. In this book, he uses international opinion poll data to understand different countries' attitudes to capitalism and get inside the mind of anti-capitalists. From there he takes on ten of the most common misconceptions about capitalism and overcomes them with a powerful blend of arguments and hard facts."

EAMONN BUTLER, DIRECTOR ADAM SMITH INSTITUTE LONDON

"Grab a pint with your friends and have a chat over current affairs. The chances are that if one of your friends talks about 'capitalism' (or 'neoliberalism,' for that matter), they are using the word as a short-cut for the status quo, and all that's wrong with it. In this remarkable book, Rainer Zitelmann clears the confusion: capitalism doesn't create poverty nor foreshadows war. Quite the contrary, actually.

Common misconceptions about capitalism are rooted less in empirical evidence than in the widespread hostility of intellectuals for an economic system which does not require their enlightened leadership to flourish. Zitelmann does not engage in the description of an ideal capitalism, but presents capitalism as it exists in our world. In capitalist economies, to a certain extent, common people have to decide their own economic future. Unleashing the ordinary person's economic liberty, even if done very partially, tends to produce more wealth and improves the lot of most individuals way better than most elaborate government plans by Economics PhDs."

PROFESSOR ALBERTO MINGARDI, DIRECTOR
GENERAL, ISTITUTO BRUNO LEONI, MILAN

In Defense of Capitalism

FIRST EDITION 2023

Copyright 2023 Rainer Zitelmann

978-1-64572-073-7 Hardcover

978-1-64572-074-4 Ebook

For inquiries about volume orders, please contact:

Republic Book Publishers
27 West 2oth Street
Suite 1103
New York NY 10011
editor@republicbookpublishers.com

Published in the United States by Republic Book Publishers

Distributed by Independent Publishers Group
www.ipgbook.com

Book designed by Mark Karis

Printed in the United States of America

IN DEFENSE OF CAPITALISM

DEBUNKING THE MYTHS

RAINER ZITELMANN

REPUBLIC

BOOK PUBLISHERS

CONTENTS

PART C: POPULAR PERCEPTIONS OF CAPITALISM

PREFACE

IN THE PUBLIC MIND, capitalism is associated with everything that has gone wrong with the world. For many, and not just adherents to the political religion of anti-capitalism, the word itself is synonymous with the ultimate evil. Wherever you look, capitalism does not seem to have many friends or allies—despite the fact that it has been the most successful economic system in human history.

The greatest trick anti-capitalists have pulled is to compare the real-world system under which we live with an ideal of the perfect world of their dreams, an ideal that does not and has never existed anywhere in the world. Anti-capitalists rely on the fact that most people know little about history and the extreme poverty and inhumane circumstances our ancestors lived in before capitalism emerged. And they know that most people today will have learned very little from their teachers at school or university about the cruel and callous conditions under socialism.

Finally, they paint the future in the blackest colors, whereby they attribute every problem and crisis not to failures of the state, but to alleged deficiencies in the market. And the fact that every single anti-capitalist system without exception has ended in failure is an argument socialists are not willing to accept. They always have a response ready— That was not "true" socialism at all!—and confidently insinuate that, after 100 years of failed socialist experiments, they have finally found the right recipe to make socialism work after all.

In essence, capitalism is an economic system, based on private ownership and competition, whereby companies themselves are free to determine what and how much they produce, aided in their decisions by the prices set by the market. The central roles in capitalist economies are played by entrepreneurs who serve to develop new products and discover new market opportunities, and consumers whose individual purchasing decisions ultimately determine the success or failure of the entrepreneur.[1] At its heart, capitalism is an entrepreneurial economic system. In fact, "entrepreneurial economics" would be the most appropriate term to describe it.

Under socialism, in contrast, state ownership dominates, and there are neither real competition nor real prices. Above all, there is no entrepreneurship. What products are produced and in what quantity is determined by centralized state planning authorities, not by private entrepreneurs.

But, neither of these systems exists in its purest form anywhere. In reality, all economic systems are mixed systems. Under socialist systems in the real world, there was and is limited private ownership of capital goods and the means of production and traces of free market economics (otherwise they would have collapsed much sooner). And in modern capitalist countries, there are numerous components of socialism and planned economy (which often hinder the functioning of the market economy and distort its results accordingly).

In my book, *The Power of Capitalism*, I developed a "theory" that I now call the "Test Tube Theory." It is less a theory and more a metaphor that can be used to better understand historical developments: Imagine a test tube containing the elements of state and market, socialism and capitalism. Then add more market to this test tube, as the Chinese have been doing since the 1980s. What do we observe? A decrease in poverty and an increase in prosperity. Or put more state into the test tube, as the socialists have been doing in Venezuela since 1999. What happens then? More poverty and less prosperity.

All over the world, we see this struggle of opposites: Market versus state, capitalism versus socialism. This is a dialectical contradiction, and the development of a country—whether it experiences more or less prosperity—depends on the development of the ratio between market and state. While in the 1980s and 1990s, we saw a strengthening of market forces in many countries (Deng Xiaoping in China, Margaret Thatcher and Ronald Reagan in Great Britain and the United States, reforms in Sweden and in the early 2000s in Germany), today it is the other side—the state—that seems to be gaining the upper hand in many countries. At the level of ideas, anti-capitalism has come back into fashion and is increasingly shaping the thinking of a new generation of journalists and politicians.

As I have toured the world, promoting *The Power of Capitalism*, I have frequently been asked questions that I did not deal with in that book, such as: What about environmental degradation? Or: Aren't human values lost in capitalism, and doesn't everything else ultimately play second fiddle to the pursuit of profit? Is there not a fundamental contradiction between democracy and capitalism? After all, when we look at the United States, people ask, isn't it clear that it is not the majority of voters but big money that determines political outcomes? What about the gap between the rich and the poor, which, as the media constantly reports, is continuously widening? And what do you say about global monopolies, such as Google and Facebook, which are becoming more and more powerful? Isn't capitalism to blame for military conflicts all around the world, and hasn't it produced terrible dictatorships—including Hitler's National Socialist regime in Germany? Finally, people who doubt or despair of capitalism ask: Shouldn't we try alternatives to capitalism? These, then, are some of the questions I address in this book.

As you read through the chapters that follow, you will soon realize that I do not argue on a theoretical level. Opponents of capitalism love to discuss theories because they know that in conceptual discussions, it is not always so easy to decide who is right and who is wrong and because they enjoy soaring to the heights of abstraction. For most people, however, theories and abstract economic models are too intangible and difficult to understand. That is the first drawback. The second, which is even more serious is: Some theories are seductive because they are consistent with what we think we know, with our preconceptions about the world. If they are coherent, engagingly formulated, well presented, and, above all, consistent with what we think we already know, they exert great appeal. I think it is more important to first ascertain whether the facts on which a theory is based are really true. And that is the sore point with the theories promoted by anti-capitalists: They do not fit with historical facts; they simply reinforce our biases about the world.

Some advocates of capitalism also like to discuss economic models. I have nothing against that, and such models have their justification. However, I think it makes far more sense to discuss historical facts rather than engage in a debate on theoretical models before deciding who is right.

In this book, I have adopted the following approach: In Part A, I focus in detail on the arguments repeatedly leveled against capitalism. In the middle section, Part B, I deal with the question of alternatives to capitalism. Socialism always looks good on paper—except when that paper is in a history book.

The third section of this book, Part C, is about popular perceptions of capitalism. Perhaps you have already read Steven Pinker's *Enlightenment Now!*, or Hans Rosling's *Factfulness*? I was fascinated by these books because they prove how wrong most people are when they believe that everything was better in the past and that the whole world is getting worse. There is a striking contradiction between survey data about how most people perceive the world around them and the facts. The same applies to people's opinions on capitalism, where there is a sharp divergence between the historical and economic facts on the one hand and people's perceptions on the other. I know this because, in a large-scale, international research project, I asked people in 21 countries what they thought about capitalism.

The primary purpose of this book is not to engage with other scholars, but to challenge popular opinions about capitalism. Nevertheless, in some chapters, I do directly address the arguments put forward by a number of prominent anti-capitalist intellectuals—such as Thomas Piketty, Naomi Klein and Noam Chomsky—and in books and articles written by scholars who are critical of capitalism. I do this primarily when I believe that their theses have now found acceptance among broader sections of the general public. Of course, most people who hold anti-capitalist opinions have never read the works of Karl Marx or the modern critics of capitalism. But many of their theses—imparted by the media, universities and schools—have found their way into the general consciousness and are even regarded, at least in part, as received wisdom, despite containing numerous errors.

You will also see that while some of these theses might appear to be quite new and innovative (e.g., the critique of consumption), they are actually much older. While the arguments put forward in support of anti-consumerism may have changed—at times, the movement was concerned about the destruction of culture, then the alleged dangers of "alienated consumption," now it is climate change—the target has always remained the same: capitalism. The constantly shifting reasoning of anti-consumerists would suggest that the rationale is not as important as the actual target. Some anti-capitalists, including Naomi Klein, have even openly admitted that they only became interested in issues such as climate change when they discovered that this issue was a new and effective weapon in the fight against the one thing they detested above all: capitalism.

Critics will probably accuse me of "one-sidedness." This is because a large number of the facts and arguments I present in this book will challenge many of the "truths" about the world that most people have come to believe. It will also contradict the narrative that is peddled by large sections of the media (I will come to that in a moment).

And that is why a prerequisite for reading this book is an openness to facts that may challenge your view of the world. In our international survey, we presented respondents in 21 countries with 18 statements to ascertain their opinions on capitalism. One statement that elicited little agreement was that capitalism has improved conditions for ordinary people in many countries around the world—far more respondents believe that capitalism is responsible for hunger and poverty. The figures I present in Chapter 1 of this book clearly show that exactly the opposite is the case.

In relation to hunger and poverty, however, it is very difficult to have a fact-based discussion. The more emotionally charged a topic is, the less willing people are to accept empirical data that contradict their own opinions, a fact that has been repeatedly confirmed by scientific experiments and studies. For example, in a series of almost identical representative surveys over the last three decades, researchers gave respondents a sheet of paper with a picture and a speech bubble and presented them with the following scenario: "I would now like to tell you about an incident that happened the other day at a panel discussion about [then followed various topics such as genetic engineering, climate change, nuclear energy, air pollution, etc., all of which are emotionally polarizing]. Experts were talking about the risks and the latest developments in the field. Suddenly, an audience member jumps up and shouts something to the panelists and the audience."

The researchers then asked respondents to look at the person and the speech bubble on the paper that contained the words, "What do I care about numbers and statistics in this context? How can you even talk so coldly when the survival of mankind and our planet is at stake?" Below the speech bubble was a question: "Would you say this person is right or wrong?" This question was repeatedly asked over a period of 27 years in 15 different representative surveys on a variety of highly emotive and controversial topics. Invariably, the majority of respondents agreed with the heckler who was not interested in the facts. On average, 54.8 percent said the fact-resistant heckler was right, only 23.4 percent disagreed.[2]

In writing this book, I am in no way interested in adopting an artificial "centrist" position or accommodating the mistaken opinions of large numbers of people when the facts are undisputable. That said, given the hundreds of books that have been written to denounce capitalism, there would certainly be nothing wrong with writing a book in its defense. In any court case, the defendant is always allowed a defense attorney. The judge—in this case that is you, dear reader—arrives at a judgment only once all of the facts have been presented. In this case, that includes the facts in favor of capitalism. A trial in which there is no defense and the prosecutor and judge are in cahoots is a show trial. Unfortunately, the debate on capitalism more often than not resembles a show trial rather than a fair trial.

I was very impressed by the clear and simple terms employed to defend the market economy used by my friend Professor Weiying Zhang, a renowned economist at Peking University. I have included his paper, which you will find on pages 350–370. For readers who have not yet studied the topic of capitalism in any depth, I recommend reading this chapter first—as soon as you have finished this preface—rather than saving it until the very end.

Finally, I would like to thank the scholars and friends who helped me with their encouragement and critical comments on this book. Some have read individual chapters, others the whole manuscript. My thanks go to Prof. Jörg Baberowski, Dr. Daniel Bultmann, Prof. Jürgen W. Falter, Prof. Thomas Hecken, Dr. Christian Hiller von Gaertringen, Dr. Helmut Knepel, Prof. Eckhard Jesse, Prof. Hans Mathias Kepplinger, Prof. Wolfgang König, Dr. Gerd Kommer, Prof. Stefan Kooths, Prof. Wolfgang Michalka, Reinhard Mohr, Dr. Kristian Niemietz, Prof. Werner Plumpe, Prof. Martin Rhonheimer, Prof. Walter Scheidel, Prof. Hermann Simon, Prof. Frank Trentmann, Prof. Bernd-Jürgen Wendt, and Prof. Erich Weede.

My special thanks go to Dr. Thomas Petersen of the Allensbach Institute, who steered the international research project over many months, and to my friend Ansgar Graw, who again brought his skills to bear in expertly editing this book.

PART A

THE TEN GREATEST ANTI-CAPITALIST

FALLACIES

1

"CAPITALISM IS RESPONSIBLE FOR

HUNGER AND POVERTY"

CAPITALISM IS OFTEN BLAMED for hunger and poverty in the world. What do you think? Has the share of the global population living in poverty decreased, increased or stayed the same over the past few decades?

In 2016, 26,000 people in 24 countries were asked for their opinions on the growth of absolute poverty over the last 20 years. Only 13 percent of respondents believed that the poverty rate had decreased. In contrast, 70 percent believed that the poverty rate had increased. This misperception was particularly strong in industrial countries: In Germany, for example, only 8 percent of respondents believed that the proportion of people living in absolute poverty around the world had fallen. A study conducted by Ipsos MORI in 2017 came to a similar conclusion. Accordingly, only 11 percent of respondents in Germany were convinced that absolute poverty had decreased globally, compared with 49 percent of Chinese interviewees.[3] Absolute poverty is defined with reference to the cost of a basket of essential goods and services. Anyone who cannot acquire this basket of goods is considered to be poor in "absolute" terms.[4]

Before capitalism emerged, most people in the world were living in extreme poverty. In 1820 around 90 percent of the global population was living in absolute poverty. Today, the figure is less than 10 percent. And most remarkably: In recent decades, since the end of communism in China and other countries, the decline in poverty has accelerated to a pace unmatched in any previous period of human history. In 1981, the absolute poverty rate was 42.7 percent; by 2000, it had fallen to 27.8 percent, and in 2021 it was below 10 percent.[5]

It is this main trend, which has persisted for decades, that is crucial. It is true—contrary to the original expectations of the World Bank, which compiles these data—that poverty has risen again over the last couple of years. But this is largely a result of the global Covid-19 pandemic and the war in Ukraine, which have exacerbated the situation in countries where poverty was already relatively high.

Other long-term trends also provide cause for encouragement. For instance, the number of children in child labor around the world has dropped significantly, falling from 246 million in 2000 to 160 million twenty years later in 2020.[6] And this decline is despite the fact that the global population increased from 6.1 to 7.8 billion over the same period.

To understand the issue of poverty, we need to look at history. Many people believe that capitalism is the root cause of global poverty and starvation. They have a completely unrealistic image of the pre-capitalist era. Johan Norberg, the author of *Progress*, was himself an anti-capitalist in his youth. However, he admits he had never really thought about the way people lived before the Industrial Revolution: "I had thought of it more in terms of a modern excursion into the countryside."[7] And Sahra Wagenknecht, the prominent German left-wing politician, writes that people had "no doubt lived in austerity" before capitalism, but she glorifies such conditions as contributing to a "far quieter, nature-loving life, integrated into cohesive communities" that was "positively idyllic" compared to capitalism.[8]

In his famous work on the condition of the working class in England, Frederick Engels denounced working conditions under early capitalism in the most drastic terms and painted an idyllic picture of home workers before machine labor and capitalism came along to destroy this beautiful life: "So the workers vegetated throughout a passably comfortable existence, leading a righteous and peaceful life in all piety and probity; and their material position was far better than that of their successors. They did not need to overwork; they did no more than they chose to do, and yet earned what they needed. They had leisure for healthful work in garden or field, work which, in itself, was recreation for them, and they could take part besides in the recreations and games of their neighbours, and all these games—bowling, cricket, football, etc., contributed to their physical health and vigour. They were, for the most part, strong, well-built people, in whose physique little or no difference from that of their peasant neighbours was discoverable. Their children grew up in the fresh country air, and, if they could help their parents at work, it was only occasionally; while of eight or twelve hours work for them there was no question."[9]

Engels goes on: "They were 'respectable' people, good husbands and fathers, led moral lives because they had no temptation to be immoral, there being no gin palaces or low houses in their vicinity, and because the host, at whose inn they now and then quenched their thirst, was also a respectable man, usually a large tenant farmer who took pride in his good order, good beer, and early hours. They had their children the whole day at home, and brought them up in obedience and the fear of God . . ." The young people, Engels writes, "grew up in idyllic simplicity and intimacy with their playmates until they married." The only negative note is when Engels continues: "but intellectually, they were dead; lived only for their petty, private interests, for their looms and gardens, and knew nothing of the mighty movement which, beyond their horizon, was sweeping through mankind. They were comfortable in their silent vegetation, and but for the industrial revolution, they would never have emerged from this existence, which, cozily romantic as it was, was nevertheless not worthy of human beings."[10]

The image many people have of life in pre-capitalist times has been transfigured beyond recognition by these and similar romanticized depictions. So let us take a more objective look back to the pre-capitalist era in the decades and centuries prior to 1820.

Poverty was by no means caused by capitalism; it had existed for a long time and had shaped people's lives for millennia. Poverty has no causes—prosperity has causes. Fernand Braudel, the renowned French historian, has written one of the most widely respected works on the social history of the fifteenth to eighteenth centuries, *Civilization and Capitalism*, in which he writes that even in relatively well-off Europe, there were constant depressions and famines. Cereal yields were so poor that two consecutive bad harvests spelled disaster.[11] In France, even then a privileged country, there were 11 general famines in the seventeenth and 16 in the eighteenth centuries. As Braudel notes, these calculations are likely to be overly optimistic. And all of the countries of Europe were in the same situation. In Germany, for example, where both town and country were persistently ravaged by hunger, one famine followed the next.

Many people believe that it was industrialization and urbanization that led to hunger and poverty. But Braudel writes that people in the countryside sometimes experienced even greater suffering: "The peasants lived in a state of dependence on merchants, towns and nobles, and had scarcely any reserves of their own. They had no solution in case of famine except to turn to the town where they crowded together, begging in the streets . . . The towns soon had to protect themselves against these regular invasions, which were not purely by beggars from the surrounding areas but by positive armies of the poor, sometimes from very far afield."[12]

If conditions in the towns had generally been worse than in the countryside, millions of people would not have flocked to the towns. The German economic historian Werner Plumpe writes: "It was not the emerging trades and industries that created a proletariat; rather, the proletariat emerged solely because there was widespread, mostly rural underemployment . . . In fact, industrialization helped large numbers of people escape structural underemployment and poverty and survive as an industrial workforce . . . Capitalism, if you will, encountered a poor population that literally had nothing to lose and much to gain."[13]

Of course, this was only true for people who found employment in the towns and were actually able to work. For everyone else, the fate was cruel. In Paris, the sick and invalids had always been put in hospitals, while those who were fit enough to work were chained together in pairs and engaged in the hard, disgusting, and endless task of cleaning the drains of the town.[14]

Hunger was one of the biggest problems in many countries. In Finland, there was a major famine in 1696/97. According to estimates, a quarter to a third of the population died. But in Western Europe, too, people often lived in inhumane conditions. In 1662, the Electors of Burgundy reported to the king that "famine this year has put an end to over ten thousand families in your province and forced a third of the inhabitants, even in the good towns, to eat wild plants," and a chronicler adds that: "Some people ate human flesh."[15]

People's diets consisted of gruel, sops and bread made from inferior flours, which was only baked once a month or every two months and was almost always moldy and so hard that in some regions it had to be cut with an axe.[16] Most people, even in the towns, had to survive on 2,000 calories a day, with carbohydrates making up well over 60 percent of their food intake expressed in calories.[17] Typically, eating consisted of a lifetime of consuming bread, more bread, and gruel.[18] Bread consumption was particularly high among the rural population and the lowest strata of the working class. According to Le Grand d'Aussy, in 1782 a working man or a peasant in France ate two or three pounds of bread a day, "but people who have anything else to eat do not consume this quantity."[19]

People back then were lean and small-boned—throughout history, the human body has adapted to inadequate caloric intake. "The small workers of the eighteenth century," Angus Deaton writes in his book *The Great Escape*, "were effectively locked into a nutritional trap; they could not earn much because they were so physically weak, and they could

7

not eat enough because, without work, they did not have the money to buy food."[20] Some people rave about the harmonious pre-capitalist conditions when life was so much slower, but this sluggishness was mainly a result of physical weakness due to permanent malnutrition.[21] It is estimated that 200 years ago, about 20 percent of the inhabitants of England and France were not able to work at all. "At most they had enough energy for a few hours of slow walking per day, which condemned most of them to a life of begging."[22]

In 1754, one English author reported: "Far from being well-to-do, the peasants in France do not even have the necessary subsistence; they are a breed of men who begin to decline before they are forty . . . With the French labourers, their external appearance alone proves the deterioration of their bodies."[23] The situation was similar in other European countries. Braudel states: "These then are the facts that go to make up the biological *ancien regime* we are discussing: a number of deaths roughly equivalent to the number of births; very high infant mortality, famine; chronic undernourishment; and formidable epidemics." In some decades, even more people died than babies were born.[24] People's "possessions" were limited to a few rudimentary items, as seen in contemporary paintings: a few stools, a bench and a barrel doing service as a table.[25]

And people died as they lived. A report from Paris says the dead were sewn up in sackcloth and thrown into paupers' graves at Clamart, just outside the capital, and then sprinkled with quick lime. The only funeral procession of the poor featured "A mud-bespattered priest, a bell, a cross." And this send-off was preceded by the indescribable conditions of the poor house, where there were only 1,200 beds available for 5,000 to 6,000 sick people, and so, "The newcomer is bedded down beside a dying man and a corpse."[26]

The reason I have described the reality of people's lives in such detail is that I wanted to show what it means to have 90 percent of the world's population living in extreme poverty. And in other parts of the world people lived in even worse conditions than the populations of Western Europe. The distinguished British economist Angus Maddison specialized in documenting economic growth and development over long periods of time. Based on a series of highly complex calculations, he estimated the historical per capita gross domestic product (GDP) for some of the world's major economies. In 1820, this amounted to 1,202 international dollars[27] in Western Europe, the region we have focused on in this chapter so far. According to Maddison, per capita GDP was at a similar level in other Western countries, such as North America, Australia, and New Zealand. In the rest of the world, however, the per capita GDP in 1820 amounted to just 580 international dollars, or about half as much as in the Western world.[28]

The positive impact of capitalism becomes clearer when you adopt a long-term historical perspective. In AD 1, per capita GDP in Western Europe was 576 international dollars, while the global average was 467, which means that in Europe it had little more than doubled in the period before capitalism, from AD 1 to 1820. And in the short period from 1820 to 2003, per capita GDP in Western Europe rose from 1,202 to 19,912 international dollars and in the West's other capitalist countries to 23,710 international dollars.[29]

In Asia, by contrast, per capita GDP rose from only 581 to 1,718 international dollars in the 153 years from 1820 to 1973. And then, in the 30 years to 2003, it rose from 1,718 to 4,434 international dollars.[30]

So what was it that triggered this dynamic development? Well, the growth in per capita GDP in Asia is primarily due to the fact that, following the death of Mao Zedong in 1976, China decided, step by step, to steadily introduce the principles of capitalism. Since the reduction of global poverty is largely a result of this development in China, I would like to present it in a little more detail below.

As recently as 1981, as many as 88 percent of the Chinese population was living in extreme poverty; today it is less than 1 percent. Never in the history of the world have so many hundreds of millions of people risen from abject poverty to the middle class in such a short period of time. Taking China as an example, then, we can learn a lot about how poverty is overcome—not in theory, but in historical reality. But first, let's take a look back. In the late 1950s, 45 million people died in China as a result of Mao's Great Leap Forward. It is staggering that most of the people who learn about the real (or alleged) problems associated with capitalism at school have never heard of the Great Leap Forward, the greatest socialist experiment in history.

I wrote about this subject in more detail in my book *The Power of Capitalism*, where I quoted Chinese journalist and historian Yang Jisheng: "The starvation that preceded death was worse than death itself. The grain was gone, the wild herbs had all been eaten, even the bark had been stripped from the trees, and bird droppings, rats and cotton batting were used to fill stomachs. In the kaolin clay fields, starving people chewed on the clay as they dug it."[31] There were frequent cases of cannibalism. At first, desperate villagers would only eat the cadavers of animals, but soon they started digging up dead neighbors to cook and eat. Human flesh was sold on the black market along with other types of meat.[32] A study compiled—and promptly suppressed—after Mao's death for Fengyang County "recorded sixty-three cases of cannibalism in the spring of 1960 alone, including that of a couple who strangled and ate their eight-year-old son."[33]

In 1958, before Mao's Great Leap Forward, life expectancy was just under 50 years. By 1960, however, it had fallen below 30! Five years later, after the starvation and killing had stopped, it rose again to almost 55. Nearly a third of those born during the darkest phase of the greatest socialist experiment in human history did not survive to see its end.[34]

In the wake of the human and economic catastrophe of the Mao era, the Chinese started to send representatives to other countries on fact-finding missions. They wanted to see for themselves what these countries were like and whether there was anything China could learn from them. From 1978, there was a flurry of travel by leading Chinese politicians and economists. They made 20 trips to more than 50 countries as they sought to identify the policies that could lead China to economic success. The scales fell from their eyes when they saw, for example, how workers in Japan were faring. They soon realized that communist propaganda had been lying to them for years when it compared the "glorious" achievements of socialism in China with the "misery" in capitalist countries. In truth, it was the other way around, as anyone on these fact-finding trips could see. "The more we see of the outside world, the more we realize how backward we are," Deng Xiaoping, the father of China's subsequent capitalist reforms, repeatedly observed.[35]

But it would be wrong to believe that China was somehow "converted" to capitalism overnight or immediately began to abolish its planned economy in favor of a market economy. The Chinese government made a slow, tentative start, gradually giving state-owned enterprises a greater deal of autonomy. The transition from a socialist, state-run economy to a market economy did not happen abruptly. Rather, it was a process that lasted years and decades—and is still far from complete. And at least as important as the top-down measures implemented from above, that is, from the party, were the bottom-up initiatives from below, for example, from the farmers.

After the bitter experience of the Great Leap Forward, a growing number of rural peasants seized the initiative and decided to reintroduce private ownership of farmland, even though this was officially prohibited. Nevertheless, it soon became apparent that the yields from private farms were much higher, so party officials let the people get on with it. The first experiments were carried out in particularly poor "beggar villages," where officials concluded that "If things go wrong here, it's not so bad, because you can't fall when you're already at rock bottom." In one of these small villages, the party leadership allowed the farmers to cultivate the particularly low-yield fields as private farmers. As soon as they were allowed to do so, the land yielded three times as much as when it had been cultivated in a collective.

Long before the ban on private farming was officially lifted in 1982, there were spontaneous initiatives by farmers all over China to reintroduce private ownership, contrary to the socialist creed. The result was extremely positive: people were no longer forced to go hungry and agricultural yields increased significantly.

And such changes were not only seen in rural areas. Beyond the large state-owned enterprises, there were numerous municipal enterprises that formally belonged to the cities and municipalities but were increasingly run like private enterprises. These companies often proved superior to the cumbersome state-owned enterprises because they were not subject to the restrictive guidelines of a planned economy. In the 1980s, a growing number of de facto privately managed enterprises were established. The socialist system, under which state ownership overseen by centralized state planning authorities was the only option, was increasingly eroded from below.

Of great importance were the newly created Special Economic Areas, where the socialist economic system was suspended and capitalist experiments were permitted. The first special economic zone was created in Shenzhen, adjacent to the then politically and economically independent capitalist Hong Kong, which was still a British crown colony at the time. Much like in Germany, where an increasing number of people fled from East to West prior to the building of the Berlin Wall, more and more people tried to leave the socialist People's Republic for capitalist Hong Kong via the then small fishing town of Shenzhen.

Deng Xiaoping was smart enough to realize that military intervention and stricter border controls would not solve the underlying issue, but the causes of people fleeing the country must be analyzed and eliminated. When the party leadership in Guangdong province, of which Shenzhen was a part, investigated the situation in more detail, they found refugees from mainland China living in a village they had established on the Hong Kong territory on the opposite side of the Shenzhen River, where they were earning 100 times as much money as their former compatriots on the socialist side.

Deng's response was to argue that China needed to increase living standards on the Chinese side of the river if it wanted to stem the flow. Shenzhen, which had fewer than 30,000 inhabitants at the time, became the site of China's first free-market experiment, enabled by party cadres who had been to Hong Kong and Singapore and seen firsthand that capitalism works far better than socialism.

From being a place where many risked their lives to flee the country, this former fishing village has today become a thriving metropolis of 13 million people with a flourishing economy centered on the electronics and telecommunications industries and a higher per capita income than any other Chinese city except for Hong Kong and Macau. The Special Economic Area model was quickly rolled out in other regions. Low taxes, low rents and low bureaucratic hurdles made these Special Economic Areas extremely attractive to foreign investors. Their economies were less heavily regulated and more market-oriented than many European countries today.

I visited this region for the first time in August 2018 and again in December 2019. On my second trip, I spoke with representatives of a private think tank. The think tank's head is a professor who does not belong to the Communist Party or any of the other eight "parties" in China. "Perhaps we will be the last defenders of capitalism," he opined. As we talked, he expressed his bewilderment at the fact that socialist thinking is experiencing such a renaissance in Europe and the United States: "Here in China, hardly anyone still believes in Karl Marx's ideas."

The official proclamation of the market economy at the Fourteenth Congress of the Chinese Communist Party in October 1992—a step that would have been unthinkable only a few years earlier—proved a milestone on China's road to capitalism. Although the Party stopped short of completely dispensing with centralized economic planning, prices for raw materials, transportation services and capital goods, all of which were set by the government, fell dramatically.

In a parallel development, attempts were made to reform state-run enterprises. Previously under exclusively public ownership, private citizens and foreign investors were now allowed to become shareholders. Privatization continued apace during the 1990s, and some companies were floated on the stock market. There were numerous spontaneous privatizations and IPOs initiated by local governments. It became clear that many state-owned enterprises were not viable under competitive conditions.

Developments in China prove that rising economic growth—even when accompanied by rising inequality—benefits the majority of the population. Today, there are more billionaires in China than in any other country in the world, with the exception of the United States; Beijing is now home to more billionaires than New York. This confirms the inherent fallacy of anti-capitalist "zero-sum thinking," which claims that the rich are only rich because they have taken something from the poor. The reason hundreds of millions of people in China are much better off today is not despite the fact that there are so many millionaires and billionaires, but precisely because—after Mao's death—Deng Xiaoping instructed: "Let some people get rich first."

Deng was right to prioritize economic growth, as can be seen from the following facts: The Chinese provinces where poverty has declined the most in recent decades are the same provinces that have experienced the greatest economic growth. Weiying Zhang, who is certainly the smartest analyst of the Chinese economy, dismisses the notion that China's extraordinary success is a result of the significant role played by the state. This misinterpretation is widespread in the West, but it is also increasingly prevalent in China itself, where some politicians and scholars believe that the explanation for the country's success lies in a particular "China model." "The advocates of the China model are wrong because they mistake 'in spite of' for 'because of.' China has grown fast *not because of*, but *in spite of* the unlimited government and the large inefficient state sector."[36]

In fact, marketization and privatization are the driving forces behind China's tremendous economic growth. Zhang analyzed data from different regions across China and concluded that "the more the market-oriented reform a province had done, the higher economic growth it had achieved, and laggards in marketization reform are also laggards in economic growth."[37] The areas where market-oriented reforms had been implemented most consistently, such as Guangdong, Zhejiang, Fujian and Jiangsu, were also those that had delivered the greatest economic growth.

Here, and this is a key insight, "the best measure of reform progresses is the *changes* in marketization scores in the concerned periods, rather than the absolute scores of a particular year."[38] The growth rate is greatest where private companies play the decisive role. Zhang's data prove it: "The provinces whose economies are more 'privatized' are likely to grow faster. It is non-state sectors, rather than the state sector, that have driven the high growth."[39]

The reform process in China over the past decades has never been uniform, never just in one direction. There were phases in which market forces quickly became stronger, just as there were phases in which the state reasserted its primacy. Even if over the longer term the main tendency was "state out and private in" (*guo tui min jin*), there were also periods and regions in which there was a backward trend, that is, "state in and private out" (*guo jin min tui*). Zhang examines the different growth rates in the "state out and private in" regions and the "state in and private out" regions. Again, the results are clear: economic output grew significantly faster in the "state out and private in" regions. As Zhang explains, this proves "that China's rapid growth of the past four decades has been driven by the power of the market and the non-state sectors, rather than the power of the government and the state-sector as claimed by the China model theorists."[40]

The most crucial factor in the future development of the Chinese economy is the degree of innovation. An analysis of the research and development intensity in industry, patents granted per capita and percentage of sales of new products in total industrial revenue makes it clear that all these key figures for innovation correlate positively with the degree of marketization.[41]

When I met Weiying Zhang in Beijing, he stressed the major danger of misunderstanding the reasons for China's growth, not only for China, but also for the West. If people in the West mistakenly conclude that China's economic success is founded on some unique "third way" between capitalism and socialism, also known as "state capitalism," Zhang worries that they will draw the wrong conclusions for their own countries. In *Ideas for China's Future*, which was published in 2020, Zhang uses a very apt metaphor: "Imagine seeing a person without an arm running very fast. If you could conclude his speed comes from missing an arm, then you naturally will call on others to saw off one of your own arms. That would be a disaster . . . Economists must not confuse 'in spite of' with 'because of.'"[42]

Advocates of a strong state in Europe and the United States want everyone to believe that China's economic success confirms that economic growth is inextricably linked with a strong state. The analyses of Weiying Zhang prove that exactly the opposite is true.

In many respects, according to Zhang, the Chinese way is less exceptional than it may appear at first sight: "In fact, China's economic development is fundamentally the same as some economic development in Western countries—such as Great Britain during the Industrial Revolution, the United States in the late 19th and early 20th centuries, and some East Asian countries such as Japan and South Korea after World War II. Once market forces are introduced and the right incentives are set up for people to pursue wealth, the miracle of growth will follow sooner or later."[43]

Indeed, there are many parallels between China and the development of early capitalism in Europe and the United States. "Early capitalism" is a horrifying phrase for anti-capitalists, despite the fact that it was a time of dramatic improvements in the living conditions of the working class. Thomas J. DiLorenzo illustrates this with the following figures for the United States: "From 1820 to 1860 wages grew at about a 1.6 annual rate, and during this period the purchasing power of an average worker's paycheck increased between 60 and 90 percent, depending on what region of the country the worker resided in. Between 1860 and 1890, during what economists call the 'second industrial revolution,' real wages—that is wages adjusted for inflation—increased by 50 percent in America. The average work-week was shortened as well, meaning that the real earnings of the average American worker probably increased more like 60 percent during that time."[44] In the next chapter, I will show that something similar is true of early capitalism in England, which is often cited as a particularly bad example of inhumane and degrading conditions.

Capitalism has done more to overcome hunger and poverty than any other system in world history. The greatest man-made famines in the past 100 years occurred under socialism. In the wake of the Bolshevik Revolution, the Russian famine of 1921/22 cost the lives of 5 million people, according to official figures in the *Great Soviet Encyclopedia* of 1927. The highest estimates put the death toll from starvation at 10 to 14 million. Only a decade later, Joseph Stalin's socialist collectivization of agriculture and "liquidation of the kulaks" (more on that in Chapter 11) triggered the next great famine, which killed between 6 and 8 million people. In relative terms, Kazakhstan was particularly badly affected, where a third of the population died.[45] Excess deaths across the Soviet Union amounted to 3.9 million in Ukraine, 3.3 million in Russia, and 1.3 million in Kazakhstan.

"When the term 'famine' is used," writes Felix Wemheuer, "the first thing most people think of is Africa. In the twentieth century, however, 80 percent of all victims of famines died in China and the Soviet Union."[46] He is not referring to the millions of victims of general malnutrition and underprovision of medical care, but defines famine as an event that causes mortality rates to jump from what is "normal" in any given country.[47] The end of communism in China and the Soviet Union was a major factor in hunger declining by 42 percent between 1990 and 2017.[48]

It is a typical misperception that when people think of hunger and poverty, they think of capitalism rather than socialism, the system that was actually responsible for the greatest famines of the twentieth century.

In North Korea, one of the few remaining socialist countries in the world, several hundred thousand people died in famines between 1994 and 1998. Jang Jing-sung, a member of the North Korean elite, describes his personal experiences in North Korea in the late 1990s, before he fled to the West. The starving were sent to parks to beg before they died. There was a special "Corpse Division," whose members would poke bodies with sticks to see if they were already dead. He saw them loading corpses on rickshaws, on which bare and skeletal feet poked out in odd directions. In a crowded market, a woman whose husband had already starved to death offered her daughter for sale for 100 won (less than 10 cents).[49]

Back to the numbers: The *Index of Economic Freedom*, which is compiled every year by the Heritage Foundation, shows that the most capitalist countries have an average per capita GDP of $71,576. That compares with $47,706 for the world's "predominantly free" countries. At the other end of the scale, the "mostly unfree" and the "repressed" countries have a per capita GDP of just $6,834 and $7,163, respectively.[50]

The United Nations' *Global Multidimensional Poverty Index* (*MPI*)[51] measures various forms of poverty (including health, standard of living and education) in 80 developing countries. If you compare the UN's *MPI* with the *Index of Economic Freedom*, you see that 35.3 percent of the populations of the "mostly unfree" developing countries live in "multidimensional poverty," compared with only 7.9 percent of people in "mostly free" developing countries.[52] The belief that everything would be better if we only "redistributed" money from rich to poor countries is naive. Economics is not a zero-sum game in which you simply have to take something from one wealthy person, group or country and distribute it to others to make everyone richer. What really conquers poverty, as demonstrated by developments in Western Europe since 1820 and in Asian countries, such as China, South Korea and Vietnam over the last 40 years, is more economic freedom.

Countless studies prove and economists have stressed that development aid has done more harm than good to countries in Africa.[53] It is a fact that I explored in detail in Chapter Two of my book *The Power of Capitalism*. Between 1970 and 1998, the peak years for the flow of development aid to Africa, poverty on the continent rose from 11 to 66 percent.[54] Foreign aid propped up corrupt governments that felt no compunction whatsoever to ensure the welfare of their people. Foreign aid payments also meant that these rulers did not depend on the consent of their people. This allowed them to unabashedly interfere with the rule of law, the establishment of transparent civil institutions and the protection of civil liberties. In turn, this discouraged both local and foreign investors from investing in these poor countries. In effect, Western development aid did much to set many African countries far back in their development.

Foreign aid inhibited the development of a functioning capitalist economy, and the high levels of corruption made investment in poor countries unattractive.[55] This led to economic stagnation and stunted economic growth. Corrupt government functionaries were more interested in serving their own interests than in serving the common good. Large sums of foreign aid and a culture of aid dependency also encouraged African governments to further expand unproductive public sectors, which was just another way to reward their cronies.[56]

Of course, rich countries should help poor countries in an emergency, such as when a natural disaster or pandemic strikes. In such cases, it should be self-evident that one country helps another, for example by providing practical equipment, medicines, food, and so forth. The same should apply to people who, despite living in a prosperous country, have fallen into poverty through no fault of their own, for example, through illness or some other stroke of fate. Here, generous help should be provided without a second thought, both from private individuals and the state. But such aid does nothing to overcome structurally induced poverty.

In Europe or the United States, the debate about the most effective methods to eradicate poverty, hunger, child labor and other problems has come to be dominated by naive ideas. Some people feel good about refusing to buy products that have been manufactured with the involvement of child workers. But quite often the anti-child-labor "victories" celebrated by "activists" have actually made the situation for people in poor countries even worse. Johan Norberg relates the following example: In 1992 it was revealed that the American retailer Walmart had been buying garments that had been manufactured by child workers. The U.S. Congress then threatened to ban imports from countries with child labor. As a result of that threat, many thousands of children in Bangladesh were immediately fired by the textile industry. When international organizations conducted a follow-up investigation to find out what had become of these children, it became apparent that many of them had moved to occupations more dangerous and less well-paid, and in several cases had become prostitutes. A similar boycott of the Nepalese carpet industry resulted in more than 5,000 girls being forced into prostitution, according to UNICEF.[57]

In the summer of 2014, a new law on child labor in Bolivia made global headlines and sparked fierce debate. The law allows children as young as ten to work under certain working conditions. Working children were even among the groups who helped write the law. A scandal? UNICEF commented, "We have to accept that child labor is a reality in many low- and middle-income countries. In Bolivia, many girls and boys said they needed their wages to survive. Supporters of the law believe that without it, children would work illegally and be at much higher risk of exploitation. Critics, on the other hand, fear that the law will weaken child protection."[58]

The situation is therefore not as clear-cut as it might appear at first glance. As previously mentioned, child labor has declined massively around the world, not primarily as a result of bans or boycotts, but because the living conditions for people in many (formerly) developing countries have improved. Parents who used to depend on their children working were now in a position to earn more themselves and finance an education for their children. Not less, but more capitalism has helped in the fight against child labor.

But what about the poor in developed rich countries? Here, it is important first of all to distinguish between "relative" and "absolute" poverty. When people talk about poverty in countries, such as Germany or Sweden, they usually mean "relative" poverty, which we will come back to in the next chapter. Relative poverty refers to people who, for example, earn less than 60 percent of their country's median income. This poverty can never be eliminated, because regardless of any increases in median income, there will always be people who earn 60 percent or less of it. This is an inevitable result of the statistical construction of the median income, which is not the average income, but the income that divides a population into two equal groups, half having an income above that amount, and half having an income below that amount.

Anti-capitalists always argue as if all (relatively) poor people living in a rich country have become poor through no fault of their own. They get downright indignant when someone points out that there are also poor people in countries, such as Germany, Great Britain, Sweden or the United States, who are either fully or partly to blame for their own situation. Nevertheless, there is no denying the fact that, in addition to people who are in need through no fault of their own, there are also people who prefer to take advantage of the state welfare system rather than work themselves. In some respects, one can even understand them: If high taxes and social security contributions mean that too little is left from a person's gross income and, at the same time, comparatively generous benefits are doled out by the welfare state, as is the case in Germany, for example, then there will always be people who prefer to live off these benefits and perhaps work cash in hand on the side. After all, they know they will end up with just as much or even more, without having to do as much as someone who works 40 hours a week. We should not direct our ire primarily at these people, but at the system that makes their behavior appear economically rational.

But does encouraging people to see themselves primarily as victims actually help anyone at all? Doesn't it just make them feel helpless and remove their sense of agency? The message of anti-capitalists is: "Your life situation is the way it is for structural reasons, so you have no chance to change it until the structures are torn down." First of all, such messages are wrong and, second, they discourage people.

Pro-capitalists encourage people to take their fate in their own hands, not to wait for others to help them out or for society to change. And one of the main reasons they do so is because they know that what the anti-capitalists promise, namely that poverty and hardship can only be alleviated through the abolition of capitalism, is in no way borne out by history. In fact, the opposite has always been true: wherever capitalism has been abolished, poverty has increased—as we will see in Chapter 11.

2

"CAPITALISM LEADS TO GROWING

INEQUALITY"

"THE POOR ARE GETTING POORER and the rich are getting richer"—
we saw in the last chapter that at least the first part of this frequently
repeated saying is not true. The billion-dollar fortunes of the super-rich
are held up in contrast to what most people have. The fortunes of the
super-rich are indeed staggeringly high, but the vast majority of that
wealth is tied up in productive corporate assets. Some people imagine
that Jeff Bezos has $100 or $200 billion sitting in his bank account.
But in fact, most of his fortune—probably over 95 percent—is tied up
in stocks in his company Amazon, which employs around 1.3 million
people worldwide. This is the source of his gigantic fortune.

But first, let's ask a more fundamental question: What about the
issue of inequality? Is it true that under capitalism the gap between the
rich and poor is widening? Before we answer this question, it is worth
asking: Is it even worth striving for equality? And what is meant by

equality? And why are so many people more concerned with the issue of inequality than they are about poverty?

The authors of the classical utopian novels were obsessed with the notion of equality. In almost every design of a utopian system, private ownership of the means of production (and sometimes even all private property) is abolished, as is any distinction between rich and poor. As early as 1517, the novel *Utopia* by the Englishman Thomas More, who established the name of this genre, states: "Thus I do fully persuade myself that no equal and just distribution of things can be made, nor that perfect wealth shall ever be among men unless this propriety be exiled and banished. But so long as it shall continue, so long shall remain among the most and best part of men the heavy and inevitable burden of poverty and wretchedness."[59]

In philosopher Tommaso Campanella's 1602 novel *The City of the Sun*, almost all of the city's inhabitants, whether male or female, wear the same clothes. And in Johann Valentin Andreä's utopian description of the Republic of Christianopolis there are only two types of clothing. "They have only two suits of clothes, one for their work, one for the holidays; and for all classes they are made alike. Sex and age are shown by the form of the dress. The cloth is made of linen or wool, respectively for summer or winter, and the color for all is white or ashen gray; none have fancy, tailored goods." Even the architecture of the houses is entirely uniform in many utopian novels.[60]

Hardly anyone who complains about "social injustice" would today advocate such radical egalitarianism. Almost everyone accepts that it is okay to have differences in income, but, many add: these differences should not be "too great." But what is "too great" and what is okay? Many critics of social inequality point out that the differences have grown larger in recent decades—for example, managers now earn much more in relation to their employees than in the past. So was the ratio right "in the past"? Hardly, because many of the people who today complain about "too much inequality" were making exactly the same complaints back then.

Both in philosophical "theories of equity" and in the everyday understanding of many people, the reward someone receives for their work should be in proportion to the amount of work they put in. "If this relationship is unequal, that is, if someone receives a greater reward with less effort, feelings of injustice arise."[61] Surveys have consistently shown that between 88 and 95 percent of Western Europeans believe that "performance" should be a major factor in determining income.[62] But we know from research that especially individuals with low socioeconomic status usually understand "performance" as the "conscientious completion of a defined quantity of tasks within a specific period of time."[63]

Most people understand "performance" to mean both the time spent and the intensity of a person's effort or endeavor. I call this the "employee mindset" because it corresponds to the personal experience of employees or workers that their wage or salary is proportional to their effort: those who work longer or harder usually earn more. This is what most people see as "fair."

What they don't understand is that this connection applies—if at all—only to blue- and white-collar workers or employees in agriculture and fishing, but it certainly does not apply to entrepreneurs. What counts most for entrepreneurs is the quality of their business idea, their creativity, their innovations.[64] The Austrian economist Joseph Schumpeter wrote that entrepreneurial profit *"arises in the capitalist economy wherever a new method of production, a new commercial combination, or a new form or organization is successfully introduced. It is the premium which capitalism attaches to innovation.* The implementation of innovation in the national economy is the true entrepreneurial function, that which actually constitutes entrepreneurial activity and distinguishes it from mere administration and the repetitive routine aspects of management."[65]

If you look at the list of the richest people in the world, they usually became rich because they had a unique entrepreneurial idea and brought a product to market that was recognized as useful by many consumers. This is the capitalist principle, but many people do not understand it. It is not the amount of work that matters, but the benefit provided to society. This benefit has very little and often even nothing to do with how much time and sweat an entrepreneur invested in their business idea.

Another misunderstanding in this context is to deride the value of such business ideas as low in retrospect, perhaps after a year or after 50 years, because most innovations, once enough time has passed, appear banal in retrospect and have been made obsolete by better, newer innovations. Those who misunderstand entrepreneurial creativity in this way have failed to understand that what distinguishes the best business ideas is rarely their technical genius, but rather being the first to market with an idea that is truly relevant to people.

Today, the Oetker Group employs over 30,000 people and generates billions in sales. It was founded back in 1891, and ten years later, August Oetker filed a patent for a baking powder that would make him one of the richest men in Germany. Later, Oetker would repeatedly quote the phrase: "In most cases, a good idea is all it takes to make a man."[66] This "good idea" does not even have to be the entrepreneur's own creation. Oetker did not invent baking powder, but he was the first to have ingenious ideas about how it could be improved and, above all, turned into a product that would satisfy the needs of millions of people.

Brian Acton and Jan Koum invented WhatsApp and sold it to Facebook for $19 billion in 2014. Two billion people around the world now use WhatsApp not only to send messages and files, but also to make free phone calls. Thanks to their innovative idea, the two WhatsApp founders have amassed a combined fortune of $13 billion. They became rich through an idea. Has inequality increased because there are now two more multibillionaires? Certainly. But has it hurt anyone, except perhaps providers of expensive phone plans?

Ideas and their timing are crucial, and it doesn't even matter whether the entrepreneur developed the idea themselves. Many successful businessmen, whether Sam Walton of Walmart, Steve Jobs of Apple or Bill Gates of Microsoft, did not develop their key business ideas themselves, but took them from others. Conversely, many inventors, whether of

Coca-Cola or of the operating system later called MS-DOS, did not become rich from their innovations. The ones who got rich were those who had ingenious ideas about how such inventions could be turned into new products that satisfy the needs of many people at a very specific point in time. It is obvious that the question of how long or how hard these entrepreneurs work is meaningless. Many people try just as hard—or perhaps even harder—and work just as long or longer, but do not become rich.

And what about the top executives employed by large companies? Their high salaries are heavily criticized by opponents of capitalism, often even more so than the (usually much higher) incomes of entrepreneurs. This is mainly because the details of executive salaries are often in the public domain. Anyone can find out how much the CEO of a listed company earns, while this is usually not the case for entrepreneurs. Moreover, top-tier managers are held in lower esteem than entrepreneurs by many people (even those with capitalist sympathies).

Managerial salaries are often so high because they are determined by the principles of supply and demand in a very tight market for top-tier executives—comparable to the market for top athletes, where even higher sums are often paid. Nevertheless, a survey I commissioned in eleven countries showed that most people believe that senior-level managers do not deserve their high salaries. I was intrigued and wanted to know why so many people feel that way.

My surveys revealed that 63 percent of Germans think it is inappropriate for managers to earn more than 100 times as much as salaried employees because, after all, they don't work so much longer or harder than their employees. This opinion was the most strongly supported when respondents were asked why managers should not earn as much as they do. This reflects the prevailing employee mindset, mentioned above, which dictates that salaries should be determined primarily by how long and how hard someone works.[67]

Employees thus project their own performance and remuneration benchmarks onto senior-level managers and believe there must be a close relationship between how hard and how long someone works, on the one hand, and the person's salary, on the other. And with regard to senior-level managers' salaries, respondents do not see such a link. Thus, they conclude that managers' salaries are excessive because no manager can possibly work 100 times as long or as hard as an average employee. Respondents barely understood that senior-level managers' salaries are determined by supply and demand in the market for top-tier executives. Only one in five German respondents agreed that companies can only hire and retain the best managers if they pay very high salaries (the survey specified salaries that are 100 times more than those of an average employee) because otherwise those managers would go to another company that pays more or would work for themselves.[68] In most of the other countries surveyed, the situation was similar: most respondents (especially, but not only, from lower income groups) seem to have implicit salary expectations, according to which the salary is, so to speak, a "perspiration premium" that compensates them for the hours they have worked.

Anyone who defends high managerial salaries should be prepared to become very unpopular. Even some defenders of capitalism criticize "excessive" managers' salaries because, after all, managers do not bear the same high levels of risk as entrepreneurs. What is frequently overlooked is that this is the very reason managers earn far less than entrepreneurs. As the owner of a small or medium-sized enterprise (SME) in Germany, I earned as much as a board member of one of Germany's largest corporations.

Severance packages are negotiated *before* a manager starts working for a company. They are part of a senior manager's overall salary package. Of course, it may turn out later that the package was overly generous because the manager did not perform as well as everyone hoped. In the same way, a manager's salary package may be too low if they end up overperforming—except you can be sure that will never be reported in the media. This is similar to elite athletes, who command huge transfer fees, which may turn out to be excessive if the athlete doesn't perform as well as expected. This point bears repeating: Whenever a company hires a top manager or a team signs a top athlete, there is no guarantee about how they will perform in the future. Their salaries are based on *forecasts*, and these forecasts are based on *past* performance. And such forecasts can be right, but they can also be wrong.

If you compare what top managers do for their companies in terms of performance, that is, in terms of added value for their companies, then on average they are not overpaid but underpaid, and this is a result of uncertainty. This is clear from studies that have looked at what happens to the value of a company when a CEO dies unexpectedly or falls ill: the value of the company falls.[69] Research, according to Tyler Cowen, shows that, "CEOs capture only about 68 to 73 percent of the value they bring to their firms. For purposes of comparison, one recent estimate suggests that workers in general are paid no more than 85 percent of marginal product on average . . . In other words, workers actually seem to be underpaid by somewhat less than CEOs are, at least when both are judged in percentage terms."[70]

The lack of understanding of these interrelationships is thus a basis for resentment about "social inequality" or "social injustice." Incidentally, it is quite revealing that many people use both terms synonymously. Clearly, they have bought into the unconvincing idea that only equality can be just.

The very concept of the "fair distribution of social wealth" is misleading. There is no wealth produced "by society"; rather, the wealth in a society is the sum of what individuals produce and exchange. The economist Thomas Sowell writes: "If there really were some pre-existing body of income or wealth, produced *somehow*—manna from heaven, as it were—then there would of course be a moral question as to how large a share each member of society should receive. But wealth is *produced*. It does not just exist *somehow*."[71]

If Robinson Crusoe and Friday live on an island and Crusoe harvests seven pumpkins and Friday harvests three, then it is nonsensical to say that Crusoe got or took 70 percent of the island's wealth. "If we keep in mind that wealth is something individuals *produce*, then there is no reason to think that economic equality is an ideal and that economic inequality is something that requires a special justification," write Don Watkins and Yaron Brook in their book *Equal Is Unfair*.[72]

By the way, even Marx criticized other socialists who advocated an "equitable distribution." It was "in general incorrect to make a fuss about so-called 'distribution' and put the principal stress on it."[73] Distribution in a society based on private property is, under this condition, "the only 'equitable' distribution on the basis of the present-day mode of production,"[74] according to Marx. "If the material conditions of production are the co-operative property of the workers themselves, then this likewise results in a different distribution of the means of consumption from the present one." On the other hand, vulgar socialists, as Marx referred to them, regard distribution as independent of the mode of production and hence present socialism as if it were principally a matter of distribution.[75]

Apart from this question, egalitarians usually take it for granted that increased equality automatically makes people happier. But is that the case? American sociologists Jonathan Kelley and Mariah D.R. Evans of the International Survey Center, Reno, Nevada, explored this question in a large-scale study. Their pool of data included 169 representative samples from 68 nations in which 211,578 people were surveyed.

On the one hand, the study drew on established questions from so-called "happiness research." Respondents were presented, for example, with the item: "All things considered, how satisfied are you with your life as a whole these days?" and asked to rate their satisfaction on a scale from 1 (dissatisfied) to 10 (satisfied). In addition, they were asked: "Taking all things together, would you say you are: Very happy, quite happy, not very happy, not at all happy?"[76]

Data from these surveys were analyzed in conjunction with data on income inequality in each of the surveyed countries. The basis for measuring income inequality is the so-called Gini coefficient. The Gini coefficient, developed by Italian statistician Corrado Gini, measures the share of income received by different groups in the population and how evenly it is distributed in society. It is zero if the distribution is equal, and one if one person receives all the income and thus the greatest possible inequality exists.

Methodologically speaking, the study from Kelley and Evans was highly sophisticated, because the researchers held all of the other factors that otherwise have an influence on happiness (age, marital status, education, income, gender, GDP per capita, etc.) constant in their calculations. "For example, we compare someone living in Israel to an otherwise similar person earning the same income but living in Finland, the two nations having the same GDP per capita but differing sharply in inequality (0.36 versus 0.26)."[77]

In addition, the researchers also distinguished between advanced societies (primarily the United States and countries in Europe) on the one hand and developing societies (primarily in Africa and Asia) on the other. Only former communist countries were not included in this study, as different relationships apply here (which the researchers analyzed in a separate study).

The study's findings are clear: It is not, as anti-capitalists would have us believe, that more inequality equals less happiness, but just the opposite—more inequality means that people are happier: "In broad overview, pooling respondents from developing nations and from advanced nations together without regard to the important differences between them, more inequality is associated with *greater* well-being."[78]

But a second look revealed clear differences: In *developing* societies, there was a statistically clear correlation between happiness and inequality—more inequality meant greater happiness. The scientists explain this with the "hope factor": People in developing countries often see inequality as an incentive to improve their own situations, for example, through better education. Some groups in society succeed in moving up the social ladder and earning more in this way, and this in turn spurs on others.

In *developed* countries, in contrast, this correlation does not hold. But even here, greater inequality did not lead to lower happiness; rather, it was clear that whether a country is more or less equal has no effect on happiness. For example, there is hardly any difference in perceptions of happiness between people in Sweden and the Netherlands on the one hand and Singapore and Taiwan on the other, even though equality is much greater in Sweden and the Netherlands (as measured by the Gini coefficient) than in Taiwan and Singapore.[79]

Admittedly, it is difficult to objectively measure levels of happiness and well-being, especially since there are many cultural differences between countries that have a bearing on how people respond to the above questions. But conversely, the self-evident assumption that more equality leads to more happiness is simply one of the many unsubstantiated anti-capitalist prejudices. Why is it that the topic of inequality is loaded with so many emotions?

Critics of egalitarians often cite envy as a cause, but egalitarians indignantly reject this. Envy is the most commonly denied, repressed and "masked" emotion. When envy becomes recognizable as such, or is openly communicated, the envious person automatically disqualifies their intentions. The anthropologist George M. Foster asks why people can admit to feelings of guilt, shame, pride, greed, and even anger without loss of self-esteem, but find it almost impossible to admit to feelings of envy. He offers this explanation: anyone who admits to themselves and others that they are envious is also admitting that they feel inferior. This is precisely why it is so difficult to acknowledge and accept one's own envy. "In recognizing envy in himself, a person is acknowledging inferiority *with respect to another*; he measures himself against someone else, and finds himself wanting. It is, I think, this implied admission of inferiority, rather than the admission of envy, that is so difficult for us to accept."[80]

Foster quotes the American psychologist Harry Stack Sullivan and raises an issue that is of key significance in exploring the sources of envy directed at rich people. Envy begins when one person recognizes that another person has something that they would also like to have. This recognition necessarily leads to the questions: "Why don't I have it? Why have they succeeded in achieving what I could not?" This insight explains why most people do not want to admit that they are envious: "Envy is not pleasant because any formulation of it—any implicit process connected with it—necessarily starts with the point that you need something, some material thing that, unhappily, someone else has. This easily leads to the question, Why don't you have it? And that is itself enough in some cases to provoke insecurity, for apparently the other fellow is better at assembling those material props of security than you are, which makes you even more inferior."[81]

Of course, critics of "social inequality" vehemently deny that they are in any way motivated by envy. In his book *Reichtum als moralisches Problem* (*Wealth as a Moral Problem*), the German philosopher Christian Neuhäuser writes: "I think that many phenomena that may seem like envy can actually be understood as wounded feelings of justice."[82] At the same time, Neuhäuser himself is a very good example of the fact that what he calls "feelings of justice" are feelings of envy: Neuhäuser is explicitly not primarily concerned with the fate of the poor, and his first concern is not to improve their situation, but to relieve the rich of their wealth.

Thus, he opposes an attitude that only takes into account "in which society the poorest people have the most goods" and explicitly *criticizes* the belief that a society in which the poorest might have €15,000 a year but everyone else is a millionaire is better than a society in which the poorest have only €12,000 but everyone else has only a little more.[83] He would prefer a society, in which the poorest have less, but the gap between them and the rich is relatively small, than a society, in which the poorest are better off and thus less poor, but the gap between poor and rich is widening.

If you take this argument to its logical conclusion, anyone who accepts Neuhäuser's line of thinking would have to approve of conditions in China under Mao, when millions of people were starving and living in abject poverty. That is because back then, inequality in China was lower than it is today, where there are millionaires and billionaires—but at the same time hundreds of millions have risen from poverty to the middle class. The Gini coefficient, which measures income inequality, was 0.31 when Mao died in 1976—a dream value from the point of view of all egalitarians. In China's cities, it was as low as 0.16 (but higher in the countryside). With the introduction of private property and the market economy, the Gini coefficient in China more than doubled over the following 20 years, from 0.23 to 0.51.[84]

Neuhäuser believes that it is necessary to *prohibit* wealth if one section of society becomes richer at a faster rate than other sections of the same society because this marks an increase in "relative poverty."[85] One could also solve the problem of relative poverty by not improving the situation of the poor, but only by taking away some of the wealth of the rich. In his view, such a "leveling down" could have a very positive impact.[86] Even without alleviating the poverty of the poor, Neuhäuser claims, a great deal could be gained simply by taking something away from the rich. He goes on to state that it would benefit society in a "substantial way if the rich are less rich as this would increase the extent to which poor people are able to act and see themselves as equal members of society."[87] It is quite wrong, he writes, for anyone to claim "that it does no good but only harm if the rich are less rich. It would make a positive difference in terms of the dignity of the poor."[88]

Neuhäuser openly admits that he is not primarily concerned with helping the poor, but with abolishing what he sees as the moral problem of wealth, even though Neuhäuser naturally does not want to be accused of being an envious person. Nevertheless, his view precisely fits the classic definition of envy: the envious person is not primarily motivated by a desire to improve their own situation or that of the worse-off, but seeks to worsen the situation of the envied (in this case, the rich).

Conversely, I am of the opinion that an increase in social inequality is not at all worthy of criticism if it is accompanied by a reduction in poverty. The Nobel Prize winner for economics Angus Deaton even goes as far as to argue that progress is always accompanied by inequality. The fruits of progress have rarely been equally distributed in history.[89] Thus, between 1550 and 1750, the life expectancy of English ducal families was comparable to that of the general population, possibly even slightly lower.[90] After

1750, the life expectancy of the aristocracy increased sharply compared to that of the general population, opening up a gap that was almost 20 years in 1850. With the onset of the Industrial Revolution in the eighteenth century and the gradual beginning of a social order that is today called capitalism or a market economy, life expectancy also increased for the general population from 40 years in 1850 to 45 in 1900 and almost 70 years in 1950.[91] "A better world makes for a world of differences; escapes make for inequality," Deaton observes.[92]

There are many earlier descriptions of the miserable situation of the industrial proletariat created by the emergence of industrialization, which we now know were false. Famously, for example, Frederick Engels wrote the work mentioned in the first chapter of this book, *The Condition of the Working Class in England*, in which he related a sympathetic account of the situation of the working class. While, as we have already seen, he glorified the living conditions of the home workers before the beginning of the Industrial Revolution, he painted a picture of the living conditions of the working class at that time that was based neither on sociological field research nor on statistical analysis and was more polemical than scientific in nature. Today, we know from precise empirical analyses that the situation of the working class in England actually improved considerably between 1781 and 1851. In an analysis published in 1983, the economic historians Peter H. Lindert and Jeffrey G. Williamson calculated that the "standard-of-living gains" for blue-collar workers in these years amounted to 86 percent. At the same time, however, the researchers note, rising social inequality was evident throughout this period.[93] That is, even during this early stage of capitalism in England, rising living standards for ordinary people and rising inequality went hand in hand. So it's always a question of which aspect you think is more important: declining poverty and a rising standard of living for the majority of people in a society, or rising inequality.

The hope of some that as equality increases, dissatisfaction over "social injustice" will decrease is, in my view, not well founded. For example, gender equality in most Western countries has risen as much as dissatisfaction over remaining inequalities has increased in recent decades. And in Germany today, welfare expenditure totals a trillion euros per year. As a percentage of Germany's gross domestic product, government spending on social programs has risen from 18.3 percent (1960) to 24.1 percent (1990) to more than 30 percent today.[94] And yet the complaints of German media and politicians about outrageous levels of social injustice are becoming increasingly shrill.

How strongly the topic of inequality and the "gap between rich and poor" inflames the media—and not only them—was shown by the outstanding success of French economist Thomas Piketty's book *Capital in the Twenty-First Century*, published in 2013. The book received an unusually enthusiastic response from the media and became a bestseller worldwide. Piketty criticizes the fact that today—or so he believes— "the distribution of wealth" is no longer at the center of economics and the social sciences. It is "long since past the time when we should have put the question of inequality back at the center of economic analysis" and "the question of inequality is again to become central," he writes.[95]

In the meantime, critics have highlighted the mistakes in Piketty's data and the serious methodological errors in his approach[96] and he has been forced to walk back his main thesis.[97] Piketty claimed to have found a magic formula according to which the capital of the rich grows faster than the economy, which inevitably increases inequality. He apparently fell for the exaggerated claims of some hedge fund and private equity fund managers about the performance of their investment vehicles. And most importantly, he completely ignores the fact that today's rich are very different people than those who were rich 10, 20, or 30 years ago—we will see below that confusing statistical categories and actual people is a mistake that is made again and again in the debate about inequality. A quick look at the list of the richest people in the world 20 years ago reveals that they are not among the top echelon of the super-rich today.

Contrary to what Piketty apparently believes, most super-rich people are not "rentiers" whose wealth increases fabulously and "passively" through ingenious financial investments, but self-made entrepreneurs whose wealth consists predominantly of the company they themselves (helped) build. And this is even more true today than in the past, as an analysis by *Forbes* shows: In 1984, less than half of those on the *Forbes 400* list of the richest Americans were self-made entrepreneurs. In 2020, the figure was 69.5 percent. This analysis is based on a scoring system that awards a score of 1 to 10 to each of the 400 richest Americans, based on how they became rich. A score of 1 means that a person inherited everything and has done nothing to grow their wealth. A 10 is awarded to anyone who rose from humble beginnings and overcame every obstacle to build their wealth and become a self-made billionaire. Individuals who score between 6 and 10 are classed as self-made.[98]

According to the 2019 *Wealth X Report*, of the 2,604 billionaires in the world, 56 percent were self-made, 31 percent had fortunes that were partly self-made, and only 13 percent had purely inherited wealth. Among UHNWIs (Ultra High Net Worth Individuals, namely those with a net worth of at least $30 million), the proportion of fortunes that were self-made was even higher at 68 percent. Twenty-four percent of UHNWIs were partly self-made and just 8 percent inherited all of their wealth.[99]

The importance of inheritance is overestimated because, in reality, most heirs are unable to preserve let alone expand their assets. In this respect, not only is it wrong to claim that "the poor are getting poorer and poorer"—as shown in the last chapter—but it is equally false to assert that "the rich are getting richer and richer." For people who have inherited their wealth, at any rate, this is usually not the case. In 1901, the German writer Thomas Mann published one of his most celebrated novels, *Buddenbrooks: The Decline of a Family*, which tells the story of how a rich merchant family, the Buddenbrooks, slowly but surely squandered its fortune over the course of four generations. As is so often the case, fact mirrors fiction, as demonstrated by the scientists Robert Arnott, William Bernstein and Lillian Wu in their research paper, "The Myth of Dynastic Wealth: The Rich Get Poorer." They ask: "Where are the current hyper-wealthy descendants of past entrepreneurial dynasties—the Astors, Vanderbilts, Carnegies, Rockefellers, Mellons, and Gettys? . . . The originators of great wealth are one-in-a-million geniuses . . . In contrast, the descendants of the hyper-wealthy rarely have that same one-in-a-million genius . . . Typically, we find that descendants halve their inherited wealth—relative to the growth of per capita GDP—every 20 years or less . . . Today, the massive fortunes of the 19th century are largely depleted and almost all of the fortunes generated just a half-century ago are also gone."[100]

Back to Piketty: He does not claim that capitalism *per se* always leads to rising inequality. On the contrary, for most of the twentieth century, according to Piketty, things went the other way—social inequality fell. It was not until the years 1990 to 2010 that inequality increased, although he concedes that "it is by no means certain that inequalities of wealth are actually increasing at the global level."[101]

To begin with, the thesis of rising inequality is not true on a global scale—and isn't the world a more relevant geographical level of analysis than a single country? Worldwide, inequality has not risen in recent years; it has fallen significantly, as the Canadian-American researcher Steven Pinker shows.[102] The years that are particularly bad from Piketty's point of view were actually the best for hundreds of millions of people all around the world. In his critique of Piketty, the French economist Jean-Philippe Delsol points out that in the 20 years for which Piketty claims inequality increased (1990—2010), 700 million people were lifted out of extreme poverty.[103]

But Piketty and other critics of inequality apparently do not care much about the fate of hundreds of millions of people in developing countries. Their critique relates mainly or exclusively to the development of inequality in developed capitalist countries, such as the United States.

As indicated above, other scholars have analyzed Piketty's figures on the evolution of inequality in the United States and in many cases have identified them as incorrect or inaccurate. According to the data Piketty and economists Emmanuel Saez and Gabriel Zucman present in the World Inequality Database, the share of U.S. income held by the richest 1 percent of Americans increased from 10 percent to 15.6

percent between 1960 and 2015. U.S. economists Gerald Auten and David Splinter have shown that these data are skewed upward and, in fact, the share of U.S. income held by the richest 1 percent increased more moderately, from 7.9 percent to 8.5 percent between 1960 and 2015. The same is true of the share of U.S. wealth held by the richest 1 percent, which Piketty and colleagues claim rose from 22.5 percent to 38.6 percent between 1980 and 2014. According to the calculations of Matthew Smith, Owen Zidar and Eric Zwick, however, it actually rose from 21.2 to 28.7 percent during this period.[104]

This does not even take into account the fact that the data on wealth exclude the present value of defined benefit pension plans and social security programs, which distort the comparison to the disadvantage of the poorer sections of the population.[105] When calculating asset values, it is also important to remember that they depend above all on how much house prices have risen in relation to share prices. In times when share prices grow much faster than house prices (the Dow Jones rose from 8,772 points in early 2009 to 36,338 at the end of 2021), wealthy people benefit more because they have a higher share of securities than less wealthy people.

Economist Thomas Sowell shows that many "statistics" about rising inequality are misleading because they fail to distinguish between developments in statistical categories over time and what has been happening with actual flesh-and-blood human beings.[106] If, for example, it is said that the income or wealth of the top 1 percent or even of the 100 richest people in a country has increased by x percent in the past decade, this refers to a statistical category, but not to the income or wealth of specific individuals. Ten years ago, the top 1 percent consisted to an (often very considerable) extent of completely different people than today. The same is true, for example, when we talk about the bottom 10 percent, which would have lost x percent. Again, this refers to a statistical category, not to specific individuals. Of those who belonged to the bottom 10 percent ten years ago, many have since moved up to a higher income bracket— they no longer belong to the bottom 10 percent because, for example, they have acquired more skills and experience and earn more, have accumulated assets or because they have a different job. Almost invariably, these statements are based on confusing what has been happening over time in statistical categories with what has been happening over time with actual flesh-and-blood individual people.[107] Many of the studies into wealth are methodologically weak because they lack the "dynamic element": the movement between income or wealth cohorts over time, also called social mobility (I will talk about this further below). It makes a big difference—economically, ethically and morally—whether the bottom 10 percent of the population in terms of income distribution in country X in decade 1 are still the same people in decade 2, or whether this "decentil" in decade 2 is now composed of completely different people. The problem is that many people who have strong opinions about inequality also have little or no understanding of statistics. This leads to grossly inaccurate numbers time and time again.

Damien Knight and Harry McCreddie have shown in their 2019 paper "Understanding the 'Facts' About Top Pay" that many statistics published in the media about executive pay inflation or about the development of the ratio between executive pay and that of ordinary employees are grossly flawed because those who make these calculations frequently lack even a rudimentary understanding of mathematical or statistical methodologies. For example, averages and medians are often confused, or no distinction is made between pay awards granted and pay awards realized, and so on. Taking the UK as an example, the authors explain how an actual increase in executive salaries of 6 percent in a given period quickly becomes an increase of 23 percent in the media, or an increase of 2 percent becomes one of 49 percent.[108]

Their conclusion: "Our view is that poor research and analysis has done more damage to social cohesion than the companies themselves have done by paying their top executives highly."[109] According to the authors, the share of compensation paid to top executives in companies in the UK's FTSE-100 as a percentage of absolute shareholder returns was only 0.19 percent in the bottom quartile 2002–2010, 0.40 percent in the median and 0.67 percent in the top quartile.[110]

So the figures about the increase in inequality in the U.S. and other countries are often exaggerated, but that does not change the fact that inequality is increasing in many countries. Walter Scheidel shows that inequality increased in Britain from 1973 onward, in the U.S. from 1976, and then in many other countries. In a sample of 26 countries, top income shares grew by half between 1980 and 2010, whereas market income inequality rose by 6.5 Gini points, only partially offset by redistribution.[111] In 11 of 21 countries for which Scheidel analyzed data on the income shares of the top groups, the portion of all income obtained by the top 1 percent rose by 50 to 100 percent between 1980 and 2010.[112]

Some explanations for this trend are more mundane than one might expect. Scheidel shows, for example, that "assortative mating" (i.e., the growing economic similarity of marriage partners) has widened gaps between households and has been credited with causing some 25 to 30 percent of the overall increase in American earnings inequality between 1967 and 2005.[113]

The German-British economist Kristian Niemietz cites technological progress as one of the "main drivers of increased inequality": In high-tech economies or economic sectors, the wage spread is greater than in less technology-heavy economies or sectors. "One conceivable, but probably not very popular, way to counteract wage spread would therefore be to erect additional hurdles against technological progress."[114]

Other causes of wealth inequality can be found where hardly anyone would suspect them, namely in the expansion of the welfare state. Chris Edwards of the U.S. Cato Institute and Ryan Bourne of the UK Institute for Economic Affairs show that increases in social security lead to people saving less, that is, building up fewer assets for their own retirement. And this is for two reasons: On the one hand, taxes and social security contributions leave them with less, making it more difficult to accumulate personal savings, but on the other hand, as the welfare state expands, people increasingly rely on the state to provide for them in times of need and when they retire. Government programs for retirement, healthcare, and other benefits have reduced the incentives and the ability of nonwealthy households to accumulate savings, which has in turn contributed to increasing wealth inequality.[115]

Another reason for rising inequality in developed countries is globalization. On the one hand, globalization and digitalization are creating career opportunities for the well-qualified, while on the other hand, workers doing basic jobs are facing competition from robots or from workers in China and other emerging countries.

These people are often called "globalization's losers," and as far as income development is concerned, that is true. Pinker points out, however, that things look quite different if you define poverty not in terms of people's earnings but in terms of their consumption. Using this approach, he says, the poverty rate in the U.S. has declined by 90 percent since 1960, from 30 percent of the population to just 3 percent. " . . . globalization may produce winners and losers in income, but in consumption, it makes almost everyone a winner."[116]

This is clear from how many hours an American had to work to be able to buy certain products: in 1973, they worked more than 100 hours to be able to buy a color TV; 30 years later it was only 21 hours. In 1973, they worked 72 hours to buy a washing machine; three decades later, they worked 23 hours. Don Watkins and Yaron Brook list 11 household appliances for which an American had to work a total of 575 hours in 1973—in 2013 it was only 170 hours.[117] This does not even take into account that the quality of products has improved considerably over the same period: The quality of a color TV in 1973 was incomparably lower than that of a color TV in 2013, and washing machines used far more electricity and water than they do today.

Lower-income households in particular benefit disproportionately as consumers from liberalization and competition. In Europe, for example, the telecommunications and airline industries were deregulated and privatized. This led to more competition and made telephoning and flying much cheaper, even for people on a budget. When I was young, air travel was so expensive that many people could afford at most one foreign vacation every few years. I flew for the first time when I was 30, and only because a government institution paid my airfare so that I could give a scientific lecture in the United States. And people kept long-distance calls (i.e., not made within one's own city) short or it would be too expensive. Today, people can fly to other countries for less than €100 in some cases, and phone calls cost only a small fraction of what they used to—and that's thanks to more capitalism in these areas.

Critics of globalization, incidentally, confirm this development—but, surprisingly, they put a negative slant on it. One example is consumer researcher Carl Tillessen, who quotes the following figures for Germany: In the early 1970s, clothing was still so expensive that people had to spend 10 percent of their disposable income on a decent set of clothes.[118] But thanks to the relocation of production to low-wage countries, we can now afford five times the amount of clothing from less than 5 percent of our disposable income with less than half the expenditure.[119]

I read the numbers this way: As far as consumption is concerned, we are almost all globalization's winners because today we get much more for our money than we used to. Tillessen, who is critical of consumerism (see Chapter 8), reads the figures quite differently. For him, they are evidence of a negative development, namely that we are buying more and more things that we don't actually need—and supposedly only because a huge group of people is being kept in slavery; the rich are getting richer and the poor are getting poorer,[120] and a "dark age has dawned" for people in poorer countries as a result of globalization.[121] Anti-capitalists also criticize what are materially clearly beneficial developments, such as that most people in the world count as globalization's winners when measured in terms of consumption.

So, why are so many people so dissatisfied? Time and again, we hear that social mobility no longer works properly, that is, the promise of advancement, whereby future generations will have a better life than people today. However, inequality and social mobility are two different issues. Rising inequality may well be associated with rising social mobility. In Germany, the opinion has become entrenched that social advancement used to work, but it is now broken. The figures contradict this thesis. The German government's 6th Poverty and Wealth Report (2021) states, "In terms of occupational status, more people continue to move further up the ladder than their father; having the same or even lower status than their father are each less common than ever before."[122]

Nevertheless, the situation should not be glossed over. The argument must be taken seriously, because if people have the impression that effort and personal endeavor are no longer worthwhile and that the path to social advancement is blocked for them or their children, this fuels dissatisfaction. And indeed, the chances of advancement could be better, and the perception that this is not the case is a source of justified criticism for many people in Western countries. If social advancement is not as easy today in countries like the U.S., however, it is not because of capitalism, but because of the state.

The first reason is that education systems in many Western countries are poor. The top ten in the PISA rankings include numerous Asian countries, such as China, Singapore, Taiwan and South Korea, whereas countries, such as Germany and the USA, no longer make the grade.[123] The state's failure in the education sector, however, is not the only barrier to advancement. As important as education is, it is only one possible path for moving up the social ladder and earning more. Another path is self-employment and entrepreneurship. But here, too, things look bleak for countries such as Germany and the U.S., where sprawling government bureaucracy and taxes stand in the way of start-ups. It is absurd that in the ranking of the countries in which it is easiest to start a company, the United States only comes in 11th place and Germany in 25th. The first five places in this ranking are all occupied by Asian countries.[124]

The welfare state in Western countries is taking away people's personal responsibility. Whereas Americans used to see themselves as masters of their own destinies, in recent decades many—as in Europe—have developed an attitude of entitlement toward the state, which they now see as responsible for guaranteeing their well-being. This paralyzes personal initiative. And politically, it leads to the strengthening of forces that tell people that other countries—such as China—are to blame for their situation. This is referred to as victim mentality. The journalist Charles Sykes lamented this development in the United States some 30 years ago.

In many countries, the state is far too strong where it should be weak—that is, in the area of the economy. And the state is very weak where it should be strong. In education, many countries could take an example from South Korea, where not only is state spending on education very high, but people also invest quite substantial sums in their own education. When anti-capitalists blame capitalism instead of the state for the fact that upward mobility often no longer works as it should, this is not supported by the facts.

Another question that is all too rarely asked is: what would be the price of eliminating inequality? In 2017, the renowned Stanford historian and scholar of ancient history Walter Scheidel presented an impressive historical analysis of this question in his book *The Great Leveler: Violence and the History of Inequality from the Stone Age to the Twenty-First Century*. He concludes that: "So far as we can tell, environments that were free from major violent shocks and their broader repercussions hardly ever witnessed major compressions of inequality."[125]

Substantial reductions in inequality have only ever been achieved as the result of violent shocks, primarily consisting of:

- War,
- Revolution,
- State failure and systems collapse, and
- Plague.

According to Scheidel, the greatest levelers of the twentieth century did not include peaceful social reforms; they were the two world wars and the communist revolutions. In Chapter 9, I will show how the two world wars reduced inequality; in Chapter 11, we will see how the communist revolutions—for example in Russia, China and Cambodia—led to the reduction of inequality.

The price of reducing inequality has thus usually involved violent shocks and catastrophes, whose victims have been not only the rich, but millions and millions of people who have had to pay with the loss of their lives, freedom, income or property. Neither nonviolent land reforms nor economic crises nor democratization has had as great a leveling effect throughout recorded history as these violent upheavals. "If we seek to rebalance the current distribution of income and wealth in favor of greater equality," Scheidel writes, "we cannot simply close our eyes to what it took to accomplish this goal in the past. We need to ask whether great inequality has even been alleviated with our great violence."[126] Scheidel's answer to this question is a resounding no. This may be a depressing finding for many adherents of egalitarian ideas.

However, if we shift perspective, and ask not "How do we reduce inequality?" but "How do we reduce poverty?"—the question posed in the previous chapter—then we can provide an optimistic answer: Not violent ruptures of the kind that led to reductions of inequality, but very peaceful mechanisms, namely innovations and growth, brought about by the forces of capitalism, have led to the greatest declines in poverty. Or, to put it another way: The greatest "levelers" in history have been violent events, such as wars, revolutions, state and systems collapses, and pandemics, but the greatest "reducers" of poverty in history have been peaceful processes.

3

"CAPITALISM IS RESPONSIBLE FOR ENVIRONMENTAL DESTRUCTION AND CLIMATE CHANGE"

IN 1977, back when I was 20 years old and a Marxist, I wrote in an essay: "The task of left-wing environmental policy must therefore not be to fight the destruction of the environment inherent in the system, because—as shown—capitalism and environmental protection are fundamentally contradictory. The purpose is therefore not to reinforce any illusions about the feasibility of environmental protection within the capitalist system, but to systematically destroy those illusions and show that protecting the environment is only possible under another economic system entirely, a system in which the means of production are socialized and production is oriented towards utility and towards the satisfaction of natural needs."[127]

Similar arguments have become popular today, almost half a century later. The popular critic of capitalism and globalization, Naomi Klein, admits that she initially had no particular interest in climate change. Then, in 2014, she wrote a hefty 500-page tome called *This Changes Everything: Capitalism vs. the Climate*. Why did she suddenly become so interested? Well, prior to writing this book, Klein's main interest was the fight against free trade and globalization. She says quite openly: "I was propelled into a deeper engagement with it partly because I realized it could be a catalyst for forms of social and economic justice in which I already believed."[128] She hoped for "a new kind of climate movement to take up the fight against so-called free trade."[129] She strictly rejects highly efficient solutions, such as climate-friendly nuclear energy, because she is not at all interested in solutions within the framework of capitalism.

Klein writes that she recognized that climate change presents a chance that "we collectively use the crisis to leap somewhere that seems, frankly, better than where we are right now"[130] and "that climate change could become a catalyzing force for positive change—how it could be the best argument progressives have ever had . . . to reclaim our democracies from corrosive corporate influence; to block harmful new free trade deals . . . to open borders to migrants."[131] The climate crisis could "form the basis of a powerful mass movement"[132] and this movement should set itself the following objectives:

- to "radically expand the commons" [i.e., state-owned property and resources].[133]

- to introduce a "carefully planned economy."[134]

- to "change pretty much everything about our economy."[135]

- to introduce "new taxes, new public works programs."[136]

- to secure the "reversals of privatizations."[137]

- to ensure "extinction for the richest and most powerful industry the world has ever known—the oil and gas industry."[138]

- to set government guidelines on "how often we drive, how often we fly, whether our food has to be flown to get to us, whether the goods we buy are built to last . . . how large our homes are."[139]

- to push for "a fundamental reordering of the component parts of Gross Domestic Product."[140]

- to seek "less private investment in producing for excessive consumption."[141]

- to guarantee "increased government spending"[142]

- and to achieve "a great deal more redistribution."[143]

Klein embraces a suggestion that the most well-off 20 percent of the population should accept the largest cuts in order to create a fairer society.[144] She argues that "our economic system and our planetary system are now at war"[145] and the only suitable response is therefore "revolutionary change to the political and economic hegemony."[146]

These quotes—to which many more such statements in Klein's book could be added—confirm that the most important goal of anti-capitalists like Klein is not to improve the environment or find solutions for climate change. Their real goal is to eliminate capitalism and establish a state-run, planned economy. That is why she consistently rejects a whole range of measures that would protect the environment and mitigate the risks of climate change because they would be compatible with the prevailing economic system: capitalism.

But what is the true relationship between capitalism, environmental destruction and climate change? If we compare the ranking of the countries with the highest environmental standards with the Heritage Foundation's *Index of Economic Freedom*, we see a different connection than the one purported by Klein.

For more than 20 years, researchers at Yale University have been publishing the *Environmental Performance Index* (*EPI*), which ranks countries according to their environmental health and ecosystem vitality.

The *EPI* uses a total of 32 performance indicators in eleven categories:[147]

1. Air Quality

2. Sanitation and Drinking Water

3. Heavy Metals

4. Waste Management

5. Biodiversity and Habitat

6. Ecosystem Services

7. Fisheries

8. Climate Change

9. Pollution Emissions

10. Water Resources

11. Agriculture

According to Yale University's analyses, Denmark, Luxembourg, Switzerland, the United Kingdom and France are the highest-ranked countries, followed by Austria, Finland, Sweden, Norway and Germany. The 2020 report states, "One of the consistent lessons of the *EPI* is that achieving sustainability requires sufficient economic prosperity to fund public health and environmental infrastructure."

The researchers find that there is a clear positive correlation between environmental performance and per capita GDP.[148]

An interesting comparison can be made between the *EPI* and the Heritage Foundation's *Index of Economic Freedom*, which has been measuring economic freedom around the globe since 1995. The *Index*, which is also referred to as the capitalism index by the sociologist Erich Weede,[149] analyzes the level of economic freedom in 178 countries and applies twelve criteria, all of which are weighted equally:

1. Property Rights

2. Judicial Effectiveness

3. Government Integrity

4. Tax Burden

5. Government Spending

6. Fiscal Health

7. Business Freedom

8. Labor Freedom

9. Monetary Freedom

10. Trade Freedom

11. Investment Freedom

12. Financial Freedom

The ten most economically free countries in the world in the 2021 *Index* are:

1. Singapore

2. New Zealand

3. Australia

4. Switzerland

5. Ireland

6. Taiwan

7. United Kingdom

8. Estonia

9. Canada

10. Denmark

According to the 2021 *Index*, the countries with the lowest levels of economic freedom are North Korea, Venezuela, Cuba, Sudan and Zimbabwe. The 178 countries are all grouped into five categories: "Free," "Mostly Free," "Moderately Free," "Mostly Unfree" and "Repressed." The Heritage Foundation's researchers compared the two indices—Yale University's *Environmental Performance Index* and their own *Index of Economic Freedom*—for the year 2020 and found that the countries with the highest levels of economic freedom also had the highest *EPI* scores, averaging 76.1, while the "Mostly Free" countries averaged 70.2. There is then a big gap to the "Moderately Free" countries, which were rated much lower (59.6 points) for their environmental performance. The "Mostly Unfree" and "Repressed" countries registered by far the worst environmental performance (46.7 and 50.3 points in the *EPI*, respectively).[150]

To smooth out the dynamic developments in the *Index of Economic Freedom*, it makes sense to take each country's average score over the 15 years from 2006 to 2020. This compensates for the kind of one-off effects that can result from short-term policy measures. These averages can then be compared with the *Environmental Performance Index* scores from 2020. The data reveal a clear positive correlation (the correlation coefficient is 0.67). A regression analysis also confirms that for every one-point increase in the *Economic Freedom Index*, there is a 1.06-point increase in the *Environmental Performance Index*. Such a high coefficient, combined with the very strong correlation between the indexes, suggests a clear statistical relationship. This correlation can be explained by the causality between increased capitalism and greater technological progress and prosperity.

The economist Daniel Fernández Méndez addressed the potential objection that countries with greater economic freedom "are 'exporting' their polluting industries to the less free third world, while keeping non-polluting industries in their country."[151] However, this is clearly not the case. His analysis of the investments made by countries with high environmental standards reveals that only 0.1 percent of their foreign investments flow to countries with low environmental standards.

Méndez's conclusions are clear: "With the data analyzed, we can see that capitalism suits the environment. The greater the economic freedom, the better the environmental quality indexes. The 'cleaner' countries do not export their pollution by relocating companies."[152]

In 2016, researchers published a study in the journal *Sustainability* that included an evaluation of the correlation between the *EPI* and the *Open Market Index* (*OMI*) compiled by the International Chamber of Commerce (ICC).[153] The *OMI* measures a country's openness to free trade and is thus an important indicator of economic freedom. The researchers found a high degree of overlap between the *OMI* and the *EPI*: 19 of the *OMI*'s 27 highest-scoring countries also appear in the top 27 of the *EPI*. The survey covered a total of 75 countries, including all G20 and EU members. Together, these countries account for more than 90 percent of international trade and investment. The researchers conclude: "It is evident that there is a strong connection between *OMI* and *EPI* scores, supporting our hypothesis that countries with an open economy score higher in environmental performance. Overall, our evidence shows that the level of the openness of an economy is associated with a country's environmental protection."[154]

Another study, "Is Free Trade Good for the Environment?" by Antweiler, Copeland and Taylor, uses sophisticated mathematical modeling to explore the correlation between free trade—a key feature of capitalism—and environmental pollution. The study finds: "Our estimates of the scale and technique elasticities indicate that if openness to international markets raises both output and income by 1%, pollution concentrations fall by approximately 1%. Putting this calculation together with our earlier evidence on composition effects yields a somewhat surprising conclusion: freer trade is good for the environment."[155]

Of course, it can be argued that capitalism leads to stronger economic growth, which in turn leads to an increase in resource consumption. Following this logic, the most economically inefficient systems should actually be best for the environment since they result in slower growth. However, the above analyses show "that, at an early stage of a country's economic growth, a high level of environmental degradation is observed, while, after a critical point of economic growth, a gradual decline in environmental degradation is reported."[156]

In addition, there are two real-world observations that also disprove the argument that stronger economic growth automatically leads to greater environmental pollution:

1. In non-capitalist countries, environmental degradation has been a far more serious problem than in capitalist countries.

2. The correlation between economic growth and increasing resource consumption is becoming ever weaker in the age of dematerialization.

Let's begin with the first point. Nowhere has environmental degradation been as bad as in the former socialist states. Is this a relevant argument? Yes, because if an economic order based on private property, competition, and freely set prices were the cause of environmental pollution, then, logically, there would have to be significantly less pollution in countries that do not have these characteristics—which is not the case. Moreover, as we have seen, anti-capitalist climate activists, such as Naomi Klein, want to establish an economic order in which the state has disproportionately greater power than under capitalism. Their prescription against climate change and pollution is more state planning. However, in countries where the state has held the most power over the economy, levels of environmental degradation were not lower. On the contrary, they were far higher than in other countries. Of course, it is not beyond human imagination to dream up numerous ideal systems in which the state commands the economy *and* solves all of the problems of pollution and climate change. However, you already know that I refuse to address such pure thought constructs or utopian models because I believe it is more instructive to deal with history and learn from it. Therefore, I will now proceed to show in detail that non-capitalist states and state-planned economies have not only failed to solve environmental problems, but have made them much worse than in capitalist countries.

In 1990, Zhores A. Medvedev took stock for the Soviet Union: "The Soviet Union has lost more pasture and agricultural land to radioactive contamination than the total acreage of cultivated land in Switzerland. More land has been flooded by hydroelectric dams than the total area of the Netherlands. More land was lost between 1960 and 1989 through salinization, changes in the water table, and dust and salt storms than the total areas of cultivated land in Ireland and Belgium put together. Amidst acute food shortages, the total acreage of cultivated land has declined by one million hectares a year since 1975. The Soviet Union is losing its forests at the same rate as rainforests are disappearing in Brazil. In Uzbekistan and Moldavia, chemical poisoning with pesticides has led to such high rates of mental retardation that the educational curricula in secondary schools and universities have had to be modified and simplified."[157] In their 1992 book, *Ecocide in the USSR*, Murray Feshbach and Alfred Friendly Jr. concluded that "no other industrial civilization so systematically and so long poisoned its land, air, and people."[158]

A well-known example of the parlous and perilous state of environmental protection in the USSR is the Chernobyl nuclear disaster, which occurred on April 26, 1986, in reactor four of the Chernobyl Nuclear Power Plant. What most people probably don't know is that this nuclear power plant proudly bore the official name Vladimir Lenin Nuclear Power Plant (*Чернобыльская АЭС им. В. И. Ленина*) in honor of the communist figurehead and state founder because, after the accident, Chernobyl became synonymous with the general dangers of nuclear energy rather than the environmental hazards allowed to run rampant under socialism.

In his definitive, 560-page work, *Midnight in Chernobyl*, the British journalist and author Adam Higginbotham demonstrates that the world's greatest-ever nuclear disaster was a direct result of endemic problems at almost every level of the Soviet economic system. This fact was clear from the moment construction of the plant commenced: "Key mechanical parts and building materials often turned up late, or not at all, and those that did were often defective. Steel and zirconium—essential for the miles of tubing and hundreds of fuel assemblies that would be plumbed through the heart of the giant reactors—were both in short supply; pipework and reinforced concrete intended for nuclear use often turned out to be so poorly made it had to be thrown away."[159]

The roof of the turbine hall of the power plant was covered with highly flammable bitumen, although this was contrary to the regulations. The reason: the more flame-retardant material that was supposed to be used was not even being manufactured in the USSR.[160] The concrete was defective and the workers lacked power tools—a team of KGB agents and informants at the plant reported a continuous series of building faults.[161] As the plant's fourth reactor approached completion, a time-consuming safety test on the unit turbines had not been completed by Moscow's deadline for completion on the last day of December 1983.[162]

Investigations in the Soviet Union after the accident confirmed that the RBMK reactor type was not up to modern safety standards and even before the accident would never have been allowed to operate beyond the borders of the USSR.[163] "The accident was inevitable . . . If it hadn't happened here and now, it would have happened somewhere else," conceded Prime Minister of the USSR Nikolai Ryzhkov.[164]

Soviet authorities initially tried to cover up the full scale of the accident, just as they had covered up a long chain of previous accidents at nuclear power plants. As one of the twelve founding members of the International Atomic Energy Agency (IAEA), since 1957 the Soviet Union had been obliged to report any nuclear accident that took place within its borders. Nevertheless, none of the dozens of dangerous accidents that occurred inside Soviet nuclear facilities over the decades that followed were ever mentioned to the IAEA. "For almost thirty years, both the Soviet public and the world at large were encouraged to believe that the USSR operated the safest nuclear industry in the world."[165] In contrast, the comparatively harmless accident at the Three Mile Island nuclear power station near Harrisburg, Pennsylvania, on March 28, 1979, was exploited by Soviet officials as an example of how unsafe nuclear power plants are under capitalism.[166] Many media outlets in

Western Europe uncritically adopted this distortion of the facts.

After the accident at the Vladimir Lenin Nuclear Plant in Chernobyl, Soviet officials stuck to the cover-up and claimed that the cause of the disaster was nothing more than human error. In a high-profile show trial, a number of the power plant's employees were sentenced. But Valery Legasov, deputy director of the Soviet Institute of Atomic Energy, finally came to the conclusion that it was the "profound failure of the Soviet social experiment, and not merely a handful of reckless reactor operators, that . . . was to blame for the catastrophe."[167] In an interview with the literary journal *Novy Mir*, he warned that another Chernobyl catastrophe could occur at any of the USSR's other RMBK nuclear power plants at any time.[168]

The expert, wracked by illness and despair over what had happened, having studied the accident and its causes more intensively than probably anyone else, recorded a memoir on tape, which was published in *Pravda* soon after his death (this was possible at the time because it was the peak of the freedoms afforded to the editors of the Party-controlled media by Gorbachev's *glasnost* in early 1986). In the September 1988 article, Legasov stated: "After I had visited Chernobyl NPP, I came to the conclusion that the accident was the inevitable apotheosis of the economic system which had been developed in the USSR over many decades . . . It's My Duty To Say This."[169]

The causes were so deeply rooted in the structure of the planned economic system that efforts by Soviet politicians and scientists to change things after the disaster were unsuccessful. An internal report to the Central Committee of the CPSU, prepared a year after the accident at Chernobyl, noted that in the twelve months since the disaster, 320 equipment failures had occurred at Soviet nuclear power plants, and that 160 of them led to emergency reactor shutdowns.[170] All of these—like the numerous accidents before them—were concealed. In the GDR, the central organ of the communist youth organization FDJ, *Junge Welt*, ran the following headline on May 2, 1986: "Western Scaremongering Seeks to Distract from Peace Initiatives."[171]

Not only was the Soviet Union's environmental record disastrous, but so was that of the second major socialist country, the People's Republic of China. Steven Pinker's book *Enlightenment Now* includes a chart that tracks carbon intensity, or CO_2 emissions per dollar of GDP, from 1820 to 2014.[172] As countries such as the United States and the United Kingdom began to industrialize, they emitted more and more CO_2 per dollar of GDP. From the 1950s onward, however, the graph clearly confirms that emissions per dollar of GDP have been falling and falling.

A closer analysis of the graph confirms that China was an extreme outlier in the late 1950s, with carbon intensity rising more dramatically than in any other country and at any other time since 1820. This was entirely due to the greatest socialist experiment in human history, Mao's Great Leap Forward. Not only did this experiment cause the greatest famine in history and kill 45 million people,[173] it was also an ecological disaster. To the outside world, Mao's propaganda constantly trumpeted new record figures in all fields as China sought to prove the progress and superiority of socialism. In particular, steel production was held up as a measure by which to demonstrate the country's progress under socialism. Mao was obsessed with steel and could recite the steel production figures for all of the world's major economies. In 1957, China's steel production was 5.35 million tons; in January 1958, Mao issued a target of 6.2 million tons; and in September, the target was doubled to 12 million.[174] These colossal goals were to be achieved primarily with small blast furnaces operated by villagers in the backyards of the people's communes. Many of these furnaces did not work properly, which is why they mainly produced low-grade material. Iron ingots produced by rural communes were piled up everywhere, and they were so small and brittle that they were unsuitable for modern rolling mills.[175] In late December 1958, even Mao was forced to admit to a top official that 40 percent of the steel was unusable. The steel that could be used had all been produced in conventional steel mills, and the worthless 40 percent came from the small furnaces.[176] At the same time, because of the backyard furnaces, emissions increased massively and economic output declined, which explains China's position as an absolute outlier in Pinker's graph on carbon intensity.

It is not the "unrestrained pursuit of profit" by capitalists, but planned economics and socialism that have caused the greatest environmental destruction—not only in the Soviet Union and China, but in all socialist countries.

China is following Western countries on the decarbonization pathway, although it did take a bit more time to get started. The same, incidentally, is true of India. In China, CO_2 emissions per dollar of GDP peaked in the late 1970s, while India's were highest in the mid-1990s, after which the previously dirigiste subcontinent moved toward a market economy. The result: carbon intensity for the world as a whole has been declining for half a century.[177]

After the collapse of socialism, it was finally possible to take stock. The socialist countries had long boasted of their pioneering role in environmental protection. As early as 1968, East Germany (also referred to as the German Democratic Republic or GDR) added protecting the environment to its constitution as a state objective. Then, in 1972— beating West Germany by 15 years—it established its own Ministry of the Environment.[178] East German propaganda constantly claimed that capitalism was to blame for environmental destruction and that only socialism, with its state-run, planned economy, could ensure a clean environment. But how did reality stack up against such claims?

In 1990, a report was published by the Federal Foundation set up to come to terms with the GDR's past. The report stated: "The ecological problems . . . are devastating. The population of the GDR encounters environmental pollution almost everywhere. Particularly serious is the air pollution caused by sulfur dioxide and carbon dioxide created by the burning of lignite. Lignite is the largest source of energy in the GDR, but the power plants are outdated; there is a lack of desulfurization equipment. The pollution is so severe that many people in the most affected regions, e.g. around the industrial centers of Leipzig, Halle, Karl-Marx-Stadt and Dresden, suffer above-average respiratory diseases and eczema. The 'industrial fog' regularly triggers smog alarms in towns and villages, leaving layers of dust on cars, windowsills and laundry hung out to dry in the open. Water bodies are also highly polluted. The chemical industry discharges untreated wastewater that pollutes rivers and lakes. The joke 'Everything is gray in the GDR, except the rivers,' which was often bandied about in the GDR, reflects this. 'Silver Lake' near Bitterfeld/Wolfen is representative of particularly drastic water pollution. The former open-cast quarry served as a wastewater pit for the Wolfen film factory, into which sludge and waste were dumped. In 1990, the layer of sludge contaminated with heavy metals was up to 12 meters thick in some places. However, it is not only industrial wastewater that contributes to water pollution, but also the generous use of fertilizers in agricultural production. Overall, many rivers and lakes in the GDR were ecologically decimated in 1990."[179]

According to the report, the soil in many areas of the former GDR was also contaminated with a wide variety of pollutants, whether through intensive agriculture or factory farming or the uncontrolled dumping of toxic industrial and municipal waste in "wild" landfills.[180]

Elsewhere in the GDR, uranium miners in Wismut were working under conditions that were extremely hazardous to their health. In compensation, they received up to seven liters of schnapps a month. No one was allowed to mention the word "uranium," and even the brochures used to advertise the area in and around Wismut strictly avoided the word.[181] This tactic of silence was designed to prevent public fears about the health risks associated with uranium.

Data on environmental performance became classified information in the GDR on March 19, 1974 at the latest, when a ministerial decision gave Günther Mittag, Secretary of the Central Committee of the State Party SED for Economics, authority over the distribution of the GDR's annual environmental assessments. From 1982, only he, State Council Chairman Willi Stoph, and Erich Mielke, the head of the Stasi (East Germany's state security service) were allowed to receive the annual environmental report. Many citizens only learned the full truth about the catastrophic state of the environment in the GDR after reunification. Here are a few facts for the purpose of comparison:

- Climate threat: The historian Hubertus Knabe, a leading expert on GDR history, states: "One of the world's biggest climate killers was, in fact, a country that had abolished capitalism—the GDR."[182] In 1989, the GDR emitted more than three times as much CO_2 for each unit of GDP than the Federal Republic.[183]

- Air pollution, sulfur dioxide: In 1988, the GDR emitted 10 times as much sulfur dioxide per km^2 as the Federal Republic (48.1 tons/ km^2 vs. 4.6 tons/ km^2).[184]

- Air pollution, airborne particles: The average load of 20.3 tons per square kilometer in the GDR was more than ten times higher than the Federal Republic (1.8 tons/km^2).[185]

- Coal-fired stoves: In private households, almost two-thirds of the apartments in the GDR were heated with solid fuels such as lignite briquettes at the time of reunification.[186]

- Pollution of rivers: Almost half of the GDR's major rivers were biologically dead in 1989, and 70 percent were no longer allowed to be used for drinking water.[187]

- Nearly half of the GDR's residents received no clean drinking water temporarily or permanently when they turned on the faucet. This was due to the high input of nitrogen, phosphorus, heavy metals and other pollutants into the waters.[188]

The historian Knabe states: "Like many climate activists today, the GDR's leadership held the view that only by abolishing capitalism could environmental problems be solved. They believed that it was the greed of corporations that led to the ruthless destruction of nature. By this logic, the profit motive needed to be replaced by reason and planning for society as a whole. And, as they saw things, this is only possible under socialism."[189]

Many people will concede that socialism is even worse for the environment than capitalism, but they are still left with reasonable doubts: Isn't economic growth in general bad for the environment? There is one argument in particular that seems logical, at least at first glance: Because the earth's raw materials are finite, infinite growth is impossible. This leads many to conclude that, somehow, growth must be curtailed.

Warnings about the limits to growth are not new; they have been around for centuries. Here are just a few examples from the last 80 years: In 1939, the U.S. Department of the Interior declared that U.S. oil reserves would last only 13 more years. In 1949, the U.S. Secretary of the Interior announced America's oil supplies would soon run out. Having learned nothing from its earlier false claims, in 1974, the U.S. Geological Survey said that the U.S. had only 10 years of natural gas left.

In 1970, the scientist Harrison Brown published a graph in *Scientific American* in which he estimated that humanity would run out of copper shortly after the year 2000. Lead, zinc, tin, gold and silver were expected to disappear before 1990.[190] Also in 1970, the ecologist Kenneth Watt predicted that the world would run out of oil: "You'll drive up to the pump and say, 'Fill 'er up, buddy,' and he'll say, 'I am very sorry, there isn't any.'"[191]

Published that same year, the Club of Rome's Limits to Growth study attracted a great deal of attention. To date, more than 30 million copies of the study have been sold in 30 languages. The book warned people to change their ways and offered a stark message: the planet's raw materials would soon be depleted, especially oil. In 20 years, the scientists predicted, the last drop of oil would be used up. And it wasn't only in relation to oil but for almost all relevant raw materials that the Club of Rome's report completely misjudged the date by which they would be exhausted. Natural gas, copper, lead, aluminum, tungsten: According to the predictions issued at the time, none of these natural resources would still be found in the earth today—based on forecasts for continued economic growth between the 1970s and the present day. Everything should have been used up by now; in some cases, decades ago. Silver was supposed to be depleted in 1985. In fact, in January 2020, the United States Geological Survey (USGS) estimated silver reserves worldwide at 560,000 tons.

Before anyone starts shaking their head at all these false predictions, it is worth pointing out that from the beginning of industrialization until about the 1970s, there was indeed a close correlation between economic growth on the one hand and energy and raw material consumption on the other.[192]

But based on numerous data series, the American scientist Andrew McAfee proves in his book *More from Less*, which was published in 2020, that economic growth has decoupled itself from the consumption of raw materials. Data for the U.S. show that of 72 commodities, only six have not yet reached their consumption maximum. Although the U.S. economy has grown strongly in recent years, consumption of many commodities is declining.[193]

As long ago as 2015, the American environmental scientist Jesse H. Ausubel confirmed in his paper "The Return of Nature: How Technology Liberates the Environment" that Americans are consuming fewer and fewer raw materials per capita. Total consumption of steel, copper, fertilizer, wood and paper, which had previously always risen in tandem with economic growth, had peaked and had been declining ever since.

Such developments are all due to the laws of much-maligned capitalism: companies are constantly looking for new ways to produce more efficiently, that is, to get by with fewer raw materials. They do this, of course, not primarily to protect the environment, but to cut costs.

What's more, innovation has promoted a trend we call miniaturization or dematerialization. One example of this trend is the smartphone. Just consider how many devices are contained in your smartphone and how many raw materials they used to consume:

- Calculator

- Telephone

- Video camera

- Alarm clock

- Voice recorder

- Navigation system

- Camera

- MP3 player (replacing the cassette / CD player)

- Compass

- Answering machine

- Scanner

- Measuring tape

- Radio

- Flashlight

- Calendar

- Encyclopedia

- Dictionary

- Foreign language dictionaries

- Address book

Many people today no longer have a fax or use paper road maps because they have everything at their fingertips in their smartphone, and some even do without a wristwatch. In the past, you had four separate microphones in your telephone, audio cassette recorder, Dictaphone and video camera. Today, the single microphone in your smartphone has replaced all of these devices.

I used to be proud of my large record collection, which spanned several shelves. As technology advanced, I bought CDs that all fit on a single shelf—and consumed far fewer raw materials. Today, my girlfriend teases me because I still buy CDs—all of her music is in digital files, which don't take up any space at all. I admit I'm a bit old-fashioned and own several thousand books. I don't have enough shelf space for them all, so most of my books are in storage. My father, despite being 93 years old, is more modern than I am and reads lots of books as e-books on his Kindle.

These are just a few of many examples of a trend toward demate- rialization.[194] The reality is more complex than it might seem at first glance when people say, "Our planet has limited resources, so we can't grow indefinitely."

So, does this all mean that the world can dispense with govern- ment regulations to protect the environment? Of course not. Even such staunch supporters of capitalism as the two Nobel Prize winners for economics Friedrich August von Hayek and Milton Friedman have always stated that the state should set the rules—the legal framework conditions—of the economic game. Hayek emphasized that free-market thinking should not be confused with a "laissez-faire" policy.[195]

And it was some of the most enthusiastic proponents of capitalism, who solved one of the world's greatest ever environmental problems: the "hole in the ozone layer." Here's the story: In the mid-1970s, U.S. scientists Mario Molina and Sherwood Rowland warned that long-lived chemicals, such as chlorofluorocarbons (CFCs), had the potential to destroy Earth's protective ozone layer. And depletion of the ozone layer, they warned, would lead to a sharp increase in skin cancers and affect terrestrial and aquatic ecosystems. At the time, CFCs were found in many household items, including refrigerators, deodorants and hair sprays.

In the mid-1980s, the American researcher Susan Solomon dis- covered that CFCs were responsible for a hole in the ozone layer over Antarctica. Then-U.S. President Ronald Reagan (a fan of Milton Friedman) and British Prime Minister Margaret Thatcher (an admirer of Friedrich August von Hayek) took the initiative and called on the global community to work together. On September 16, 1987, more than 30 countries agreed to phase out CFCs. The resulting "Montreal Protocol" remains an outstanding example of global environmental protection and has helped to ensure that the hole in the ozone layer has become significantly smaller. Ex-UN Secretary-General Kofi Annan later described the "Montreal Protocol" as "Perhaps the single most successful international environmental agreement to date." In one fell swoop, Reagan and Thatcher, the two arch-capitalists, thus did more to protect the environment than Greenpeace and all the other left-wing "environmental activists" ever had.

Government regulations are therefore not bad per se, but often government guidelines on environmental protection do not achieve their well-intentioned goals and instead end up doing the exact opposite. German environmental and energy policy is a case in point: Between 1957 and 2004, about 110 nuclear power stations were commissioned. In the 1970s and 1980s, the primary focus of environmentalists in Germany was to demand a phase-out of nuclear power. No issue was as important to the country's environmental activists as the decommissioning of every single nuclear power plant.

A coalition government of Social Democrats and Greens was formed in 1998 and, two years later in 2000, regulated the end of nuclear energy for the first time in a contract between the Federal Republic and the nuclear power plant operating companies. In 2002, the German Atomic Energy Act was amended on the basis of this contract. A decision was made to extend the operating lives of nuclear power plants in 2010, but this decision was reversed in 2011 following the natural disaster at Fukushima. The last German nuclear power plant is scheduled to be decommissioned in 2022.

It was the Fukushima disaster in 2011 that prompted Angela Merkel's government, in a lightning-swift move, to decide to shut down Germany's nuclear power plants much earlier than originally agreed. And yet it was not the accident itself (which did not even cause Japan to turn its back on nuclear power), but the fact that there were elections in the German state of Baden-Württemberg roughly two weeks afterward that led to Angela Merkel's swift policy shift. In the heated pre-election atmosphere, Merkel wanted to rob the Greens of one of their key election issues. But even that did not work, and the Greens attracted a record number of votes and, for the first time in German politics, a German state elected a Green politician as minister president.

One of the main reasons Germany has not made greater progress in the fight against climate change, despite its extensive efforts, is this decision to phase out nuclear power. It has resulted in the country failing to reduce its CO_2 emissions by as much as it could have. In terms of environmental protection, France, for example, is in many respects no better than Germany, but while Germany has successively shut down its nuclear power plants, France's share of nuclear power in its national energy mix is higher than any other country at about 70 percent (2019). Germany ranks 10th in the overall *Environmental Protection Index 2020*, while France ranks 5th. And this is mainly due to nuclear energy, because in the *EPI's* separate *Climate Protection Index 2020*, Germany ranks just 14th, with France in 4th place.

In their 2020 *EPI* report, Yale researchers cautiously and diplomatically explain that "some analysts" may be of the opinion that Germany's nuclear phase-out could harm the country's progress in environmental performance. Less diplomatic, but more accurate, the *Wall Street Journal* claimed that Germany is pursuing the world's dumbest energy policy.[196]

The main justification for Germany's nuclear shut-down is the risks associated with using nuclear energy. But these risks are exaggerated beyond measure. A comparison of deaths per unit of energy generated (TWh) shows that nuclear energy kills 0.07 people, oil 18.4 and coal 24.6.[197] Even hydropower is significantly more dangerous than nuclear energy. And the "kill ratio" is actually higher for wind power, photovoltaics and renewable fuels than for nuclear power.[198]

Bill Gates makes a strong case for nuclear power in his book on climate change, insisting that "it's hard to foresee a future where we decarbonize our power grid affordably without using more nuclear power."[199] That's because "Nuclear is the only carbon-free energy source we can use almost anywhere, 24 hours a day, 7 days a week."[200]

Opponents of nuclear power have repeatedly implied, either directly or by employing vague formulations, that 20,000 people died as a result of the reactor meltdown in Fukushima in 2011. The number 20,000 is approximately correct, but these people died as a result of an earthquake and subsequent tsunami, but by no means due to radioactivity.[201]

You'll hardly ever hear about the fact that the latest generation of nuclear power plants is safer than its predecessors—most people aren't even aware of the advances that have been made. In addition, the problems with the final disposal of radioactive waste are hugely exaggerated,[202] and little publicity is given to the new reactors, which have almost entirely dispensed with this problem.[203]

As the climate scientist Kerry Emanuel from the Massachusetts Institute of Technology (MIT) in Cambridge succinctly observes: "They can't have it both ways. If they say this [climate change] is apocalyptic or it's an unacceptable risk, and then they turn around and rule out one of the most obvious ways of avoiding it [nuclear power], they're not only inconsistent, they're insincere."[204]

In the United States (as elsewhere), there was a long period during which no new nuclear power plants were built—but this had nothing to do with capitalism. On the contrary, the anti-capitalist movement around the U.S. lawyer Ralph Nader led a massive campaign that deliberately stoked people's fears and led to an almost complete stop in the construction of new power plants.[205] Over the last few years, discussions about nuclear power have become more objective in some countries. As a result, a growing number of environmental activists have even come out in favor of building new nuclear power plants. In California, a good 50 start-ups are currently working on the development of new nuclear technologies. Experts are already talking about "Nuclear Valley" as an offshoot of "Silicon Valley."[206] Bill Gates founded the company TerraPower in 2008 and, if it is successful, reactors could be operated with nuclear waste from other nuclear facilities.[207]

The example of nuclear energy shows that government intervention in the economy, even when environmental protection is given as a motive, is often not driven by rational environmental considerations but by populism and ideology. Nuclear energy is not the only example. The author Alexander Neubauer cites dozens of examples of government environmental regulations that have achieved the opposite of what was intended. *Deutsches Ärzteblatt* (the German medical journal) has published numerous articles reporting that the use of thermal insulation to hermetically seal homes has caused a significant increase in mold infestations in apartments, causing asthma, pneumonia and other life-threatening conditions. Some U.S. states have already banned this kind of insulation because of the associated health risks—in Germany, it is mandatory.[208] This does not, however, mean that we should get rid of all government regulations for environmental protection, but it does prove that economic freedom as a whole is far better at protecting our environment than government edict.

For many so-called "climate activists," environmentalism is little more than a pretext for their fight against capitalism. Some advocate extremely radical solutions that would in fact lead to an eco-dictatorship. They argue that when the survival of mankind is at stake, there should be no taboos. By this logic, we should entertain even the most radical solutions and dispense with values, such as freedom and democracy. When it comes to survival, the argument goes, we can't afford the luxury of being squeamish. However, as I have shown above, planned economies have always failed, especially on the issue of environmental protection.

When it comes to utopias and radical solutions, I am generally skeptical. Nevertheless, if you are willing to engage in a radical thought experiment for a moment, then you might like to consider the arguments put forward by radical supporters of capitalism. Among them is the German economist Thorsten Polleit, who argues that environmental degradation comes from the state overusing, wasting and embezzling scarce resources: "It has no interest or incentive in working for the efficient management of scarce resources; moreover, it also usually lacks the necessary knowledge (competence)."[209] This, he writes, is evident from socialist planned economies, but also applies to states in the Western world, that have also nationalized a host of natural resources—land, parks, roads, waters, and airspace. By monopolizing legislation and jurisdiction, Polleit says, states have been the originators of many environmental problems: "For example, by allowing companies and consumers to dump pollutants on roads and into rivers, oceans, and the air at no cost. Often, this practice is justified on the basis of the 'common good,' which places the rights of polluters above the rights of the aggrieved (property owners). For example, owners of property located near an airport must endure increasing aircraft noise without being compensated by the airport operator."[210]

Polleit proposes a radical capitalist solution. Given the state's poor record as the owner and manager of natural resources, coupled with the positive potentials of the free market being appointed to safeguard scarce resources, Polleit raises the questions: "*Why not privatize everything? Why not convert every piece of state-owned property into private property?*"[211] Under the utopian "pure capitalism" envisioned by Polleit, everything would be in private hands—land, roads, rivers and oceans. The owners of waterways and ocean parcels, or any other resource for that matter, Polleit explains, would be scrupulous in ensuring that their resources are in no way damaged by others. After all, their resources have a market value—they can be marketed as drinking water, for example, or for recreational and sporting use. Polleit's premise is that anyone who is responsible for damaging the resource/property of others would be pursued and held accountable by the owners. He outlines similar principles for other environmental problems, such as air pollution and noise pollution.[212]

As I have already mentioned, I am, as a matter of principle, skeptical about utopias. Nevertheless, Polleit's utopia would be more likely to solve the world's environmental problems than the models propagated by etatists, which amount to an eco-planned economy, of which you can be 100 percent certain that they would exacerbate environmental problems rather than solving them. At the very least, it is perhaps worth considering how we can incorporate some of the ideas proposed by capitalist thinkers, such as Polleit, as we strive to identify market-based solutions to the world's most pressing environmental problems.

4

"CAPITALISM REPEATEDLY LEADS TO NEW

ECONOMIC AND FINANCIAL CRISES"

FOR AS LONG as there have been anti-capitalists, they have been anticipating the great crisis that would bring about the final, irreversible collapse of capitalism. Karl Marx believed he had discovered various economic "laws" that would necessarily lead to the downfall of capitalism, such as the "tendency of the rate of profit to fall" or the impoverishment of the proletariat. In his major work, *Capital*, Marx formulated this as follows: "Along with the constantly diminishing number of the magnates of capital, who usurp and monopolise all advantages of this process of transformation, grows the mass of misery, oppression, slavery, degradation, exploitation; but with this too grows the revolt of the working class, a class always increasing in numbers, and disciplined, united, organised by the very mechanism of the process of capitalist production itself. The monopoly of capital becomes a fetter upon the mode of production, which has sprung up and flourished along with, and under it. Centralisation of the means of production and socialisation of labour at last reach a point where they become incompatible with their capitalist integument. This integument is burst asunder. The knell of capitalist private property sounds . . . But capitalist production begets, with the inexorability of a law of Nature, its own negation."[213]

Marx called his "law" of the tendency of the rate of profit to fall "in every respect the most important law of modern political economy, and the most essential for understanding the most difficult relations. It is the most important law from the historical standpoint."[214] He wrote these sentences in his *Grundrisse: Foundations of the Critique of Political Economy*, and proudly added: "It is a law which, despite its simplicity, has never before been grasped and, even less, consciously articulated."[215] From this law, Marx explains, follows the inevitable collapse of capitalism "in bitter contradictions, crises, spasms."[216] In *The Making of Marx's 'Capital'*, a work that is highly regarded by Marxists, the economist Roman Rosdolsky referred to this as Marx's "prognosis of 'breakdown.'"[217]

Marx formulated his prognosis in the mid-nineteenth century. But the breakdown, the final, great crisis of capitalism, he and others repeatedly predicted has still not happened. His predictions, such as the aforementioned "tendency of the rate of profit to fall" as a harbinger of capitalism's collapse, or the increasing impoverishment of the workers, have proved to be wrong—which, however, does not prevent Marxists to this day from considering his theory, from which these predictions necessarily followed, to be correct.

For anti-capitalists, economic crises have always, above all, been a source of hope—that capitalism would finally collapse on itself. Unfortunately for them, their hopes have been dashed time and time again. In many ways, anti-capitalists are a bit like a doomsday cult, undauntedly announcing new dates for the end of the world after their previous prophecies went unfilled and life carried on as normal.

In the 2008 financial crisis—which we will come to later—anti-capitalists believed that the long-awaited end of capitalism had finally arrived. When capitalism survived this crisis, they were forced to wait and draw hope from the coronavirus crisis of 2020. Even in the earliest days of the Covid-19 pandemic, left-wing intellectuals frequently expressed their wistful expectations that the pandemic would finally achieve what they had been hoping for during the financial crisis of 2008, namely a fundamental reorganization of society and the final defeat of capitalism.[218] William Davies, a British sociologist, published an article in the left-wing British daily newspaper *The Guardian* under the headline: "The Last Global Crisis Didn't Change the World. But This One Could": "We can already identify a few ways that 2020 and its aftermath will differ from the crisis of the 1970s. First, while its transmission has followed the flightpaths of global capitalism—business travel, tourism, trade—its root cause is external to the economy. The degree of devastation it will spread is due to very basic features of global capitalism that almost no economist questions—high levels of international connectivity and the reliance of most people on the labour market. These are not features of a particular economic policy paradigm, in the way that fixed exchange rates and collective bargaining were fundamental to Keynesianism. They are features of capitalism as such . . . It will take years or decades for the significance of 2020 to be fully understood. But we can be sure that, as an authentically global crisis, it is also a global turning point. There is a great deal of emotional, physical, and financial pain in the immediate future. But a crisis of this scale will never be truly resolved until many of the fundamentals of our social and economic life have been remade."[219]

In an economic sense, it is obvious that the crisis triggered by the coronavirus pandemic was the result of an exogenous shock that had nothing to do with the structure of the capitalist economic system. Since the Stone Age, humanity has been struggling with the most severe and serious epidemics—and although globalization did indeed allow the Covid-19 virus to spread (more) rapidly, it was ultimately capitalism that led to the swift development and deployment of equipment, treatments and vaccines so soon after the crisis began—from protective masks and corona tests to the vaccines developed by the detested, capitalist "Big Pharma" companies.

In his 1912 work *Theory of Economic Development*, the Austrian economist Joseph Schumpeter devoted a chapter to "The Nature of Economic Crises." The term "crisis," according to Schumpeter, subsumes quite different phenomena that have no more "in common with each other than . . . that they are all events that call a halt on the previous economic development."[220] He objected to the "popular and scientific conviction that crises are always one and the same phenomenon."[221] Schumpeter differentiated between two categories of crises, namely crises that are "purely economic phenomena . . . resulting from . . . the economic system" and "crises that are not purely economic phenomena."[222] The first of these, according to Schumpeter, are elements or regular, if not necessary, incidents "of a wave-like movement of alternating periods of prosperity and depression."[223] Schumpeter would have counted the crisis triggered by the coronavirus pandemic as one of the second category of crises, whose causes "exist outside the purely economic sphere."[224]

Capitalism differs from previous, "stationary" economic processes, Schumpeter wrote in his 1942 work *Capitalism, Socialism and Democracy*, by its dynamism: "Capitalism, then, is by nature a form or method of economic change and not only never is but never can be stationary."[225] He famously claimed that capitalism "incessantly revolutionizes the economic structure *from within*, incessantly destroying the old one, incessantly creating a new one. This process of *creative destruction* is the essential fact about capitalism."[226] He accused economists of looking only at the problem of how capitalism administers existing structures, "whereas the relevant problem is how it creates and destroys them."[227]

In this respect, crises are something positive—much like a cleansing thunderstorm. In a crisis, companies that do not manage well will go under and other, more innovative companies with better products, better production processes, better distribution structures and lower costs will take their place.

Schumpeter emphasized that many incompetent entrepreneurs could make a short-term profit and that errors and misconduct were common in a boom phase. One element of a crisis, he wrote, is "that everything that is unsound for either reason shows up when prices break and credit ceases to expand in response to decreased demand for it."[228] In his 1927 work *Der moderne Kapitalismus*, the German sociologist and economist Werner Sombart observed that periods of decline are perhaps essential to the development of the capitalist economy: A "selection process" filters entrepreneurs and enterprises—the weak enterprises disappear and the strong survive.[229] "So, blessing upon blessing flows to capitalism from the existence and progress of the expanding economy."[230]

On the question of how economic crises arise in capitalism, there are now about as many theories as there are theorists—and there is not the space here to present them all. Basically, however, I would like to distinguish between two classes of crises: crises that are a result of normal economic cycles, and those that are rooted in structural weaknesses—especially in the relationship between the state and the economy.

The biggest problem today is this second class of crises: In principle, free-market societies tend to constrict the market and expand the role of the state in economic life over time. One reason—aside from the activities of vested interests and the hopes of politicians to maximize votes by making lofty social promises—is the inevitable cyclical waves and crises of capitalism, to which governments often respond with stimulus programs, new regulations, and the general expansion of government action.

Crises are as much a part of economic life as physical weaknesses and illnesses are of life itself—human, animal and plant. In the case of most illnesses that people go through in the course of their lives, their bodies' defense systems and self-healing powers ensure that they get well again. Even if we do nothing about a cold, except to rest for a few days, we get well again. Capitalist crises strengthen the economy in the medium and long terms because unproductive companies are swept from the market. Crises serve a positive, cleansing function, even if the immediate effects are unpleasant for the hardest-hit companies and employees.

But just as lots of people would regard a doctor as incompetent if they were sent home without a prescription and merely advised to rest in bed for a few days to cure the common cold, so voters would doubt the competence of a politician who told them, "Let's wait until the crisis is over. In the long run, things will be much better, even if a few big companies go bankrupt during the crisis." The opposition would denounce such a politician as heartless or incompetent, and most people would probably agree.

This analogy can be taken further: Some people would describe a doctor who prescribes antibiotics for a cold, fever-reducing drugs for a raised temperature, or drugs to suppress the urge to cough as a good doctor because the treatments help them. They are not aware that the doctor's short-term "help" is often associated with undesirable side effects, a slower healing process or even more serious long-term complications. Fever and coughing are the body's natural responses as it fights infection. While there are, of course, situations in which medication is required, it is often better to do nothing. This is because those who suppress their body's natural responses in order to feel better are delaying the self-healing process. If you take antibiotics every time you have a cough or the sniffles instead of relying on your body's self-healing powers, you risk not only a number of undesirable side effects but also help speed up antibiotic resistance.

Most people have internalized the belief that taking action is almost always better than "doing nothing," not only in the field of healthcare, but also in politics and business. Many patients do not understand that inaction is often better than actionistic resistance. And most citizens are just as unlikely to understand that in normal economic crises, waiting and trusting the system's self-healing powers would often be best, at least better than economic stimulus programs, government intervention and printing money, which may help in the short term, but which will first have undesirable side effects; second, delay economic recovery for an unnecessarily long time; and third, weaken economic growth in the long term.

Schumpeter was convinced that any artificial stimulation of the economy to mitigate a crisis, even with the best of moral intentions, would only ever make things worse because it would prevent the crisis from correcting maladjustments, thereby creating new maladjustments. Schumpeter emphasized "that recovery is sound only if it does come of itself."[231]

The U.S. economist Thomas J. DiLorenzo compares the approach adopted by the American government under President Martin Van Buren to deal with the depression of 1837 with the response of President Franklin D. Roosevelt to the Great Depression of 1929. Van Buren pursued an unequivocally laissez-faire policy and resisted all proposals for direct government action and interventionism, which led to a very rapid end to the crisis.[232] In contrast, Franklin D. Roosevelt launched his "New Deal," which relied on a comprehensive series of government programs and pursued an anti-capitalist, interventionist policy. Contrary to the myth spread by anti-capitalists that the "New Deal" ended the crisis, Roosevelt's policies actually prolonged it. Unemployment, which had been as low as 3.2 percent in 1929, climbed to 14.6 percent by 1940. The average unemployment rate from 1933 to 1940 was as high as 17.7 percent.[233] Per capita GDP in the United States had been $857 in 1929 and, at $916, was still barely above that level eleven years later in 1940. Personal consumption expenditure, which had totaled $78.9 billion in 1929, fell to $71.9 billion in 1940.[234]

Japan, in seeking to survive a crisis when its stock and real estate bubbles burst in 1990, delivered another sad example of how damaging government intervention can be. Instead of relying on the self-healing powers of the market and initiating free-market reforms, Japan tried to ease the "pain" caused by the crisis by increasing its national debt over and over again. By 2020, the national debt of Japan amounted to an incredible 266 percent of GDP, which is even higher than the national debts of Greece (200 percent), Italy (155 percent) and the United States (131 percent). Significantly, from 1980 to 2003, inflation-adjusted welfare spending in Japan grew at an annual rate of 4.37 percent, faster than in any comparable country (U.S. 2.84 percent, Germany 1.94 percent).[235]

While politicians would be best advised to do nothing in the case of economic slumps or when speculative bubbles burst, this is the wrong recipe in the case of serious crises that have deep-seated, structural causes. In the face of such structural crises, politicians must indeed act, just as you can't wait for serious illnesses or injuries to heal by themselves. In my book *The Power of Capitalism*, I showed how Margaret Thatcher and Ronald Reagan led their countries out of deep crises in the 1980s. They did so not by relying on social programs and tax increases, but by creating more room for market forces through decisive privatizations, tax cuts and deregulation.

On a smaller scale, these types of reforms were implemented in Sweden in the 1990s to reverse the excessive taxation and regulation introduced by previous governments. This approach put Sweden back on the path to growth. The same is true for many other countries where capitalist reforms have resulted in more growth and prosperity. In Germany, too, the free-market reforms initiated by Gerhard Schröder at the beginning of the millennium helped the economy recover and drove unemployment ever lower.

Unfortunately, capitalist reforms take place far too rarely. It is easier to win elections with welfare promises and redistribution programs than it is with the announcement of free-market reforms, which often go hand in hand with cuts in social spending.

From the point of view of most politicians, there is no limit to the extent to which the welfare state can be expanded because whatever level they reach is soon deemed insufficient. Politicians are always discovering new "injustices" (i.e., inequalities) that they claim can only be corrected by redistribution or higher borrowing. They calculate that, when the next elections roll around, the beneficiaries of such "generous measures" will remember which politicians campaigned for them. The benefit for the recipients of government welfare schemes is more than questionable.

Capitalism even gets the blame for crises that clearly have nothing to do with capitalism. This applies to the coronavirus crisis just as much as it does to the Global Financial Crisis of 2008, which peaked with the bankruptcy of Lehman Brothers. In my book *The Power of*

Capitalism I devoted an entire chapter to this crisis—here I will present a condensed analysis.

The U.S. central bank, the Federal Reserve, or Fed for short, had radically cut interest rates after the Dot Com bubble burst in 2000. This response may have eased the pain of one crisis, but it also led to a new bubble, this time in the real estate sector. The new real estate bubble did not develop evenly across the United States—it mainly became a problem in states that had restricted the supply of real estate through heavy government regulation of the building code. Years before the American house price bubble burst, a number of forward-looking economists had warned of the link between low interest rates and rising house prices. William R. White, a proponent of the market-oriented Austrian school of economics, warned in August 2003 that "the unusually buoyant behavior of housing prices in the current slowdown may well be related to the substantial monetary easing undertaken by central banks . . . [This] has encouraged a further rise in indebtedness in the household sector in a number of countries, raising the risk of contributing to balance sheet overextension there, especially if housing prices were to soften."[236]

It is notable how a leading American economist who is more sympathetic to active state interventions than White saw the matter. Paul Krugman even *recommended* to the Fed the very strategy White had *warned against*: "To fight the recession the Fed needs more than a snapback; it needs soaring household spending to offset moribund business investment. And to do that, as Paul McCulley of Pimco put it, Alan Greenspan needs to create a housing bubble to replace the Nasdaq bubble."[237]

One cause of the real estate price bubble was that banks had increasingly been granting a growing number of home mortgages to unqualified borrowers who would clearly never be able to repay their loans. In fact, loans to minority borrowers from lower-income sectors of society were precisely what politicians, including President Bill Clinton, wanted. It was enforced by the legislature and backed by the semi-public mortgage companies Freddie Mac and Fannie Mae. Banks throughout America actually ran the risk of being sued for discrimination unless they met certain quotas for lending to minorities.

In his autobiography, Alan Greenspan, Chair of the Federal Reserve of the United States at the time of the crisis, admitted that such lending policies had increased the level of financial risk. "But I believed then, as now, that the benefits of broadened homeownership are worth the risk."[238] It was not "unfettered markets" that caused the subprime mortgage crisis; it was socio-politically motivated government quotas and the Fed's low interest rates.

The subprime loans were securitized as collateralized debt obligations (CDOs) and sold to investors, including state-owned banks in Germany (Americans even spoke of "stupid German money"). As soon as property prices started to fall, the value of these CDOs collapsed as many borrowers were no longer able to service their loans. This caused serious problems for banks, insurance companies and investment funds, and led to a chain reaction that culminated in the collapse of Lehman Brothers in September 2008.

As mentioned above, the companies Fannie Mae and Freddie Mac played a major role in these developments. The Federal National Mortgage Association (FNMA) was founded in 1938 and formally "privatized" in 1968. At that time, the company was rebranded as Fannie Mae, from the abbreviation FNMA. Thanks to regulatory privileges and tax benefits, the company retained its status as a government-sponsored enterprise even after it was formally privatized. Its counterpart, Freddie Mac (Federal Home Loan Mortgage Corporation), buys mortgage loans from banks and packages them for the financial market as mortgage-backed securities.

The two companies had an extremely high and inexpensive credit line with the U.S. Treasury. Because they were guaranteed by the state, their refinancing bonds were treated as "government securities" with low interest rates similar to government bonds. The two quasi-state mortgage companies fell back on this state guarantee in 2008–2009.

Fannie Mae and Freddie Mac were the largest mortgage companies in the world and guaranteed the lion's share of U.S. mortgage loans. Without them, the rapid spread of subprime loans—that is, risky mortgages to low-income homebuyers—would never have been possible. They had a close relationship with Countrywide, a financial services provider notorious for its subprime activities, which, at its peak, had 60,000 employees and 90 branches and was the largest seller of mortgages to Fannie Mae. At the time, real estate insiders joked that Countrywide was, in effect, a subsidiary of Fannie Mae.[239]

The two quasi-state mortgage companies played an important role in implementing government requirements for politically correct lending. As early as September 1999, *The New York Times* reported that Fannie Mae had relaxed the requirements for the loans it bought, thus making it possible "to extend home mortgages to individuals whose credit is generally not good enough to qualify for conventional loans." Fannie Mae would stand "under increasing pressure from the Clinton administration to expand mortgage loans among low and moderate-income people." One of the aims of the Clinton administration's policy was "to increase the number of minority and low-income owners who [tended] to have worse credit ratings than non-Hispanic whites." Even then, *The New York Times* pointed to the considerable risks this would entail, especially during an economic downturn.[240]

In 1996, the Department of Housing and Urban Development demanded that 12 percent of all mortgages purchased by Fannie and Freddie should be "special affordable" loans, typically granted to very low-income homebuyers. That number was increased to 20 percent in 2000 and again, to 22 percent, in 2005. The goal for 2008 would have been 28 percent. The two government-sponsored enterprises implemented these requirements. Fannie Mae bought $1.2 billion of subprime loans in 2000, $9.2 billion in 2001 and $15 billion in 2002. By 2004, Fannie Mae and Freddie Mac together had already spent $175 billion on subprime loans.[241]

In 2008, Paul Krugman defended the two companies against their critics and stressed that they had never granted a single subprime loan.[242]

In any case, mortgage lending was not a service provided by the two companies. Nevertheless, without them, the real estate crisis would never have occurred, as they were by far the largest and most reckless buyers of subprime loans. More than 40 percent of the mortgage loans that the two companies bought between 2005 and 2007 were subprime loans or so-called Alt-A loans, which was usually just a nicer label for subprime loans.[243]

As soon as property prices started to fall, all of the statistical calculations that the value of CDOs and mortgage-backed securities had been based on were no longer worth the paper they were printed on. And this is exactly what happened in the following years: the Case-Shiller Home Price Index for 20 regions in the U.S. fell by 35 percent between July 2006 and February 2012. In San Francisco, house prices fell 46 percent, in Tampa 48 percent, in Detroit 49 percent and in Miami 51 percent. When adjusted for inflation, the drops were even more drastic.

Many homebuyers who had bought at the height of the house price bubble lost their homes and all of the equity they had invested in their properties. The market value of many properties often fell below the outstanding amount of the mortgages secured against them, which meant that homeowners who were unable to raise additional equity had to watch as their banks foreclosed on their homes.

This is what triggered the Global Financial Crisis of 2008. The securitized real estate loans, which had been awarded such good ratings by the rating agencies, collapsed in value because house prices fell and many borrowers were no longer able to service their loans. This caused serious difficulties for banks, insurance companies and investment funds, and led to a chain reaction that culminated in the collapse of Lehman Brothers in September 2008.

Anti-capitalists claim that the financial crisis was a result of excessive deregulation. They portray the financial industry as if it had been a "free-market" economy with little regulation. If this were the case, how is that Yaron Brook and Don Watkins list eight different regulatory authorities?:

- U.S. Securities and Exchange Commission (SEC)

- Financial Industry Regulatory Authority (FINRA)

- Commodity Futures Trading Commission (CFTC)

- Federal Reserve (Fed)

- Federal Deposit Insurance Corporation (FDIC)

- Office of the Comptroller of the Currency (OCC)

- National Credit Union Administration (NCUA)

- Office of Thrift Supervision (OTS)

Brook and Watkins commented: "If you want to take a ride through hell, spend some time perusing the thick sea of regulations issued by these agencies. If this is a free market, we can't imagine what a regulated one would look like."[244] In their book, they include a table of 28 different measures to regulate or deregulate the financial industry from 1980 to 2009, the years in which there was supposed to have been unrestrained deregulation of the U.S. financial industry: Of the 28 measures, just five cut red tape; the remaining 23 added regulations.[245]

Indeed, there was nothing like laissez-faire capitalism in the financial markets. Immediately before the financial crisis, 12,190 people were working full-time on regulating the financial market in Washington, DC, alone—five times as many as in 1960. Moreover, U.S. annual spending on federal agencies charged with regulating the financial market had increased from $725 million to an inflation-adjusted $2.3 billion since the 1980s, which is when the laissez-faire phase is said to have begun.[246]

Even the British economists Paul Collier and John Kay, who have wrongly argued that "market fundamentalism" has come to dominate economic policy in Western societies over recent decades,[247] are forced to concede: "Those who blame the financial crisis on deregulation fail to recognize that there is today, and was in 2008, far more financial regulation than ever before: the state was increasingly active, yet decreasingly effective."[248]

Nowhere are there fewer free-market economic principles than in the financial world, and no sector is so heavily regulated and supervised by the state, with the possible exception of the healthcare industry. The fact that precisely the two areas of the economy that are most strictly regulated by the state are the most unstable should give critics of capitalism pause for thought. Of course, regulations are necessary in both of these areas. But the slogan "more regulation helps more" is patently wrong. The opposite is true. In a detailed analysis, the American economist Richard Bookstaber concludes that increasing regulation has exacerbated the problems in the finance market. "Attempts . . . to add safety features, to layer on regulations and safeguards, will only add to the complexity of the system and make accidents more frequent."[249] Too often, regulations create precisely the opposite effect to what was intended, which is an often-overlooked problem with government intervention in general. That is why we should not overestimate the positive effects of regulatory intervention and underestimate the problem of undesirable side effects.

In *The Power of Capitalism*, I wrote: "Misdiagnosing the causes of the financial crisis means that the proposed therapies are also wrong. The financial crisis was caused by excessively low interest rates, heavy-handed market interventions and over-indebtedness. Are we seriously to believe that the right therapy involves even lower interest rates, stronger market interventions and more debt? These measures may well have a short-term impact, but markets are becoming increasingly dependent on low interest rates. Such low interest rates do nothing to solve the underlying problems—they only suppress the symptoms and push them into the future."[250]

The biggest problem today is not that capitalism causes crises, but the way the state and central banks deal with them. "Each crisis, recession or depression," writes the German economist and libertarian thinker Roland Baader, "is only prolonged and exacerbated when central banks, acting in accordance with the principles of a planned economy, attempt to fight it with the same means with which they brought about the disaster, namely with even lower interest rates and an even greater supply of money and credit. This prevents the correction of imbalances in the production structure and adds further, even greater imbalances."[251]

Some crises are triggered by politicians and central banks intervening in the first place; other crises are made worse by their actions. Ultimately, it is a problem of the welfare state, which constantly promises its citizens that it will insure them against all risks. The moment the government proclaims that it is responsible for every respect of the well-being of its citizens, including their financial well-being, it puts itself under pressure to act in every crisis to suppress any and all symptoms to the fullest possible extent. Short-term, pseudo-solutions may be rational from the point of view of a politician who wants to be re-elected, but they usually make problems worse in the long term. And this is a game that will not work indefinitely. When it stops working, you can be sure that politicians and large sections of the media will look to blame capitalism and the groups that have always been popular scapegoats, such as "the rich," "greedy bankers" and "fat cat managers." A crisis that is essentially caused by government and central bank intervention is thus reinterpreted for the public consciousness as a crisis of capitalism.

Overall, there can be only one conclusion: Yes, crises in the form of temporarily negative economic growth—accompanied by a temporary increase in unemployment—are part and parcel of capitalism. These crises can be triggered by purely market-related factors or by "exogenous shocks" such as natural disasters, epidemics, wars or political interventions[252] that have little or nothing to do with the structure or system of the free market economy.

The vast majority of crises are simply features of the regular ebb and flow of normal economic waves, that is, cyclical intensifications and slowdowns of economic growth, which fade away after a few months or even a year. And, unarguably, many of the crises that have occurred over the last 120 years or so have been triggered, or at least considerably aggravated and prolonged, by populist interventionism from political leaders.

5

"CAPITALISM IS DOMINATED BY THE RICH; THEY SET THE POLITICAL AGENDA"

"THE TRUE RULERS OF THE WORLD" are the super-rich, writes Swiss sociologist Jean Ziegler in his 2018 book *Was ist so schlimm am Kapitalismus?* (*What's Really So Bad about Capitalism?*): "The tiny group of men and women of different nationalities, religions, origins, but all similar to each other in their energy, greed, contempt for the weak, indifference to the common good, blindness to the fate of the planet and the fate of the people who live on it."[253] They are, according to Ziegler, "cold monsters,"[254] these "oligarchs of globalized financial capital" that have become "the real world government."[255] But very few people realize this shocking truth because "a handful of billionaires control most of the media . . . They make sure that no overly shocking information about the victims of their cannibalistic world order enters the collective consciousness."[256]

Every day, the media runs articles and reports about powerful lobby groups that influence politics or even dictate to governments which legislation they should pass. The battle between mavericks (the good guys), who uncover sinister conspiracies initiated by powerful corporations (the bad guys), who are frequently the capitalist puppet-masters of corrupt politicians, is a common Hollywood trope.

In American election campaigns, it is widely accepted that if you want to become president, you will only succeed if you can raise hundreds of millions of dollars in donations—from Wall Street, from powerful pharmaceutical companies, from the weapons lobby, and from very large unions and other special interest groups. In the minds of right-wing conspiracy theorists, politics is controlled by (left-wing) billionaires, such as George Soros, while from the point of view of left-wing conspiracy theorists, the strings are being pulled by libertarian billionaires, such as the Koch brothers. Even the media is in the pockets of a handful of billionaires. Take *The Washington Post*, for example, which has belonged to one of the richest men in the world, the founder of Amazon, Jeff Bezos, since 2013. In the face of this overwhelming burden of proof, there can seemingly no longer be any doubt: Money rules!

And that is not all: Critics of "social inequality" claim that the problem is getting worse, that with rising inequality, the influence exerted by the rich on politics is growing. Ten years ago, the economist Paul Krugman wrote in *The New York Times* that we live in a "society in which money is increasingly concentrated in the hands of a few people, and in which that concentration of income and wealth threatens to make us a democracy in name only."[257] And his colleague Joseph Stiglitz, winner of the Nobel Prize in Economics, said in his 2015 collection of essays, *The Great Divide*, that politics "increasingly represents the interests of the 1 percent."[258] Noam Chomsky, perhaps the most popular critic of capitalism in the U.S., writes that "the real concentration of power is in a fraction of 1 percent" of the population: "They get exactly what they want, because they're basically running the place."[259]

I would like to counter this prevailing perception with three theses, which I will illustrate with a few examples:

1. The rich do exert political influence, but they are nowhere near as powerful as the media, Hollywood movies and some academics with an anti-capitalist bias would have us believe.

2. The rich helping to shape the political agenda, for example, through lobbying, is not only legitimate in a pluralistic democracy, but important. And often, laws that are in the interest of the rich also benefit society's weakest members (e.g., tax cuts and deregulation).

3. Anyone who believes that rich lobbyists, in pursuit of their own particular special interests, exert too much influence over politics must surely advocate *less* and not *more* government, that is, more capitalism. After all, the more the state intervenes in the economy (through subsidies and overregulation), the greater the influence lobbyists can exert.

If the rich were so omnipotent and were increasingly strengthening their grasp on power, you would expect them to be very satisfied with recent political developments. In Germany at least, however, this is by no means the case (I will focus on the United States later). In 2013/2014, researchers conducted a total of 160 in-depth interviews (60–90 minutes) with leading members of the German business community.[260] The researchers found a decidedly negative attitude among the business elite toward politics: "The tenor is pessimistic. Today, [Germany] is still in a healthy position—not least thanks to companies as the engines of society—but if countermeasures are not initiated soon, this status is in danger of being forfeited as a result of prevarication and wrong-headedness on the part of politicians . . . Mendacity, incompetence, egoism—such accusations and disparaging remarks against leading politicians are frequently heard from within the ranks of Germany's business elite."[261] A number of the entrepreneurs and managers even described the country's political leaders as "a collection of chatterboxes, clueless ignoramuses and egoists who are ruining the country."[262] The left-leaning researchers were so shocked by the attitudes they encountered that they suggested some members of the business elite would benefit from a "thorough political education."[263]

In early April 2021, one of Germany's most influential managers gave an interview that caused quite a stir. Wolfgang Reitzle, chairman of Linde, one of Germany's most valuable companies, said: "After almost 16 years of Merkel, Germany is, in so many respects, a basket case. There are shortcomings almost everywhere you look: our bureaucracy is stuck in the fax age, there's a digitalization backlog, a high-speed internet blackhole, massive deficiencies in infrastructure and ailing schools. And these are just a handful of examples of failings that are shameful for a leading industrial nation."[264]

With his comments, Reitzle was addressing issues that are important not only for the economy, but for society at large, and which have long been neglected by Germany's political elite. In countries across the Western world, social spending has massively increased over the last few decades, while far too little has been spent on infrastructure and education. If "big business" set the political agenda, then political priorities would certainly be very different. The exasperation with politics and politicians expressed by the business elite is all too understandable.

I benefited from an insider's perspective for 15 years because I was the owner of the leading public relations consultancy for the German real estate industry. Our clients included two of the German real estate industry's leading associations ("lobbyists"), Immobilienverband Deutschland (which we advised for 14 years) and the German Property Federation—ZIA (which we advised for eight years). During these 15 years, I never had even the slightest impression that powerful companies were determining the government's policy agenda.

Quite the opposite. Real estate companies and associations were in a constant defensive struggle against the politicians who were making life ever more difficult for them. The work of the industry's "lobbyists" was not to push a business-centric agenda, but rather to fight to prevent the worst from happening. Where I had direct insight into the workings of politics, the associations did not wield great influence.

Far from it. Unfortunately, they usually failed to get the government to enact their proposals. For example, the associations were constantly suggesting measures that would streamline the building code, but the opposite has happened—there are now 25,000(!) different regulations in German building law.

Of course, the associations proudly trumpeted each of their small victories. There was a peculiar congruence of interests here: Critics of capitalism are eager to paint business lobbyists as being all-powerful, and the lobby groups themselves have an interest in presenting themselves as being more powerful than they really are. After all, they are under pressure from the elevated expectations of their members, who are all too often disappointed when their lobbyists do not achieve more, and who often do not understand the ins and outs of the political decision-making processes.

It is an essential characteristic of pluralistic societies that various interest groups—companies, trade unions, environmental organizations, and so forth—all advocate their interests and points of view. And the fact that the rich also help to shape the political agenda is not always worthy of criticism, even if it is generally seen that way. In the past, Prussia and other states had a three-class electoral system in which the votes of citizens who paid more taxes counted for more than those who paid little or no taxes. Those days are long gone. But the fact that the rich—mostly entrepreneurs—try to ensure that their voice as a minority within society is heard is just as legitimate as it is for other groups. Contrary to the widespread misunderstanding, democracy does not equate to the unrestricted rule of the majority over the minority, not even over the rich. This would be a "dictatorship of the proletariat," as propagated by Marx and Lenin, not a pluralistic democracy.

Those who want to limit the influence of the rich should first and foremost limit the power of government and the political class. After all, it is only when the government strengthens its grip on the distribution of economic resources that the rich are more likely to try to gain influence or even bribe politicians.

The United States is generally regarded as the country in which the rich exert a particularly strong influence over political developments. For years, anti-capitalists, such as the two politicians Bernie Sanders, a formally non-partisan senator, and Alexandria Ocasio-Cortez, a left-wing Democrat, have been beating the drum about the ever-increasing influence of the rich on American politics. But if money alone bought political power, Donald Trump would never have become the Republican candidate for the U.S. presidency in 2016. That honor would more likely have gone to Jeb Bush, who was able to raise far more in political donations. Even Benjamin I. Page and Martin Gilens, political scientists and two of the most prominent proponents of the thesis that U.S. politics is determined by the rich, concede that "most of the big-money contributors—and most Republican think-tankers and officeholders—supported other candidates."[265] And: "Trump's positions went directly contrary to the views of wealthy donors and wealthy Americans generally."[266]

Furthermore, if money determined political outcomes, Trump would not have won the 2016 election. Democratic candidate Hillary Clinton would have, as Page and Gilens themselves recognize: "The better-funded candidate sometimes loses, as Hillary Clinton herself did."[267] Clinton and her allies, including her joint committees with the Democratic Party and the super PACs that supported her, raised more than $1.2 billion for the full cycle, according to the Federal Election Commission. Trump and his allies collected about $600 million.

Moreover, "not one CEO in the Fortune 100 donated to Trump's election campaign by September 2016. His victory did not stem from influence by the wealthy but more from grassroots opposition to wealthy coastal elites."[268]

If money alone could buy political power, then Joe Biden would also not have become president. Perhaps the White House would have gone to the wealthy entrepreneur Michael Bloomberg, who at the time of his application for the Democratic candidacy was the eighth richest man in the world, worth $61.9 billion according to *Forbes*. In all likelihood, Bloomberg spent more of his own money (and spent it quicker) on his election campaign than any other candidate in history, namely $1 billion in just over three months. This was revealed in the Federal Election Commission (FEC) report on campaign financing.[269] Bloomberg financed his campaign himself and did not accept any donations.

Bloomberg is by no means the only candidate whose wealth did not help him realize his political ambitions. Republican Steve Forbes spent $69.2 million on his bids for the 1996 and 2000 nominations, but won only a handful of delegates. In 2020, billionaire hedge fund manager Tom Steyer put up $200 million of his own fortune and ended up without a single delegate.[270] In the 2008 GOP primaries, Mitt Romney spent more than twice as much as John McCain—much of which was his own money—but he dropped out of the race in February and McCain went on to secure the Republican nomination.[271] The Koch brothers have always been portrayed by critics of capitalism as among the most dangerous pro-capitalists on the planet, but David Koch learned just how hard it is to turn money into political power back in 1980, when he was one of the main supporters of the Libertarian Party and threw his hat into the ring as a candidate for vice president: he earned just 1 percent of the vote.[272]

In the history of American elections, some Democratic candidates have mainly raised money from large donors, and others, such as Bernie Sanders, have relied far more on smaller donations. In the 2016 primaries, 60 percent of donations to the Sanders campaign came from people who gave less than $200.[273]

The same is also true of Republican candidates. Barry Goldwater and Patrick Buchanan, for example, both mobilized large numbers of small donors, whereas candidates, such as Jeb Bush, were supported primarily by large donors.

In an op-ed in *The New York Times* in 2016, Bradley A. Smith, the former chairman of the Federal Election Commission, concluded that "The Power of Political Money Is Overrated": "But while money is critical to inform the public and give all views a hearing, this election proves once again that money can't make voters like the views they hear.

Jeb Bush is not the only lavishly funded candidate to drop out of the race . . . The evil of 'money in politics' is vastly overstated."[274]

In his book, *Unequal Democracy*, Larry M. Bartels criticizes inequality and the influence of the wealthy in the United States. He examined the "estimated effect of unequal campaign spending" in 16 U.S. presidential elections from 1952 to 2012, concluding that "Republican candidates outspent their Democratic opponents in 13 of those elections." But in only two elections, namely that of Richard Nixon in 1968 and that of George W. Bush in 2000, does Bartels conclude that "Republican candidates won close elections that they very likely would have lost had they been unable to outspend their Democratic opponents."[275] And with Hillary Clinton—as shown above—raising considerably more in donations than Donald Trump in the 2016 election, there were just two out of 17 elections over the past 64 years in which unequal campaign spending was the decisive factor in an election.

Nevertheless, the thesis that "money makes the world go around" remains popular, especially in relation to the United States. One of the most frequently cited academic studies purporting to prove the power of money in the U.S. is the 2013 paper "Democracy and the Policy Preferences of Wealthy Americans" by Benjamin I. Page, Larry M. Bartels and Jason Seawright.[276] If anything, it is quite surprising that this paper is repeatedly cited as evidence of the extent to which the wealthy determine politics. After all, with only 83 respondents, the research base for a quantitative study was very small. Moreover, all of the study's respondents came from the Chicago metropolitan area. And many of the respondents were not really rich as only 36 of the 83 owned assets worth more than $10 million.[277]

The above study was published in 2011. It would certainly be interesting to find out, 11 years later, whether the wealthy respondents got what they wished for from America's politicians. As the title of the study indicates, above all, the researchers wanted to identify the "Policy Preferences of Wealthy Americans." Of eleven items mentioned by the wealthy respondents, "budget deficits" were of greatest concern. Thus, from the perspective of 87 percent of the wealthy, this was the biggest issue that U.S. policymakers should address. In last place, scoring only 16 percent, was climate change. The authors conclude that "the contemporary emphasis in Washington on reducing the federal budget deficit addresses what is, by far, the most important problem in the minds of wealthy Americans—though not of the American public as a whole."[278]

Ten years later and the national debt, the reduction of which was the top goal of the wealthy in America according to the survey, has risen from $15.6 trillion to $28.4 trillion, almost doubling. At the time of the survey, national debt stood at just under 100 percent of U.S. GDP; today it is more than 133 percent. If, above all, the rich wanted to see a significant reduction in the national debt, they did not get it from Barack Obama or Donald Trump—and certainly not from Joe Biden.

In fact, Joe Biden's political agenda is dominated by the very issue that wealthy Americans mentioned least frequently in the survey 11 years ago, namely the fight against climate change via the Green New Deal (which goes hand in hand with a significant rise in the national debt).

So, do the rich exert any influence on politics? Of course they do, but less so on the big-ticket issues that are the subject of heated public debate and that determine the overall direction of policy. The authors of the study cited above state: "One key finding is that, for contacts that could be coded, just under half (44 percent) acknowledged a focus on fairly narrow economic self-interest." So the rich were not really concerned about the "big issues," instead choosing to focus on their immediate economic interests. The authors cite, for example: trying "to get the Treasury to honor their commitment to extend TARP funding to a particular bank in Chicago," "to better understand the new regulations of the Dodd-Frank Act and how it will affect my business [banking/finance]," "Fish and wildlife . . . permitting on development land," or "seeking regulatory approvals" for their clients.[279]

The American political analyst John York, who posed the question "Does Rising Income Inequality Threaten Democracy?" in a 2017 essay, concluded that the activities of lobbyists are more likely to be directed at pushing such specific interests than at redefining the broad brushstrokes of government policy. And this, he argued, could best be prevented by limiting the influence of the government on the economy: "Constraining government would also have the advantage of reducing the amount of money in politics . . . Getting rid of regulations that distort the free market and rig the game for the politically connected, cutting wasteful government contracts and kickbacks for cronies, and calling out politicians who engage in these practices would stanch the river of cash flowing to D.C. at its source."[280]

York cites several examples of how companies that refused to make major donations or engage in lobbying suffered political disadvantages and were ultimately forced by politicians to change their stance. Such practices could most likely be prevented by limiting the power of the government. "If the federal government were kept within its constitutional limits, Washington insider status would not count for nearly as much as it does now." In 2017, the author also saw no sign that the political influence wielded by America's wealthiest citizens had increased: "There is no evidence that the influence of the affluent on major policy outcomes has increased as income inequality has grown. Contrary to what one would expect from reading the studies on inequality and democracy, spending on welfare programs benefiting the poor has gone up dramatically and the tax burden on the wealthy has increased in recent decades."[281] In the United States, which is always held up as a particularly stark example of glaring and rising inequality, social spending as a share of GDP rose from 9.6 to 14.3 percent between 1980 and 2018, a 50 percent increase.[282]

In his 2012 book, *Affluence and Influence*, Martin Gilens argues that wealthier voters hold greater sway over politics in the United States than voters from lower income groups. He examined 1,923 questions from public opinion polls conducted in the U.S. between 1981 and 2002, supplemented by datasets from 1964 to 1968 and 2005/2006.[283] He proceeded to analyze the political views of members of lower-, middle- and upper-income groups and then compared their responses in opinion polls with government policies in the years following each election. He highlighted what he called "representational inequality," which he claimed was evident in the fact that the opinions of the lower- and, in some cases, middle-income groups had less chance of being implemented by the government than those of the upper-income group.

It is worth noting, however, that while this "representational inequality" applies to religious issues, foreign policy and economic policy, it does not apply to social welfare, as Gilens acknowledges: "The social welfare domain is the only policy domain examined in which the divergence of preferences across income groups does not lead to a substantial decline in responsiveness to the preferences of less-well-off Americans." According to Gilens, this was because "poor and middle-income Americans have powerful allies that tend to share their preferences on these issues," such as the American Association of Retired Persons (AARP), one of the most influential lobbying groups in the United States.[284]

In the domain of economic policy, on the other hand, Gilens reports that the opinions of lower-income groups are less likely to be heard. So, what policies does Gilens think would lead to "greater representational equality in the economic sphere"? Well, Gilens suggests that to address representational inequality, policies would have to "result in a higher minimum wage, more generous unemployment benefits, stricter corporate regulation . . . and a more progressive personal tax regime in general."[285]

But whether a higher minimum wage, higher taxes on the rich and stricter regulation are really in the interests of the working classes is open to doubt. The two American presidents who have been most vehemently castigated in recent decades for one-sidedly representing the interests of the rich and for cutting too much red tape were Ronald Reagan and Donald Trump. Both indeed pushed through substantial tax cuts for the rich and deregulated in some areas, but this helped low-income earners more than many policies in the social arena.

The American Dream of income mobility, which for many today has turned into a nightmare of discontent, was alive and well in the 1980s: 86 percent of households that were in the poorest income quintile in 1981 had moved up the economic ladder into a higher quintile by 1990. The percentage of poor households that moved all the way up to the richest income quintile between 1981 and 1990 was even slightly higher than the percentage of those who remained in the poorest quintile. The number of Americans earning less than $10,000 a year fell by 5 percent during the 1980s, while the number of those earning more than $50,000 rose by 60 percent and the number of those whose annual income exceeded $75,000 rose by a staggering 83 percent.[286]

There are many fables about the Reagan years, such as the persistent and pernicious claim that wealthy whites were the sole beneficiaries of Reagan's policies at the expense of poorer African Americans.[287] During Donald Trump's presidency—before the coronavirus pandemic—unemployment in the United States fell to an all-time low, and the economic situation improved for low-earners, African Americans and Latinos, factors that allowed Trump, in his second presidential election in 2020, to make significant gains among these groups of voters who traditionally shun the Republican party. So the claims made by critics of capitalism that policies that benefit the rich must be bad for the poor are patently not true.

But what about the argument that most members of the United States Congress are themselves very wealthy? "Virtually all U.S. senators, and most of the representatives in the House, are members of the top 1 percent when they arrive . . . By and large, the key executive-branch policymakers on trade and economic policy also come from the top 1 percent," criticizes leftist economist Joseph Stiglitz.[288] So, to what extent does their personal wealth influence the policies of these decision-makers?

There has been a great deal of research into the relationship between the wealth of American congressmen and their voting behavior. Martin Gilens, who generally criticizes the influence of the rich on U.S. politics, concedes on this issue that there is no evidence of a connection between their wealth and the political decisions made by members of Congress or the House of Representatives: "Taken together, the analyses described above suggest that legislators' personal interests and preferences can shape their congressional voting, but that concern over the growing wealth of members of Congress is probably misplaced. At least in terms of economic policy broadly conceived, liberals and conservatives are equally likely to be found among Congress's wealthiest members and among those with the fewest resources. It's impossible to say with any confidence whether U.S. representatives would behave differently if their salaries put them in the middle of the U.S. income distribution rather than towards the top. But it does appear that the substantial existing differences in economic status among members of Congress are not related to broad patterns of voting on economic policy."[289]

Incidentally, representatives of the National People's Congress in China, which includes a number of billionaires, would probably only smile pityingly at the fortunes of their American colleagues. At the same time, in other Western countries, including Germany, members of the legislature are by no means as affluent as in the United States.

But is it always a disadvantage to have wealthy politicians? A wealthy politician is often far more independent and unfettered in their decision-making than one who is entirely dependent on their party. One example from Germany would be the long-serving CSU representative Peter Gauweiler, who is a brilliant lawyer and frequently registered the highest income of all members of the German parliament, the Bundestag. His financial independence enabled him to follow his own convictions and to hold opinions that did anything but toe the party line. A representative who has spent their entire life in politics—and can do nothing else—does not have this intrinsic independence.

In earlier times, wealth was actually an explicit requirement for holding political office. From the earliest days of Rome all the way through the Roman Republic and the imperial period up to late antiquity, it was wealth above all that determined a citizen's position and influence. The economic elite always doubled up as the political elite. For example, Emperor Augustus stipulated that only those who possessed one million sesterces could become senators; 400,000 sesterces were the prerequisite for entering the nobility.

The problem with many parliaments today is not that too many entrepreneurs are active there, but quite the opposite. After the 2017 federal elections in Germany, the daily broadsheet *Frankfurter Allgemeine Zeitung* published an article under the headline "Twice as Many Entrepreneurs in the Bundestag."[290] Their number had risen from just 35 in the previous legislative period to 76 in the 2017 elections (out of 706 representatives). More economic expertise and more entrepreneurial thinking would certainly make politics better rather than worse. In the Bundestag elected in 2021, the share of entrepreneurs among newly elected representatives fell from 2 percent to 1.4 percent.[291]

If the rich in Western countries can be reproached, it is not for being excessively involved in politics, but that they are not involved enough. At any rate, this is true for those rich people who are also advocates of capitalism. While the voices of critics of capitalism such as George Soros or Tom Steyer, who vehemently argue for higher taxes on the rich, can be heard loudly, supporters of capitalism rarely speak out in public. Page and Gilens speak of the "public silence of most billionaires." David Koch, who provides financial support for libertarian viewpoints, himself made just one public comment on tax policy in a 10-year period; his brother Charles Koch made no public comment at all on these issues.[292] "The public silence of most billionaires," report Page and Gilens, "contrasts markedly with the willingness of a small, unusual group of billionaires— including Michael Bloomberg, Warren Buffett, and Bill Gates—to speak out about specific public policies . . . All three have favored a substantial social safety net, progressive taxes, and moderate regulation of the economy. An ordinary American who tried to judge what U.S. billionaires think and do about politics by listening to Bloomberg, Buffett, or Gates would be badly misled."[293]

This observation is correct and points to one crux of the problem: The public pressure to criticize capitalism is so great that it even silences billionaires, while rich people who advocate higher taxes on the rich and more government regulation are free to speak their minds without concern. Clearly, rich people who think capitalism is the superior system and who are skeptical of the outsized role of government should be bolder and participate more actively in the public discourse.

The relationship between money and politics is particularly problematic in countries where wealth does not depend primarily on entrepreneurial ideas, but on political influence, access to the levers of power and corruption. This is true, for example, in Russia, where, after the collapse of communism, a handful of oligarchs seized control of the sources of raw materials—especially oil and gas—and where "rent-seeking" industries play the decisive role. They are often also the same countries in which corruption is widespread. Russia, for instance, ranks a lowly 129th out of 176 in Transparency International's *Corruption Perceptions Index* and even ranked first in *The Economist's* 2016 crony-capitalism index.[294] In the *Index of Economic Freedom*, the Heritage Foundation's capitalism index, Russia ranks a distant 92nd. Many other countries are as bad, if not worse, than Russia. From these examples, it is clear that the world needs more capitalism, not less, to loosen the ties between politics and business.

Many people associate "capitalism" with "corruption." And yet, according to the American economist Alan H. Meltzer: "Offenses such as bribery can be either public or private and are common in many nations, but they are most common where government officials have the most authority."[295] The view that corruption is particularly widespread in capitalist countries is simply wrong, as confirmed by a comparison of Transparency International's *Corruption Perceptions Index* (*CPI*) with the *Index of Economic Freedom*. The countries with the lowest levels of corruption are the same countries that have high levels of economic freedom. Of the 10 countries with the lowest corruption, every single one is in the "Free" or "Mostly Free" categories in the *Index of Economic Freedom*. Denmark, New Zealand, Finland and Singapore are the countries with the lowest levels of perceived corruption in the world. Three of these countries (Denmark, New Zealand, and Singapore) are also among the ten most economically free countries in the world, while Finland ranks a respectable 17th in the *Index of Economic Freedom* (ahead of countries such as the United States and Germany, for example).[296]

Conversely, countries that rank in the bottom ten in the *CPI* are the same countries that are classed as "Repressed" in the *Index of Economic Freedom*, such as North Korea (170th in the *CPI* and 178th in the *Index of Economic Freedom*) and Venezuela (176th in the *CPI* and 177th in the *Index of Economic Freedom*). The more government intervenes in economic life, the more opportunities there are to bribe government officials. Anyone who wants to limit wealthy citizens' unethical or even criminal influence on politics should therefore advocate *less* not *more* government.

6

"CAPITALISM LEADS TO MONOPOLIES"

THE IRRATIONALITY OF THE DEBATE about "monopolies" was noted by the economist Ludwig von Mises as early as 1922 in his epochal work *Socialism*: "The mere mention of the word monopoly," Mises wrote, "usually stirs up emotions which make clear judgement impossible and provokes, instead of economic arguments, the usual moral indignation evinced in etatist and other anti-capitalist literature."[297] Mises observes that the monopolist's scope in a capitalist economy free from government interference is much smaller than the "popular writers on cartels and trusts" commonly tend to assume.[298]

In fact, the supposed tendency toward monopoly is one of the oldest arguments against capitalism. This thesis states that free competition will inevitably destroy itself and, at the end of the process of concentration and centralization of capital, a small number of remaining monopolies will dominate the economy. Lenin described this process in his 1917 work "Imperialism: The Highest Stage of Capitalism," in which he writes: "This transformation of competition into monopoly is one of the most important—if not the most important—phenomena of modern capitalist economy."[299] Lenin continues, stating that monopoly is a "fundamental law" of the present stage of capitalism.[300]

When Lenin and other theorists speak of monopolies, they are not just referring to companies that control 100 percent of a given market, which is in any case very rare for non-state-owned companies. Adam Smith, too, in his work *Wealth of Nations*, employed the term "monopoly" to refer not only to trading companies that are the sole suppliers in their fields, but to firms that never fully supply "the effectual demand" in order to sell their commodities at "much above the natural price." Smith understood the "natural price" to be the price that could be obtained under conditions of free competition.[301] Some modern economists also define monopolies in this broader sense as "firms that have some control over price through control over market supply, even though they may not be the only seller in their market."[302]

Lenin wrote that in the United States in 1904, almost half of the total production of all enterprises in the country was in the hands of one percent of the total number of enterprises: "From this it can be seen that, at a certain stage of its development concentration itself, as it were, leads right up to monopoly; for a score or so of giant enterprises can easily arrive at an agreement, while, on the other hand, the hindrance to competition, the tendency towards monopoly arises from the very dimensions of the enterprises."[303]

Lenin did not see this tendency in a negative light at all. The consequence of the formation of monopolies was "immense progress in the socialization of production."[304] At its most developed stage, capitalism "leads right up to the most comprehensive socialization of production; it, so to speak, drags the capitalists, against their will and consciousness, into some sort of a new social order, a transitional one from complete free competition to complete socialization."[305] He sharply opposed the "reactionary, petty-bourgeois critics" of capitalism, who dreamed of going back to free competition.[306]

The German economic historian Werner Plumpe points out that

analyses, such as Lenin's, were inaccurate because they generalized trends in a number of particularly capital-intensive sectors, such as heavy industry, and extrapolated them into the future.[307] As Plumpe points out, hardly anything remains of the large companies that dominated in the early to mid-twentieth century and provided the basis for Lenin's forecasts. A few of these companies do still exist today under the same historic names, although, as Plumpe observes, they no longer have much in common with their forebears.[308]

As Josef Schumpeter wrote in his 1942 book, *Capitalism, Socialism and Democracy*, pure cases of long-run monopoly must be very rare and "that even tolerable approximations to the requirements of the concept must be still rarer than are cases of perfect competition."[309]

A monopoly could "under the conditions of intact capitalism hardly persist for a period long enough to matter for the analysis of total output, unless buttressed by public authority, for instance, in the case of fiscal monopolies."[310]

Why, asks Schumpeter, is there so much talk about monopoly? The answer, he posits, must lie the realm of the "psychology of political discussion."[311] In the United States, he says, economists, government officials, journalists and politicians have an obvious fondness for the word because it has become a "term of opprobrium" and people attribute practically everything they dislike about business to that sinister power.[312] In the short term, however, he concedes, "genuine monopoly positions or positions approximating monopoly" are much more frequent, although this does not mean that they have a wholly negative impact and, as he also observes, monopolies need by no means have a "soporific influence."[313]

Schumpeter was one of the few economists who did not regard the economic function of monopolies in a wholly negative light, but also described their positive contribution to the process of "creative destruction." The American economists Richard B. McKenzie and Dwight R. Lee therefore refer to Schumpeter in their work *In Defense of Monopoly*, in which they write: "Hidden in Schumpeter's analysis is a theory of *optimum monopoly* required for maximum economic growth."[314]

Both economists adopt a not-uncritical view of monopolies and concede that such market positions may well be harmful to economic growth. They do add, however, "that not all monopolies and not all levels of monopolization are welfare destroying, a perspective that suggests economists should pay more attention to the institutional conditions for what might be called *optimum monopoly*."[315]

In particular, they distinguish between monopolies for goods that are *given*—that is, not actually created by the monopoly—which they judge negatively "because the monopoly had no role in creating the good and bringing the net value into existence," and monopolies for goods which are *developed* by the individuals and firms in question and which could serve a useful function.[316] From their point of view, a situation of—in economists' jargon—"perfect competition" is, first, unachievable in the real world and, second, undesirable.[317]

The prospect of monopoly profits is a key driver of innovation. Competition is an essential factor in economic progress, not in terms of perfect competition or a perfect market—which can only exist in abstract economic models, not in reality—but in the form of competition that is always subject to temporary monopoly tendencies. Schumpeter emphasized that a perfect system "that at *every* given point of time fully utilizes its possibilities to the best advantage" may, in the long run, be inferior to an imperfect system "that does so at *no* given point of time, because the latter's failure to do so may be a condition for the level or speed of long-run performance."[318]

Monopolies unlock the possibility of surplus profits—and these surplus profits are drivers of efficiency and innovation, as Marx aptly recognized in Volume III of *Capital*: "Furthermore, the surplus-profit which some individual capital otherwise realises in a particular sphere of production—for deviations of the rates of profit in various spheres of production are continually balanced out into an average rate—is due, aside from the fortuitous deviations, to a reduction in cost price, in production costs. This reduction arises either from the fact that capital is used in greater than average quantities, so that the *faux frais* of production are reduced, while the general causes increasing the productiveness of labour (cooperation, division of labour, etc.) can become effective to a higher degree, with more intensity, because their field of activity has become larger; or it may arise from the fact that, aside from the amount of functioning capital, better methods of labour, new inventions, improved machinery, chemical manufacturing secrets, etc., in short, new and improved, better than average means of production and methods of production are used."[319]

Developing completely new products and markets involves very different risks and requirements than operating in established markets. Entrepreneurs are most likely to accept this increased risk when there is the prospect of—at least temporary—monopoly profits significantly above normal profit margins. "Hence, in a more dynamic, real-world economy in which *development* or *progress* is to be anticipated in some systematic way, some supranormal profits must occur, and this level of profitability must be above the level achievable in a perfectly competitive environment."[320]

When people are asked to compare the advantages and disadvantages of monopolies, they usually mention the following disadvantages:[321]

- Higher prices and less choice for consumers

- Less incentive to cut costs

- Less incentive to innovate and invest

- Monopolies can gain political power to protect their vested interests

There are, however, also advantages that are often overlooked:

- Economies of scale—lower average costs from increased scale

- High profit can be used for research and development

- The reward of getting a patent (a monopoly power) can encourage investment

These advantages and disadvantages should not, however, be understood as applying to every company that is considered a monopoly. For example, companies that are now regarded as monopolies can be exceptionally innovative. Amazon, Facebook, and Google, for example, are among the companies that have seen numerous competitors—including companies that were once considered monopolies themselves—rapidly lose their monopoly position or disappear from the market altogether due to technological innovations and the emergence of new competitors (I will come back to this with a few examples). Even when there is no serious competition today, such companies are aware of the possibility that new entrants with innovative technologies could appear to usurp their dominant positions.[322] This, in turn, is one of the reasons why these companies are so determined to keep innovating even though they already dominate their markets. If they fail to innovate, if they underestimate this danger, they will lose their market position.

Any company that appears omnipotent today is actually far from such omnipotence—and they are aware of it. The Franco-Belgian economist Nicolas Petit cites the main threats as being technological innovations that quickly render existing solutions obsolete, the entry of new, innovative companies to the market, and government regulations that call existing business models into question.[323] Real or perceived monopolies are usually much less stable than they might appear at first glance, especially when they are at the height of their power.

The positive functions of monopolies are too seldom recognized, yet these by no means apply only to the gigantic corporations usually associated with the term, but can also apply to smaller companies that hold a de facto monopoly position in a niche market. I myself established a company in a niche market in Germany (Dr.ZitelmannPB.GmbH, today PB3C), which held a de facto monopoly position for over fifteen years—as a public relations service provider in the German real estate industry. For more than ten years, we had almost no competitors, which meant we could charge high fees and enforce contract terms that allowed us to plan our revenues with a high degree of certainty. Of course, word eventually got out that our company was making very high profits (the return on sales averaged 48 percent over the fifteen years before I sold the company), and new providers with lower prices and less restrictive contractual terms entered the market to compete with us.

But without my company as a role model, these competitors would probably never have come into being. In this respect, my company's "monopoly" helped to create a market for professional PR services in the German real estate industry. And certain innovations, such as offering an expanded range of services and enhancing the level of professional specialization across different departments, which had been almost unheard of among PR firms until then, could only be implemented by protecting this quasi-monopoly. This monopoly arose—as is often the case—from my company's superior market position.

This shows that even in highly specialized and niche markets, monopolies can perform a positive function. The company I sold in 2016 is still doing business today and is still the market leader, but of course, because of competition, the high profit margins we enjoyed in the company's early days are no longer achievable. This example shows that the word "monopoly" refers to far more than just the gigantic international corporations we normally think of when we hear the word.

But let's turn our focus back to the world's leading tech giants. All around the world, companies, such as Google, Amazon, Facebook, Microsoft, and Apple, are regarded as a threat. Almost everyone uses them, but hardly anyone likes them. Some concerns are valid, especially about the political bias of companies such as Facebook—I'll come back to this later. But many of the criticisms normally leveled at monopolies do not apply to these companies. The U.S. economist Tyler Cowen uses the example of Google, Facebook and Apple to show that these companies are by no means hostile to innovation—quite the opposite. "Yet in practice the major tech companies have proven to be vigorous innovators. Furthermore, the prospect of being bought up by Google or one of the other tech giants has boosted the incentive for others to innovate, and it has given struggling companies access to capital and expertise when they otherwise might have folded or never started in the first place."[324] Big tech companies today spend vast sums on research and development—in 2018 alone, the six giants, Amazon, Google, Microsoft, Netflix, Facebook and Apple, are estimated to have spent at least $22.6 billion on research and development.[325]

It is not only this figure that contradicts many of the characteristics normally attributed to monopolies. In a major study in 2020 ("Big Tech and the Digital Economy"), Nicolas Petit presents a series of arguments that relativize the common concept of monopoly and coined the term "moligopoly." Tech giants, such as Amazon, Google, Microsoft, Netflix, Facebook and Apple, are active in a growing number of domains, and they compete with each other and other serious competitors in a whole host of market segments: "Google has developed an email service, a browser, a mobile OS, and a social network. Amazon has grown from a specialist online bookseller to a generalist online retailer as well as a cloud computing services provider, and it now owns a brick-and-mortar grocery chain. And Facebook is a firm structured along two market segments, that is global networks and messaging."[326] And the tech giants keep opening up new segments where they lock horns with each other and other companies—Microsoft in the games segment, Google in self-driving cars, Facebook in payment systems, and Amazon in video production and streaming. It's interesting when you look at these companies, not from an anti-trust perspective, but from a stock analyst perspective. In any analysis, there are references to quite a few existing or potential competitors, as Petit demonstrates with a range of different examples.[327]

I recently read Brad Stone's biography of Jeff Bezos[328]—and the entire biography relates the constant battles Bezos has had to fight against competitors from day one. These have included specialty players, from an online supplier of diapers to major companies, such as eBay, Apple, Barnes & Noble, Walmart and others. The claim that a company like Amazon is able to eliminate its competitors is downright absurd.

Petit concludes: "The picture of big tech firms as monopolists is intuitively attractive, but analytically wrong. Monopoly findings based on observations of limited rivalry in the tech giants' origin market constitute a narrow view of competition. In spite of patent dominant positions, big tech firms do not live the quiet life. Their intense degree of effort is inconsistent with standard monopoly theory. A better picture is one of big tech firms as moligopolists, that is firms that coexist as monopolists and oligopolists."[329]

What most critics who call for governments to step up their regulation of certain markets or to break up monopolies overlook is the fact that monopolies tend to be far less durable than people believe. The Belgian economists Dirk Auer and Nicolas Petit analyzed media coverage of monopolies over a 150-year period. They evaluated a total of 1,399 articles from 1850 to 2000.[330] Among its conclusions, their analysis confirms that media coverage of monopolies is overwhelmingly negative: 61 percent of the articles the two researchers evaluated had a negative slant, 30 percent were neutral and only 9 percent mentioned any positive aspects of monopolies.[331] This is not surprising in itself, since the media usually run negative rather than positive stories. However, it should give pause for thought that the emergence of monopolies is reported much more extensively and frequently than the end of monopolies.[332] "If the press articles covered a random sample of monopolies, then we should see roughly as many articles about disappearing monopolies as emerging ones. This is because very few monopolies have survived the entire timespan of the dataset."[333] Their analysis of press coverage confirms what Milton Friedman wrote about monopolies as early as 1962, namely that their importance is vastly overstated, partly because "monopoly is more newsworthy and attracts more attention than competition."[334]

You don't even have to go that far back in history to prove Friedman's point. In 2019, Tyler Cowen wrote in his book *Big Business* that the following companies, among others, have been criticized as monopolies in the United States in recent decades: Kodak, IBM, Microsoft, Palm, BlackBerry, Yahoo, AOL, Digital Equipment Corporation (DEC), General Motors, and Ford. "On that list, only Microsoft remains a dominant entity."[335]

The American economist Ryan Bourne provides numerous examples of companies that were identified as monopolies and went on to sacrifice their dominant market position in his article "Is This Time Different? Schumpeter, the Tech Giants, and Monopoly Fatalism."[336] The social network Myspace, for example, was founded in 2003 and quickly gained millions of users. By June 2006, Myspace was the most-visited website in the U.S., even ahead of Google. In 2007, the UK's leading left-wing newspaper *The Guardian* asked, "Will Myspace ever lose its monopoly?" By early 2008, Myspace had a 74.4 percent share of the social network market, and by December 2008, it had 75.9 million visitors in the United States alone. But just six months later, Facebook overtook Myspace in the U.S., and the company's market share had fallen to just 30 percent by the end of 2009. Today, Myspace has become almost entirely irrelevant. Bourne concludes: "Importantly, the Myspace history shows that the very network effects that lead to massive growth can also lead to a rapid demise when a superior product comes along."[337]

In November 2008, *Forbes* magazine ran a major story on the cell phone manufacturer Nokia. The headline of the magazine's cover story read "One Billion Customers—Can Anyone Catch the Cell Phone King?" After consistently being the world's largest cell phone manufacturer from 1998 to 2011, Nokia was overtaken by Samsung in the first quarter of 2012 as the South Korean company took an estimated 25.4 percent share of the market. Nokia still accounted for a respectable 22.5 percent of the market and Apple had 9.5 percent. Nevertheless, Nokia's share had fallen by more than a third since 2008. Strikingly, Nokia developed the world's very first smartphone in the 1990s, "but it did not foresee the importance of apps to the appeal of the phone until it was too late."[338] In 2013, Microsoft bought Nokia's cell phone division, which at the time had a global market share of just 3 percent.[339]

Another example is Xerox, which invented the first photocopier in 1960 and dominated the market in 1970 with a market share of almost 100 percent. Just as people today say "I Googled it" when they searched the internet, people back then (and to a certain extent still today in the

U.S.) referred to "Xeroxing" whenever they photocopied something. In 1973, Xerox was accused of violating antitrust laws and a drawn-out legal battle ensued. But then more so than today, the problem was settled by the market, as companies, such as IBM, Eastman-Kodak, Canon, Minolta, Ricoh and others, all launched smaller and cheaper photocopiers.[340] The competitors' machines used low-maintenance liquid toner and were built with inexpensive, standardized parts. They were sold through ordinary office supply stores rather than through an expensive proprietary network. All of a sudden, the Japanese were selling low-end copiers at prices below the manufacturing cost of Xerox's machines, while Xerox wanted to continue making money on copy volume like a reliable subscription, as it had always done. Xerox's market share shrank from 95 percent in 1972 to 49 percent in 1979, before dipping below the 30 percent mark for the first time between 1998 and 1999.[341] Today, Xerox is stuck on less than 2 percent of the global photocopier market.[342]

Another example is Kodak, which in 1976 held over 90 percent of the U.S. film market and 85 percent of the U.S. camera market.[343] Kodak fully underestimated the shift to digital cameras before the market evolved again to come to be dominated by high-spec cell phone cameras. In 2012, the company filed for bankruptcy and later tried its luck with other business models. Kodak is an example of how some companies can hold a monopoly position for an extensive period of time. But this is not true for the vast majority of monopolists, as the stories of Myspace and Nokia confirm.

In some cases, one might argue, a monopoly is no more than a temporary phenomenon, which exists only to be replaced by another monopoly, as exemplified by Myspace and Facebook. These types of monopoly are referred to as "serial monopolies." There are countless examples of industries in which consumers flock to a "best-in-class" provider at a particular point in time. "In such markets, firms will compete to be the monopolist. It is in this competition that products that create more value for consumers prevail against those that create less value. Notice what that means. The very acts of competition that bring about the market tests of these products [...] will look like monopolizing acts. That is because they are. They determine which monopoly prevails until better products prompt new campaigns to capture an increasing returns market."[344]

One company that is often criticized today as a monopolist is Amazon. From its origins as an online bookseller, Amazon has expanded its services to include an ever-growing roster of product categories. Of course, more traditional booksellers complain that they cannot profitably compete against Amazon, but this is simply because Amazon offers a far greater variety of products—including used books—than any regular bookseller. But that doesn't mean that Amazon is unbeatable in the long run. Largely below the radar of the general public, new successful models are growing that work without Amazon and, "Which in the long run could even gnaw at the root of the world's most valuable company. The principle sounds simple, but many things have to work together: Manufacturers of consumer goods make direct contact with customers via social networks and organize every stage of the processes all the way through to the delivery of goods to customers' doorsteps. This allows companies to retain control of every single link in the value chain. Experts refer to this as 'direct-to-consumer' or D2C for short. The result: manufacturers bypass the major eCommerce platforms and cut out all intermediaries. The D2C trend, market experts believe, could become the seed of a movement capable of undermining Amazon's current dominance in eCommerce in the long term."[345]

Some large companies have already taken a pioneering role in D2C, including the sporting goods companies Nike and Adidas. Of course, this is only a snapshot, and it may have become apparent by the time you read this book that Amazon has also stamped out these new business models.

Competition and monopoly are not absolute opposites, but they are a dialectical contradiction: Competition creates monopoly because the best product prevails. High monopoly profits attract new competitors, who gradually destroy the monopoly, but at a certain point may themselves temporarily become a monopoly, only to be destroyed again by their competitors. It is only in the case of public monopolies that this cannot happen, since government power prevents it from being subject to competition. Milton Friedman stressed that the fundamental disadvantage of both public regulation and public monopoly is the extraordinary difficulty of reversing such developments: "I reluctantly conclude that, if tolerable, private monopoly may be the least of the evils," Friedman observed.[346]

Monopolies that are not public monopolies will typically disappear sooner or later because the monopolists become overly bureaucratic as they grow larger, because they are subject to minimal competitive pressures and because their mentality becomes more and more like that of government-owned enterprises. "They become more bureaucratic, they fail to foresee new and important products, market conditions turn against them, foreign competitors enter the market, disruptive technologies can 'change everything,' or their costs rise as they lose their dynamism."[347] Within such companies, however, there are creative minds that may eventually leave to start new companies.

A telling example of this very phenomenon is the emergence of SAP, Germany's leading software development company. It all started when IBM made the mistake of frustrating some of its best employees who were better at recognizing market opportunities than the company's own management. One of these disgruntled employees was Claus Wellenreuther, who had started working for IBM as a systems consultant in 1966 after graduating from the University of Mannheim. Wellenreuther, who as a business administration graduate was more of an outsider among all the physicists, mathematicians and engineers at IBM, became a specialist in the development of financial accountancy systems. "At IBM, accounting and Wellenreuther," explains SAP co-founder Dietmar Hopp, "went together like bread and butter."[348]

At the time, IBM was focused almost exclusively on the sale of hardware, and it would be years before the company recognized the importance of software. In mid-1971, IBM decided to centralize the development of a package of financial accountancy software, robbing Wellenreuther of his hobbyhorse. "I had imagined," Wellenreuther explains, "that I would be considered to manage the project. After all, I had been working on almost nothing but financial accountancy systems all along."[349] He was told, however, that he would not be considered for the new role, which would instead go to one of IBM's established managers. Wellenreuther realized that his career was at a dead end and that he could no longer move up the ranks at IBM. He decided to take his accrued vacation of two months to consider his options. Having done so, he quit and went into business for himself in early October 1971. The sign next to his doorbell now read "System Analysis Program Development" (SAP).

Another of IBM's employees, Dietmar Hopp, was also starting to think about a future away from the company. At IBM, Hopp was considered a specialist in the field of dialog programming—a classical programming method that allows computers to execute program commands immediately after input, thereby eliminating the delays in processing that were a common feature of earlier PCs.

Until then, IBM had largely left the development of application programs to its customers and consultants, providing them with individual support in each case. Each time, software engineers were reinventing the wheel, at considerable cost to IBM's customers. "What we do at IBM," Hopp realized, "is always the same for every customer. That's something we can standardize."[350] Hopp took it upon himself to develop standardized software that could be used in as many companies as possible. And it is with this idea that he, Wellenreuther, Hasso Plattner and two other former IBM employees went into business for themselves.

It was clear to SAP's founders that they had to be very fast. After all, they knew that if they were successful, other companies—perhaps even IBM—would copy their idea. It was not enough to have a brilliant idea for standardized software and to be able to program efficiently; they also needed a professional approach to sales. The founders of SAP soon realized that there was little point in presenting their ideas to computer specialists within large companies, who at first glance seemed to be the right people to talk to. But these IT specialists were afraid that SAP's new software would make them and their teams largely redundant.

They were also afraid that SAP's programs would highlight the errors and shortcomings in existing processes, which no one in their companies had noticed because the IT staff were the only ones who really understood anything about computers. So instead of offering their new software to IT managers, SAP started at the top, with the companies' board members and CFOs. That was their first good sales idea. But even more important was the fact that, from the very beginning, the company relied on partnerships with major auditing firms and hardware manufacturers. After all, it was much easier to sell software to a company if you didn't have to market it yourself because it was recommended by independent consultants who were already trusted by business executives.

SAP was thus able to concentrate primarily on the continuous further development and optimization of its software. "For us, the ability to innovate," says Hopp, "is synonymous with profitability." At the same time, he says, constant self-doubt, "whether others might not be better and overtake us," is embedded in the culture of SAP. "That uncertainty is what has always driven us."[351] As a cautionary example, he cites Nixdorf, which focused entirely on sales while flagrantly neglecting to optimize its products—and failed as a result.

SAP was more consistent and faster than its competitors because it focused exclusively on developing standardized software. "For years, our competitors continued to vacillate between producing standardized software packages on the one hand and developing bespoke software in specialized fields on the other."[352] SAP quickly succeeded in securing the business of almost all of Germany's leading corporations, and within a few years had established a virtual monopoly on the German market. Today, SAP is the largest European software developer. Only the U.S. still has three larger companies in this segment. And it all started because the monopolist IBM did not appreciate new developments quickly enough and, at the same time, did not give employees, who were better at recognizing new opportunities than the company's entrenched managers, the chance or the freedom to develop within the company.

Incidentally, according to Thomas J. DiLorenzo, IBM is a fine example of how the market does a much better job of preventing monopolies than government antitrust legislation: "Beginning in 1969 the federal government spent 13 years prosecuting IBM for allegedly monopolizing the computer market. The government finally abandoned the case after causing IBM to spend many millions of dollars and untold hours responding to its requests. Meanwhile, IBM's competitive position had been eclipsed by such companies as Microsoft and Wang Computers."[353] Wang Computers? Yes, you've most likely never even heard of this once-powerful brand because it disappeared completely in 1999 after almost half a century.

It wasn't only the computer giant IBM that made mistakes that led to the company losing its monopoly position. Another company Xerox, which I already mentioned above, did much the same. Xerox operated a top-secret development lab, the Palo Alto Research Center, which was reverently referred to in the industry as "Xerox PARC." Apple founder Steve Jobs was all too curious to see what was being researched here. And with his usual powers of persuasion, he finally succeeded in taking a peek inside the sanctuary, along with some of Apple's best computer experts.

Jobs was sent into raptures of excitement by what he saw. He walked back and forth across the room, jumping up and down, experiencing a thrill unlike any he had ever felt before. There, on display for the first time, was everything we now come to expect from a computer, including individual windows on the computer's screen for each document, and a device we have come to know as the mouse. It is impossible today to imagine a PC any other way, but back then, what Jobs saw was absolutely revolutionary and sensational. The Xerox employee who demonstrated the invention to Jobs and the Apple team was delighted to be met by such enthusiasm and pestered by such intelligent questions. One can only imagine what was going through the Xerox employee's mind as he realized that what he and his team had invented was so significant, while at the same time not receiving the appropriate attention and recognition within his own company. By the end of the demonstration, the Xerox man had decided to quit his company and join Apple.

These stories of IBM and SAP, Xerox and Apple, both have one thing in common: The big companies had very smart employees with incredible ideas, but weren't able to recognize their potential and quickly turn them into marketable products.

Companies, such as Google, Facebook, Amazon and Apple, appear omnipotent today—as was the case with earlier monopolies. But history teaches us that, more frequently than we might think, monopolies are far less enduring than they might appear at the height of their power. And each time, the critics tell us that this time, everything is going to be very different; this time, the monopoly will endure unless the government intervenes to clip its wings.

There is ample proof that measures enacted by the government to eliminate real or perceived monopolies are almost always superfluous or counterproductive. "A government agency," writes Martin Rhonheimer, "cannot possibly judge whether a monopoly—the same applies to cartels—is harmful or useful . . . Therefore, it seems more efficient to leave the assessment of its efficiency to the free market."[354]

While the economist Israel M. Kirzner stresses that monopolies that arise from competition, where one company creates attractive buying and selling opportunities in the market and satisfies the needs of consumers better than others, are not at all harmful, but are actually an important factor in achieving economic growth,[355] some thinkers belonging to the ordoliberal tradition, such as the German economist Walter Eucken, saw a great danger in any monopoly or cartel. Some of these ordoliberals—alongside Eucken, the economist Alexander Rüstow in particular merits a mention here—envisioned an ideal state of free competition among large numbers of small companies. This unrealistic utopian model, combined with the assumption that cartels and monopolies are always damaging, leads ordoliberals to advocate powerful antitrust authorities to break up trusts and cartels. Although they are otherwise skeptical about the government playing too large a role in economic affairs, in this case they call for omnipotent government agencies to prevent concentrations of power in the economy.

The Russian-American author Ayn Rand took a contrary position and—criticizing U.S. antitrust legislation—wrote cynically: "The concept of *free* competition, *enforced* by law is a grotesque contradiction in terms. It means: forcing people to be free at the point of a gun. It means: protecting people's freedom by the arbitrary rule of unanswerable bureaucratic edicts."[356] It is impossible to legislate competition, Rand argued, because there are no standards by which to define who should compete with whom, how many competitors there should be in a given field, what their relative strength or so-called "relevant market" should be, what prices they should charge, and what methods of competition are "fair" or "unfair." "None of these can be answered, because *these* precisely are the questions that can be answered only by the mechanism of a free market."[357] The only meaning and purpose of antitrust laws, Rand writes, is "the penalizing of ability for being ability, the penalizing of success for being success, and the sacrifice of productive genius to the demands of envious mediocrity."[358]

The Chinese economist Weiying Zhang dismisses the fiction of "perfect competition." "So called perfect competition is a lack of competition."[359] Antitrust legislation, he continues, is almost entirely also anticompetition: "According to the theories currently provided by economics, there is no way firms can be competitive. If you set prices higher than others, it is monopolistic pricing. If you set prices lower than others, that is dumping. If you set prices equivalent to others, that is conspiracy. Any type of pricing behaviour can be called monopolistic behaviour."[360]

Large companies that occupy (or supposedly occupy) a monopoly-like position have a hard time because they are surrounded by so many opponents: Less successful competitors, that is, those who have not been as successful at producing good-quality products at reasonable prices, are their enemies, as is the media, which is often steered by anti-capitalist resentment. Less successful companies and the media form an unholy alliance with government agencies and regulators who share the task of breaking the "power of the monopolies." They do this ostensibly on behalf of consumers, although in reality, their efforts are largely motivated by vested interests or ideology. Monopolies have a hard time standing up to these attacks because they have staunch opponents even among the ranks of what are normally ardent supporters of the market economy. Ludwig Erhard, whose greatest achievement as Minister of Economics was to ensure a free market economy in West Germany after World War II, is one such person. Erhard sharply opposed all monopolies and cartels, which he regarded as harmful per se.[361] Monopolies—and large companies in general—thus have many opponents and very few defenders.

Many leftist critics who fiercely attack private monopolies simultaneously accept or even justify the existence of public monopolies. Attacks on real or perceived monopolies by anti-capitalists and governments also serve a diversionary function because the most dangerous monopoly is the public monopoly. As Thomas J. DiLorenzo writes: "That is, government generates tremendous publicity for itself by prosecuting high-profile firms primarily for engaging in *competitive* behavior. Meanwhile, government itself is the main cause of real monopoly—with its protectionist tariffs, with its regulation of certain industries (from cable television to taxi services) that creates franchise monopolies; with its occupational licensing regulation, which makes it difficult or impossible to enter hundreds of occupations; and with antitrust regulation itself, which is often used as a political weapon against the most successful businesses."[362]

In terms of monopolies, government is far more of a culprit than a problem solver not only because government so often becomes a monopolist itself, but also because its overregulation favors the emergence of monopolies or oligopolies in certain sectors. After all, the more regulatory hurdles a government introduces, the more challenging it is for newcomers to enter the market. It stands to reason that only very large companies can afford to pay for the vast ranks of employees who are forced to ensure that their company complies with regulatory requirements, rather than being engaged in productive activities. "There is some evidence," explains Tyler Cowen, "that observed increases in concentration ratios are correlated with rising government regulation of business."[363] In some cases, government regulations directly restrict competition and lead to higher prices, as Cowen demonstrates with the example of the U.S. airline industry, where the government prohibits foreign carriers from operating domestic flights.[364]

Even some of the most disparaged practices of companies, such as Facebook, are caused by government regulation rather than the companies themselves. Take the censorship of political content, an annoyance that rightly attracts universal opprobrium. The fact of the matter is that Facebook and other companies are not the originators of this idea. From their perspective, it is expensive and entails a great deal of effort. They have been forced to hire thousands of additional employees and constantly develop new algorithms that detect or delete undesirable content. They censor content on this scale above all because legislators in various countries force them to do so. And if they don't do it, they run the risk of being sued.[365] So the right place to address such justified criticism of Facebook and others is, often enough, government—and not first and foremost the companies themselves.

However, the greatest paradox in the criticism of monopolies raised by anti-capitalists is that they are precisely the same people who so frequently advocate nationalization, even though public monopolies are the most durable and least vulnerable monopolies of all. Is it not absurd for anti-capitalists to criticize large firms for restricting competition while at the same time advocating more government-owned enterprises that eliminate competition not only temporarily and partially, but permanently and completely? The enemy of permanent monopoly is not socialism, it is capitalism.

7

"CAPITALISM PROMOTES SELFISHNESS AND GREED"

THE VERY THOUGHT of the word "profit" makes many people feel uncomfortable. They associate it with greed and other base motives. In 2019, Hermann Simon, a leading German entrepreneur and management thinker and author of the seminal book *Hidden Champions*, stood in the pedestrian zone of a German city and approached 100 people. This method of conducting a survey is known as "convenience sampling" and should not be expected to deliver representative results. But Simon wasn't really concerned with the numbers; he was most interested in observing people's reactions. He asked passersby, "How much remains as profit after costs and taxes when a company collects €100 in revenue?" Many of the people he spoke to found the question difficult, and some refused to answer, arguing that they rejected the idea of profit on principle. "It dawned on me that every student of business or economics should be required to ask normal people about the topic of profit. I never did that myself in my time in academia, neither as a student nor as a professor."[366]

On average, the pedestrians surveyed by Simon guessed a net return on sales (ROS)[367] of 22.8 percent; the median estimate was 19 percent. Despite the small sample size, these values were very close to the results of representative surveys. The answers Simon's interviewees gave were significantly overestimated: The true mean value of the net return on sales of German companies over a period of 14 years was actually 3.24 percent.[368]

What seems most curious is that although profit is so important to business, there are hardly any books on it. Hermann Simon has written one. He begins by declaring that the statement "I support profit maximization!" would cause outrage in wide circles of society. Yet, according to Simon, profit maximization is essentially just the opposite of waste, or to put it in other words, the minimization of waste.[369]

Companies that fail to maximize their profits are, in fact, acting antisocially—especially toward their own employees, whose jobs they are endangering. It is a well-known fact that most start-ups do not survive for very long and tend to go bankrupt a few years after being founded. What is less well known is that, across the board, many companies are hardly making a profit at all. That is extremely dangerous because it is only one small step from a very low profit to a loss. And that is something that everyone who opposes "profit maximization" should bear in mind.

Even many entrepreneurs underestimate the importance of profit. In his book, Simon reports on companies that serve as examples for many others: At a highly respected company, the boss is 66 years old and works 60 hours a week. When asked about profit, he replies, "Actually we don't make any money. But we have always stayed afloat, we have always invested enough, and we are in good shape." The fact is that in the last eight years, the company had posted a slight profit in four years and had posted losses, though not dramatic ones, in the other four years. The figures were close to zero each time, so the losses were not dramatic, but the profits were also minimal. The owner was looking to sell his company and did not understand why no one was willing to buy it from him at his unrealistic price.[370] Another German company that Simon profiles is a world-leading plant engineering company that has been run for the last 36 years by an enthusiastic engineer who is now 70 years old. Not a single employee has ever been laid off, the workforce is highly skilled, and the machinery is state of the art. The company seems to be in good shape and posts revenues of between €50 and €100 million. However, the company had posted a loss in four of the previous nine years, and in four others, it barely broke even. In the remaining year, it achieved a net profit margin of 5 percent. The proprietor is pleased about his company's "knowledge capital," his brand, and his real estate holdings and is surprised that he cannot find a buyer. "He simply did not want to accept that the miserable profit history had reduced the company's value to such an extent that it might make a sale impossible."[371]

The company's owner explains: "In my world, the primary motive behind business is not big financial results. For me, that is not the most important part of my activity. When a normal financial result covers basic needs, that is enough for me. Beyond that, there are other motives, such as the quest for perfection, the thrill of discovery, the passion for working with others, and the shared joy in our successes."[372] Here is an entrepreneur who would gain a great deal of approval from those who criticize profit because he is not interested in filthy lucre but in self-realization. And yet his approach to running a business is highly risky and irresponsible toward his employees. Anyone who posts such small profits is, in effect, no more than one meter from the abyss.

"Profit," Simon writes, "is and will remain the sole criterion for the sustainable success and viability of a company."[373] He doesn't accuse entrepreneurs of striving for too much profit but too little. Many companies are far too interested in sales revenues and market shares, he argues, and too little in profit. And that is despite the fact that profit is such an important indicator of performance and a prerequisite for entrepreneurial independence and, subsequently, for the survival of the company—and, of course, for the prosperity of the entrepreneur. Conversely, negligible profits or even losses, according to Simon, produce the opposite effects: frustration, self-doubt, demotivation and, in the event of insolvency, the destruction of assets.

Many people equate profits and earnings with selfishness and greed. Whether you are speaking with advocates of capitalism or anti-capitalists, you will often hear that selfishness and greed are the system's main drivers. Some defenders of capitalism say, "Well, people are inherently selfish. That's why socialism does not work. Capitalism is more in tune with human nature." Anti-capitalists, in turn, will claim that capitalism promotes the worst qualities in people, especially greed.

Some people call for capitalism to be abolished; others feel it needs to be "improved." The British economist Paul Collier has put together a series of proposals on how capitalism should be "reformed." He criticizes the "moral deficit" facing "modern capitalism" and claims that "greed is good"—the iconic catchphrase of Gordon Gekko in the 1987 film *Wall Street*—has supposedly become the maxim of modern capitalism, and that capitalism is therefore in urgent need of an ethical correction.

In 2020, Collier co-wrote the book *Greed Is Dead* with his British colleague John Kay, in which they paint a biased picture of a capitalism dominated by "market fundamentalism" and "individualism": "Markets are not seen as mechanisms for mutually beneficial exchange but places where people try to outsmart each other for their individual profit."[374] Collier and Kay also distort the thinking of economists, including Milton Friedman, by claiming that their "arguments provided both a pragmatic and a philosophical basis for an ideology which acquiesced in, or even embraced, greed as a dominant human motivation."[375]

With twenty-first century capitalism so out of kilter, Collier believes the solution is to restore the concept of "public interest" to the center of economic life and require companies to align themselves with the "public interest" rather than solely with the pursuit of profit.

Collier describes how this should be achieved in his earlier book *The Future of Capitalism: Facing the New Anxieties*: "The best way to overcome these limitations is not to strengthen regulation, but to put the public interest right in the engine room where decisions are being taken: the public interest needs direct representation on the board."[376]

Collier's proposal might make you think of the kind of "political commissars" that exist in totalitarian systems and monitor compliance with political directives. But Collier has a different idea. He calls for laws to be changed in such a way as to force corporate leaders to make decisions not solely in the best interests of their companies, but in accordance with the "public interest." This, he claims, would curb selfishness and greed.

And, according to Collier, any company that fails to act in line with the public interest should be punished: "How can the public interest best be incorporated into the board? The law could be changed to make due consideration of the public interest mandatory for *all* board members. Being legally liable, if board members chose to ignore an important aspect of the public interest, they could face civil or criminal challenge in the courts."[377] This would open the floodgates to arbitrariness. After all, "public interest" is such a vague and elastic term that it could be used in any way by anyone. Collier is not suggesting that companies and board members should adhere to government regulations (which they are already legally obligated to do), but that in his model of "social capitalism" every entrepreneurial decision should be evaluated to determine whether it serves the "public interest," which today probably means that it promotes "sustainability," does not contribute to climate change and, of course, complies with all "gender" aspects. Collier advocates a series of policies that he refers to as "social maternalism." But that is by no means all. He has even more radical ideas. He wants citizens to play the role of "policemen" who watch over companies to make sure they are acting in the public interest. He isn't proposing a state police force, but self-empowered activists, legitimized by no one, to spy on and monitor companies. "Every regulation can be subverted by clever box-ticking; every tax can be reduced by clever accounting; every mandate can be fudged by motivated reasoning. The only defence against such actions is an all-seeing police force . . . This gentle policing role does not require everybody to be a part of it: there is a critical mass of participants above which the risks arising from corporate misconduct become too high to entertain."[378]

Collier is banking on the fact that there would be enough self-appointed activists in every company to happily take on this monitoring and snitching job: "All firms have a large pool of decent people who would be willing to take on a new identity alongside their existing identities; they would feel proud to become guardians of the public interest . . . There is no shortage of well-motivated people working purposively in large corporations."[379] Although Collier repeatedly professes pragmatism in his book and rages against ideologues and populists, his ideas are frighteningly similar to totalitarian systems. If private individuals without any legitimation are to assume the role of Collier's "all-seeing police force" to make sure that the boards of corporations are acting in the "public interest," this no longer bears any relation to a market economy or capitalism. In the end, nothing remains of capitalism but the word itself—ten letters that have been robbed of their actual meaning.

I have dealt with this at length because Collier is not a radical Marxist, but one of the many authors who thinks he needs to come up with suggestions on how to "improve" capitalism and place limits on the supposed "greed" that pervades our modern economic system.

The question is: Are greed and unbridled egoism really—and today more than ever—the driving forces of capitalism? The self-interest of every human being is one, though certainly not the only, driver of every human action. But this has nothing to do with a specific economic system. Rather, it is a primordial anthropological constant. "In popular usage," writes Ayn Rand, "the word 'selfishness' is a synonym of evil; the image it conjures is of a murderous brute who tramples over piles of corpses to achieve his own ends, who cares for no living being and pursues nothing but the gratification of the mindless whims of any immediate moment. Yet the exact meaning and dictionary definition of the word 'selfishness' is: *concern with one's own interests.*"[380]

The word "selfish" combines the pronoun self-, meaning to or for yourself, with the suffix -ish, for "having the character of." In his book on egoism, Julien Backhaus writes: "The 'ego' is the starting point of all of your experiences on this planet. It is neither good nor bad. It simply is. It forms the center of your life. It is what separates you from your environment."[381]

Totalitarian ideologies seek to diminish the "I." They want nothing more than to subordinate it to the "we," as demonstrated by two of the maxims of National Socialism: "*Du bist nichts, dein Volk ist alles*" ("You are nothing, your people are everything") and "*Gemeinwohl vor Eigenwohl*" ("Public interest before self-interest.") In a speech in November 1930, Adolf Hitler said: "In the entire sphere of economic life, in the whole of life itself, one will have to do away with the idea that the benefit of the individual is the essential thing and that the benefit of the whole is built on the benefit of the individual, i.e., that the benefit of the individual is what gives rise to the benefit of the whole in the first place. The reverse is true: the benefit of the totality determines the benefit of the individual . . . If this principle is not recognized, then a selfishness must inevitably set in and tear the community apart."[382]

This conviction unites all totalitarian thinkers, revolutionaries and dictators, from Robespierre in the French Revolution to Lenin, Stalin, Hitler and Mao. Hannah Arendt, one of the greatest thinkers of the twentieth century, wrote in her work *On Revolution*: "It was not only in the French Revolution but in all revolutions which its example inspired that the common interest appeared in the guise of the common enemy, and the theory of terror from Robespierre to Lenin and Stalin presupposes that the interest of the whole must automatically, and indeed permanently, be hostile to the particular interest of the citizen."[383] Yes, absurdly, Arendt claims that selflessness is the highest virtue, and the value of a man may be judged by the extent to which he acts against his own interest and his own will.[384]

Adam Smith emphasized the benefits of selfishness, not primarily in terms of pure self-interest, but precisely because people need help from others all the time. However, he also highlighted the fact that no one can rely solely on the goodwill of others: "He will be more likely to prevail if he can interest their self-love in his favour, and show them that it is for their own advantage to do for him what he requires of them . . . It is not from the benevolence of the butcher, the brewer, or the baker that we expect our dinner, but from their regard to their own interest. We address ourselves, not to their humanity but to their self-love, and never talk to them of our own necessities but of their advantages."[385] Ludwig von Mises emphasized that it is a mistake to contrast egoistic and altruistic actions. Fortunately, "The power to choose whether my actions and conduct shall serve myself or my fellow beings is not given to me . . . If it were, human society would not be possible."[386]

In addition to equating the pursuit of profit with greed, many people are uncomfortable with the pursuit of profit because they believe economic life functions as a zero-sum game. Scientific research has proved that people who experience feelings of envy toward the rich adhere to zero-sum beliefs. But what does zero-sum mean? It is the belief that one person's gain must always be another person's loss—like in a tennis match where there is always a winner and a loser. Zero-sum believers imagine that a rich person can only become rich at the expense of others—especially workers, whom he exploits. They imagine the economy as a pie that always stays the same size: If one person takes a larger slice, all that is left is a correspondingly smaller piece.

But that is not how capitalism works. Trade and productivity gains increase the size of the pie. When the economy grows, many people benefit—not only the capitalists, but also the employees. And if there is an economic crisis, then in the worst case, the entrepreneur must fear for the existence of their company and employees for their jobs. The class contradiction between capitalists on the one hand and workers and employees on the other does not exist as such. More often, the interests of both sides are congruent because in a flourishing company, both the owner and the workers are usually better off than in a company that makes little profit and is perhaps even threatened with bankruptcy.

But back to the topic: Selfishness has always been a human trait. But in capitalism, it is restrained by the fact that only the entrepreneur who primarily focuses on the needs of customers can be successful. Empathy, not greed, is the basis of capitalism. Empathy is the ability to recognize and understand another person's feelings and motives. And this is the most important quality of successful entrepreneurs.

Let's take Steve Jobs as an example. He invented products such as the iPhone because he understood better than others the needs and desires of people in modern society. The same goes for Mark Zuckerberg, today one of the richest people in the world. He invented Facebook because he recognized his contemporaries' desire to connect with other people via the internet better than other entrepreneurs. Steve Jobs and Mark Zuckerberg became successful—like all successful entrepreneurs—through their customers.

The brothers Karl and Theo Albrecht were, for many years, the richest people in Germany. They became rich as the founders of the discount grocery store Aldi, which supplies quality products at low prices. They employed the same strategy as Sam Walton, the founder of Walmart, who was, for many years, one of the richest Americans. Through their buying decisions, consumers have confirmed that Jobs, Zuckerberg, the Albrecht brothers and Sam Walton were right about the wants, needs and feelings of other people; indeed, all of these entrepreneurs knew what consumers wanted before the consumers knew themselves.

Of course, there are also companies that act in an excessively selfish manner, losing sight of the interests of their fellow man. One example is Deutsche Bank, which contested thousands of legal claims with its private customers. But such companies are punished under capitalism—by the market. Deutsche Bank forfeited its position as one of the world's leading banks because it put the interests of its own investment bankers over and above the interests of its customers and shareholders.

Again and again, individual cases of companies or board members acting dishonestly are used as accusations against capitalism itself. The examples are legion, such as the American energy company Enron's fraud scandal in 2001, the "dieselgate" scandal of 2015 involving Volkswagen and other German car manufacturers, or the billion-dollar fraud committed by the payment processor Wirecard, which was exposed in Germany in 2020. Sometimes, as in the Wirecard case, such large-scale fraud was only possible because government regulators completely failed to do their jobs. There were detailed reports in the business press, but Germany's financial regulator, the BaFin, did not follow them up. In this, as in many other instances, it is more a case of state failure than market failure.

Swindlers and criminals have existed since the dawn of human civilization—under every system. It is a typical trick employed by critics of capitalism to portray basic anthropological facts—for example, the existence of fraudsters—as a system feature. However, there is not the slightest evidence that there is more fraud under capitalist than under non-capitalist systems. In fact, there is much to suggest that it is the other way round. Companies that abuse the trust of their customers suffer damage to their reputation and are punished by their customers or the financial market. Customers lose confidence and migrate to the competition, while investors sell the company's stocks or even punish it through so-called short selling. We saw in Chapter 6 that even monopolies can lose their power and eventually cease to be monopolies or even disappear from the market altogether. That is how powerful the market is under a capitalist system.

I worked in the real estate industry for roughly 20 years, and unfortunately I also came into contact with a few entrepreneurs who acted unethically or even broke the law. But first, this was a tiny minority, and second, the vast majority of unethical entrepreneurs sooner or later suffered at least significant image problems and often disappeared from the market altogether, while others were punished by the legal system. And often, the financial markets and customers are quicker to punish a company than the judiciary.

In socialist systems, on the other hand, consumers are helplessly at the mercy of state-owned enterprises because they are monopolies that cannot go bankrupt or face the economic or legal consequences of their actions. Under socialism, if a state-owned company acts against the interests of its customers, they have no alternative because there is no competition. Under capitalism, consumers can easily punish companies that lose sight of their needs. Every day, customers vote on a company— by buying its products or not.

And of course it is by no means the case that morally reprehensible actions are the exclusive preserve of capitalist companies. Such problems also exist in churches, in trade unions and in non-governmental organizations (NGOs) that are supposedly committed to fighting for the poor and the environment and against capitalism. One such recent example involved the organization Oxfam, which year after year publishes "studies" that denounce the rich and capitalism to extensive media fanfare. In February 2018, it was revealed that Oxfam employees forced women who volunteered in Oxfam stores to perform sexual acts in exchange for assistance in crisis situations. This was reported by Helen Evans, a former senior-level Oxfam manager and former head of the security team at Oxfam UK. Oxfam had failed to adequately investigate these incidents, she alleged. According to Evans, an internal survey in a number of countries had revealed that one in ten employees had personally been victims of sexual misconduct or had at least observed such harassment and assault. This is just one of many cases where non-profit organizations have failed to fulfil their moral duties. Just as it would be unfair to generalize such reports and put the NGOs in the dock, it is unfair to blame capitalism for the moral failings of individual companies.

Of course, some entrepreneurs are greedy, but it would be absurd to regard the pursuit of profits in general as an expression of greed. "Greed," writes the economist Thomas Sowell, "may well explain an individual's *desire* for more money, but income is determined by what *other people* pay, whether those other people are employers or consumers. Except for criminals, most people in a market economy receive income as a result of voluntary transactions. How much income someone receives voluntarily depends on other people's willingness to part with their money in exchange for what the recipient offers, whether that is labor, a commodity or a service."[387]

On an economic level, companies need to make a profit, otherwise they will not survive. This is true not only under capitalism, but in any economic system: If, for example, in a socialist system, the majority of companies were to post losses, the system would quickly collapse. Ultimately, this is why the Soviet Union "went bankrupt" in the late 1980s, some 70 years after its founding. The system—that is, all Soviet enterprises combined—had accumulated so many losses that the economy was no longer viable.

Hermann Simon emphasizes that profit and freedom go hand in hand. "Business owners who generate a profit reduce their dependence on banks, customers, and suppliers. They can decide on their own what they do with their profits. They can distribute them, re-invest them in the existing business, build new businesses, or donate them to a cause or charity of their choice. Profit grants freedom."[388] But the reverse is also true: If an entrepreneur does not make a profit, they have less freedom. Banks restrict their room to maneuver, they depend on every single order, their employees worry about losing their jobs and may even move to a competitor.

Freedom, incidentally, is also a key motive for entrepreneurs to become entrepreneurs in the first place. I wrote my doctoral dissertation on the psychology of the super-rich and wanted to find out what money means to the very wealthy. When most people think of the rich, they immediately think of luxurious cars, expensive yachts and magnificent villas. Television shows are full of such images. And of course, there are rich people for whom material possessions are important.

I conducted in-depth interviews of between one and two hours with 45 wealthy people for my dissertation. In the end, the transcripts of these conversations comprised 1,700 pages—plus a psychological test with 50 questions that each interviewee filled out. The result:[389] My interviewees associated having money, that is, a large fortune, with very different advantages in their lives. In order to better understand their individual motives, all of the interviewees were presented with six statements to find out what they associate with money. They were asked to rate each of these statements from 0 (completely unimportant) to 10 (very important).

The variety of the interviewees' responses reveals the range of their individual motivations. For example, the motive of "being able to afford the finer things in life" (i.e., expensive cars, houses or vacations) played a very important role for 13 interviewees, while ten affirmed that this was not of the slightest importance to them. For the remaining interviewees, this point was neither extremely important nor completely unimportant. The motive of "security" was cited as being particularly important by about half of the interviewees, but there were also nine who attached no importance to it at all.

Only one motive was shared by almost all respondents: they associated wealth with "freedom and independence." The self-image of being financially free united almost all respondents and no other motive was rated as highly. Only five interviewees rated this statement with a score that was not in the highest range between 7 and 10 points, while 23 awarded it the maximum value of 10.

The second most important point was: "The opportunity to use the money for new things, to invest," which was rated as very important by 23 interviewees and less important by only one.

Now some people are sure to object: "Freedom is all well and good, perhaps even profit. But where is the humanity in all of this?" Socialist systems promise people happiness and a solution to all of their problems, a kind of paradise on Earth. We know from the socialist experiments of the twentieth century that this promise of paradise all too often ended in hell. Scientists have counted more than 100 million deaths as a result of these socialist experiments—I present three examples of the inhumanity of socialist systems in Chapter 11.[390]

Capitalism does not promise people paradise on Earth but an order that ensures a reliable supply of goods. I have shown in previous chapters that capitalism is not only the best remedy against hunger and poverty, but also, for example, for the environment. But one thing capitalism cannot offer people is individual meaning in life and the promise of happiness. Man should be free to strive for happiness, but whether it is achieved is not the responsibility of the economic system. The free-market philosophy is based on the self-responsibility of every individual person.

"Non-capitalist economic systems," writes the German economic historian Werner Plumpe, "have not yet succeeded anywhere in providing the material background relief without which it is difficult to imagine a 'good life' of any kind. Material background relief does not mean happiness in life, especially since it is not always and everywhere given—even under capitalist conditions. All in all, the capitalist order is far superior to all other conceivable arrangements. And if this is so, the coldness of the economy is at least a necessary condition of a satisfying life, if not its fulfillment. But the economy is not responsible for that either; that is down to people themselves."[391]

Socialists always speak of the "we." Advocates of free markets believe that people should be the masters and shapers of their own destinies, that they themselves are responsible for living "a satisfying life" and not the government. As I was researching for an earlier book, I devoted a great deal of attention to successful people with disabilities and found that there is much to learn from them. First and foremost is taking responsibility—not to blame society, not to blame other people or external circumstances, but to take responsibility for yourself.

One example that really impressed me was the life of one particular American: He was born in 1930 into one of the poorest families in his town. He never knew his father. His mother died at the age of 31. He was black, which was even more of a problem in the U.S. back then than it is today. And on top of that, he contracted an incurable eye disease and went blind at the age of seven.

You have probably heard many of his songs. His name is Ray Charles. He is revered as the "High Priest of Soul." On *Rolling Stone* magazine's list of the "Best Singers of All Time," he is ranked first among men, ahead of superstars such as Elvis Presley, John Lennon, Bob Dylan and Paul McCartney. Only one female singer, Aretha Franklin, ranks ahead of him, relegating him to second place overall in the "100 Greatest." He was not only a singer, but also a songwriter and producer, and received the coveted

Grammy Award 17 times from 37 nominations. With a net worth of $100 million, he was also one of the wealthiest singers of his day and age.

But there was also a dark side to his life. Ray Charles spent 16 years as a heroin addict. But he did not blame his drug use on external circumstances, his disability or the discrimination he had suffered. In his autobiography, he writes: "No one did it to me. I did it to myself. It wasn't society that did it to me, it wasn't a pusher, it wasn't being blind or being black or being poor. It was all my doing."[392]

That is it: to be the author of one's own life, for better or for worse. The German philosopher and cultural scientist Peter Sloterdijk calls this an existentialist philosophy.[393] It is characteristic of successful people— "the figure of self-choice, whereby the subject makes something out of that which was made out of it."[394] Contrast this with the philosophy of socialists, which declares, "You are a victim of circumstances and you have no chance for a better life within these capitalist structures—so join us and help tear these structures down." Declaring people victims in this way makes them helpless and powerless. In contrast, examples of people who took their fate into their own hands despite—and sometimes even because of—adverse external circumstances can be a valuable source of encouragement and inspiration.

Admittedly, capitalism is the more challenging system because not everyone loves freedom and personal responsibility. Many find it easier when it is the system that gives them their sense of purpose. Islamic states offer their citizens religious meaning, socialist states promise a classless society in a communist future, and the National Socialist state gave many Germans a sense of life and value within the *Volksgemeinschaft* (national community). All of these collectivist systems provide amazingly precise instructions as to what role each individual should play in the community—and what role they should not play. But for people of other convictions, for people of other faiths (or, under National Socialism, for groups that were excluded from the *Volksgemeinschaft*), these systems were a living hell, and many met their end in Hitler's concentration camps or Stalin's Gulag.

Classical liberalism is based on the principle that neither the state nor the economy conveys a meaning of life that is binding for all citizens. Can you define the meaning of your life? For example, I can understand Arnold Schwarzenegger, who said, "The meaning of life is not simply to exist, to survive, but to move ahead, to go up, to achieve, to conquer."[395] Even in his youth, he said, he set big goals for himself. "With my dreams and ambition," Schwarzenegger explained, "I was definitely not normal. Normal people can be happy with a normal life. I was different. I felt that being alive had more in store for me than just giving me an average existence."[396] I'm fascinated by people who think that way. But I would never dream of advocating a society in which everyone is obliged to think and feel that way.

People have very different dreams and ideas of what a fulfilling life means to them. A free society gives people, such as Schwarzenegger, who came from a small Styrian village in Austria, then became the world's most famous bodybuilder and one of the highest-paid action stars in Hollywood (and was twice elected governor of California), more opportunities than other societies to realize their very individual dreams. But it does not oblige anyone to dream a particular dream or to demand anything special from life at all. That, too, is part of every person's self-choice.

8

"CAPITALISM ENTICES PEOPLE TO BUY PRODUCTS THEY DON'T NEED"

IN HIS 2015 ENCYCLICAL "Laudato si'," a blazing indictment of capitalism, Pope Francis proclaimed, "Since the market tends to promote extreme consumerism in an effort to sell its products, people can easily get caught up in a whirlwind of needless buying and spending. Compulsive consumerism is one example of how the techno-economic paradigm affects individuals." Like other anti-capitalists, he goes on to claim that this is done only in the interests of the rich: "This paradigm leads people to believe that they are free as long as they have the supposed freedom to consume. But those really free are the minority who wield economic and financial power."[397] And just like all anti-capitalists, Pope Francis proves himself to be a zero-sum believer when he proposes that the solution to the problem is "to accept decreased growth in some parts of the world, in order to provide resources for other places to experience healthy growth."[398]

In 2018, the Swiss sociologist Jean Ziegler wrote: "Consumer society is based on a few simple principles: Its members are customers who are seduced into buying, consuming, and throwing away goods in ever-increasing numbers, and acquiring ever-new goods even when they don't really need them."[399] Ever new desires "are instilled into the consumer's brain, implanted"[400] and, as result, a "compulsion to consume" prevails under capitalism.[401]

Such criticism of consumerism is nothing new. When the thesis that capitalism leads to the ever-greater impoverishment of the broad masses of the working class was refuted by developments in the United States and Western Europe after the Second World War, the "New Left" virtually turned the argument around: Not too little, but too much consumption was the true evil of capitalism, they claimed. There was even talk of "the terror of consumption." This involved capitalist companies first artificially creating "needs" among consumers through advertising, then partly satisfying them with cheap, inferior goods, in the epitome of the "throwaway society." The British philosopher Roger Scruton characterized the critique of "over-abundance" and "consumer society" when he wrote, "This story turns the proof of our freedom—namely, that we can obtain what we want—into the proof of our enslavement, since our wants are not really ours."[402]

Of great influence was Herbert Marcuse, the mastermind of the Frankfurt School, who argued in his book *One-Dimensional Man* that people could no longer distinguish their "true" from their "false" needs because their ability to refuse what existed had been overridden by the enormous progress of commodity production. The goods and services of the capitalist world "indoctrinate and manipulate; they promote a false consciousness which is immune against its falsehood . . . Thus emerges a pattern of *one-dimensional thought and behavior*."[403] For Marcuse, these were inhumane conditions: "Those whose life is the hell of Affluent Society are kept in line by a brutality which revives medieval and early modern practices."[404] Accordingly, consumption reinforces "alienation," a term that remains so vague that it allows everyone to develop their own ideas of what it might actually mean and, in any case, "recognize" their own problems as problems of society.

The term "terror of consumption" became one of the favorite phrases of the '68 generation. At its most extreme, this radical criticism of consumption prompted the first spectacular acts of terrorism in Germany by Andreas Baader and Gudrun Ensslin, who would go on to form the core of the Red Army Faction (RAF) with Ulrike Meinhof and later killed 33 people. On April 3, 1968, two incendiary devices exploded in the Kaufhof and Schneider department stores in Frankfurt. The terrorists justified their bombings: "We set fires in department stores so that you will stop buying. The compulsion to consume terrorizes you, we terrorize the goods."[405] According to their logic, the terror of consumption must be fought with another form of terror, thereby legitimizing violence and attacks in the fight against consumer slavery.

For some leftists, consumerism was and is even worse than fascism—which meant there was a certain logic to fighting it with all means. The leftist Italian film director Pier Paolo Pasolini attacked "consumerism" and asserted: "No fascist centralism ever managed to do what the centralism of consumer civilization has successfully accomplished."[406] This new ideology, he said, was "the worst kind of repression in human history," a new form of totalitarianism that was "all-embracing and alienating to the uttermost limit of anthropological degradation or genocide."[407] He stated that "Superfluous goods make life superfluous," and called for a new culture of poverty.[408]

In many parts of the world, including Europe, criticism of consumerism became entwined with anti-Americanism: American cultural imperialism, so the argument ran, was destroying true culture and causing the capitalist world to become increasingly superficial and uniformly boring.

Although this critique took on great importance in the 1960s in the U.S. and Europe, it is actually as old as capitalism itself—in fact, it is even older, going back to philosophers, such as Plato in antiquity. Werner Plumpe argues that early critiques of nascent capitalism in the eighteenth century did not focus on social issues. According to Plumpe, capitalism was a problem in the eyes of the earliest critics "because it provided cheap consumer goods for a mass market, goods that were inferior in the eyes of the hitherto dominant, affluent classes. It was, one might say, the critique of consumption with which the educated world confronted the emerging capitalism and by means of which the first unease about it was expressed."[409]

This criticism manifested many resentments: the resentment of the "educated" toward the "profane economy," coupled with an uneasiness of the Christian tradition toward a world in which "abundance, money, and individualism not only changed the social-moral order but threatened to dissolve it."[410]

In the nineteenth century, this criticism intensified, and the United States became the object of a biting critique of capitalism. U.S. capitalism, however, did not come into focus so much for social reasons, "which would also have been quite absurd in view of the mass flight from European misery and the news coming back from the U.S. of life there; rather, it met with widespread revulsion from the 'arrogant' European world, which rejected mass consumption as much as the supposed immorality of a pursuit of individual advantage unrestrained by any tradition."[411] From the perspective of the educated middle classes, capitalism was at heart a project of the lower classes, and developments in North America seemed to confirm this strikingly.[412]

The criticism of supposed superficiality and consumerism has always been formulated primarily by intellectuals and based on their fear that the criteria for esteem and recognition within society were evolving. Whereas individual reputation in the eyes of the educated bourgeoisie used to depend on how well-read someone was, how aptly he mastered the classical educational canon, now under capitalism, anyone with the financial means could buy "status symbols."

In his book *The Intellectuals and the Masses*, the British literary historian John Carey cites the British writer George Gissing as an example of this criticism. Gissing, according to Carey, was the earliest English writer to "formulate the intellectuals' case against mass culture."[413] In his novels, Carey continues, Gissing employs two standard procedures to introduce a new character. One of them, Carey explains, is to look at the character's bookcase: "Shelves which contain poetry, literature, history and no natural science belong to sensitive, imaginative, intelligent characters. Shelves which contain politics, social science, technology and modern thought of virtually any description brand their owner indelibly as at best semi-educated and at worst cruel, coarse, and dishonest."[414]

Commerce, Carey writes, "lay at the heart of Gissing's discontent with the modern. Intellectuals, he implies, should by rights be immune from the sordid pressures of the marketplace."[415] Gissing abhorred advertising in any form, associating it with vulgarity and ill-breeding.[416]

Anti-capitalist cultural criticism took aim at the department store as early as the late nineteenth century. In his novel *The Ladies' Paradise*, published in 1883, Émile Zola indicts the moral turpitude of the department store and depicts the decline of small retailers in a Paris neighborhood. In researching his novel, Zola conducted extensive business and sociological studies and interviews, and his work was based on an actual department store. In another novel, *Warenhaus Berlin* by Erich Köhrer, the successful department store owner Friedrich Nielandt ends up burning his own store to the ground. Even then, department stores were accused of undermining people's morals and whipping them into a buying frenzy.[417]

The German historian Wolfgang König distinguishes three strands in the critique of "consumer society": a "culture-critical" position that attacks the superficiality of consumption; the "domination-critical" position, in which the consumer appears as the mindless subject of total manipulation and a puppet on the strings of capital; and the "environment-critical" position that vilifies consumption as the culprit of environmental degradation: "Over time, the focus of consumer critique shifted from positions critical of culture to those critical of domination to those critical of the environment. The individual manifestations of consumer critique spanned a broad political spectrum from far left to far right, although the emphasis of the cultural-critical position was more on the conservative spectrum, that of the domination- and environment-critical positions more on the left."[418]

One of the most influential conservative intellectuals in postwar Germany was Karl Korn, editor of one of Germany's leading newspapers, *Frankfurter Allgemeine Zeitung*, until 1973, and head of its Talk of the Town cultural section: "Does anyone seriously believe," he once asked, "that anyone can assimilate to the modern, automobile-centric way of life and remain an unchanged cultural subject? Anyone who drives a car and listens to the radio with the same regularity that applied to Europeans' church-going habits, who attends his or her local movie theater, swallows sulfonamides or hormone drugs, and controls their reproduction, is changed in his or her consciousness and social being."[419]

While a majority of West Germans rejoiced in a greater selection of goods after the horrors of dictatorship, the World War and the deprived postwar period, Korn sensed the "barbarism" of consumption: "In a world whose supreme law is the satisfaction of consumer needs, which displaces death and pain from human consciousness, insecurity nevertheless increases, as we all know and have experienced, because fear and emptiness increase. Thus hypercivilization and barbarism eventually coincide."[420] Korn was suspicious of everyone except scholars, religious people, artists and villagers,[421] who were not involved in the process of what he called "massification."

For intellectuals—whether on the left or the right of the political spectrum—criticism of consumerism was and is a means of distinguishing themselves from both the economic elite and the broad masses. The intellectuals, the bearers of the critique of capitalist-driven consumerism, fundamentally despise everyone who is not like them: the masses, who indulge in superficial consumption, and the capitalists, who also lack proper education and culture. Both the masses and the capitalists, these critics posit, are united by disdainful materialism, which stands in complete contrast to the idealism of true values and elevated culture that characterize the educated bourgeoisie.

This critique of capitalism and its representatives became especially popular in the 1960s. Ferdinand Lundberg, a professor of social sciences and economics at New York University, published a widely acclaimed book titled *The Rich and the Super-Rich* in 1968, in which he stated: "As to the general human type of American wealth-builder, new and old, it can be said that he is usually an extrovert, given to little reflectiveness until perhaps he approaches senility. He is more often unschooled than schooled, and unread, and has for the most part a naive view of the world and his role in it . . . By his position alone he is alienated."[422] Most of the "capitalists" that make up the *Fortune* list of the wealthiest individuals in America, he continued, could easily be described as "truants from high culture."[423] The leftist Canadian-American economist John Kenneth Galbraith began his widely acclaimed world bestseller, *The Affluent Society*, which was published in 1958, with the assertion "But, beyond doubt, wealth is the relentless enemy of understanding."[424]

Criticism of consumer capitalism continues to be formulated by intellectuals right up to the present day, and it is becoming increasingly strident and relentless. In 2009, the British author Neal Lawson published an article in the left-wing British newspaper *The Guardian* under the headline "Do we want to shop or to be free? We'd better choose fast." His critique: "We consume to buy identity, gain respect and recognition, and secure status. Shopping is the predominant way in which we know ourselves and each other, and it is at the point of ruling out other ways of being, knowing and living. This is because of the consumer industrial complex of designers, advertisers, psychologists and retail consultants who create an endless stream of new wants and turn them into needs. The market competes like a shark; it has no morality but feeds incessantly on us to get us to buy more because sales and profits must go up and up."[425]

Lawson's critique culminates in equating the Gulag Archipelago, the network of forced labor and concentration camps in Stalin's Soviet Union where millions died, with the Italian luxury brand Gucci, which he regards as the incarnation of consumer capitalism: "Totalitarianism, a society where alternatives are ruled out, was meant to arrive in the jackboots of the communist left or the fascist right. It now arrives with a smile on its face as it seduces us into yet another purchase. The jackboots are in this season's colour and style. We are watched, recorded and ordered not by our political beliefs but by our shopping desires. The gulag is replaced by Gucci."[426]

The intellectual critique of the capitalist consumer society holds the values and tastes of the educated bourgeoisie as absolutes and denounces all of the wants and needs of anyone who does not accord with these preferences as "false needs" created by cunning advertising to increase the profits of the capitalists.

The cultural scientist Thomas Hecken aptly criticizes the view that the "true needs" of buyers are disregarded and that "false needs" are artificially and manipulatively created by the capitalist market as an "act of highly manipulative rhetoric": "The suggestion that you are the only one (in contrast to everyone else, who are all being misled) who knows what people's true, authentic needs are remains empty and presumptuous given the cultural malleability of man as a deficient being. One's own political intentions and aesthetic preferences are thus subsumed behind the false, ill-founded notion of a natural human destiny."[427]

This distinction between legitimate and "natural" needs, on the one hand, and nonsensical, "artificial" needs, on the other, is above all a method used by intellectuals to reassure themselves of their own identity and establish their values, tastes and consumption habits as the only valid benchmark.

The French sociologist Pierre Bourdieu applied the term "habitus," which he describes in a somewhat complicated way as "a socially constituted system of structured and structuring dispositions, acquired in practice and constantly aimed at practical functions."[428] This includes an individual's style of dress, the hobbies and leisure activities they favor, their mode of speech, the social circles in which they move, the sports they practice, the general knowledge they possess, and, ultimately, the self-confidence they exhibit. Differences in habitus, according to Bourdieu, demarcate the various classes within a society.

Individuals, according to Bourdieu, are born into specific class groups within society and, from childhood onward, learn particular behaviors and, from their parents and social environments, assimilate modes of comporting and articulating themselves, and develop specific taste preferences. These behaviors and preferences combine to create a lifestyle in keeping with their specific class group and the group's individual members, and to differentiate their class group from other social strata.

For his empirical research, Bourdieu developed a questionnaire in which, for example, he asked respondents about the furniture they owned; the hobbies they pursued; their favorite musicians, singers, writers, artists, and films; their taste in clothing; and the food they served to guests.[429] According to Bourdieu, the totality of these preferences defines the lifestyles that distinguish the classes and groups within a society from one another.

As we have seen from the quotations from Gissing and Lundberg, the typical intellectual has clear ideas about what constitute "true" and "false" needs. Accordingly, anyone who has read only a small number of books has discredited themselves by this very fact alone, as has anyone who has read the wrong books, who by doing so has demonstrated that they lack true culture and education. And this failure to be "well-read" and appreciate "true culture" is, from the intellectuals' point of view, the common bond between the scorned capitalists and the masses, who have been manipulated by advertising.

But for the intellectual, being well-read is only one (though perhaps the most important) distinguishing criterion. Musical taste is another characteristic feature. Anyone who listens to popular music rather than classical, or even atonal music, is deemed to exhibit a frightening degree of superficiality. Theodor Adorno, mastermind of the Frankfurt School, for example, loved the twelve-tone music of Viennese composer Arnold Schönberg and regarded popular music, such as the music produced by the Beatles, as an aesthetic cruelty. One's own, very personal tastes thereby become identity-forming commonalities in the critique of the prevailing society.

Of course, capitalism creates a whole host of products that you or I would call useless and superfluous, simply because they are useless and superfluous to you and me. But capitalism is a free and democratic system in that it lets people decide for themselves what they need or don't need (with the exception of products that are banned for good reason, such as child pornography). The alternative would be a government-run, command economy in which politicians and civil servants decide what products people need or don't need. Ludwig Erhard, who introduced the market economy in West Germany after the Second World War, once ironically observed of critics of the capitalist consumer society: "If the ladies want cuckoos on their hats, let them have cuckoos. I am certainly not about to ban the production of hats adorned with cuckoos."[430]

Indeed, who would even want to determine what are "true" and what are "false" needs? In 2020, the consumer researcher Carl Tillessen published a book to widespread acclaim in Germany. The book certainly creates the impression that everything used to be better than it is today. Globalization and digitalization, in Tillessen's eyes, have had a primarily negative impact on the world. In the past, he claims, "when everything was still manufactured domestically," price structures were "reasonably coherent." He continues: "But globalizing the production of so many everyday consumer goods has turned our world of goods upside down . . . Today, a short-sleeved shirt can cost twenty times as much as a long-sleeved shirt because the short-sleeved shirt comes from Switzerland and the long-sleeved shirt comes from China . . . That doesn't just feel wrong, it is wrong."[431] It is wrong, he says, because "for people who are not so close to us geographically and culturally, globalization has ushered in a very dark age."[432] As far as this line of thinking is concerned, we have already seen in Chapter 1 that this is simply not true.

So, what were the good old days like? Consumption was supposedly governed by rational principles back then, compared with today's rampant irrationality. As evidence of this, Tillessen writes: "When our consumption was still rational, the lower class could be relied upon to shop in the lower-price segment, the middle class in the mid-market segment and the upper class in the upper segment. Homo economicus of earlier centuries was rational and always automatically adjusted his consumption to his wealth."[433] But you could put it another way: In earlier centuries, the majority of people all over the world were destitute and, as a result, could not afford anything except what they absolutely needed to live. Were those the good old days? Today, according to Tillessen, everything has become worse: "And if you can't actually afford to buy a Louis Vuitton bag today, you don't buy a cheaper bag, you save until you can afford the Louis Vuitton bag with the monogram print."[434] What is actually so wrong with ordinary people being able to buy more today than they used to? And who is to decide whether they "need" it or not?

Tillessen dismisses "pleasure purchases" as entirely irrational—thereby also implying that rational purchases are only made to satisfy immediate physical needs: "Without financial remorse, we now regularly make pure pleasure purchases. When we buy one thing, we no longer have to do without another. As a result, our consumption becomes less rational day by day. Never in human history has shopping had so little to do with meeting a tangible need."[435] He cites perfume as an example of "superfluous" products.[436]

We should feel guilty about almost all of our purchases, or at least more than 90 percent of them because, as Tillessen explains, "more than 90 percent of the products we buy are produced under unfair conditions."[437] And if you buy a cheap T-shirt, for example, you might as well have the receipt "framed and hung on the wall, because it makes you a certified supporter of modern slavery."[438] So buying cheap goods is the greatest sin you could possibly commit. On the other hand, if you buy a Gucci T-shirt for €299 that bears a "Made in Italy" label, it is more likely that it was made under "fair conditions," but, even then, you still can't be 100 percent certain.[439] By buying luxury, branded items, Tillessen explains, "we certainly have not prevented modern slavery, but at least we have not knowingly supported or encouraged it."[440]

Why, one wonders, do people buy so many things every day, all of which, according to anti-consumerism critics, they don't need? The simple explanation, according to Tillessen, is that they are sick—so sick they would need therapy. Tillessen speaks of shopping addiction. Such a disease undoubtedly exists, but for him, we are all addicted to shopping. He cites extreme examples, such as someone who was addicted to classical music CDs and ended up spending $8,000 a day on them.[441] We are addicted because we "increasingly buy things that we don't need in the slightest, even though the economic futility and ecological harmfulness of our behaviors are becoming increasingly clear to us. If we were honest with ourselves, we would have to admit our growing mental and physical dependence on regular pleasure purchases. Without realizing it, we've all been addicted to consumption for years."[442] People never even unpack some of their purchases or take the time to read the instructions, Tillessen writes, so they remain unused after they're purchased. As we can see from these examples, critics of consumerism take extreme behaviors and turn them into mass phenomena that supposedly affect all of us.

Even if you buy what are deemed to be the "right" things by consumer critics, you should feel guilty if you are not buying them for the "right" reasons. Because, "If someone prefers to buy organic fruit and vegetables primarily because they believe they are healthier for them, then that is not ethical consumption. And if someone buys organic bread and organic eggs because of the taste, that has nothing to do with morality."[443] Tillessen concludes that 99.9 percent of shopping decisions are made largely independent of moral considerations.

And who is behind all of this? Globe-spanning conspirators, such as Amazon, who dream of world domination: "Today it is the E-tailers (retailers + eCommerce = E-tailers) who, like James Bond villains, dream of wiping brick-and-mortar retail completely off the face of the earth and achieving total world domination."[444]

Of course, such critics of consumerism are well aware that barely anyone could or would want to live in a way that would consistently align with the logic of their arguments. Tillessen openly admits: "But if we were to follow all of these precepts, our lives would be nothing but root vegetables, sauerkraut and shriveled apples, and unwashed, crumpled, second-hand clothes. The multiplicity and rigor of the requirements makes a radically sustainable life seem like something we can neither achieve nor want to achieve. Living exclusively in harmony with the principles of sustainability and only ever buying fair trade goods would set us back decades in the progress of humanity, as would claiming not to use Google products, either directly or indirectly. And in the end, the perceived magnitude of the personal sacrifices every one of us would have to make would be absurdly disproportionate to the tiny contribution we could make to improving the world. So, most people simply abandon the attempt to live more sustainably and carry on as they always have. Unfortunately."[445]

So Tillessen knows that there is no chance of people consistently changing in their lives as he so vehemently complains about. But they can at least change small things, he says, such as riding a bicycle to work from April to September or only using the train rather than airplanes for domestic travel. In addition, he suggests, we should all constantly measure our carbon footprint, "even though this is only one of many aspects toward achieving net zero carbon emissions and completely ignores the issue of the social compatibility of our consumption."[446]

His proposals, when you boil them down, amount to symbolically doing "something"—with the permanent burden of a guilty conscience because whatever you do is far too little, as we are nevertheless still destroying the environment, promoting climate change, consuming nonsensical products and, above all, are still responsible for the exploitation and slavery of people in Asia, Africa and Eastern Europe. As you will remember: if we buy the right things for the wrong reasons, that does not count. As a result, whatever we do, we are always left with a feeling of guilt. So, bad consumption is the consumption that leaves us with a good feeling and the less condemnable consumption is the one that leaves us with a guilty feeling. That begs the question: Are people with permanently guilty consciences happier? Are they self-confident citizens?

Or are they more open to manipulation by politicians who build their political strategies on guilty consciences and promises of psychological relief if citizens join the anti-capitalist movement or at least put their crosses next to the "right" party's name at the polls?

All of which leads to the next question: How do we resolve this contradiction of ideologically condemning consumption on the one hand and one's own existence as a consumer on the other? The "solution" to this contradiction is "to refer to only very specific purchases made by private individuals as 'consumption'—namely other people's acts of purchase and acquisition. The objects one buys oneself seem to be much less commercial and undemanding than those of the petit bourgeois and workers; the perception of the objects with which members of the (upper or aspiring) middle class surround themselves, as well as their dealings with them, seem to them to be much less distracted and apathetic. In short, only what seems worthless and uncreative is labeled and rejected as consumption."[447]

According to the German professor of cultural studies, Thomas Hecken, left-wing intellectuals' rejection of consumerism only applies to domains populated by other objects and tastes. It is easy to dismiss such a "domain" if you do not appreciate it anyway, while at the same time accusing those who do enter it "of cultural and sometimes also moral failure," and declaring that "one would prefer to prohibit its spread."[448]

What "consumption critics" fail to mention in their differentiation between "true" and "false" needs is that almost all needs that go beyond food and sexuality are subject to cultural shifts. This has always been the case. In his book *Empire of Things*, the historian Frank Trentmann writes, for example, about the desire for Indian cotton in eighteenth-century Europe, for European dress in nineteenth-century Africa, and the emergence of new European tastes for exotic goods such as coffee, tea, and chocolate: "Preferences for these goods were neither pre-existing nor stable but had to be created."[449]

At some point in history, all needs that went beyond meeting basic survival needs were considered superfluous or luxuries—and only very few could afford them. In the past, windows and indoor toilets were regarded as a nonsensical luxury; today, they are as natural as they are indispensable for most people in the world. In the late Middle Ages and early modern era, spending on fashionable dresses, lavish weddings and beautiful furniture met with widespread condemnation and even prohibition: "It was denounced for setting off a spiral of emulative spending—what is often called 'keeping up with the Joneses'—and for undermining values and social hierarchies . . . Perhaps most troubling, avarice and the lust for things were said to distract Christians from the true life of the spirit."[450]

According to the sociologist Helmut Schoeck, the war against luxury is as old as the hills. Legislation against luxury can be found in the most diverse societies, among primitive peoples, in antiquity, among the Far Eastern advanced civilizations, in the European Middle Ages, and even into modern times. "Sometimes a man who could afford inequality could pay ransom for the privilege, could buy off the envy of the community, as it were, by paying, say, a special tax if his house had more than a certain number of windows or stoves, or his waistcoat more than the minimum number of buttons; today in some countries his car is taxed according to its horsepower." On some occasions, Schoeck continues, a commoner in West Africa who put too many leaves on the roof of his hut, or who consumed honey he had found in the jungle, was even forced to pay for this "luxury" with the loss of a limb, if not his life.[451]

Trentmann, who analyzes the history of consumerism, writes that it was usually well-off commentators, such as the Roman philosopher Seneca, who berated others for giving in to material temptations: "It is rarely common people," Trentmann observes.[452] And strangely enough, even the harshest critics of capitalist "consumption" make excessive use of the products produced under capitalism. A study in Germany found that Green Party parliamentarians, who often call for personal sacrifice, limits on consumption and, for environmental reasons, for people to stop flying, use domestic flights more often than politicians from any other party. And you would be hard pushed to find an anti-capitalist willing to live without the computers, internet and smartphones that help them spread their criticism of capitalism.

Incidentally, it was not only capitalism that promised people unfettered consumption and consumer goods, but also the regimes of socialism and National Socialism. "Of course," Trentmann writes, "the track record of delivering the goods differed. What is remarkable, though, from a world-historical perspective, is how the vision of high and rising levels of consumption managed to install itself as the undisputed cultural ideal. Ideals of frugal self-reliance have been no match, or have been limited to short-lived and self-destructive experiments like that of the Khmer Rouge in Cambodia, between 1975 and 1979."[453]

The Empire of Things, as Trentmann calls it, has expanded in part because possessions have increasingly become important carriers of identity, memory and emotions. Clothes, cars, watches, smartphones, and so forth, are valued "for the feelings they generate within their owners, as well as their practical use."[454]

The anti-capitalist critics of consumption also reject any and all forms of advertising. Let's let the well-known critic of capitalism, Jean Ziegler, have his say again: "The instruments with which the capitalists create these needs are called marketing and advertising, two of the most unfortunate and stupid activities ever invented by mankind."[455] The "ad men," according to Ziegler, are "cunning" and they "hunt the consumer wherever he goes, encircle him, harass him with calls, bombarding him with their so-called messages."[456] These mercenaries of marketing "direct the behavior of the consumer."[457]

Of course, some advertising seems ridiculous and superfluous—to you, to me, and to many other people—but to anti-capitalists, *any* form of advertising is reprehensible. Noam Chomsky criticizes the advertising industry, which aims to have everyone "trapped into becoming consumers" in order to "control *everyone*."[458] He criticizes the fact that people do not decide rationally and presents the economic model of homo economicus in such a way that people make their decisions without any emotion. In his view, the fact that this is not the case confirms that the model is wrong and also proves the perfidious nature of advertisers' manipulation techniques: "If advertisers lived by market principles [i.e., that informed consumers make rational decisions, R.Z.], then some enterprises, say General Motors, would put on a brief announcement of their products and their properties, along with comments by *Consumer Reports* magazine, so you could make a judgement about it . . . If you've ever turned on your television set, you know that hundreds of millions of dollars are spent to try to create uninformed consumers who will make irrational choices—that's what advertising is."[459] According to this line of reasoning, you could also say that any woman who does not receive a marriage proposal from her lover in the form of a sober, factual email with a brief summary of the arguments in favor of marriage is hopelessly uninformed and manipulated.

Critics of advertising portray companies as omnipotent and try to create the impression that consumers are helpless victims in their clutches. To prove the advertising industry's omnipotence, critics have been repeating some myths for more than half a century. One is based on Vance Packard's 1957 book *The Hidden Persuaders*, which generated a great deal of media coverage when it was first published. The book reported one particularly manipulative advertising technique, which involved a cinema flashing split-second advertising images onto the screen during film showings. These images appeared and disappeared so quickly that audiences did not even consciously notice them. The press referred to subliminal advertising as the "most hidden, hidden persuasion," and those who used such techniques as "invisible monsters," who were guilty of "brainwashing."[460]

The book attracted so much attention because, in the same year, James M. Vicary, owner of an advertising agency, allegedly conducted an experiment in which he subliminally inserted the slogans "Drink Coca-Cola" and "Eat Popcorn" during a film screening. Vicary claimed that this increased sales of Coca-Cola by 18.1 percent and popcorn by as much as 57.7 percent. However, it later emerged that the experiment was faked or had never taken place. "The alleged study merely served as a marketing ploy to boost sales for Vicary's marketing company."[461] I have lost count of the number of times in my life that people have told me about this alleged experiment, portraying it as a particularly reprehensible example of consumer terror and manipulation through advertising.

I must admit, though, that I also long believed that the experiment had actually taken place, although I could never quite understand other people's outraged indignation. After all, what was supposedly happening? People were watching a movie that might have been about murder and manslaughter, but they weren't overcome by violent urges; instead, they ordered a bottle of Coke during the intermission because they had been shown it for a split second. But, as I said, all this never actually happened anyway, and Vicary, the supposed king of subliminal advertising, suffered the ignominy of bankruptcy just one year after the alleged experiment.

Of course, advertising can work—it can and should "manipulate"—but it is by no means as omnipotent and devious as its critics pretend. Far more frequently, it is actually ineffective. The American entrepreneur Henry Ford is credited with once stating that "Half the money I spend on advertising is wasted; the trouble is I don't know which half." In the mid-1980s, social psychologist and advertising expert Eva Heller wrote that the phrase attributed to Henry Ford no longer held true: "Today, it can be assumed that at least three-quarters of advertising budgets are spent without delivering the expected results."[462]

And David Ogilvy, the great advertising guru, repeatedly ridiculed the advertising campaigns created by other advertising agencies in his book *Confessions of an Advertising Man*, accusing them of being inefficient, often doing nothing to increase sales, and serving to entertain rather than to sell. He accused other advertisers of being more concerned with winning awards for their campaigns than with selling their clients' products.

Since 2003, the German marketing expert Bernd M. Samland has regularly asked more than 3,000 people about various advertising slogans—and most of the English slogans were either not fully understood or even completely misunderstood by the (potential) customers.[463] The advertising copywriters had apparently forgotten their cardinal task, namely to increase sales.

Great sales successes, such as Harry Potter, were not achieved primarily through advertising. Howard Schultz, the founder and former chairman of Starbucks, once said: "It is now difficult to launch a product through customer advertising because customers don't really pay attention as they did in the past, nor do they believe the message . . . I look at the money spent on advertising, and it surprises me that people still believe they are getting returns on their investments."[464]

In January 2021, American advertising experts Bradley Shapiro, Günter Hitsch and Anna E. Tuchman published a study based on their meticulous scientific analysis of TV advertising for 288 consumer goods. Their shocking finding: Not only did advertising not pay off for 80 percent of brands, it even had a negative ROI (Return On Investment).[465]

Of course, you could argue that targeted online advertising via social media is much more effective today, but there are doubts about that too. A few years ago, Procter & Gamble and Unilever reduced their online advertising spending by 41 and 59 percent, respectively—with no negative impact on the bottom line. Uber also cut its online budget by two-thirds after a massive ad fraud—with no change to the number of app installations.[466]

Advertising is not as omnipotent as advertising agencies and anti-capitalists would have us believe—for a variety of reasons—and the image of the mindless consumer being seduced by ingenious advertisers into spending all day, buying unnecessary items, is a massive exaggeration. If anyone is being cheated, it is more often than not the companies that spend so much money on ineffective advertising and who only join in the advertising game because their competitors are doing so too. Advertising agencies are most successful at convincing their clients to spend money, not the customers of their clients.

On a personal level, I frequently find myself annoyed by primitive advertising, but I also can't stand many modern opera productions and still wouldn't get the idea that opera houses should be closed down for that reason (the difference is, of course, that as a taxpayer, I have no choice but to help finance high culture in Germany whether I want to or not; whereas as a consumer, I only finance advertising when I buy the products that are being advertised).

At the same time, when I picture a world without advertising for products and services, I think of the dreariness of socialism, where boring posters dominate the streetscape, proclaiming propaganda messages from the party and slogans calling for the fulfillment of the plan. I much prefer advertising under capitalism, which, at its best, has achieved the status of art, as was the case with Andy Warhol, who was himself a commercial artist by profession. The sociologist Schoeck wrote that as soon as anyone mentioned "the terror of consumption" in his presence, he asked them to describe which process in their everyday life they were referring to: "Neither in university seminars nor at other events did I ever find anyone who confessed to being a victim. It seems that it is always the wrong needs of others that are being satisfied."[467]

Another major bugbear of anti-capitalist consumer criticism is what is known as "obsolescence." The term itself is ambiguous, because it covers very different issues that basically have little to do with each other. Wikipedia defines the term as follows: "Obsolescence is the state of being which occurs when an object, service, or practice is no longer maintained, required, or degraded even though it may still be in good working order."[468] In a second entry, this time for "planned obsolescence," Wikipedia states: "In economics and industrial design, planned obsolescence (also called built-in obsolescence or premature obsolescence) is a policy of planning or designing a product with an artificially limited useful life or a purposely frail design, so that it becomes obsolete after a certain pre-determined period of time upon which it decrementally functions or suddenly ceases to function, or might be perceived as unfashionable."[469]

Technical obsolescence and psychological obsolescence are frequently and deliberately conflated to make the problem seem as big as possible. The fact that products are disposed of even though they still function perfectly well is not in itself worthy of criticism. At some point, I disposed of my record player and my cassette recorder because the CD had been invented. Both devices would certainly have lasted for many more years. Had I become a victim of manipulation by capitalist advertisers? No, I was often annoyed by scratched records (for younger readers, scratches caused the record to "skip") and tape getting jammed or tangled up in my cassette recorder (again, for younger readers, this caused the cassettes to break) and was glad that there was now a device that spared me the annoyance of these two problems.

I also loved my old Nokia phone, which had a battery that lasted for days. I even stocked up on several, just in case my favorite model might eventually be discontinued. Later, I switched to iPhone. Did I do that because evil advertising strategists at Apple manipulated me? No, it was simply because the new device offered me many useful features that were missing from my old Nokia phones. I used to be the proud owner of a VCR, but again, I was always annoyed by the tape getting tangled, twisted or even torn. So I was glad when the DVD was invented because that proved far more reliable. I threw away the video recorder, although it was still technically functional.

The topic of obsolescence is not new, as the German technology historian Wolfgang König confirms. Anti-capitalists and so-called consumer activists speak of a great conspiracy operated by business and industry, which, they allege, systematically and en masse pursues a strategy of "planned obsolescence," that is, manufacturing products specifically so that they break faster.

But as early as 1976, a study by the economist Burckhardt Röper concluded that the alleged evidence that manufacturers were deliberately shortening the life of their products did not hold up. Many other studies in recent decades have arrived at similar conclusions. Even the German Öko-Institut admitted in 2015 that many such criticisms were exaggerated. At the same time, however, the Öko-Institut's analysis confirmed that the initial useful life of most of the product groups studied had indeed decreased in recent years. It was found, for example, that many electronic devices had been replaced by newer ones, even though the old ones still functioned well enough.[470]

In contrast to such differentiated analyses, we are frequently confronted by striking media reports that create the impression that planned obsolescence is a common and widespread phenomenon and that devices are deliberately produced in such a way that they break more quickly—a topic that has also been taken up by some politicians. Wolfgang König writes that it is striking that in "conspiracy theory literature, the same examples are used again and again, some of them going back a century."[471] The fabricated story of the light bulb whose life span had been shortened intentionally to the disadvantage of consumers has been repeated hundreds of times, says König.[472]

Time and again, the example of the car manufacturer General Motors, which offered a series of constantly updated models in the 1920s, has been cited as evidence for the thesis of planned obsolescence. With each new model, General Motors took market share away from Henry Ford, who stubbornly stuck to his one-size-fits-all model. In order to fully understand this, you probably need to know that Henry Ford reacted with passionate emotion whenever someone told him he had to move with the times and change anything about his famous Model T. On one occasion, when an employee had developed a successor model in Ford's absence and left it outside the door, Ford went crazy, as one onlooker described: "He takes his hands out, gets hold of the door, and bang! He ripped the door right off! God! How the man done it, I didn't know! He jumped in there, and bang goes another door. Bang goes the windshield. He jumps over the back seat and starts pounding on the top. He rips the top with the heel of his shoe."[473]

For years, Ford succeeded in preventing his employees from developing new models, but he could not stop the competition. General Motors responded to evolving customer expectations and launched new model after new model. Ever since, the example has been cited again and again as evidence of the sinister strategies of capital and the reprehensibility of capitalist consumer society. König comments, "What this is supposed to have to do with planned obsolescence in a conspiracy-theoretical sense remains incomprehensible."[474] Other frequently cited examples—including everything from modern cars supposedly rusting faster to inkjet printers' making consumers buy ink more often than is actually necessary—do not stand up to further scrutiny. An investigation by the German consumer organization Stiftung Warentest concluded that the thesis of built-in obsolescence is illogical: "The ideal case would be that all parts fail at the same time after reaching the end of their planned service life. Against this background, the strategy of purposefully built-in weak points makes little sense and would be wasteful because many other parts in the device would then be oversized and overly expensive to produce."[475]

Moreover, what sense does it make to produce devices to last forever when it is clear that they will be technically obsolete in a few years anyway? I suspect that even die-hard critics of capitalism today have neither a tape recorder nor an old film projector at home, nor do they have an old Nokia cell phone or a black-and-white television—and old record players are at best something for home audio purists.

The example of performance throttling in older iPhones is also frequently cited. Apple has admitted that its software tempers the peak performance of devices with older, non-replaceable lithium-ion batteries to ensure they remain functional and prevent unexpected shutdowns due to a sudden drop in power supply. A lawsuit was filed against Apple in the U.S., which ended in a settlement in March 2020; Apple agreed to pay a total of up to $500 million to the injured parties. Is that evidence that the plaintiffs were right? Was it an admission of guilt by Apple? Not necessarily. It is well known that in the U.S., even the most nonsensical consumer lawsuits can end with the award of massive sums in compensation. Red Bull, for example, paid $13 million to resolve two consumer class action lawsuits—consumers had complained about the slogan "Red Bull gives you wings" because they felt it falsely claimed performance-enhancing benefits.

Even if there are isolated examples of companies deliberately building weaknesses into their products, these still do not prove that this is a widespread strategy employed by profit-hungry capitalists. Every company knows that being exposed for such practices would lead to them being pilloried on the internet and in the media, severely damaging their brand value and stock price. Under capitalism, it is the consumer who has the final say—and, from the point of view of a company acting rationally, the risk that consumers will punish the company for such practices is higher than any potential short-term profit that could be made. Which, as we all know, does not mean that there are not, from time to time, companies that lose sight of their own best interests.

The critique of consumerism is accompanied by a critique of the status of money in capitalist systems. Capitalism appears to critics of consumption as a system in which money is the be all and end all. But money, so the thesis goes, does not make people happy. And this skepticism has apparently been confirmed by scientific studies. As early as 1974, the economist Richard Easterlin claimed that there is no positive correlation between higher incomes and greater levels of happiness, at least above a certain annual income.[476] The two Nobel Prize winners in economics, Daniel Kahneman and Angus Deaton, qualified Easterlin's finding somewhat and related it only to certain expressions of the feeling of happiness. But they did also conclude that the correlation between higher incomes and greater happiness only applies up to a certain limit, namely an annual income of $75,000. Anything above that level, the two economists explained, no longer has a significant impact on a person's happiness as they had already become accustomed to living in financial security and would only make minimal adjustments to their lifestyle with each subsequent salary increase.[477]

New research has disproved this thesis. The most recent analysis comes from the psychologist Matthew A. Killingsworth, who found that both "experienced well-being" and "evaluative well-being" did increase with income.[478] "Experienced well-being" was measured by analyzing 1.73 million experience-sampling reports from 33,391 Americans. They were contacted at random times on their smartphones and asked the question, "How do you feel right now?" Their evaluative well-being was measured by the question, "Overall, how satisfied are you with your life?" The result: the $75,000 limit advanced in Kahneman and

Deaton's study did not exist. For incomes over $80,000, Killingsworth's study also confirms a clear correlation between having a higher income and being happier. Methodologically, the study had some advantages over older studies. For example, in older studies, respondents could only answer "yes" or "no" to questions about their happiness, whereas the current study used a continuous scale. Another major advantage was that contacting respondents via their cell phones allowed the researcher to measure respondents' current emotional state. In previous studies, people were merely asked to recall how they had felt at a given point in the past. However, such memories are often distorted and strongly colored by respondents' current emotional states at the time they are asked.

The pursuit of material values is nevertheless considered superficial and "materialistic" from an anti-capitalist, anti-consumerism perspective. The renowned German-Polish literary critic Marcel Reich-Ranicki saw it quite differently: "Respectable people work in pursuit of glory and money. Indecent people want to change the world and save others." Of course, this is a pointed and exaggerated statement, and we immediately think of counterexamples of idealists such as Henry Dunant or Albert Schweitzer who brought about good, and power-hungry and corrupt dictators who brought much misfortune to humanity.

Nevertheless, Reich-Ranicki has hit on a salient point: The legion of idealists who wanted to improve the world and redeem people—and in the process brought endless suffering upon them—is long. It includes mass murderers, such as Adolf Hitler and Mao Zedong, as well as fanatical cult leaders and the followers of the Islamic State. On the other hand, there are countless examples of entrepreneurs whose "materialistic" pursuit of profit has improved millions of people's lives.

One of the biggest mistakes is to judge people or companies by their intentions and not by the results of their actions. Someone who *only* strives for profit can create immense benefits for society—by bringing new products to market to make people's lives easier or by managing to offer products of the same quality at a significantly lower price so that more people can afford them.

9

"CAPITALISM LEADS TO WARS"

THAT WARS ARE WAGED primarily because they are in the economic interests of capitalists was initially a Marxist thesis, but now seems to have become an accepted element of common thought. From the colonial wars to the First World War to the war in Iraq—according to anti-capitalists, these conflicts were all waged in the interests of big business, hoping to secure new sources of raw materials and open up new markets. First, it is important to note that wars were far more common in the pre-capitalist era—roughly speaking, before the beginning of the nineteenth century—than in the capitalist era. "For most of human history, war was the natural pastime of governments, peace a mere respite between wars," writes Steven Pinker.[479] In his book *Enlightenment Now*, he includes a graph that illustrates the percentage of years that great powers were at war. In the sixteenth and early seventeenth centuries, this percentage ranged from about 75 to nearly 100 percent; in the early nineteenth century, the percentage was still well above 50, only to drop to 25 and much lower in the twentieth and twenty-first centuries.[480] In contrast, the number of deaths in battle per million people reached all-time highs in the twentieth century during World Wars I and II. Since then, both the number of wars and the number of casualties have declined sharply.[481]

First of all, it can be stated that even on the basis of pure statistics, the thesis of war-mongering capitalism does not stand up to scrutiny. With the rise of capitalism 200 years ago, the frequency of wars did not increase; it significantly decreased.

I would like to devote this chapter to an examination of three wars by way of example: the First and Second World Wars and the Iraq War of 2003. I will pursue the question of the extent to which these wars were "capitalist wars," that is, were triggered exclusively or predominantly by capitalist interests.

Before we turn to these examples, however, I would like to present some of the findings of war and conflict research. For many years, a majority of researchers maintained that democratic countries do not wage war against each other, or at least very infrequently.[482] Some researchers qualified this finding somewhat and applied it only to democracies that also happen to be developed, industrialized nations. But overall, there was broad consensus on this finding, and the thesis was tested statistically by forming so-called dyads, pairs of states. These dyads represent the units of investigation to examine how often and for what reason such states engaged in military conflict with each other.

There was and is no agreement among researchers as to *why* democracies rarely—or perhaps never, given a narrow definition of democracy—wage war against each other.[483] The German sociologist Erich Weede, who has conducted extensive research on these issues, stated in 2005 that "the danger of conflict is particularly low in dyads where both states are governed democratically and trade significantly with each other or are otherwise economically interdependent."[484]

Since throughout history most democratic states have, at the same time, been capitalist and most capitalist states have, at the same time, been democracies, it has never been easy to decide which is more important for peace: whether a country had a democratic order or whether it had a capitalist system. As I said, both have typically existed simultaneously, although there have always been exceptions. Chile under Pinochet, for example, was capitalist but a dictatorship. Today, China, too, is increasingly adopting features of capitalism, but it is still a dictatorship.

In 2007, the American political scientist Erik Gartzke published an extensive empirical analysis in which he explored precisely this question: Which plays the greater role in ensuring that there are fewer wars: democracy or capitalism? Gartzke analyzed dyads from 1950 to 1992 and examined a total of 222 wars.[485] He employed metrics for all of the countries to show to what extent they were democratic (politically) or capitalist (economically). Using these ratios, Gartzke then applied a regression analysis relating to whether or not the country was engaged in a military conflict. He concludes: "This study offers evidence suggesting that capitalism, and not democracy, leads to peace."[486]

In a further study in 2010, Gartzke and Joseph Hewitt also analyzed military conflicts from 1950 to 1992, this time examining only those conflicts "that elicit decisions from a state's highest ranking foreign policy leaders." Conflicts that may have resulted "from clashes between frontline forces not directly authorized by leading officials" were not considered.[487] This analysis once again focused on the question of whether a country's democratic political order or its capitalist economic order was more likely to prevent military conflicts. Once again, the result was that capitalism, not democracy, was the most important factor in the absence or reduced frequency of military conflicts. Gartzke and Weede agree "that it is economic development and market freedoms, rather than political liberty, that precipitate interstate peace."[488]

Supporters of the theory of "capitalist peace," however, have different answers as to *why* capitalism results in less frequent conflicts. On this point, Weede more strongly emphasizes the factor of countries' interdependence through trade relations, while Gartzke believes that financial market integration is more important for peace than trade.

The topic of trade and war is not new. The British manufacturer and political campaigner Richard Cobden (1804–1865), a leading champion of the free trade movement, was at the same time a committed pacifist and emphasized the importance of trade and mutual economic dependence in preventing war. "I believe," Cobden writes, "that the desire and the motive for large and mighty empires, for gigantic armies and navies, for those materials which are used for the destruction of life and the desolation of the rewards of labour, will die away."[489] Gartzke, on the other hand, argues that trade plays a more ambivalent role in preventing war: "Economic development, financial markets, and monetary policy coordination all arguably play a more critical role in promoting peace."[490]

In 2018, Weede questioned the methodological validity of studies that conclude that trade does not play a decisive role in whether military conflicts become less likely and "if all of these shortcomings are avoided, then almost all studies support the proposition *'peace by free trade.'*"[491] Thus, states that are closely linked by trade are significantly less likely to engage in military conflict with one another.

Although researchers are still debating which characteristics of capitalism play the greatest role in ensuring that there are fewer military conflicts between capitalist states,[492] at least researchers such as Weede and Gartzke have presented convincing arguments to support the view that capitalism and not democracy is the decisive factor. "Since democracy depends on capitalism or economic freedom as well as the prosperity generated by it, the democratic peace becomes a mere component of the capitalist peace."[493]

Regarding the frequently cited counter-argument of the First World War, in which capitalist countries (including Germany on one side and France and Great Britain on the other) fought each other, Weede argues that trade dependencies were weaker between France and Germany (who fought against each other) than was the case between Great Britain and France (who did not go to war with each other).[494] "As far as trade linkages were concerned they were strongest where least needed—between Britain and France, between Britain and the United States, between Germany and Austria-Hungary. These pairs ended up on the same side of the war."[495]

For me, there is another, more fundamental argument that holds more weight: Of course, capitalist countries can also wage wars against each other, and the First World War is just one example of this. Researchers working on the theory of "capitalist peace" have analyzed long lists of military conflicts and then examined whether the countries involved were capitalist or not. However, in my opinion, this method alone does not lead to a satisfactory conclusion. First of all, it is possible for capitalist countries to wage war against non-capitalist countries, and above all, it is conceivable that countries whose economic system is capitalist do wage war against each other—but for reasons that have nothing to do with their economic systems. For by no means is capitalism always ultimately responsible when countries with capitalist economic systems wage war against each other. After all, decisions relating to war and peace are not made by capitalist entrepreneurs, but by politicians, that is, states. In Marxist theory, of course, the state under capitalism is always only an agent and executor of the interests of big business—an argument I refuted in Chapter 5.

From my point of view, it is necessary to analyze and determine for each specific conflict whether and to what extent representatives of the business class exerted a decisive influence in the run-up to the outbreak of war or whether politicians allowed their actions and policies to be directed by business interests. Taking the First World War as an example, I will show that this was not the case and that leading representatives of the business communities in both Germany and Great Britain were opposed to military action and war.

Obviously, there are a number of reasons why countries wage wars. Alongside economic considerations, geopolitical reasons can also play a role; sometimes wars are the result of the escalation of diplomatic threats and ultimatums that lead to a military conflict by accident rather than design. The nations of Europe "slithered into war" as a result of blunders and accidents, explained Britain's First World War Prime Minister David Lloyd George. In some cases, rulers use wars to divert attention from conflicts at home, and in centuries gone by, a common motive for waging war was a ruler's need or thirst for prestige. And of course—in earlier centuries even more so than today—religion played a role. Wars have multiple causes and a handbook of theories of war contains ten chapters on anthropological, biological, psychological, socio-psychological, political, geopolitical, social, economic, ecological, and theological theories of war.[496]

When states with capitalist economic systems wage wars, it is not necessarily the case that the reasons for military action are economic or that they correspond to the interests of the country's capitalist entrepreneurs. The First World War was and is always cited by Marxist historiography as a particularly clear example of the capitalist nature of a war. Critics of the theory of capitalist peace also frequently cite the First World War as a counter-argument. It is for this reason that I would like to deal with the First World War in more detail.

Seven years before the outbreak of the war, the resolution against militarism and imperialism passed by the Second International, a federation of socialist parties and trade unions, stated: "Wars between capitalist states are as a rule the result of their rivalry for world markets, as every state is not concerned in consolidating its own market, but also in conquering new markets . . . Wars are therefore inherent in the nature of capitalism, they will only cease when the capitalist economy is abolished."[497]

In the 1920 preface to the French and German editions of his book *Imperialism, the Highest Stage of Capitalism*, Lenin wrote that his writing had "proved . . . that the war of 1914–1918 was imperialistic (that is, an annexationist, predatory, plunderous war) on the part of both sides; it was a war for the division of the world, for the partition and repartition of colonies, 'spheres of influence' of finance capital, etc." As long as private ownership of the means of production existed, such wars were "absolutely inevitable."[498]

In an analysis of the causes of the First World War, however, the historian Werner Plumpe concludes that there is no evidence from the period before August 1914 that German companies were seeking war or in any way supporting the initiation of military action.[499] How could a war have benefited the German economy? In the decades leading up to the war, the country's large, export-oriented companies had experienced an unprecedented surge in business. Even major heavy industry groups such as Krupp and Thyssen had substantial export quotas, and a war did not align with their interest in any way.[500] "War was indeed also the *worst-case scenario* for Germany's highly successful industry, which had gained such a strong position in expanding world markets that war could only be detrimental, especially since it was most likely to be waged against its own clientele."[501]

Plumpe cites leading industrialists, most of whom were clearly opposed to war. Their fears proved well-founded following the outbreak of war: a general ban on exports was imposed, foreign demand collapsed, and domestic demand also declined. "In view of the comprehensive collapse of major markets, the shock of war was violent."[502]

The situation was no different in other countries. In London, as British historian Niall Ferguson reports in his major work on the First World War, the overwhelming majority of bankers were horrified by the prospect of war, "not least because war threatened to bankrupt most if not all of the major acceptance houses engaged in financing international trade."[503]

The Rothschilds, the great bogeymen of anti-Semites and anti-capitalists, strove in vain to avert an Anglo-German conflict and, for all their efforts, were accused by the foreign affairs editor of *The Times*, Henry Wickham Steed, of "a dirty German-Jewish international financial attempt to bully us into advocating neutrality."[504] Ferguson concludes that there is no evidence of a capitalist appetite for a major European war.[505]

It is sometimes argued that companies became active proponents of military conflict once the war had started and that some of them earned huge amounts from the war. This is true: business usually adapts to changes in circumstances and political conditions, but so do most people, not just entrepreneurs. The same is true under any system. Business and industry can hope for the best external conditions for their economic activities—but they cannot determine them. In any case, the war did not benefit the German economy, quite the opposite. The postwar decades were marked by economic misery—inflation, unemployment, and so forth—that contrasted sharply with the capitalist economic prosperity of 1896 to 1914. "The First World War," writes Ferguson, "undid the first, golden age of economic 'globalization.'"[506]

Capitalism has significantly reduced the economic importance and the concomitant benefits of conquering foreign territories. Before capitalism, when economies were largely static, the conquest of foreign territories to expand economic power and secure raw materials played an important role. But today, neither a country's size nor its raw material deposits matter for its economic weight. "States always have dissimilar interests when it comes to resource or territorial issues, but changes in modern economies often make these differences trivial, as resources can be had more easily through commerce," explains Gartzke.[507]

The largest country in the world by land mass is Russia, covering an area of 6.6 million square miles. At the same time, Russia has the largest raw material deposits in the world, worth an estimated US$75.7 trillion.[508] But its GDP per capita was just US$11,774 in 2019.[509] In comparison, tiny Singapore, which measures just 274 square miles and has virtually no raw material deposits, had a GDP per capita of US$65,233,[510] five and a half times that of Russia. The market capitalization of the Singapore stock exchange, at around US$700 billion[511] was almost as high as that of Russia (US$745 billion).[512] One explanation for this is that Singapore is the most economically free (i.e., most capitalist) country in the world, ranking first in the *Index of Economic Freedom 2021*, while Russia comes in a poor ninety-second.[513]

Germany has an area of only 137,882 square miles and few raw materials by international standards. Despite its disproportionately smaller area and raw material deposits, Germany's GDP of US$3.8 trillion[514] is more than twice that of Russia; and its GDP per capita, at US$46,445,[515] is four times higher than that of Russia.

In fact, large deposits of raw materials represent an economic disadvantage for many countries. Economists refer to the "Dutch disease" and the economist Paul Collier refers to a "natural resource trap."[516] Thus, the most important factors for the economic strength of a country are different today than in earlier history.

If we analyze the causes of the Second World War, how important were economic considerations? Well, they were more important than is often assumed in research because, in the thinking of Adolf Hitler, who was responsible for triggering the Second World War, economic aspects played a key role.[517]

Hitler's goal was to conquer new "living space in the East," that is, in the Soviet Union. He had never made any secret of this aim and stated it openly in his book *Mein Kampf,* and in numerous speeches.

Hitler adhered to a theory that had also been advocated by Marxist theorists such as Rosa Luxemburg and Nikolai Bukharin,[518] the theory of "shrinking markets." He considered the path that German companies had taken, namely relying primarily on exports, to be a major mistake. In Hitler's opinion, sales markets would continue to shrink as a result of the industrialization of former developing countries. Therefore, the country's export orientation was a dead end; only new living space in the East could solve the problems.

"Man does not live by ideas, but by grain and corn, by coal, iron, ore, all of those things that lie in the land. And if this land is missing, all theories become useless. It is not a problem of the economy itself, but of the land," Hitler argued.[519] In a speech on May 30, 1942, Hitler repeated his theory, which he had already regularly espoused in earlier speeches and in *Mein Kampf:* "If one does not want to extend the *Lebensraum* [the additional territory, literally "living space," in Russia and Ukraine that Hitler wanted to conquer, R.Z.], then one day a disparity must occur between population, which constantly grows, and *Lebensraum,* which stays the same. This is nature's intention: by this she forces man to fight, just like every other creature in the world. It is the battle for food, the battle for the foundations of life, for raw materials which the earth offers, the natural resources which lie within her, and the fruits she offers those who cultivate her."[520] And it was this additional *Lebensraum* that Hitler sought to conquer in the Soviet Union.

Is this not proof that the Second World War was waged in the capitalist interest? On the contrary: Hitler, after all, firmly rejected what he called the policy of the "economically peaceful conquest of the world."[521] In his opinion, Germany's economic policy oriented toward export was a dangerous aberration. Hitler wanted to make Germany self-sufficient and independent of the world economy by conquering living space in the East.

He was by no means concerned with opening up new sources of raw materials and new markets for private capitalist companies, for he had in mind a planned economy for the period after the war and in the conquered territories. Shortly after the attack on the Soviet Union, on July 28, 1941, he declared: "A sensible employment of the powers of a nation can only be achieved with a planned economy from above."[522] About two weeks later he said, "As far as the planning of the economy is concerned, we *are still very much at the beginning*."[523] He repeated this thought about a year later: Even after the war, it would not be possible "*to renounce state control of the economy*" because then every interest group would think exclusively of the fulfilment of its own wishes.[524]

Hitler increasingly admired the Soviet economic system, which he considered far superior to the capitalist one.[525] In a conversation with the Italian dictator Benito Mussolini at the end of April 1944, he confessed that he had come to the conclusion that capitalism had run its course and that the peoples would no longer tolerate it. Only National Socialism and Fascism and "maybe Bolshevism in the East" would survive the war.[526]

So, economic considerations played a decisive role in Hitler's *Lebensraum* concept—and thus in the origins of the Second World War—but this is certainly not proof that capitalism leads to war.

Incidentally, the fact that the position and influence of capitalists over economic policy, society and politics were massively weakened by these wars also speaks against the thesis that the First and Second

World Wars were waged in service of the capitalist pursuit of profit or that the rich instigated these wars for their own economic best interests. In *Capital in the Twenty-First Century*, Thomas Piketty even argues that "progressive taxation was as much a product of two world wars as it was of democracy."[527] Prior to the First World War, "tax rates, even on the most astronomical incomes, remained extremely low . . . This was true everywhere, without exception."[528] Until 1914, top income tax rates in developed countries were incredibly low. In France, Piketty writes, income tax law provided for a top rate of just 2 percent in 1914, rising to 72 percent by the mid-1920s—largely a result of the First World War.[529] In Prussia, the top rate remained stable at 3 percent from 1891 to 1914, before rising to 40 percent in 1919–1920. In the United States and Great Britain, the top rates were abruptly raised to 77 and more than 40 percent respectively after the First World War.[530]

"Of course, it is impossible to say," explains Piketty, "what would have happened had it not been for the shock of 1914–1918. A movement had clearly been launched. Nevertheless, it seems certain that had the shock not occurred, the move toward a more progressive tax system would at the very least have been much slower, and top rates might never have risen as high as they did."[531]

Inheritance and gift taxes in Germany also rose abruptly after the First World War, from 0 to 35 percent on larger inheritances. "The role of the war and of the political changes it induced seems to have been absolutely crucial."[532] The same is true for other countries. In other words, the First World War led to a significant increase in taxes levied on high-income and high-wealth individuals.

The Second World War resulted in an even harsher tax burden on the wealthy. In 1942, the Victory Tax Act was passed in the United States, causing the top tax rate to skyrocket to 88 percent, a level that, through various surtaxes, rose to 94 percent in 1944.[533] The thresholds for the application of the top tax rates in the United States were also lowered significantly, which meant that they applied to larger numbers of taxpayers.

In Great Britain, the rates applicable to the highest incomes and inheritances in the 1940s peaked at 98 percent.[534] In Germany, the top tax rate climbed to 64.99 percent in 1941,[535] while in France, the income share of the richest citizens fell 68 times faster during the Second World War than in the following 38 years: 92 percent of the total decline in the income share of the top 1 percent from 1939 took place in the seven years to the end of the war in 1945.[536]

In Japan, the country's richest 1 percent of the population received 19.9 percent of all reported income before taxes and transfers in 1938. Within the next seven years, however, their share shrank by two-thirds to 6.4 percent. And more than half of this loss was incurred by the richest tenth of this top bracket, whose income share plummeted from 9.2 to 1.9 percent, a decline of almost four-fifths.[537] The declared real value of the richest 1 percent of Japanese estates shrank by 90 percent between 1936 and 1945 and by almost 97 percent in the period 1936 to 1949. The top 0.1 percent of estates lost even more during this period, 93 and more than 98 percent, respectively.[538] The Japanese economic system was gradually transformed into a planned economy "that preserved only a facade of free market capitalism."[539] Executive bonuses were capped, rental income was fixed by the authorities, and between 1935 and 1943, the top marginal income tax rate in Japan doubled.[540]

Walter Scheidel's analysis proves that wars have been among the biggest causes of massive wealth losses for the rich in modern history. According to Scheidel, the two world wars were "among the greatest levelers in history."[541] The average percentage decline in the top income shares in countries that actively fought in the Second World War as front-line states was 31 percent of the pre-war level, which is deemed a robust finding considering that this sample includes a dozen countries.[542] The only two countries in which inequality increased during this period were also those farthest from theaters of war (Argentina and South Africa).[543]

"Low savings rates and depressed asset prices, physical destruction and the loss of foreign assets, inflation and progressive taxation, rent and price controls, and nationalization all contributed to varying degrees."[544] The wealth of the rich was dramatically reduced in the two world wars, regardless of whether countries lost or won, suffered occupation during or after the war, and were democracies or run by autocratic regimes.[545]

For the rich, the economic impact of the two world wars was therefore devastating, a fact that stands against the thesis that capitalists instigated the wars to serve their own economic interests. Contrary to the popular perception that it was the lower classes who suffered most during the two world wars, it was actually the capitalists who were the biggest losers in economic terms, measured in both absolute and relative income and wealth losses.

But what about more recent wars? The United States has been involved in several military conflicts since the Second World War, and it has, in each case, been claimed by critics of capitalism that these wars were instigated to further the economic interests of big business. Perhaps the most prominent example for this thesis relates to the Second Iraq War, which the United States and other countries waged in March and April 2003 and which led to the overthrow of Saddam Hussein.

Even before the war began, an international poll found that 76 percent of people in Russia, 75 percent in France, 54 percent in Germany and 44 percent in Great Britain agreed that the United States was keen to invade Iraq in order to control Iraqi oil.[546] The major German news magazine *Der Spiegel* ran the provocative cover story "Blood for Oil. What Is Really at Stake in Iraq," which featured interlocking gasoline pump nozzles and assault rifles superimposed over the stars of the U.S. flag.[547] And left-wing activist and film director Michael Moore spread the same theory in 2004 in his film *Fahrenheit 9/11*, which became the most successful documentary feature of all time in the United States.[548] Anti-capitalists, such as Noam Chomsky, also wrote that the goal of the war was for the United States to secure Iraq's oil resources.[549] From their perspective, the Second Iraq War provided striking confirmation of the thesis of war-mongering capitalism.

These theories seemed all the more convincing because the official U.S. rationale for war—that Iraqi dictator Saddam Hussein was in possession of weapons of mass destruction and working with international terrorists—did not stand up to scrutiny after the war ended. Intelligence sources were proved to have been at least partially wrong and, moreover, intelligence had been unilaterally interpreted by the U.S. government. Subsequent investigations conclusively revealed that Iraq was not in possession of weapons of mass destruction, as the U.S. had claimed. This added fuel to the "war for oil" theory fire.

However, scholarly analyses of this popular view have arrived at a clear conclusion: "There is no evidence that the U.S. oil industry in any way beat the drum for the invasion of Iraq. If anything, the opposite was true: U.S. oil companies had long wanted U.S. and UN sanctions lifted so that they would not fall further behind their competitors from France, Russia, and China in the race for Iraqi oil concessions. As almost always, big business wanted business, not war. The idea that American companies could extract and sell Iraqi oil unmolested and without payment under an occupation regime is unrealistic."[550]

If the United States had been concerned with securing access to better oil supplies and lower oil prices, all it would have had to do was give in to Russian and French admonishments in the UN Security Council to end export restrictions. "There is also the fact that Saudi Arabia, which has larger stocks of oil and would have been an easier adversary, would have made a far more suitable military target—not heavily armed and populous Iraq."[551] Incidentally, there is also no evidence that the United States made any attempt, either during the occupation or afterward, to award American corporations a privileged position in the Iraqi oil industry.[552]

In his book on the Iraq war, the political scientist Stephan Bierling arrives at the unequivocal conclusion: "No matter how much people twist and turn the 'no blood for oil' argument, it remains totally devoid of any sufficient basis in fact."[553] The main reason for the war, according to his analyses, was for the United States to set a precedent by demonstrating its military might and, as a result, to change the risk calculus of all potential enemies of the United States after the September 11 attacks. The war was intended to demonstrate to friend and foe alike that the

U.S. should be taken seriously, was fully capable of taking decisive action, and to send out a stark signal that countries that cooperated with terrorists would pay a high price.

In terms of the correlation between capitalism and war, there is another point of view that needs to be considered. The American political scientist John Mueller argues that the causal direction is actually the other way around: it is not primarily that free-market capitalism leads to peace, but that peace causes—or facilitates—capitalism and its attendant economic development.[554] He also points out that capitalism's characteristic fixation with economic well-being and the pursuit of wealth stand in tension with the idea of war as it has been advocated for centuries—if not millennia. That prolonged peace degrades and weakens the character of a nation by favoring cowardice and effeminacy was a thesis advanced by numerous philosophers, from Aristotle to Nietzsche.[555] Time and again, thinkers and politicians complained that hedonism, superficiality and selfishness took the place of supposedly higher values such as heroism, sacrifice and honor during extended periods of peace, or that war was the real engine of progress.[556] Only at the moment when other ideas replaced these convictions, for example, that trade created more benefits than conquest, peace served progress more than war, and economic growth and prosperity were chief goals, did such convictions, which served to legitimize wars, lose their significance.

Another popular thesis among anti-capitalists today is that capitalism is primarily rooted in colonialism. Colonial wars are blamed on capitalism, even though capitalism has been most successful in the very countries that were least active in terms of colonial expansion. North America or the United States were, to use the language of the anti-capitalist critics of colonialism, not "perpetrators"; they were themselves initially among the victims of colonialism. Its own colonial activities played a completely subordinate role in the U.S. and its economic development. And even though there is much talk today about Germany's colonial past, the fact that Germany's colonial ventures since the 1880s were of minor economic importance speaks against the emphasis on colonialism as the root of capitalism. "Developments in the United States and the German Empire were characterized by the replacement of hitherto colonially sourced raw materials, at least where technically possible, with domestic products, thus emancipating the two economies in some respects from colonial sources of supply."[557] What were initially the leading nations, Great Britain, the Netherlands, and France, fell behind in relative terms in the second half of the nineteenth century.[558] Portugal and Spain, the first imperialist powers with colonies from Mexico to Macau, were the poorest in Western Europe at the time capitalism emerged. And countries such as Sweden and Austria became wealthy even without significant overseas colonial territories.

Thus, there are many arguments against the thesis that wars have their roots in capitalism or that capitalism is an especially war-mongering system: Wars were far more frequent in pre-capitalist times than in the age of capitalism, and those wars that are repeatedly cited as evidence for the thesis (from the First World War to the Second Iraq War) had causes that were unrelated to the economic interests of capitalists.

10

"CAPITALISM MEANS THAT THERE IS

ALWAYS A DANGER OF FASCISM"

MAX HORKHEIMER, the leading philosopher of the Frankfurt School, famously coined a phrase that is still quoted today: "But whoever is not willing to talk about capitalism should also keep quiet about fascism."[559] With his use of the term "fascism," Horkheimer was referring to National Socialism. Leftist theorists avoid the term "National Socialism" and prefer to speak of fascism because they believe that the socialism contained in National Socialism discredits the "good," "real" kind of socialism. "Fascism," according to the classic definition offered by Georgi Dimitrov, General Secretary of the Communist International, was "the open terrorist dictatorship of the most reactionary, most chauvinistic and most imperialist elements of finance capital."[560] In the Marxists' view, capitalists sought to secure their rule by the means of "fascist dictatorship." To this day, many people believe that the real cause of fascism was capitalism and that Adolf Hitler came to power only because he was backed by the money of big business.

Since National Socialism is always cited by anti-capitalists as offering what they claim to be conclusive proof of the link between capitalism and fascism (much more frequently than, for example, Italian fascism), and since I myself have done a great deal of research in this field, I will proceed to examine whether the historical facts support this thesis.

In his early speeches, Hitler sharply attacked "finance capital" and "stock market capital" as surrogates for his descriptions of the Jews: "Therefore this capital grew and today rules practically the whole world, immeasurable as to the amounts, inconceivable in its gigantic relationships, uncannily growing and—the worst part—completely corrupting all honest work, because that is the horrible part, that the normal human being who today has to bear the burden of the interest on this capital has to stand by and see how despite diligence, industry, thrift, despite real work, hardly anything is left to him with which only to feed himself, and even less to clothe himself, at the same time as this international capital devours billions in interest alone which he has to help pay, at the same time in which a racial class is spreading itself out in the state which does not do any other work than to collect interest for itself and to cut coupons."[561]

In his speeches in the early 1920s, Hitler advocated the "nationalization of all the banks and the whole sector of finance"[562] and the "nationalization of mineral resources, of artificial fertilizers [and] chemical products,"[563] although he did oppose "total nationalization." Somewhat confusedly, the National Socialist Party's 1920 manifesto program stated: "We demand the nationalization of all the (already) socialized companies (trusts)."[564]

In parliament, the National Socialists often voted together with the two left-wing parties, the Social Democrats and Communists, on social policy issues.[565] The National Socialists introduced motions in parliament demanding the nationalization of all major banks and the prohibition of trading in securities. The party's deputies also introduced motions calling for the confiscation of "the fortunes of the princes of

bank and stock market" and all "profits derived from the war, the inflation and—later—the depression."[566]

In the face of such demands, the business-affiliated *Deutsche
Bergwerk-Zeitung* (*Zeitung* means "newspaper") commented that the
National Socialist Party represented a threat to private property and
differed only marginally from the communists. *Deutsche Allgemeine
Zeitung* in Berlin, which was owned by a consortium of Ruhr industrial-
ists, bankers and shipping company owners, observed that even as the
Social Democrats distanced themselves from Marxism, the National
Socialists seemed intent on assuming that heritage.[567]

Very early on, Walter Rademacher, a leading figure in the Saxon coal
industry, who had formerly served as a German National People's Party
(DNVP) deputy, recognized that the National Socialists' commitment
to private property was not worth much. This was because the National
Socialists qualified that recognition with the proviso that the pursuits
of private businessmen were acceptable only so long as they served the
public interest. The authority to determine what served that public
interest, Rademacher observed, seemed to rest wholly with the state. If,
he concluded, the state could contravene the rights of entrepreneurs at
any time simply by declaring that they had used their property improp-
erly, nothing would remain of private enterprise or the entrepreneur's
control over his property.[568]

He had thus understood something that was much later formulated
by the German economist Frederick Pollock. Pollock was a co-founder
of the Institute for Social Research in Frankfurt, which later became the
nucleus of the Frankfurt School mentioned above. At the same time, a
close friend of Horkheimer, Pollock wrote an essay on the economic order
of National Socialism in 1941 in which he stated: "I quite agree that the
legal institution of private property has been retained and that many of
the characteristics shown to be inherent in National Socialism are already
apparent, perhaps only in an embryonic stage, in non-totalitarian countries. But does it mean that the function of private property is unchanged?
Is the 'increased power of a few groups' really the main result of the change

that has taken place? I think that it goes far deeper and should be described as the destruction of all but one of the essential characteristics of private property. Even the mightiest combines have been deprived of the right to establish a new business where the highest profits can be expected; or to discontinue production where it becomes unprofitable. These rights have been transferred to the ruling groups as a whole. It is the compromise between the controlling groups which decides on the scope and direction of the productive process; against such decision the property title is powerless even if it is derived from ownership of an overwhelming majority of a stock, not to speak of a minority stock owner."[569]

This is certainly one of the most accurate characterizations of the National Socialist economic system. Few recognized this later development during the phase of the National Socialist Party's rise to power before 1933. Nevertheless, most entrepreneurs at the time were suspicious of the National Socialists' goals. In late 1929, Paul Reusch, one of the most influential business leaders at the time,[570] wrote a set of guidelines on editorial policy for the editors of the newspapers his company controlled in which he named the National Socialist Party, together with the Communists, the Social Democrats and the trade unions, as among the bearers of Marxism, its pernicious "idea of class conflict" and its "utopian goals in the field of economic policy."[571]

Such fears were fueled by National Socialist Party publications, such as the fortnightly magazine *Arbeitertum*, the organ of the National Socialist Workers' Cell Organization, which called for an end to the "liberal-capitalist economic system," "state socialist nationalization of basic industries" and for the removal and prosecution of the "hyenas of the economy."[572]

For tactical reasons Hitler, Hermann Göring and other leading National Socialists attempted to convince German businessmen that the party was harmless. Since Hitler, as he explained in numerous speeches, was of the opinion that it was actually the capitalists who ruled the state,[573] he tried to "neutralize"[574] and appease big business in discussions in confidential circles.

After the National Socialist Party's first major electoral successes in the 1930 Reichstag elections, some members of the business community also joined the National Socialists, but they were mainly outsiders. The best known of these was the industrialist Emil Kirdorf, who joined Hitler's party in 1927 but left again out of disappointment only a year later (he then did not rejoin until 1934).[575]

Like Kirdorf, a number of business people hoped that they could somehow influence the National Socialist Party and exert a moderating influence on its economic policies, which admittedly proved to be an illusion.[576] But the legend that the National Socialist Party was largely financed by "big business" is false. As a result of his extensive research on this question, the American historian Henry A. Turner concluded "that the funds reaching the Nazis from big business were but a small fraction of those that went to their opponents and rivals. On balance, big business money went overwhelmingly against the Nazis."[577]

Unlike bourgeois parties such as the DVP, which was favored by many entrepreneurs and received large donations over many years, Hitler's party was not dependent on major donors. The National Socialist Party had succeeded in tapping into sources of funding that made it independent of donations from big business or wealthy individuals. From the late 1920s, the party took in more and more money through membership fees as membership rose from 25,000 in 1925 to 919,000 in 1932.[578] The party amended its membership fee several times; in 1930, the standard fee was 0.80 reichsmark—a skilled worker earned 200 reichsmarks a month and a welfare recipient received 50 reichsmarks.[579] In addition, there were special collection campaigns among regular members. Members of the party's paramilitary wing, the SA, had to buy their own brand of cigarettes and also paid into a private insurance scheme.

Moreover, unlike other parties, the National Socialists charged admission fees for their numerous party rallies. According to the police, the party held an average of 100 rallies a day throughout Germany—and earned money with each one. The entrance fee was one reichsmark—at that time, a typical postal employee earned less than 0.90 reichsmarks an hour.[580]

In the 1932 Reichstag elections, the NSDAP became by far the strongest party in Germany, attracting 37.4 percent of the vote, ahead of the SPD (21.6 percent). Participation in government seemed close at hand. Now the party was able to secure more donations from the German business community. "This did not happen," writes Henry Ashby Turner Jr. in his major work, *Big German Business & the Rise of Hitler*, "because increasing numbers of big businessmen had undergone conversion to National Socialism. Despite the efforts of Hitler and other Nazi spokesmen to allay misgivings about their movement, all but a very few figures in big business remained aloof from it . . . Virtually all the contributions that flowed to the Nazis from big business sources during the first half of 1932 thus sprang from motivations other than conviction. Nor did most result from a desire to see the Nazis succeed."[581]

Some entrepreneurs specifically gave money to those National Socialists whom they considered comparatively "business-friendly" (e.g., Hermann Göring) and whom they hoped could hold the party's radical socialists at bay. Others donated money to several parties, including the National Socialists, to cover all bases in case the latter came to power. The industrialist Friedrich Flick and the company IG Farben gave money to all of the "bourgeois" parties and the National Socialists, but the latter received much less than the others. IG Farben, for example, donated a total of 200,000 to 300,000 reichsmarks to several parties in 1932, of which the National Socialists received no more than 10 to 15 percent.[582]

Faced with the possibility of the National Socialists gaining a strong place in government, some businessmen who considered their situation particularly insecure or vulnerable politically "began to regard the Nazis with the fear such men customarily feel toward rulers or even potential rulers. They began, as a consequence, to include the Nazis among the recipients of the political 'insurance premiums' with which they sought to buy security against shifts in Germany's internal distribution of power. Others responded opportunistically to the prospect of the NSDAP's attainment of a share of power."[583]

In the decisive months before Hitler's appointment as Reich

Chancellor, big business, contrary to the anti-capitalist myth, played no role. Hitler was very unpopular in business circles during these months because his party launched a series of scathing attacks on Franz von Papen's government,[584] which was regarded favorably by the country's big industrialists. The intrigues that preceded Hitler's appointment, at the center of which was Reich President von Hindenburg, did not involve big business, if only because—unlike the military, for example—it had no access to Hindenburg. "Germany's leading capitalists," Turner writes, "remained passive, ill-informed bystanders during the backroom intrigues in the circles around President Hindenburg that resulted in Hitler's installation as chancellor."[585]

After Hitler's appointment on January 30, 1933, large sections of the business community reacted as many Germans did: with opportunism. The membership of the National Socialist Party tripled within a few months from 922,000 to 2.63 million.[586] Civil servants, workers, the self-employed—people from all classes—flocked to the party. The influx was so strong that on May 1, 1933, the National Socialists decided to suspend new admissions.[587] The party had already succeeded in winning over a substantial proportion of workers in the elections in the Weimar Republic. And even among the party's members, workers played a much greater role than has been previously assumed, accounting for 40 percent of memberships, as the German political scientist Jürgen W. Falter has demonstrated.[588]

The business community also turned to Hitler's regime—partly out of enthusiasm, partly out of opportunism, and partly because they misjudged the true character of the new government: they believed that Franz von Papen was still the strong man, not Hitler. Many thought that, once in power, Hitler would moderate his behavior and abandon his radical program. As we know today, this proved to be a grandiose deception and self-delusion.

Leftist fascism theorists claim that the National Socialist Party's anti-capitalist propaganda in the period prior to seizing power served only to deceive voters, while, in reality, Hitler was acting in the interests of the capitalists. Historical research, however, has shown that this claim is also false.

The year 2005 saw the publication of *Hitler's Beneficiaries* by Götz Aly. The German historian notes that one reason for the popularity of National Socialism was its "borrowings from the intellectual tradition of the socialist left."[589] In his memoirs, Adolf Eichmann, the architect of the mass murder of the Jews, repeatedly affirmed: "My political sentiments inclined toward the left and emphasized socialist aspects every bit as much as nationalist ones."[590] For millions of Germans, the appeal of National Socialism lay in "the promise of real equality," asserts Aly: "For all those who legally belonged to the German racial community—about 95 percent of the population—social divides became ever smaller. For many people, the regime's aims of leveling out class distinctions was realized in the Hitler Youth, the National Labor Service, the major party organizations, and ultimately even in the Wehrmacht."[591]

Aly explains how, when it came to decisions on wartime taxation, the Nazi leadership "intervened to protect lower- and middle-income Germans."[592] He even speaks of "tax breaks for the masses,"[593] while at the same time, the regime pursued a parallel policy Aly refers to as "tax rigor for the bourgeoisie." Aly puts forward many examples of the government's readiness to tax businesses and the country's wealthy, including the so-called *Hauszinssteuer* (real estate inflation tax), which cost German property owners 8.1 billion reichsmarks in 1942 alone.[594] "In the case at hand, the Nazi leadership at no point even considered legislation that would have placed a comparable burden on working people. On the contrary, discussions of the property tax were framed by the general principle that materially better-off Germans were to bear a considerably larger share of the burden of war than poor ones."[595]

Between September 1939 and March 1942, according to Aly, the Reich treasury recorded 12 billion reichsmarks in revenue from war taxes of various kinds. Looking at the distribution among the social classes, only the additional tax on tobacco, spirits and beer, which yielded a total of 2.5 billion reichsmarks from September 1939 to the

beginning of 1942, affected the wallets of the majority of Germans.[596]
Companies and high-income earners provided 75 percent of the
increased domestic revenue required to pay for the war. Neither blue-
collar workers nor lower and middle-income employees or civil servants
were to be burdened with war taxes to any significant degree, and "the
Nazi leadership at no point even considered legislation that would
have placed a comparable burden on working people. On the contrary,
discussions of the property tax were framed by the general principle that
materially better-off Germans were to bear a considerably larger share
of the burden of war than poor ones."[597]

However, Aly's theses were recently challenged by the German
historian Ralf Banken in his book *Hitlers Steuerstaat* (*Hitler's Tax State*).
Banken claims that Aly overstates the burden placed on high earners in
the Third Reich and criticizes the fact that Aly's research is based on too
narrow a selection of sources.[598] However, Banken also details the sharp
rise in the tax burden on German companies before the war. He notes
a "clear trend of a sharply rising tax burden on German businesses, who
were frequently subject to the maximum corporate income tax of nearly
35 percent and the assessed income tax of almost 52 percent."[599] But such
tax rates alone are not even the most decisive factor. At least as important,
Banken explains, was that depreciation allowances were dramatically
reduced. "In addition, tax auditors became increasingly better trained
after 1935 and were able to refer taxpayers to averages and benchmarks or
other ratios of the audit material for the respective industry, against which
they measured and assessed specific individual cases . . . Moreover, legal
recourse via the tax courts became increasingly restricted for companies,
or smaller companies without a lobby did not even get through to the
Ministry of Finance with their petitions."[600]

During the war, the tax burden rose to more than 70 percent in
some cases, affecting large companies in particular.[601] The situation was
quite different for National Socialist Party functionaries and especially
for the leading representatives of the regime, who were able to secure
numerous concessions and generous tax gifts from financial authorities.

Hitler adopted an increasingly strident tone on matters relating to the economy. In his "Memorandum on the Four-Year Plan 1936" in August 1936, Hitler wrote: "The Ministry of Economics only has to set the national economic tasks, and private industry has to fulfil them. But if private industry does not believe it is capable of doing so, then the National Socialist state will find its own way of solving this problem." And he threatened openly: "German industry, however, will learn to understand these new economic tasks, or it will have proved itself to be incapable of continuing to exist in these modern times, in which the Soviet state sets up a gigantic plan. *But then it will not be Germany which will go under, it will at most be a few industrialists.*"[602]

In the same year, Hitler declared at the Reich Party Congress: "Had Communism really only intended to do a certain cleaning up by removing individual decayed elements from the camp of the so-called upper ten thousand or out of that of our just as useless *petit bourgeois*, we would easily have been able to let it run on for a while."[603]

Hitler repeatedly warned that if private companies were unable to perform the tasks assigned to them by the state, the state would step in and take over. And he did not stop at threats. In 1937, for example, he initiated the creation of the Reichswerke Hermann Göring, which by 1940 employed 600,000 people. The Salzgitter plant eventually became the largest in Europe. With this, the National Socialist state had shown that its oft-proclaimed "primacy of politics" was deadly serious, and that it would not hesitate to become active itself and to build up state-controlled enterprises in areas where private industry resisted the execution of state directives.[604]

Let us return to Pollock, who in his 1941 analysis of the National Socialist economic system, stated: "Whereas until recently in the capitalistic era social power mainly derived from one's property, under National Socialism one's status is determined by his social function."[605] He goes on to add that, "Money alone gives only limited power or (as in the case of the Jews) no power at all. Political power, in turn, which is equivalent to the control of the means of production, may become the source of practically unlimited income."[606] Respect for an economic sphere in which the state may not interfere, a feature so essential to private capitalism, was completely disregarded under National Socialism, Pollock writes. "In consequence, execution of the program is enforced by state power and nothing essential is left to the functioning of the laws of the market or other economic 'laws.' The primacy of politics over economics, so much disputed under democracy, is clearly established."[607]

The German-Israeli historian Avraham Barkai, in his seminal study of the National Socialist economic system, concludes that "the scope and depth of state intervention in Nazi Germany had no peacetime precedent or parallel in any capitalist country, Fascist Italy included."[608]

Wages and prices, which in capitalism are formed by the free interplay between supply and demand, were fixed by the state under National Socialism. Although there had been a Reich Price Commissar in Germany since 1931, the appointment of a Reich Commissar for Price Formation at the end of October 1936 was, according to the economic historian Dietmar Petzina, "more than just the restoration of an already well-known institution under a new name; rather, it developed into a central steering institution of economic policy within the framework of the Four-Year Plan."[609] The task of the Price Commissioner was by no means merely to "monitor" and correct market prices, but to "officially determine prices."[610]

Aly explains that social equalization on the one hand and brutal Aryanization on the other corresponded and describes the enthusiasm with which the property of European Jews was nationalized in favor of the German majority: "Indeed, such enthusiasm can generally be observed whenever a part of society claims the right to nationalize other people's property, justifying that act with the rationale that the beneficiaries make up a homogeneous and therefore underprivileged majority, the 'people' itself. The eagerness with which individuals have assumed this position is a fundamental element in the history of twentieth-century violence."[611]

The policy of exterminating the Jews on the one hand and the social policy initiatives on the other were not opposites but interwoven. "The Nazi leadership established a framework for directly sharing the spoils of its military victories with the majority of Germany—the profits derived from crippling the economies of occupied and dependent countries, the exploitation of work performed by forced laborers, the confiscated property of murdered Jews, and the deliberate starvation of millions of people, most notably in the Soviet Union."[612] Thus National Socialism shares many of the features of other socialist-totalitarian systems. "Upward mobility for the common people—in various forms and not infrequently at the cost of others—was one of the fundamental political innovations of the twentieth century. The Nazi brand of socialism was part of this tradition."[613]

Hitler and the National Socialist propaganda machine referred to a *Volksgemeinschaft* (national community) in the Third Reich. From the point of view of left-wing fascism theory—but also of some other historians—this term was a deceptive maneuver and had no basis in reality. But in recent years, research has shown that this thesis cannot be sustained.

The German historian Norbert Götz emphasizes the fact that the widely held view that dismisses *Volksgemeinschaft* as a "simple myth" or a mere "promise" of National Socialism is just as shortsighted as the view that claims that the Third Reich implemented the concept of *Volksgemeinschaft* as a social reality. [614] Although the precise meaning of the term *Volksgemeinschaft* is still fiercely debated, there is much to be said for the findings published by Schmiechen-Ackermann in 2012: "Interpretative approaches that completely ignore the efficacy and at least short-term integrative power of the 'Volksgemeinschaft' phenomenon will no longer be deemed plausible."[615]

The National Socialists intended to expand the planned economy for the period after the war, as we know from many of Hitler's remarks.[616] He increasingly admired the Soviet economic system. "If Stalin had continued to work for another ten to fifteen years," Hitler said at one of his "table talks" in August 1942, "Soviet Russia would have become the most powerful nation on earth, 150, 200, 300 years may go by, that is such a unique phenomenon! That the general standard of living rose, there can be no doubt. The people did not suffer from hunger. Taking everything together we have to say: They built factories here where two years ago there was nothing but forgotten villages, factories which are as big as the Hermann Göring Works."[617] On another occasion, also to his inner circle, he said that Stalin was a "genius" for whom one must have "unqualified respect," especially given his comprehensive economic planning. There was no doubt in his mind, Hitler added, that in Soviet Russia, unlike in capitalist countries such as the United States, there has never been any unemployment.[618]

On several occasions, the dictator mentioned to his closest associates that it was necessary to nationalize the large joint-stock companies, the energy industry and all other branches of the economy that produced "essential raw materials" (e.g., the iron industry).[619] Of course, the war was not the right environment in which to implement such radical nationalizations. Hitler and the National Socialists were well aware of this, and in any case, they had been making every effort to allay the nationalization fears of the country's business community. Thus, a memo from SS chief Heinrich Himmler in October 1942 states that "during the war" a fundamental change of Germany's capitalistic economy would not be possible. Anyone who "fought" against this would provoke a "witch-hunt" against himself.[620] In a report prepared by an SS Hauptsturmführer in July 1944, the question "Why does the SS engage in business activities?" was answered as follows: "This question was raised specifically by circles who think purely in terms of capitalism and who do not like to see companies developing which are public, or at least of a public character. The age of the liberal system of business demanded the primacy of business, in other words business comes first, and then the state. As opposed to this, National Socialism takes the position: the state directs the economy, the state is not there for business, business is there for the state."[621]

As we have seen, this had been Hitler's maxim from the very beginning, which explains why most entrepreneurs in the Weimar

Republic were hostile toward or at least skeptical of the National Socialists. Those who actively provided financial support to Hitler were the exception. However, the closer Hitler came to power, the more opportunists emerged from the business community to pander to the National Socialists in anticipatory obedience. And in the first years of the regime, many entrepreneurs also enthusiastically joined the ranks of Hitler's acolytes. But in doing so, they were not behaving any differently from many workers, employees and civil servants. The thesis, however, that fascism was a form of rule by finance capital or that big business brought Hitler to power through their donations and influence is refuted by historical research.

PART B

ANTI-CAPITALIST ALTERNATIVES

11

SOCIALISM ALWAYS LOOKS GOOD ON PAPER (EXCEPT WHEN THAT PAPER IS IN A HISTORY BOOK)

THE PREVIOUS TEN CHAPTERS, in which the most frequent arguments against capitalism have been refuted, show that there is no need for alternatives to capitalism because capitalism is not—as many people believe—responsible for hunger, poverty, war, and so on. Nevertheless, nothing is without an alternative, and this chapter will explore the question of what counter-models to capitalism exist.

Every day, somebody, somewhere, is dreaming up new alternatives to capitalism. There are countless books and theories, for example, about the "post-growth economy" or new spins on socialism. I do not want to deal with such theories, which exist only on paper but have never been tried out in practice. First, there are far too many of them, and second, I think it is unfair to compare reality with a theory, a book or a thought construct. That would be like measuring your marriage against the descriptions of ideal love in a trashy romance novel, rather than comparing it with other, real-life marriages. Logically, your marriage—just like any other marriage—has its ups and downs and will never be perfect. In short, it would not beat an idealized fantasy. If I were to criticize your marriage because it is not as perfect as one of the relationships a novelist has dreamed up, you would rightly object that it would make far more sense to compare your relationship with other, actual marriages. And that is the advice I will follow in this chapter.

The biggest mistake anti-capitalists make is to create a perfect social or economic order in their heads and believe that, if only enough people shared their vision, it would be possible to implement their intellectual construct in the real world. Incidentally, there are also pro-capitalists who fall into the same trap: they rightly criticize the shortcomings of the existing mixed systems and dream up an ideal libertarian utopia of "pure" capitalism, which, however, does not and never has existed anywhere in the world. They, too, compare a real, existing system with an intellectual construct.

Capitalism, unlike socialism, is not a system devised by intellectuals; it is an economic order that has evolved organically, just as animals and plants have evolved and continue to evolve in the natural world, without the need for a central, guiding plan or theory. One of the most important insights provided by Friedrich August von Hayek is that the origin of functioning institutions lies "not in contrivance or design, but in the survival of the successful,"[622] via "selection by imitation of successful institutions and habits."[623]

Of course, capitalism will also develop and evolve. In fact, one of the key strengths of capitalism as a system is that it is constantly changing and adapting—otherwise it would not be so successful. And just as capitalism has changed again and again over the past 200 years, it will continue to change in the future. These changes will be triggered by major crises and evolutionary developments, but this will happen in the reality of economic life and not in the ivory tower of an intellectual dreaming up a perfect society.

In his book *Socialism: The Failed Idea That Never Dies,* Kristian Niemietz counts a total of more than two dozen socialist experiments over the past 100 years. A vast majority of these experiments invoked Karl Marx. Many people today know nothing or almost nothing about these experiments, which is why I would like to discuss some of them in more detail in this chapter. However, I would like to note at the outset that socialists will not be impressed by this. They will argue that none of these experiments deserves the title of "true socialism" because the world has not yet seen "true socialism."

Anyone who points to the fact that, over the last 100 or so years, every system that has claimed to be based on the ideas of Karl Marx has failed, will be met by accusations that these systems somehow co-opted his name and misapplied his intrinsically correct thoughts. This is the primary immunization strategy employed by anti-capitalists: decoupling the "good Karl Marx" from the failed political practice of Marxism.

Can you blame a thinker or prophet for being misunderstood? Of course not. It is, after all, a common phenomenon. How often have people cited Jesus Christ, despite behaving in a completely un-Christian way! Nevertheless, there were and are also many Christians all over the world who understand his teachings quite correctly. And Jesus, after all, never claimed to have designed a utopia for the realization of paradise on Earth: "My kingdom is not of this world,"[624] he told his disciples. Karl Marx's kingdom, however, was supposed to be of this world.

Above all, it is quite different to claim that a thinker has *always and without exception* been misunderstood and *not a single system* has implemented his ideas "correctly." And yet, this is exactly what anti-capitalists say about Marx. If you ask anyone who wants to decouple the thoughts of the man who invented Marxism from its real-world implementation, in which countries his ideas have never been "properly" executed, you will get no answer. The reason is simple: All socialist systems that invoke or have invoked Marx have failed without exception, whether in the Soviet Union, in China, in Yugoslavia, in the GDR, in North Korea, or in Albania. Each of these countries experimented in a different way with Marxism, but all ultimately failed because they were economically inefficient.

The thesis that a theory has always and exclusively been misunderstood over a period of more than 100 years is extremely brazen and would basically be a damning indictment of any theorist. After all, that would mean that they had failed to express themselves clearly and only succeeded in sowing confusion. However, this would do Marx an injustice. His writing is deliberate, and he was determined to remain extremely vague in formulating his notions of a future socialist or communist society. There are only a small number of isolated statements, for example, in his early writings. Marx declared that he did not want to be a "Utopian socialist" who designed a ready-made model of a socialist society. But this much is clear: Socialism—as a transitional phase on the road to the classless society of communism—was to be based on the abolition of private ownership of the means of production. That is one of the points Marx stated with extreme clarity over and over again. And that is precisely what happened in every single socialist system the world has ever seen. The abolition of private ownership of the means of production and the replacement of a market order, in which entrepreneurs decide what is produced and prices are the essential source of information, with a state-run economy has been—despite the many differences—the common feature of all socialist systems, whether in the Soviet Union or China, in Cuba or North Korea, in the GDR or in any other Eastern bloc country. Lenin and Mao, Fidel Castro and Kim Il-sung, Walter Ulbricht and all the other Communist leaders understood Marx quite correctly on this most important point.

The reasons such a system is always destined to fail were theoretically explained by Ludwig von Mises in 1922 (i.e., five years after the establishment of the first socialist state in the Soviet Union) in his book *Socialism: An Economic and Sociological Analysis*. According to Gertrude E. Schroeder, Professor of Economics at the University of Virginia, historical developments over the past 100 years have confirmed everything that Ludwig von Mises wrote,[625] as well as categorically disproving Karl Marx in practice with probably the clearest repudiation of any theory in history.

After a number of attempts to implement socialism, most of which failed quickly (such as the Paris Commune in 1871), the first major attempt was launched in the Soviet Union as a result of the October Revolution.

Today, hardly anyone will defend the Soviet system, but it was different in the 1930s. Leading intellectuals, writers, poets and journalists were all united in their enthusiasm toward the Soviet Union and its leader Stalin. The renowned French writer Henri Barbusse detailed his thoughts as he walked through Red Square in Moscow, where he was struck that, there in Lenin's tomb, "is the only person in the world who is not asleep . . . he is the paternal brother who is really watching over everyone. Although you do not know him, he knows you and is thinking of you." And when the gaze of the late walker turns to the Kremlin, where a light still burns (Stalin was a night owl), it is in the calm assurance that up there, "Whoever you may be, the finest part of your destiny is in the hands of that other man . . . who also watches over you and who works for you—the man with a scholar's mind, a workman's face and the dress of a private soldier."[626]

Many intellectuals downplayed Stalin's terror—or even supported it. After a trip to the Soviet Union in 1931, the Irish playwright George Bernard Shaw, who would go on to win the Nobel Prize for Literature in 1939, adapted Hamlet's famous words: "Our question is not to kill or not to kill, but how to select the right people to kill."[627] The distinguished German writer and theater critic Alfred Kerr wrote in 1933: "The reality of the 'Soviet Republic' is for my consciousness one of the greatest and most gratifying facts. Because here, for the first time in 2,000 years, a very honest attempt is being made to bring justice into the world through energy. If I die tomorrow, the thought of this isolated phenomenon in the midst of a timid and backward world will be the last, the only solid consolation."[628]

Such praise for Bolshevism and Stalin were by no means rare, and those who extolled him were by no means outsiders in intellectual circles, but literary figures honored to this day, such as Jean-Paul Sartre and Bertolt Brecht. If you look for evidence, you will find dozens of quotes in books, such as those by the Hungarian-American historian Paul Hollander and Kristian Niemietz. The Russian philosopher Michail Ryklin writes that the "vast majority" of European writers "either praised the Soviet system or refrained from passing judgement."[629]

Even if hardly anyone defends Stalin today, there are still plenty of leading politicians from left-wing parties who revere Lenin and Trotsky. They speak of "Stalinism" with disdain, but then go on to profess their support for Lenin and Trotsky. One such example is John McDonnell, until a few years ago one of the leading figures in the British Labour Party. In the party's 2015 leadership election, he supported Jeremy Corbyn, who subsequently appointed him to his shadow cabinet as shadow chancellor. McDonnell cited his most significant intellectual influences as "Marx, Lenin and Trotsky."[630] Janine Wissler, leader of Germany's left-wing Die Linke party, was also a member of the Trotskyist Marx21 group until her election as the party's leader in February 2021. According to Trotskyists, the socialist Soviet Union was at its best when Lenin and Trotsky shaped policy, but bad times followed under Stalin after Lenin's death.

In fact, however, the crimes of communism began as soon as the Bolsheviks seized power and started their war against a majority of the Russian people. It began with the struggle against the bourgeoisie, against the rich. In December 1917, Lenin demanded that extreme force be used against "this offal of humanity, these hopelessly decayed and atrophied limbs, this contagion, this plague, this ulcer," specifically "the rich and their hangers-on," and the bourgeois intellectuals.[631] His aim was "to *purge* the land of Russia of all vermin," the rich and other rogues. How this should be done, he explained in drastic words: "In one place half a score of rich, a dozen rogues, half a dozen workers who shirk their work . . . will be put in prison. In another place they will be put to cleaning latrines . . . In a fourth place, one out of every ten idlers will be shot on the spot."[632]

In December 1917, the Bolsheviks nationalized land and real estate.

In all cities with more than 10,000 inhabitants, property owners were expropriated. In February 1918, the Bolsheviks began to evict affluent families from their apartments to house unemployed proletarians and soldiers. "Housing Committees," appointed by councils, registered property owners and threw them out of their lodgings. "The new era offered many new opportunities for workers and peasants, but for the old elite it meant the end of everything that had made life worth living."[633]

In some places, workers took bloody "revenge" on factory managers and engineers, but sometimes simply on anyone they considered bourgeois—which, when in doubt, was anyone who wore a suit or did not perform manual labor.[634] Peasants drove out their landlords and took the land. "The revolution allowed the lower classes to loot estates and expel landlords. It also enabled workers to advance from their ghettoes into the city centers, conquer public spaces, and force their rules upon what was left of society."[635]

As a result of war, civil war, revolution and socialism, agricultural production fell by 57 percent between 1914 and 1921. Livestock decreased by 33 percent between 1916 and 1922, and the amount of land in agricultural use decreased by 35 percent.[636] In terms of food, the situation was, therefore, very difficult. Nevertheless, the Bolsheviks used hunger as a weapon in the class struggle against the bourgeoisie. Lenin blamed "the rich" for the hunger—they were the scapegoat to whom hatred was to be directed: "The famine is not due to the fact that there is no bread in Russia," Lenin explained, "but to the fact that the bourgeoisie and the rich generally are putting up a last decisive fight against the rule of the toilers, against the state of the workers, against the Soviet government, on this most important and acute of questions, the question of bread. The bourgeoisie and the rich generally, including the rural rich, the kulaks, are doing their best to thwart the grain monopoly; they are dislocating the distribution of grain undertaken by the state for the purpose of supplying bread to the population."[637]

In Petrograd, now St. Petersburg, the per capita calorie allocation was proclaimed on posters in the fall of 1918: workers were entitled to a daily ration of 100 grams of bread, 2 eggs, 10 grams of fat, and 10 grams of dried vegetables, while "bourgeois, real estate owners, merchants, shopkeepers, etc." were to receive only 25 grams of bread and were not entitled to eggs, fat or vegetables.[638] In contrast, party members could eat in canteens, were given "food parcels" (*pajoks*), and enjoyed exclusive access to special stores set up for the families of senior party officials.[639]

Martin Ivanovich Latsis, one of the first leaders of the Soviet political police, instructed his subordinates on November 1, 1918: "We don't make war against any people in particular. We are exterminating the bourgeoisie as a class. In your investigations don't look for documents and pieces of evidence about what the defendant has done, whether in deed or in speaking or acting against Soviet authority. The first question you should ask him is what class he comes from, what are his roots, his education, his training, and his occupation."[640]

Many of the bourgeoisie fled the big cities, including to the Crimea. But wherever they were tracked down, they were met with terror. In one massacre, 10,000 to 20,000 people were shot or lynched: "From Nakhimovsky [in Sevastopol in the Crimea] all one could see was the hanging bodies of officers, soldiers, and civilians arrested in the streets. The town was dead, and the only people left alive were hiding in lofts or basements. All the walls, shop fronts, and telegraph poles were covered with posters calling for 'Death to the traitors.' They were hanging people for fun."[641]

Where the "bourgeoisie" were not immediately expropriated, they faced extremely high taxes. In order to ensure that their taxes were paid, hundreds of "bourgeoisie" were taken hostage and locked up in concentration camps. "In accordance with the resolutions of the Workers' Soviet, 13 May has been declared the day of expropriation of the property of the bourgeoisie," announced the newspaper *Izvestia* of the Council of Workers' Delegates of Odessa on May 13, 1919. "The property-owning classes will be required to fill in a questionnaire detailing foodstuffs, shoes, clothes, jewels, bicycles, bedding, sheets, silverware, crockery, and other articles indispensable to the working population . . . It is the duty of all to assist the expropriation commissions in this sacred task. Anyone failing to assist the expropriation commissions will be arrested immediately. Anyone resisting will be executed without further delay."[642]

A popular theme that recurred in many articles in Bolshevik newspapers was the humiliation of the bourgeoisie who were forced to clean the latrines and barracks of the Chekists—the members of the Cheka, the Extraordinary All-Russian Commission for Combating Counterrevolution, Speculation and Sabotage—and the Red Guards. The same Odessa newspaper mentioned above reported: "If we execute a few dozen of these bloodsucking idiots, if we reduce them to the status of street sweepers and force their women to clean the Red Army barracks (and that would be an honor for them), they will understand that our power is here to stay."[643]

All these acts of violence were justified by the "noble" goal of eliminating exploitation and oppression once and for all. And as this goal was so great, all means were justified, as the editorial of the newspaper *Krasnyi Metsch* (*The Red Sword*) of the Cheka in Kiev explained to its readers: "We reject the old systems of morality and 'humanity' invented by the bourgeoisie to oppress and exploit the 'lower classes.' Our morality has no precedent, and our humanity is absolute because it rests on a new ideal. Our aim is to destroy all forms of oppression and violence. To us, everything is permitted, for we are the first to raise the sword not to oppress races and reduce them to slavery, but to liberate humanity from its shackles . . . Blood? Let blood flow like water! Let blood stain forever the black pirate's flag flown by the bourgeoisie, and let our flag be blood-red forever! For only through the death of the old world can we liberate ourselves forever from the return of those jackals."[644]

Grigory Zinoviev, party leader in Petrograd and member of the Bolshevik inner leadership circle, wrote in September 1918: "To dispose of our enemies, we will have to create our own socialist terror. For this we will have to train 90 million of the 100 million Russians and have them all on our side. We have nothing to say to the other 10 million; we'll have to get rid of them."[645]

Hatred was first directed against the rich and the bourgeoisie, but soon the Bolsheviks waged war against the population as a whole, especially the workers and peasants in whose name they claimed to act. Trotsky saw the militarization of labor as a means to increase production, which had fallen massively after the turmoil of the Civil War and the campaign of expropriations. Between 1914 and 1921, industrial output in Russia fell by 85 percent.[646] Strikes by workers were a frequent occurrence and were heavily repressed. Strike leaders were often shot, drowned or otherwise summarily executed.

Nevertheless, in the spring of 1920, nearly three-quarters of all industrial workers in Russia went on strike. The Bolsheviks stormed the factories, the ringleaders were shot, and family members were sent to concentration camps as a deterrent.[647] The brutality of these measures by a supposed workers' government was even more severe than the workers had experienced in the tsarist era.

In February and March 1921, workers downed tools and went on strike across Russia—one of the centers of this industrial action was Petrograd. Special units of the Cheka opened fire on demonstrating workers. Panic broke out among Bolsheviks as workers and soldiers fraternized. Kronstadt, a naval base and port city on an island off Petrograd, was the site of a mutiny by marines from two armored cruisers. On March 1, more than 15,000 people gathered, representing a quarter of the civilian and military population of the naval base. The strikes and demonstrations were violently suppressed, and the death toll was in the thousands. As many as 8,000 insurrectionists fled to Finland and later returned to Russia, having been promised amnesty. Despite the pledge of leniency, they were immediately arrested and transported to a concentration camp, where many died.[648] The historian Gerd Koenen provides the following assessment: "The triumph and dictatorship of the Bolsheviks rested not least on the complete annihilation of the Russian workers' movement."[649]

Lenin had no choice but to recognize that continuing a radical economic policy would have threatened the foundations of Soviet power.

Industrial production had already fallen to a tenth of its 1913 level, and people all across Russia were starving.

In response, Lenin initiated a U-turn and proposed a New Economic Policy (NEP), which was adopted at the Tenth Congress of the Russian Communist Party in March 1921. Lenin conceded that "we have sustained a very severe defeat on the economic front."[650] The economic policy of the Bolsheviks, he euphemistically put it, had failed "to produce that development of the productive forces which the Programme of our Party regards as vital and urgent."[651] In clearer terms: the socialist planned economy had failed as soon as it was introduced. After all, Lenin was clever enough to realize that the only available solution was "reverting to capitalism to a considerable extent." Those were the very words that Lenin used to formulate his policy shift.[652]

The NEP legalized profit-oriented production, private ownership in the production of consumer goods and the acquisition of wealth. It also incorporated peasants into the economic system through the introduction of a "natural tax." The Communists allowed state-owned enterprises to lease their factories to private individuals and place matters of finance, logistics, and entrepreneurship in private hands. In July 1921, freedom of trade was even restored for craftspeople and small industrial enterprises.[653]

The new guidelines adopted in the fall of 1921 resolutely opposed egalitarianism for workers with different levels of qualifications. Free distribution of food, mass-produced consumer goods and state services—having just been celebrated as great socialist "achievements"—were canceled, and rents were reinstated. There was no longer any talk of abolishing money. The historian Helmut Altrichter writes: "The state had retained control of the 'command heights of the economy': banking, the currency, the transport system, foreign trade, large and medium-sized industry. Below this threshold, however, it strove for greater productivity and efficiency, for more competition, for less dominance from above and for more initiative from below."[654]

What happened next was what always happens when even a small dose of free-market capitalism is added to a state-run economy: the economy recovered. Hunger (in 1921/22, at least 5 million of 29 million hungry people died of starvation; some estimates cite as many as 14 million deaths from starvation[655]) declined between 1923 and 1928, productivity rose and, by 1925/26, had been restored to pre-war levels in many major industries.[656] The New Economic Policy was the Communists' admission that the official narrative, which blamed "foreign saboteurs and agents" and other external factors for crop failures, starvation and declines in production, did not correspond to the facts. The main causes of Russia's woes lay in socialist economic policies.

But for the Communists, the NEP represented nothing more than a tactical retreat. In December 1926, Stalin declared that "we have introduced NEP, have permitted private capital, and have to some extent retreated in order to regroup our forces and later on pass to the offensive."[657] In 1929, Stalin initiated the next stage of the socialist revolution, and this time his focus was on agriculture. To that point in time, the Bolsheviks had never really been able to assert their rule in the countryside. Jörg Baberowski impressively describes how large sections of the peasantry lived far removed from their communist rulers, not only geographically, but also ideologically and economically. In many villages, there was no communist party cell or state organ, and if there was, they had little power. "To the peasants, the Communist functionaries were generally nothing more than representatives of an alien authority that demanded taxes and spoke an incomprehensible language."[658]

In truth, the Bolsheviks did not understand the reality of the peasants' lives. They thought in terms of their ideology of class struggle and believed they could establish their rule in the countryside by setting the poor peasants against the richer kulaks, just as they had set the workers against the capitalists. "For the peasants, however," writes Baberowski, "the supposed antagonism between rich and poor made no sense whatsoever. When peasants came into conflict over land or influence these were disputes between families or clans . . . The kulaks were not simply the masters of the village, but they were also its protectors. In times of misery and poverty their power and influence among the other peasants actually increased."[659]

"Eliminating the kulaks [i.e., the wealthiest peasants] as a class" was an official Bolshevik objective. In *History of the Communist Party of the Soviet Union (Bolsheviks): Short Course*, the standard textbook that all communists in the world had to study, in contrast, it is claimed that the distinguishing feature of the revolution against kulakism was "that it was accomplished *from above*, on the initiative of the state, and directly supported *from below*, by the millions of peasants, who were fighting to throw off kulak bondage and to live in freedom in the collective farms." This revolution had eliminated the "most numerous class of exploiters in our country, the kulak class, the mainstay of capitalist restoration."[660] In 1929, Stalin justified the decision to liquidate the kulak class thus: "The last hope of the capitalists of all countries, who are dreaming of restoring capitalism in the U.S.S.R.—'the sacred principle of private property'—is collapsing and vanishing. The peasants, whom they regarded as material manuring the soil for capitalism, are abandoning en masse the lauded banner of 'private property' and are taking the path of collectivism, the path of Socialism. The last hope for the restoration of capitalism is crumbling."[661]

In June 1930, Stalin proudly declared at the Sixteenth Congress of the Russian Communist Party "that the process of eliminating the kulaks as a class in our country is going full steam ahead."[662] The method of "complete collectivization," Stalin continued, was "essential": "How can it be abandoned without betraying communism, without betraying the interests of the working class and peasantry?"[663]

Vyacheslav Molotov, one of Stalin's closest associates from 1930 to 1949 as Soviet head of government and eventually foreign minister, told a meeting of party secretaries in February 1930 that kulaks who offered resistance should be drowned like cats in rivers. "We will welcome all useful proposals coming from the provinces (*na mestakh*)." Some would have to be shot, others deported to Siberia.[664]

In 1930–31, during the campaign to collectivize agriculture, two million people were deported as kulaks and 30,000 were shot.[665] Many peasants resisted collectivization and slaughtered millions of their own animals in protest against the collectivization of livestock. In addition, millions of animals perished during a new famine. Between 1928 and 1933, the number of pigs and cattle decreased by half and sheep by a third. The number of working horses and oxen decreased from 29.7 million in 1928 to 18.8 million in 1932.[666]

The Communists continued to increase the levies on agricultural products produced by the peasants, and those who did not comply could be shot as "thieves of socialist property." In 1932, a law was passed that specified a ten-year prison sentence or the death penalty for "any theft or damage of socialist property." From August 1932 to December 1933 alone, more than 125,000 people were sentenced under this law, and 5,400 received death sentences.[667]

Even the *History of the Communist Party of the Soviet Union (Bolsheviks)*, which was authorized by Stalin himself, had to admit that "the *voluntary* principle of forming collective farms was being violated, and that in a number of districts the peasants were being *forced* into the collective farms under threat of being dispossessed, disfranchised, and so on"[668]—an unusual critique for a Stalinist work, but which, in fact, downplayed the barbaric killings and the coercive regime, speaking only of "distortions and mistakes committed by the local organizations."[669] In fact, it was a bloody campaign against the peasants, in which millions fell victim to starvation, deportation and death.

Many intellectuals and journalists in the West downplayed or even praised the terror and collectivization campaign. Walter Duranty, *The New York Times*' Moscow correspondent, who was awarded the Pulitzer Prize for best foreign correspondent in 1932, addressed collectivization: "Future historians . . . may well regard the Russian struggle for collectivization as a heroic period in human progress . . . The most backward section of the population would have the chance to obtain what it most needed, namely education . . . women would have the chance for leisure and freedom as well . . . whether the villages preferred their dirt and ignorance to Progress or not, Progress would be thrust upon them."[670]

The American historian and literary critic Waldo Frank praised the Soviet economic system because the workers did not work for a boss: "Here are happy workers, because they are whole men and women . . . Dream, thought, love collaborate in the tedious business of making electric parts, since these toilers are not working for a boss."[671]

The background to the policy of collectivization was Stalin's goal of industrializing Russia by force. Foreign exchange from the sale of grain was used to build up heavy industry, which grew rapidly. The price was high—the historian Helmut Altrichter writes of the "terrorist mobilization of the entire population" in service of expanding industry.[672] In the agricultural districts around Moscow, the mortality rate rose by 50 percent between January and June 1933. In the early 1930s, there were 6 million more deaths than usual and about 300,000 people died during the deportations.[673]

At the same time, the Communists began to create a nationwide system of concentration and labor camps, the so-called Gulag. By early 1935, there were 965,000 prisoners in the Gulag system, 725,000 in "work camps" and 240,000 in "work colonies."[674] Although there were also many political and common criminal prisoners, most of the inmates were ordinary citizens who had violated the increasingly harsh laws, for example, for "breaking the passport law" (which eliminated freedom of movement within the country), for "nonfulfillment of the minimum number of working days" or for "destruction of Soviet property."[675]

On January 1, 1941, the Gulag camps contained more than 1.9 million inmates.[676] The regime, which had set out to liberate the workers, increasingly developed into a system of forced labor and domination. Since there were no economic incentives, as they exist in capitalism, the process of industrialization could only be enforced with the most brutal force.

Of course, the system did not only create losers; there were also winners. When so-called technical specialists, that is, engineers, technicians, factory directors, and so forth were arrested or shot, space was created for new social climbers. At the beginning of the second Five-Year Plan, Baberowski writes, more than half of all factory directors were former workers. In universities and schools, the system of quotas prevailed, giving preferential treatment to workers and their children in the allocation of university places.[677] Stalin had positioned himself as a man of the people, an ally of the proletarian upstarts, a man who came from below, from humble beginnings, and who—unlike the intellectual Trotsky— spoke the same simple and crude language as the ordinary people.[678]

Communist policy was characterized by a constant interplay of the most brutal terror and phases in which the terror subsided somewhat and economic concessions were made to the peasants, before moving on to a new wave of terror. The Communists were always testing the limits and, at most, extreme famines could persuade them to deviate from their pure doctrine and implement at least some elements of private property ownership and market principles.

If the Communists had consistently enforced their line in agriculture as well, and allowed only state ownership, the system would have collapsed completely, and even more people would have starved to death.

For as a result of collectivization, agricultural production collapsed, even though Stalin proclaimed at the Sixteenth Congress that it was a "fact that we are now in a position not only to replace kulak production by collective-farm and state-farm production, but to exceed the former several times over."[679] The opposite was true, and even Stalin had to back down and allow more private ownership in agriculture. Peasants were granted small pieces of farmland for private use. The superiority of private property and the market over socialism is evident from the following figures: "Although privately used land accounted for less than 5 percent of total farmland, by the 1950s it provided more than 70 percent of potatoes, about 70 percent of milk, and close to 90 percent of eggs. In the 1930s, it secured the livelihoods of collective farmers. What they received in wages from the collective farms was not enough to survive."[680] Industrialization was achieved primarily at the expense of agriculture— as evidenced by the fact that it was not until the 1950s that per capita agricultural production returned to the level it had been in 1928.

The disaster of collectivization did not deter communists in other countries. True, Stalin had specifically advised Chinese revolutionary leader Mao Zedong in 1950, based on his own experience, to leave the assets of rich peasants unmolested in order to speed China's agricultural recovery after years of civil war. But Mao ignored Stalin's advice. He regarded redistribution of the land as an easy way to win the support of the peasants. The land was measured and distributed to the poor. The rich were humiliated, dispossessed, and even murdered. "By implicating a majority in the murder of a carefully designated minority, Mao managed permanently to link the people to the party," writes Dutch historian and China expert Frank Dikötter. He estimates the number of murdered "class enemies" between 1947 and 1952 to have been 1.5 to 2 million people.[681]

After the death of Stalin in 1953, Mao increased the pace of collectivization in China. That same year, a grain monopoly was introduced, forcing peasants to sell their crops at prices fixed by the state. In 1955–56, agricultural collectives, similar to the state farms in the Soviet Union, were introduced. They took back the land that had just been given to the poor peasant farmers, and the rural population was transformed into bonded servants at the beck and call of the state.[682]

In 1958, the greatest socialist experiment in human history, Mao's Great Leap Forward, began. I described this in detail in the first chapter of my book *The Power of Capitalism* and briefly addressed it in Chapters 1 and 3 of this book.

The atrocities committed during this time are indescribable. In total, about 45 million people died, either from starvation or being murdered. Frank Dikötter describes this horrific period: "People who did not work hard enough were hung up and beaten; some were drowned in ponds. Others were doused in urine and forced to eat excrement. People were mutilated. A report circulated to the top leadership, including Chairman Mao, describes how a man named Wang Ziyou had one of his ears chopped off, his legs bound with wire, and a 10-kilo stone dropped on his back before he was branded—as punishment for digging up a potato. There were even cases of people being buried alive. When a boy stole a handful of grain in a Hunan village, local boss Xiong Dechang forced his father to bury his son alive. The man died of grief a few days later."[683]

After these terrible events, Mao was subject, at least temporarily, to criticism. At a meeting of party cadres in Beijing, head of state Liu Shaoqi (president of the People's Republic of China from 1959 to 1968) described the famine as a man-made disaster, and support for Mao reached an all-time low.

Now at least some private ownership of property was permitted, and peasants were allowed to farm small plots of land for themselves. But Mao repeatedly stressed that the class struggle was far from over; everywhere he looked he saw evidence of capitalist forces.

He was not even entirely wrong in this, for spontaneous and illegal enterprises were set up all over China. In Shenyang (Manchuria), there were an astounding 20,000 private entrepreneurs, while in Wuhan, the commercial and industrial center on the middle Yangtze River, 3,000 profiteers made a living by exploiting loopholes in the planned economy. "Many carried out their trade across several provinces. Private networks were constructed far and wide, involving not only agricultural products but also gold and silver . . . A shadow economy flourished in the interstices of the collectives. There were underground factories, underground construction teams, underground transportation corps."[684]

Without permission for peasants to cultivate private plots of land and without the shadow economy, the socialist system would certainly have collapsed. But Mao was not ready to accept these capitalist degenerations. He declared that a third of the power in the country was no longer in the hands of the Communists,[685] and Liu Shaoqui launched a major "Socialist Education Campaign." Entire provinces were accused of "taking the capitalist road." More than 5 million party members were punished and more than 77,000 people were hounded to their deaths.[686]

Mao, unlike Stalin, believed that the class struggle had to continue from below, from among the people, in order to eradicate the risk of a restoration of capitalism. He decided to unleash the Great Proletarian Cultural Revolution, which began on June 1, 1966, with an appeal in the *People's Daily*. The headline exhorted readers to "Sweep Away All Monsters and Demons!" It was the starting signal for the Cultural Revolution. The people were urged to rise up and seek out the representatives of the bourgeoisie who were allegedly trying to transform the dictatorship of the proletariat into a dictatorship of the bourgeoisie.[687]

Schoolchildren and students in particular were mobilized. They rioted in the streets and turned against "filthy rich peasants," "son-of-a-bitch landlords," "bloodsucking capitalists," "neo-bourgeoisie" and "alien class elements,"[688] but often simply against their own teachers or professors, who were accused of capitalist thinking. The first death occurred in a girls' school administered by Beijing Normal University, where the vice-principal was tortured. Students spat in her face, filled her mouth with soil, tied her hands behind her back and then beat her, including with nail-spiked clubs. After several hours of torture, the vice-principal lost consciousness and died.[689]

A school principal in Beijing was ordered to stand in the scorching sun while Red Guards poured boiling hot water over him. A biology teacher was tortured for hours until she died, after which the other teachers were forced to beat her corpse. In elementary schools, where students were no older than thirteen, some teachers were forced to swallow nails and excrement, others had their hair shaved off and were forced to slap each other in the face.[690] Fellow students were also humiliated and sometimes tortured to death because they had "bad family backgrounds" or came from "exploiting families."[691]

In an outlying district of Beijing, local Communist Party cadres ordered all landowners and all other "bad elements," including their family members, to be exterminated. Some were beaten to death, others stabbed with chaff cutters or strangled with wire. Several were electrocuted, and children were hung by their feet and whipped. An eight-year-old girl and her grandmother were buried alive.[692]

The young Red Guards raided houses of people from "bad class backgrounds." The widow of a former manager of the Shell oil company in Shanghai was beaten in her apartment; everything in it was smashed and vandalized. A Party official asked her, "Is it right for you and your daughter to live in a house of nine rooms with four bathrooms when there is such a severe housing shortage in Shanghai? Is it right for you to use wool carpets and have each room filled with rosewood and black-wood furniture when there is a shortage of wood and basic furniture for others? Is it right to for you to wear silk and fur and sleep under quilts filled with down?" Shortly thereafter, the widow was carted off to a local jail, and several working-class families moved into her home.[693] There was a wave of expropriations in Shanghai, and 30,000 families were forced to surrender their property to the state. Many were granted a small living space for which they were charged rent. The vast majority of victims were classified as "bad elements exploiting the proletariat."[694]

While the Cultural Revolutionaries persecuted "capitalist elements" for allegedly living in luxury, 50 estates were built for Mao during the 27 years of his rule, no fewer than five in Beijing alone. The estates were set in enormous grounds, mostly in grandiose locations. In many places of great beauty, a whole mountain or a long stretch of lakeshore was cordoned off for his exclusive use.[695] Since Mao loved swimming, his villas were equipped with luxurious swimming pools that were heated for months on end, just in case Mao should suddenly fancy a dip.[696] Mao was also a gourmand and had his favorite delicacies shipped in from 1,000 kilometers away,[697] In addition, Mao, who demanded sexual renunciation from his compatriots, was constantly supplied with young and beautiful women who had to do his bidding.[698] Mao earned a fortune from the sale of his books, which everyone was required to own. His biographers Jung Chang and Jon Halliday state: "Mao was the only millionaire created in Mao's China."[699]

But the Chinese knew none of this. Since things like decent clothes, high-heeled shoes, makeup, porcelain, and so forth, were considered capitalistic and anyone who owned them was at risk of ridicule or beat-ings, the production of all these items was soon stopped. Instead, several billion(!) Mao badges were produced all over China to pin on people's lapels, just above the heart.[700] Loudspeakers were set up on every street corner and in the fields, blaring slogans against capitalism and in favor of socialism at full volume from morning till night. Everywhere stores and streets were renamed, erasing potential reminders of the capitalist or feudalist past. The most common new names for stores were Red Flag, Red Guard, The East Is Red, Workers, Peasants, The People, and the like. In Shanghai more than a hundred were called Red Guard.[701]

Quotations from Chairman Mao Zedong, also known as *The Little Red Book* in the West, was printed in the millions and enthusiastically waved and recited by Red Guard activists. One of Mao's quotes was, for example, "A revolution is not a dinner party, or writing an essay, or painting a picture, or doing embroidery; it cannot be so refined, so leisurely and gentle, so temperate, kind, courteous, restrained and magnanimous. A revolution is an insurrection, an act of violence by which one class overthrows another."[702] The ruling class had long since been overthrown, but, according to Mao's philosophy, the struggle between the capitalist and socialist lines was a permanent one—and the Cultural Revolution was a means to that end.

Mao claimed that capitalist elements had taken root in the Party. Initially, party officials succeeded in directing the hatred of the young Red Guards against their teachers and professors—or against ordinary people who were made scapegoats because they had "bad class backgrounds." But soon the Red Guards shifted the focus of their attacks to party officials. "It looked like a people's revolution. Just as Mao had incited students to rebel against their teachers months earlier, he now unleashed ordinary people against their party leaders. In doing so he tapped into a deep pool of resentment. There seemed to be no end to the number of people who harboured grievances against party officials."[703]

Initially, the army was ordered to stay out of the fighting but soon intervened. The fronts were unclear. Many army personnel considered the rebels to be counterrevolutionaries, agitators who were only using the Cultural Revolution as a pretext to attack the Party and socialism.

The situation became ever more confused as uprisings against the army broke out nationwide, soon followed by direct attacks on the military. By June 1967, China was in chaos. Counterrevolutionaries were arming themselves, and the situation threatened to spiral completely out of control until Mao signed a decree authorizing the army to defend itself against the rebels.[704] Open civil war broke out in some parts of the country, using machine guns, mortars and napalm.[705]

In Guangxi province alone, 80,000 people were killed in the summer of 1968. The local militia allied with the army to hunt down alleged rebels. In Liujang, some of the victims were publicly decapitated, their heads displayed with a note reading "counterrevolutionary." In one people's commune, rumors circulated about an imminent counterrevolutionary plot in which landlords would come and claim back their old land. As a result, some 60 people were frogmarched to a field and forced to kneel as their heads were smashed with hammers.[706]

In some places, "class enemies" were cut open while they were still alive; their hearts and livers were taken out and eaten. This was not cannibalism, the rebels said, because it was the flesh of landlords and spies.[707]

In September 1968, state leader Zhou Enlai announced an "all-round" victory. But now began a campaign from above to cleanse the party of "spies" and "traitors." Between 1968 and 1980, 17 million students were banished from the cities to the countryside, where they were supposed to be "re-educated" by the peasants. In fact, most of those sent to the countryside lived apart from the peasants. Many lived in caves, pigsties or sheds, and many suffered from malnutrition or other deficiency diseases. Numerous young women were molested or raped.

And it was not only young people who were banished to the countryside. They were joined by the weakest in society—unemployed people, vagrants, invalids, and retired workers who had never farmed in their lives and were now expected to fend for themselves far from the cities. Many were sent to re-education camps in rural areas, but the camps were not even capable of sustaining their residents.

The Cultural Revolution led to chaos, and the party partially lost control as its officials became consumed in the conflicts. This allowed people in several provinces to reclaim freedoms that the Communists had taken from them. Many farmers started cultivating vegetables for their own consumption. "The desire to own land was driven from below and only ratified by local authorities much later."[708]

Those who stayed in the people's communes and obeyed the Party's directives had a much worse life than those who disobeyed. "It was a socialist world turned upside down, as those who answered the call of the market thrived while members of the collective remained mired in poverty."[709]

Large, illegal markets sprang up all over the countryside, where people offered their products. The Party's inspectors were powerless because if they tried to intervene, they were threatened by the traders. A process of decollectivization occurred as many thousands left the people's communes into which they had been forced, or expanded their private farmland far beyond what was allowed. In Guangzhou province, underground factories sprang up, entirely devoted to feeding the black market.[710] Since the planned economy could not produce enough goods to satisfy demand from the ordinary population, market economy structures spontaneously emerged everywhere. In some parts of the country, there was no wood, so unfinished houses could be seen everywhere, abandoned for lack of timber and other building materials. In response, hundreds of factories sprang up to illegally trade in timber.[711]

Dikötter describes a longstanding "silent revolution," which gained momentum after the Cultural Revolution: "Throughout the country people started quietly reconnecting with the past, from local leaders who focused on economic growth to villagers who reconstituted popular markets . . . Sometimes a farmer merely pushed the boundaries of the planned economy by bringing some corn to market or spending more time on a private plot. In other cases they were bolder, opening underground factories or speculating in commodities normally controlled by the state. But everywhere, in one way or another, people were emboldened by the failure of the Cultural Revolution to take matters into their own hands. As one shrewd observer has noted, 'people decided they did not want to go on living the way they were doing, and they were setting up ways to get themselves out of their predicament.' It was an uneven, patchy revolution from below, and one that remained largely silent, but eventually it would engulf the entire country."[712]

A crucial factor in understanding the dynamics of the Chinese reforms initiated by Deng Xiaoping after Mao's death is that they were only partially initiated "from above." Many developments were sponta-neous—the forces of the market prevailed, as it were, against the state. The Chinese economist Weiying Zhang writes that Deng Xiaoping has been called the "architect" of China's reforms: "However, Deng Xiaoping understood, economic and social reforms are different from building construction. It cannot be built according to predesigned blueprints. Instead a 'cross the river by feeling the stones' approach must be taken."[713]

Deng, Zhang argues, pursued a strategy of reform through experi-mentation. Nothing of importance was simply decreed—not price reform, labor market reform, tax reform, or foreign trade reform. Deng's approach was always to experiment with new approaches in certain areas or sectors (e.g., special economic zones). If they worked, they were expanded; if not, they were ditched.[714] A key role was played by the encouragement given to initiatives "from below" as opposed to determining initiatives centrally. Deng's most important skill, as Zhang puts it, was that "Deng Xiaoping knew what he did not know!"[715]

Western intellectuals tempered their enthusiasm for China as capi-talism took hold. During and after the Cultural Revolution, Mao and China were a source of inspiration to intellectuals everywhere. Simone de Beauvoir, the famous French feminist and social theorist, wrote at the time, "Life in China today is exceptionally pleasant . . . Plenty of fond dreams are authorized by the idea of a country . . . where generals and statesmen are scholars and poets."[716] And her partner, the philoso-pher Jean-Paul Sartre, a confessed admirer of Stalin who had previously downplayed the Gulags, wrote of Mao's China, "A revolutionary regime must get rid of a certain number of individuals that threaten it and I see no other means for this than death; it is always possible to get out of a prison; the revolutionaries of 1793 probably didn't kill enough people."[717]

In France, where anti-capitalism is more pronounced than in any other Western country, admiration for dictators such as Stalin and Mao has always been particularly strong in intellectual circles. The book *Generation Stalin: French Writers, the Fatherland and the Cult of Personality*[718] provides numerous testimonies from admirers of Stalin. And so, it is no coincidence that the most radical socialist experiment in history, the Khmer Rouge regime in Cambodia, was conceived in Paris universities.

In the process, between a fifth and a quarter of Cambodia's population perished from mid-1975 to early 1979—estimates range from 1.6 to 2.2 million people.[719] This experiment, which the Khmer Rouge leader Pol Pot (also referred to as "Brother 1") called the "Super Great Leap Forward"[720] in honor of Mao's Great Leap Forward, is most revealing because it offers an extreme demonstration of the belief that a society can be artificially constructed on the drawing board.

Today, it is sometimes claimed that Pol Pot and his comrades wanted to implement a puritan form of "primitive communism," and their rule is painted as a manifestation of unrestrained irrationality. In fact, this couldn't be further from the truth. The Khmer Rouge's masterminds and leaders were intellectuals from upstanding families, who had studied in Paris and were members of the French Communist Party. "Based on borrowings from Marxist and Maoist concepts, the party's intellectual elite developed its own theory of world capitalist exploitation, its own model of Cambodian society and the historical fault lines that trapped the country in a circle of underdevelopment and dependence."[721]

Two of the masterminds, Khieu Samphan and Hu Nim, had written Marxist and Maoist dissertations in Paris.[722] The intellectual elite who had studied in Paris occupied almost all of the government's leading positions after the seizure of power.[723]

They had worked out a detailed Four-Year Plan that listed all the products the country would need in exacting detail (needles, scissors, lighters, cups, combs, etc.). The level of specificity was highly unusual, even for a planned economy. For example, it said, "Eating and drinking are collectivised. Dessert is also collectively prepared. Briefly, raising the people's living standards in our own country means doing it collectively. In 1977, there are to be two desserts per week. In 1978 there is one dessert every two days. Then in 1979, there is one dessert every day, and so on. So people live collectively with enough to eat; they are nourished with snacks. They are happy to live in this system."[724]

The party, the sociologist Daniel Bultmann writes in his analysis, "planned the lives of the population as if on a drawing board, fitting them into pre-determined spaces and needs."[725] Everywhere, gigantic irrigation systems and fields were to be built to a uniform, rectilinear model. All regions were subjected to the same targets, as the Party believed that standardized conditions in fields of exactly the same size would also produce standardized yields. "With the new irrigation system and the checkerboard rice fields, nature was to be harnessed to the utopian reality of a fully collectivist order that eliminated inequality from day one."[726]

Yet the arrangement of irrigation dams in equal squares with equally square fields in their center led to frequent floods. The Party's strict designs had totally ignored natural water flows and most Party officials had little to no technical knowledge of dam construction. The irrigation systems were built by forced labor, who painstakingly followed the plans issued by headquarters—and 80 percent of them did not work.[727]

Private property was to be completely abolished—in the same way as we have seen in numerous utopian novels. But "Brother 1" and his comrades did not restrict themselves to collectivizing land and the means of production. From September 1976, people had to surrender absolutely everything, including their watches, radios, tools, plows, seeds, kitchen utensils, and so forth.[728] Everyone had to wear the same black uniform, and each gender had its own "revolutionary" haircut. There was no jewelry; however, party cadres could get hold of notepads, bicycles and pens that set them apart from the crowd—and which they proudly displayed.[729]

In order to wipe the slate clean and start to construct a just society, almost everyone was expelled from the cities. In the process, the communists lied to the people and told them that they were about to be bombed by the U.S. and would only have to leave their homes for a few days. That also meant that they would not have to take many of their possessions with them or even lock their doors. They were given 24 hours to leave their homes, but from the beginning, the plan was to never let them return. Families were often torn apart, communities were separated and people were squeezed together in collectives. In most cases, people were not just moved once; they were taken to new places again and again.

Most insidiously, people were asked whether they wanted to return to their homes. But this was just a trick question to identify those who were ideologically unsound and in need of more intensive re-education. Anyone who answered the question with a yes was taken to another place—not their former home—where living conditions were even more unbearable.[730]

The communists compared people to cattle: "Watch this ox as it pulls the plow. It eats when it is ordered to eat. If you let it graze in the field, it will eat anything. If you put it into another field where there isn't enough grass, it will still graze uncomplainingly. It is not free, and it is constantly being watched. And when you tell it to pull the plow, it pulls. It never thinks about its wife or children."[731] The collective even assumed the role of choosing who people should marry. Anyone who rejected a spouse more than once was quickly branded an enemy of the system.

On the day the Khmer Rouge seized power, April 17, 1975, their leader Pol Pot set out his plan for the coming weeks and months. It contained a raft of measures, including:

- the evacuation of all people from the cities,

- the abolition of all markets,

- the abolition of money.

On that same day, the central bank was blown up, and money was completely abolished. Banknotes fluttered worthless through the deserted city streets. Gold and jewelry were confiscated by the state, as was all private property.

The planned economy failed quickly and radically. The people suffered from hunger. But of course, the communists did not see the cause of their failures in the inherent impossibility of designing a society on the drawing board. They blamed alleged saboteurs. Tens of thousands were arrested and locked up in torture prisons. The Khmer Rouge themselves claimed that they had no prisons, and in some ways, this was true because they were places of torture and death, which hardly anyone ever left alive.[732]

Under torture, "confessions" were extorted, such as this one: "I gave instructions to destroy the crops by harvesting them while they were still unripe. I ordered Chaet to burn rice . . . My goal was to create unrest among the people, especially between the New People and the Old People. This hindered the Party's plan."[733] Or: "I am a fake revolutionary. In reality I am an enemy, an enemy of the people, of the nation of Cambodia, and of the Communist Party of Cambodia. I am a cheap, reactionary intellectual who merely poses as a revolutionary."[734]

People had to confess that they worked for the CIA, although many did not even know what the CIA was (some thought it was the name of a person). Some of the confessions were absurd and self-contradictory, such as, "I am not a member of the CIA. I confessed to belonging to the CIA when confronted with my guilt. I ask the Party to kill me because I did not follow the revolution."[735]

The entire country was crisscrossed with a network of 196 so-called security and re-education centers that were exactly identical in structure, function and internal procedures. Schools and Buddhist pagodas were closed and turned into internment camps for the class enemy.

The core of the security apparatus relied most heavily on the recruitment of children between the ages of 12 and 16, who in Pol Pot's opinion were blank sheets ready to be filled with socialist thinking. One element of the children's training involved being forced to watch prisoners being tortured or horrifically murdered under drawn-out torture. They were not allowed to show any emotion, as this was interpreted as a sign of sympathy with the enemy and was to be punishable accordingly.[736]

In the beginning, the terror was directed primarily against the "wealthy" and well-educated. "Rich and educated city-dwellers suddenly—and literally—found themselves at the very bottom of the food chain. Reports of sadistic behavior by cadres who themselves lived in opulence and tormented the old elite were accordingly abundant."[737] The Communist Party declared the upper economic and educational classes in particular to be enemies of the people and murdered them for even the smallest offenses in the re-education camps.[738] "Candidates who wished to join the Party must come from low classes, such as the poorer or middle peasantry, primarily from the lower classes."[739]

But soon the circle of enemies grew larger and larger, and no section of the population was spared. Anyone could be exposed as an enemy of the system at any time, even if they belonged to the Communist Party—at least half of its own cadres were murdered.[740] Anyone who did not want to be considered an "enemy" had to constantly expose and denounce other "enemies." This created a spiral of violence. Later, almost 20,000 mass graves containing the regime's victims were found all across the country.

The power that ruled everything called itself "Angkar" ("Organization") and people did not even know who this organization was. They only knew that they could not resist it and that it ruled every area of their lives—just like Big Brother in George Orwell's *1984*. "All revolutionary laws and regulations were promulgated in the name of Angkar; all transgressions were known to and were punished by Angkar. Angkar was everywhere, a pervasive presence that none could escape. 'Angkar has more eyes than a pineapple', the cadre said. Husbands and wives spoke of Angkar only in private, in a whisper, fearful of being overheard. No-one criticized Angkar in public; even the most minimally critical passing allusion could be enough to ensure arrest, interrogation, and subsequent disappearance for re-education. Danger was ever present; at no time did one know whether the spies of Angkar were listening."[741]

The regime collapsed a few years later. The Khmer Rouge provide an extreme example of the strategy of creating socialist utopias through extreme constructivism. Pol Pot and his comrades believed that radical equality would lead to a just and happy society. He could and should have known better, especially after Mao's Great Leap Forward in China had already failed so resoundingly, costing the lives of 45 million people. For Pol Pot, the socialist experiment of Mao's Great Leap Forward served as a template—it just had not been implemented radically and consistently enough, which is why he referred to his experiment as the "Super Great Leap Forward." The new national anthem ended with: "Let us build our fatherland so that it may take a Great Leap Forward! An immense, glorious, prodigious Great Leap Forward."[742]

An intellectual functionary with experience abroad proudly declared: "We are making a unique revolution. Is there any other country that would dare abolish money and markets the way we have? We are much better than the Chinese, who look up to us. They are trying to imitate us, but they haven't managed it yet. We are a good model for the whole world." Even after Pol Pot was ousted, he continued to believe that April 17, 1975 was the greatest date in the history of all revolutions, "with the exception of the Paris Commune in 1871."[743]

Thus we see a continuous procession of failed socialist experiments—from the Soviet Union to China to the most radical variant in Cambodia. As different as they were in detail, they were all united by the constructivist delusion that it is only by abolishing private property, fighting "the rich" and implementing a planned economy that people can be freed from the misery of feudalism and capitalism.

And all of these regimes—from Stalin to Mao to Pol Pot—found apologists and admirers among renowned intellectuals. Among the intellectuals who have trivialized the socialist terror regime in Cambodia, for example, was Noam Chomsky, who objected to the defamation of the regime, saying that the reports of mass killings were fabricated.[744]

The anti-capitalist philosopher Slavoj Žižeks even went as far as to declare that the Khmer Rouge had not gone far enough: "The Khmer Rouge were, in a way *not radical enough*: while they took the abstract negation of the past to the limit, they did not invent any new form of collectivity." All the same, he added: "revolutionary violence should be celebrated as 'redemptive' and even 'divine.'"[745]

It should also be noted here that Žižek was an admirer of Che Guevara and described Stalin's terror in the 1930s as "humanist terror": "Stalinism effectively saved what we understand as the humanity of man."[746]

Paul Hollander comments: "Žižek's beliefs appear to be rooted in an unshakeable conviction that nothing exceeds the evils of capitalism and the violence it generates. It was a conviction shared to varying degrees by many Western intellectuals who were attracted to dictators of different political persuasion and who had in common an anti-capitalist disposition."[747]

Anti-capitalism is the root of admiration for even the worst socialist terror regimes in history. Of course, not all socialist regimes were as violently bloodthirsty as those of Stalin, Mao and Pol Pot. But then, even those socialist experiments that began much more innocuously soon led to economic collapse and curtailed freedoms in a process of cumulative radicalization, as the most recent example of a failed socialist experiment confirms: Hugo Chávez's "Socialism of the 21st Century" in Venezuela. Chávez was democratically elected and in the early days of his regime, he promised to uphold property rights and vowed that he would never "expropriate anything from anyone."[748] Before the election, Chávez employed a surprisingly conciliatory rhetoric, casting himself as a great admirer of Western values who welcomed foreign investors, a "Tony Blair of the Caribbean."[749] To a certain extent, this was a deliberate deception. Nevertheless, Chávez did not set out to lead his country into economic disaster and dictatorship. However, this is precisely what happened. For there is a certain inherent logic in the fact that the elimination of economic freedom always leads to economic decline and then, at some point, to the elimination of political freedoms.

We should not believe the words and assurances of socialists when they speak of freedom and democracy. The Communist Party of Germany (KPD) affirmed in its program declaration of June 11, 1945: "With the destruction of Hitlerism, it is also important to complete the democratization of Germany, that bourgeois-democratic transition that began in 1848 . . . We are of the opinion that forcing the Soviet system onto Germany would be the false path . . . Rather, we are of the opinion that the most compelling interests of the German people in the present situation call for Germany to take a different path, the path of establishing an anti-fascist, democratic regime, a parliamentary, democratic republic with all the democratic rights and liberties for the people."[750]

As history shows, the exact opposite happened in the GDR over the next few years. Under the pretext of anti-fascism, land and the essential means of production were nationalized, and a dictatorship modeled on the Soviet Union was established.

Frederick Engels promised that after the socialization of the means of production the state would completely "die out": "The first act by virtue of which the state really constitutes itself the representative of the whole of society—the taking possession of the means of production in the name of society—this is, at the same time, its last independent act as a state. State interference in social relations becomes, in one domain after another, superfluous, and then dies out of itself; the government of persons is replaced by the administration of things, and by the conduct of processes of production. The state is not 'abolished.' *It dies out*."[751] And, "In proportion as anarchy in social production [for Engels, synonymous with the capitalist economy, R.Z.] vanishes, the political authority of the state dies out. Man, at last the master of his own form of social organisation, becomes at the same time the lord over Nature, his own master—free."[752]

In *The State and Revolution*, Lenin described his final aim as "abolishing the state, i.e., all organised and systematic violence, all use of violence against people in general."[753] All that was needed was an intermediate stage of socialism and the dictatorship of the proletariat to bring about this final state of communist society. Marx had already written in his "Critique of the Gotha Program": "Between capitalist and communist society there lies the period of the revolutionary transformation of the one into the other. Corresponding to this is also a political transition period in which the state can be nothing but *the revolutionary dictatorship of the proletariat.*"[754]

In fact, there was no dictatorship of the proletariat in any socialist state. As we have seen, the early Soviet Union was based precisely on crushing the workers' movement and rapidly developed into the dictatorship of a party and ultimately of a despot. According to the ideas of Marx, Engels and Lenin, a transitional period was to be followed by a final state in which there would be no state. "Lastly," Lenin writes, "only communism makes the state absolutely unnecessary, for there is *nobody* to be suppressed—'nobody' in the sense of a *class*, of a systematic struggle against a definite section of the population."[755] Thus, according to this logic, when the means of production are socialized and the classes are deprived of their economic basis, the state will die out of its own accord.

As is well known, never, in any country in the world, has such a thing ever occurred. Not only did the state not die out, it constantly grew stronger; violence did not become unnecessary, it was one of the characteristic features of socialist systems—from the Soviet Union to Venezuela. And this was still true in the periods following the worst phases of Stalin's rule: The post-Stalin Soviet Union did not see the same excesses of the 1930s, but it was still a dictatorship in which people were deprived of basic rights, such as freedom of the press, freedom of speech and freedom of assembly.

Again and again, people were consoled with promises of a communist utopia, which, they were assured, was no longer a far-off dream. At its 22nd Party Congress in 1961, the Communist Party of the Soviet Union (CPSU) adopted a program that promised to build communism in 20 years. "Communist construction," it said, "has become the practical task of the Party, the cause of all the Soviet people."[756] By 1970, the program promised, the Soviet Union would surpass "the strongest and richest capitalist country, the U.S.A., in production per head of population." Then, by 1980, "*a communist society would in the main be built in the U.S.S.R.*"[757] The Soviet Union would secure for its citizens a living standard "*higher than that of any of the capitalist countries*"[758] and would become the country "with the shortest and, concurrently, the most productive and highest-paid working day."[759] The entire population would be able "adequately to satisfy its need in high-quality and varied foodstuffs,"[760] and by 1980 such "an abundance of material and cultural benefits for the whole population will be attained" so that it would be possible to transition "to the communist principle of distribution according to need" proclaimed by Marx.[761]

The program thus expressly referred to Marx's "Critique of the Gotha Program," in which he had promised: "In a higher phase of communist society, after the enslaving subordination of the individual to the division of labour, and therewith also the antithesis between mental and physical labour, has vanished; after labour has become not only a means of life but life's prime want; after the productive forces have also increased with the all-round development of the individual, and all the springs of co-operative wealth flow more abundantly—only then can the narrow horizon of bourgeois right be crossed in its entirety and society inscribe on its banners: From each according to his ability, to each according to his needs!"[762]

This was what the CPSU promised to achieve by 1980 at the latest. But none of their promises were ever fulfilled. The Soviet Union had a population of 270 million in 1982, 16 percent more than the U.S. (232 million). Nevertheless, 44 million radios were sold in the U.S. that year, compared to just 6 million in the U.S.S.R.; 8 million cars were sold in the U.S., against just 1.4 million in the U.S.S.R.; and 29 million tape recorders were sold in the U.S., while the U.S.S.R. managed just 3.2 million.[763]

In 1981, the year in which the program promised a communist society would have been built, a comparison between the United States and the Soviet Union revealed: "In the 1980s, living standards in the

USSR are likely to improve much more slowly than in the past because of the projected severe constraints on economic growth. These are some of the major findings of an extensive comparison of per capita consumption in the USSR and the United States in 1976 based on detailed expenditure data and new purchasing power parities. In 1976, real per capita consumption in the Soviet Union was 34.4 percent of that in the United States: this value is the geometric mean of comparisons in rubles (27.6 percent) and in dollars (42.8 percent). These comparisons, moreover, are believed to be biased in favor of the USSR because of the inability to allow fully for the notoriously poor quality and narrow assortment of Soviet consumer goods and services. The comparisons also cannot take into account the erratic, primitive distribution system and random shortages that make shopping difficult for Soviet consumers. Based on a geometric mean comparison, Soviet consumers come nearest to their American counterparts in consumption of food, beverages, and tobacco (54 percent) and soft goods (39 percent). The Soviet lag is massive (less than 20 percent of the US level) in consumer durables and household services."[764]

When Mikhail Gorbachev launched far-reaching reforms in the Soviet Union in the mid-1980s, the system slid completely into chaos. What emerged, however, was not a free, capitalist society, but a system of "Crony Capitalism,"[765] which is economically inefficient and whose gross domestic product is even lower than Italy's, despite the size of the country and its vast raw material resources.[766]

Advocates of "democratic socialism" distance themselves from systems such as those that prevailed in the Soviet Union and the Eastern bloc countries. But they act as if it is possible to arbitrarily separate the two—economics and politics—from each other: When they do criticize socialist systems, they tend to criticize the economic constitution almost as a side issue, rather than putting it at the heart of their condemnation. What they instead focus on are the elimination of political and democratic freedoms (e.g., freedom of speech, freedom of the press, etc.). The economic prescriptions issued by many supporters of "democratic socialism" are quite similar to those of their non-democratic comrades, characterized as they are by a deep distrust of market forces and almost boundless trust in the state. "Democratic socialists" simply want to correct the "mistake" made by the real-world socialist states of the past 100 years by combining the socialist economic system with a democratic state constitution. This is ultimately what the term "democratic socialism" means. Although Marx couldn't have been clearer in emphasizing the close interdependence of economics and politics, of base and superstructure, the "democratic socialists," for all their other reverence for the thinker from Trier, seem to deny any such connection.

The famous passage from the preface to *A Contribution to the Critique of Political Economy* in which Marx describes this connection reads: "My inquiry led me to the conclusion that neither legal relations nor political forms could be comprehended whether by themselves or on the basis of a so-called general development of the human mind, but that on the contrary they originate in the material conditions of life . . . In the social production of their existence, men inevitably enter into definite relations, which are independent of their will, namely relations of production appropriate to a given stage in the development of their material forces of production. The totality of these relations of production constitutes the economic structure of society, the real foundation, on which arises a legal and political superstructure and to which correspond definite forms of social consciousness. The mode of production of material life conditions the general process of social, political and intellectual life."[767]

It is a striking contradiction that socialists, who are otherwise keen on referring to Marx, deny this connection between economics and politics as soon as they start to criticize socialist societies. For them, it is apparently a coincidence that societies with a non-capitalist base, characterized by the absence of economic freedom, also have a "superstructure" entirely lacking in political freedoms.

Niemietz provides an apt summary of this connection: "Limitation of personal liberty are therefore inevitable, and, within the logic of the system, justifiable. Emigration restrictions are an example of this."[768] An example of the connection between the elimination of economic and political freedom was the GDR: First, economic freedom was eliminated through the nationalization of land and the means of production. As a result, there was a massive disparity between the economic performance of East and West Germany. The standard of living in the West was much higher, and so 2.8 million people fled the GDR—mainly, but not only, entrepreneurs and well-educated professionals. So the fact that the Wall was built in 1961 certainly corresponded to an economic inevitability because otherwise the system in East Germany would have been bled dry immediately. "This is why," explains Niemietz, "the Berlin Wall was not an aberration from the 'noble' ideal of socialism, but a logical correlate of a planned economy."[769]

The elimination of economic freedom inescapably leads to an expansion of state power, since politics and bureaucracy are no longer restricted to making political decisions, but also economic ones. Whereas in capitalist countries there is an economic elite that exerts power and influence alongside the political elite, in a state-run economy there is only one elite that dominates all domains.

Of course, it is possible to dream up systems in which freedom and socialism coexist. And, at most temporarily, it may even be possible for them to coexist. Examples include the flirtations with "democratic socialism" in Britain and Sweden in the 1970s. In both systems, the state gained more and more power as taxes were hiked, while, in parallel, major economic sectors were nationalized. At some point, these countries arrived at a crossroads: The most radical supporters of "democratic socialism," for example, in the British Labour Party, demanded an ever-bigger role for government. In their view, any economic problems their countries were experiencing stemmed from the fact that there was still too much capitalism. If they had prevailed, economic decline would have been accelerated, and at some point there would have been a transition from quantity into a new quality, and democratic socialism would have evolved into the normal form of socialism, that is, a system of political repression—as happened later, for example, in Venezuela.

Fortunately, the socialists' opponents succeeded in convincing majorities in Great Britain and Sweden to vote for them, and launched capitalist reforms that pushed back the power of the state over the economy—through tax cuts, privatizations and deregulation.

PART C

POPULAR PERCEPTIONS OF CAPITALISM

12

WHAT PEOPLE IN THE UNITED STATES

THINK OF CAPITALISM

THE PREVIOUS 11 CHAPTERS examined the facts about capitalism and socialism. This and the next two chapters deal with opinions about capitalism. Before I present figures and graphs on how Americans feel about capitalism (followed by the results for the UK in the next chapter and for 19 other countries in Chapter 14), I would like to provide details of the items and methods used in the survey.

In the past, surveys have frequently been conducted to find out what the population of a country—or even several countries—feel about capitalism and the market economy. Often, such surveys merely asked respondents a general question about whether they think capitalism is a good economic system or not. *The Edelman Trust Barometer 2020*,[770] a survey of 28 countries, reports an average of 56 percent of respondents believe that "Capitalism as it exists today does more harm than good in the world."

In Europe, people in France agreed most strongly with this opinion (69 percent), followed by Italy (61 percent), Spain (60 percent), Germany (55 percent) and the United Kingdom (53 percent). In both the United States and Canada, 47 percent of respondents agreed with this critique of capitalism. The survey found the smallest proportions of capitalist critics in Japan (35 percent), Hong Kong (45 percent), and South Korea (46 percent). In the Edelman and similar surveys, however, only one question on capitalism was asked, which means that although we know whether people are for or against capitalism, we don't know why.

I wanted to find out more, so, together with the Allensbach Institute and Ipsos MORI, I designed an international survey of 21 countries that went into much greater detail. Even before the survey began, I suspected—based on previous surveys—that majorities in most countries would tend to be critical of capitalism. Nobody needed a new survey to confirm this.

Above all, I wanted to find out why such large numbers of people around the world reject capitalism. What negative—and, of course, positive—characteristics do people associate with the term "capitalism"? What exactly do they criticize about capitalism (and what do they find good)? How do perceptions differ in different countries? And within countries, how do people in different income and age brackets feel about capitalism? What kind of relationship do people with more left-wing and more right-wing mindsets (and, of course, among those "in the middle") have with capitalism?

The survey was conducted in June 2021 to June 2022 in a total of 21 countries. In the United States, Ipsos MORI surveyed a representative sample of 1,090 people. The survey differs from many other surveys on capitalism not only in its depth (i.e., in the level of detail of the questions asked), but also in a particular method: the hypothesis before the survey began was that some people are repelled by the word "capitalism" in particular, even though their actual views would put them more in the pro-capitalist camp. Some people have only vague and unclear associations with "capitalism," others connect the term with all of the evils of this world.

Thus, one set of questions (on economic freedom) consistently avoided the word "capitalism." Respondents were presented with a total of six statements, of which three statements favored economic freedom and a market economy and three advocated a strong role for the state. You can find the exact wording of all of the survey items in the Questionnaire on pages 371–375.

The set of questions on economic freedom included, for example, the statement: "We need a lot more state intervention in the economy, since the market fails time and again." Another, in contrast, stated: "I am for an economic system in which the state sets the rules but ideally does not interfere otherwise."

Supporting one statement or the other does not automatically make someone a pro- or anti-capitalist, but we were able to make a clear distinction between respondents who, for example, supported two or three pro-economic freedom statements while also rejecting statements in favor of more state intervention and those who were in favor of more state control and were skeptical about the free market. For each country, we calculated the average levels of support for the "pro-economic freedom" and the "pro-state" items and used these data to calculate how people in any given country feel about economic freedom.

In contrast, the term "capitalism" was used in two other sets of questions. First, we wanted to know exactly what the survey's respondents associate with the word "capitalism." The survey included a list of 10 terms, namely "prosperity," "innovation," "greed," "coldness," "progress," "corruption," "freedom," "constant pressure to achieve," "a wide range of goods," and "environmental degradation." Again, we determined the average percentage of respondents who associate positive characteristics (e.g., prosperity, progress) or negative characteristics (e.g., greed, environmental degradation) with the word "capitalism."

The most important set of questions was the third one. Each respondent was presented with a total of 18 statements about capitalism. Negative statements included, for example: "Capitalism is responsible for hunger and poverty," "Capitalism leads to growing inequality," and

"Capitalism entices people to buy products they don't need." Positive statements included, for example: "Capitalism has improved conditions for ordinary people in many countries," "Capitalism is an especially efficient economic system," and "Capitalism means that consumers determine what is offered, and not the state." Again, as with the previous sets of questions, we analyzed the data to determine the average percentage of respondents who supported these positive and negative statements.

If we combine the data for the last two sets of questions, we are able to determine what people think when the word "capitalism" is mentioned. It is interesting to compare this with the first set of questions, where the answers reveal how people feel about capitalism when the word is not mentioned. By comparing responses across the three sets of questions, we can see exactly what role the word "capitalism" plays. We can then combine the findings from each of the three sets of questions into a single coefficient, and the figures for each set of questions can also be distilled into a single coefficient to provide an overall indication of what people in any given country think of capitalism.

And that is not all: For each country, for example, we can depict precisely what male and female, younger and older, low- and high-income and less- and better-educated respondents—as well as respondents who place themselves to the right, in the center or to the left of the political spectrum—think of capitalism. We also investigated whether there is a connection between being a pro- or anti-capitalist and believing in conspiracy theories.

ATTITUDES TO ECONOMIC FREEDOM IN THE UNITED STATES

A majority of Americans are in favor of economic freedom. Respondents were presented with a total of six statements about economic freedom. Three of these statements had a clear pro-market tendency, for example: "I think private business alone should decide what products to manufacture and what prices to charge for them; the state should not be involved in that." Three statements had a clear pro-state tendency, for example: "We need a lot more state intervention in the economy, since the market fails time and again." Agreement with the three pro-market statements averaged 30 percent, while agreement with the pro-state statements averaged 18 percent (Figure 12.1).

FIGURE 12.1

UNITED STATES: SIX STATEMENTS ON
A GOOD ECONOMIC SYSTEM

Question: "Below is a list of various things that people have said they consider
to be a good economic system. Which of the statements would you say too?"

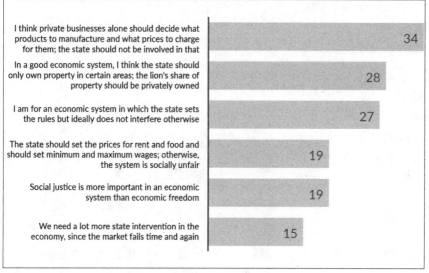

Note: All data are in percentage of respondents
Source: Ipsos MORI survey 20-091774-30

The biggest differences in the United States are between age groups. How someone feels about economic freedom in the U.S. depends more on their age than on any other sociodemographic factor (such as income, gender or education). It is interesting to note that pro-market statements attract similar levels of support across different age groups, with very little difference in approval ratings. At the same time, variations in responses to the statements about government intervention are all the greater. The younger our American respondents are, the more likely they are to support government intervention in the economy. Agreement with the three statements advocating a stronger role for the state averages 27.7 percent among those under the age of 30, but only 8.3 percent among those over the age of 60 (Figure 12.2).

FIGURE 12.2

UNITED STATES: STATEMENTS ON ECONOMIC
SYSTEMS—AVERAGES BY AGE GROUP

Question: "Below is a list of various things that people have said they consider to be a good economic system. Which of the statements would you say too?"

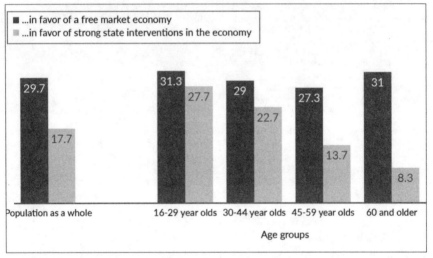

Note: All data are in percentage of respondents

Source: Ipsos MORI survey 20–091774-30

The differences are also very clear in relation to each of the individual statements: For example, 32 percent of Americans under the age of 30 believe that the state should set the prices for rent and food and minimum and maximum wages, while only a small minority of 7 percent of respondents over the age of 60 feel the same. And 23 percent of Americans under the age of 30 would like to see a lot more state intervention in the economy, compared with only 6 percent of those over the age of 60.

As expected, low-income earners (annual household incomes of less than $25,000) are less pro-market than high-income earners and are more likely to support government intervention: An average of 24 percent of low-income earners agree with the survey's pro-market statements, compared with an average of 34 percent of high-income earners (annual household incomes of more than $75,000). However, and again this is an important finding, support for pro-market statements predominates in all income groups, from low-income to middle-income to high-income earners, although the gap between pro-market and pro-state statements is much smaller among low-income earners (24 percent to 20.3 percent) than among high-income earners (34 percent to 16.3 percent), as Figure 12.3 confirms.

FIGURE 12.3

USA: STATEMENTS ON ECONOMIC
SYSTEMS—AVERAGES BY INCOME

Question: "Below is a list of various things that people have said they consider
to be a good economic system. Which of the statements would you say too?"

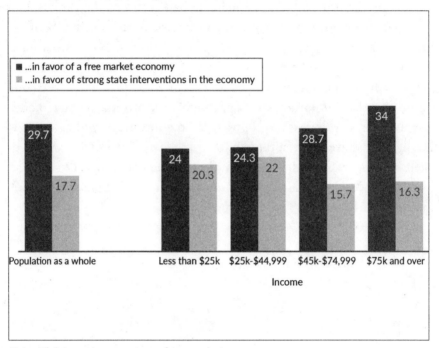

Note: All data are in percentage of respondents
Source: Ipsos MORI survey 20-091774-30

Americans with far left-wing political views are most strongly in favor
of government intervention in the economy (29.7 percent on average).
It is interesting to note, however, that in contrast to the other surveyed
countries, even among Americans who describe themselves as moderately left-wing, an average of 25.3 percent register their support for pro-
market statements and 24.0 percent support pro-state statements. The
ratio of support for a free market economy and support for government

intervention is thus finely balanced among left-wing moderates in the United States. Here, especially in relation to other countries, there is a clear cultural imprint in favor of a market economy, which is even recognizable among those on the (moderate) left of the political spectrum.

Among Americans who define themselves as political centrists, pro-market statements clearly dominate (28.7 percent versus 16.3 percent). The difference is even more pronounced among right-wing Americans, who are three times as likely to agree with pro-market statements than pro-state statements. On this point, it is striking that among respondents in many other countries support for economic freedom is higher among moderately right-wing respondents than is the case for far right-wing respondents. The situation is different in the United States: the further to the right respondents rank themselves, the stronger their approval of economic freedom and their skepticism toward the state (Figure 12.4).

FIGURE 12.4

USA: STATEMENTS ON ECONOMIC SYSTEMS—
AVERAGES BY POLITICAL AFFILIATION

Question: "Below is a list of various things that people have said they consider
to be a good economic system. Which of the statements would you say too?"

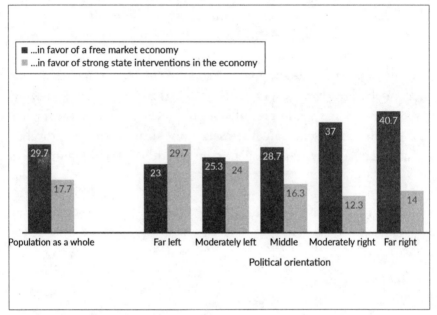

Note: All data are in percentage of respondents
Source: Ipsos MORI survey 20-091774-30

WHAT DO AMERICANS ASSOCIATE WITH CAPITALISM?

Americans are more likely to associate the term "capitalism" with positive than negative things. On average, 68 percent of American respondents selected positive associations, such as "prosperity" and "freedom."
In contrast, negative terms such as, for example, "greed" or "corruption"
were chosen by an average of 62 percent. However, the rather small
difference between the two figures also shows that the frequency with
which Americans associate positive and negative terms with capitalism
differs only slightly, as can be seen from Figure 12.5.

FIGURE 12.5

USA: ASSOCIATIONS WITH CAPITALISM

Question: "Please now think about the word capitalism. For each of the following statements, select whether that is something you associate with capitalism."

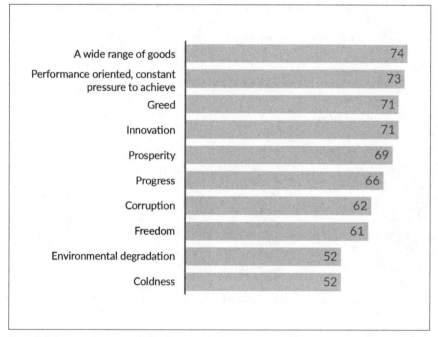

Note: All data are in percentage of respondents
Source: Ipsos MORI survey 20-091774-30

And what role does income play? While there are differences in attitudes toward capitalism among income groups, they are much smaller than the differences among age groups. For individuals in households earning less than $45,000 per year, negative associations only slightly outweigh positive associations, and the ratio is nearly even. For persons in households earning more than $45,000, positive associations outweigh the negative and responses to our survey items are different to those given by individuals earning less than $45,000, although these differences are smaller than might be expected (Figure 12.6). To put it simply, not every American on a lower income is opposed to capitalism, and not every American on a higher income is in favor of capitalism.

FIGURE 12.6

USA: ASSOCIATIONS WITH CAPITALISM—ANALYSIS BY INCOME

Question: "Please now think about the word capitalism. For each of the following statements, select whether that is something you associate with capitalism."

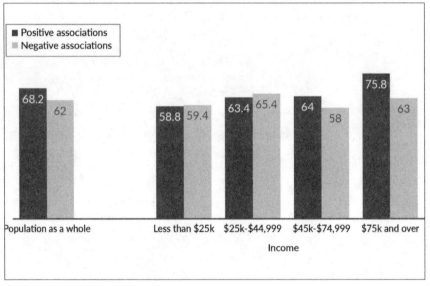

Note: All data are in percentage of respondents
Source: Ipsos MORI survey 20–091774–30

Respondents were asked to indicate their political orientation by placing themselves on a left-right scale. As might be expected, negative associations with capitalism are strongest among respondents on the left of the political spectrum. For example, most left-leaning Americans associate capitalism with environmental degradation, while a majority of right-leaning Americans do not. Among Americans who place themselves on the far left, 47 percent associate capitalism with "freedom," compared with 80 and 81 percent, respectively, of Americans who are moderate or far right.

Dividing the average percentage of positive associations by the average percentage of negative associations yields a coefficient of 0.75 for respondents with far left-wing attitudes (the lower the number, the more negative the attitude toward capitalism). The coefficient for moderate leftists is 1.01, and for self-described centrists, the coefficient is 0.99. The further to the right our American respondents classify themselves, the more positive their associations with capitalism: moderately right respondents have a coefficient of 1.48, while far rightists have a coefficient as high as 1.74 (Figure 12.7).

FIGURE 12.7

USA: THE ASSOCIATION COEFFICIENT—
ANALYSIS BY POLITICAL ORIENTATION

Question: "Please now think about the word capitalism. For each of the following statements, select whether that is something you associate with capitalism."

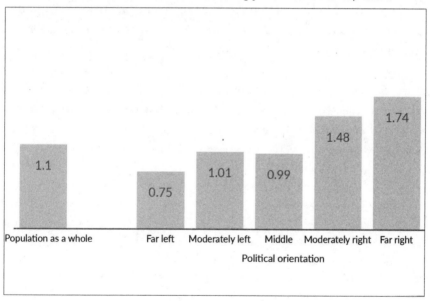

Note: The lower the coefficient, the stronger the anti-capitalist attitude
Source: Ipsos MORI survey 20-091774-30

EIGHTEEN POSITIVE AND NEGATIVE
STATEMENTS ABOUT CAPITALISM

Respondents were presented with a total of 18 statements about capitalism, 10 of which were negative and 8 of which were positive. The level of agreement with the positive statements (averaging 28 percent) is slightly higher than the level of agreement with the negative statements (averaging 25 percent). Dividing the percentage for the positive statements by the percentage for the negative statements gives us a coefficient of 1.12.

The most frequently selected negative statements about capitalism included, for example, that capitalism is determined by the rich who set the political agenda. Many Americans also blame capitalism for promoting selfishness and greed. In contrast, other negative statements, such as that capitalism leads to hunger and poverty, to economic and financial crises, to wars or even to fascism, were cited far less frequently (Figure 12.8).

The pro-capitalism statement that received the strongest support (33 percent) is also the one that is the most defensive among the available options: "Capitalism may not be ideal, but it is still better than all other economic systems." About one-third of respondents are also of the opinion that capitalism encourages people to do their best, that capitalism means economic freedom and that consumers determine what is offered, and not the state (Figure 12.9).

FIGURE 12.8

USA: STATEMENTS ABOUT CAPITALISM—10
NEGATIVE STATEMENTS

Question: "Which of the following statements about capitalism, if any, would you agree with?"

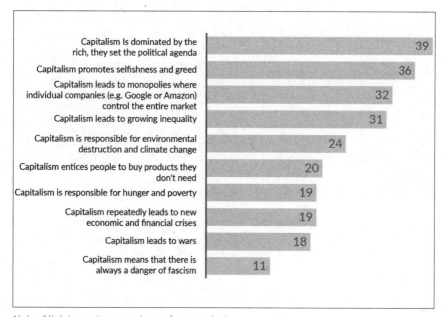

Note: All data are in percentage of respondents

Source: Ipsos MORI survey 20-091774-30

FIGURE 12.9

USA: STATEMENTS ABOUT CAPITALISM—8 POSITIVE STATEMENTS

**Question: "Which of the following statements about
capitalism, if any, would you agree with?"**

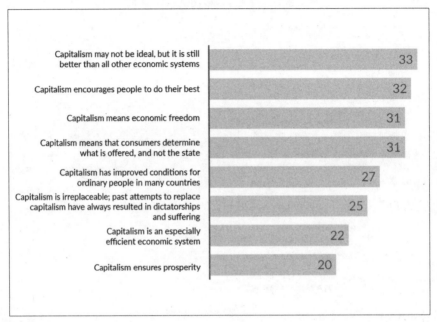

Note: All data are in percentage of respondents
Source: Ipsos MORI survey 20–091774–30

According to our data, younger Americans under the age of 30 are the most critical of capitalism, with an attitude coefficient of 0.63 (27.5 percent negative and 17.3 percent positive statements). Again, for these 18 statements, it is clear that as the age of our respondents increases, the more positive they feel about capitalism. Capitalism has the most supporters among those over the age of 60, with a coefficient of 1.77 (38.6 percent positive and 21.8 percent negative statements, as depicted in Figures 12.10 and 12.11). For example, only 21 percent of those under the age of 30 agree that capitalism may not be ideal, but it is still better than all other economic systems. Of those over the age of 60, this is a view held by 51 percent. Conversely, 26 percent of Americans under the age of 30 blame capitalism for hunger and poverty, compared with only 12 percent of those over the age of 60.

FIGURE 12.10

USA: 18 STATEMENTS ABOUT CAPITALISM—
AVERAGES BY AGE GROUP

Question:"Which of the following statements about capitalism, if any, would you agree with?"

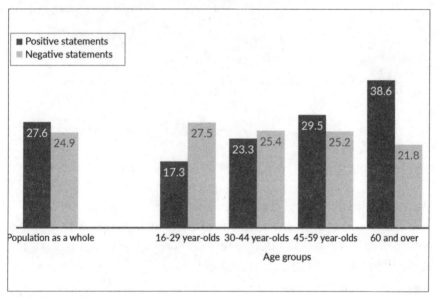

Note: All data are in percentage of respondents
Source: Ipsos MORI survey 20-091774-30

FIGURE 12.11

USA: 18 STATEMENTS ABOUT CAPITALISM—
AGE-GROUP COEFFICIENT

Question: "Which of the following statements about
capitalism, if any, would you agree with?"

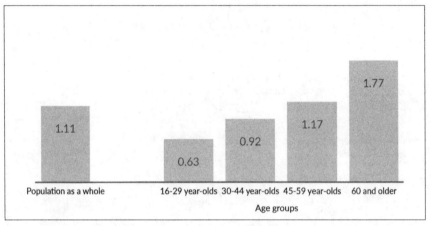

Note: The lower the coefficient, the stronger the anti-capitalist attitude
Source: Ipsos MORI survey 20-091774-30

In terms of income groups, this set of 18 statements elicits the responses one would expect: low-income earners with net household incomes of less than $25,000 tend to be critical of capitalism with a coefficient of 0.69 (25.2 percent negative and 17.5 percent positive statements)—although their negativity is not all that pronounced. High-income earners with net household incomes of more than $75,000 are clearly pro-capitalist, with a coefficient of 1.46 (33.6 percent positive and 23 percent negative statements). For more details, please see Figures 12.12 and 12.13.

FIGURE 12.12

USA: 18 STATEMENTS ABOUT CAPITALISM—AVERAGES BY INCOME

Question: "Which of the following statements about capitalism, if any, would you agree with?"

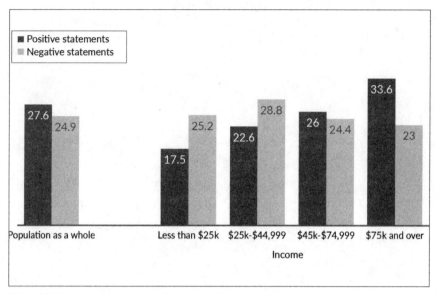

Note: All data are in percentage of respondents
Source: Ipsos MORI survey 20–091774–30

FIGURE 12.13

USA: 18 STATEMENTS ABOUT CAPITALISM—
INCOME-GROUP COEFFICIENT

Question: "Which of the following statements about
capitalism, if any, would you agree with?"

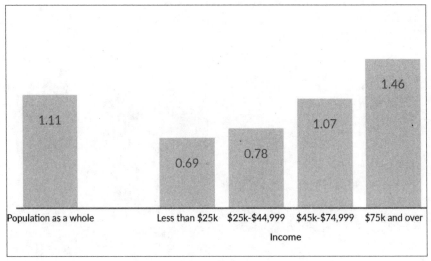

Note: The lower the coefficient, the stronger the anti-capitalist attitude
Source: Ipsos MORI survey 20-091774-30

And what picture emerges when we compare responses to these statements in terms of respondents' classifications on the left-right spectrum? The differences are particularly clear in relation to this set of 18 statements. For example, 50 percent of far-left Americans say capitalism leads to growing inequality, while only 10 percent of those on the far right say the same. And 63 percent of far-left Americans believe that capitalism is dominated by the rich; they set the political agenda. Among far-right Americans, only 21 percent share this opinion (Figure 12.14).

FIGURE 12.14

**USA: 18 STATEMENTS ABOUT CAPITALISM—
THE LARGEST DIFFERENCES BETWEEN FAR-
LEFT AND FAR-RIGHT RESPONDENTS**

Question: "Which of the following statements about
capitalism, if any, would you agree with?"

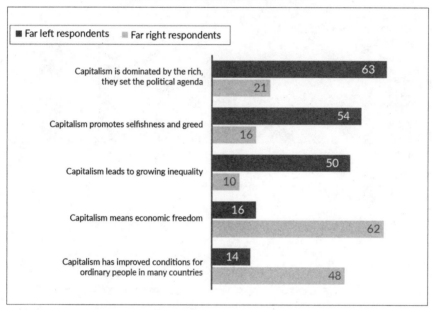

Note: All data are in percentage of respondents
Source: Ipsos MORI survey 20–091774-30

All in all, Americans on the far left of the political spectrum are the strongest anti-capitalists with a coefficient of 0.33, followed by those on the moderate left with 0.60. For this set of questions, approval and disapproval of capitalism are more or less evenly balanced among those who place themselves in the middle of the political spectrum (0.95). The pro-capitalist groups are moderately right respondents (2.87) and far-right respondents, who registered a very high coefficient of 4.0. See Figure 12.16 for more details.

FIGURE 12.15

USA: 18 STATEMENTS ABOUT CAPITALISM—
AVERAGES BY POLITICAL ORIENTATION

Question: "Which of the following statements about capitalism, if any, would you agree with?"

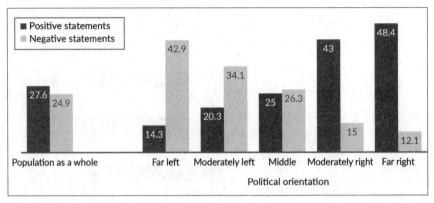

Note: All data are in percentage of respondents
Source: Ipsos MORI survey 20-091774-30

FIGURE 12.16

USA: 18 STATEMENTS ABOUT CAPITALISM—
COEFFICIENT BY POLITICAL ORIENTATION

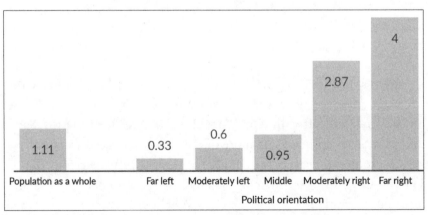

Note: The lower the coefficient, the stronger the anti-capitalist attitude
Source: Ipsos MORI survey 20-091774-30

GENDER AND EDUCATION

Women in the United States value economic freedom slightly less than men, although the differences are far less pronounced than those for age and political orientation (Figure 12.17).

FIGURE 12.17

USA: ECONOMIC FREEDOM COEFFICIENT—ANALYSIS BY GENDER

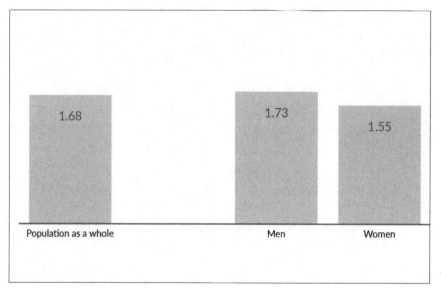

Note: The lower the coefficient, the stronger the anti-capitalist attitude

Source: Ipsos MORI survey 20–091774–30

Analyzing the responses to the capitalism association test in combination with the 18 positive and negative statements on capitalism confirms that women in the United States are slightly less pro-capitalist than men (Figure 12.18).

FIGURE 12.18

USA: OVERALL COEFFICIENT ON ATTITUDES TOWARD CAPITALISM—ANALYSIS BY GENDER

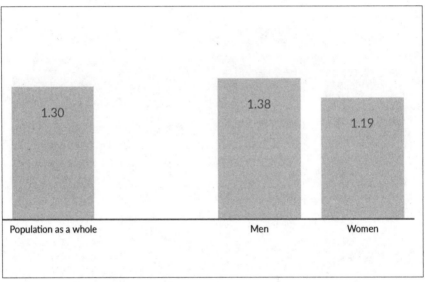

1.30	1.38	1.19
Population as a whole	Men	Women

Note: The lower the coefficient, the stronger the anti-capitalist attitude
Source: Ipsos MORI survey 20–091774–30

In Figure 12.19, you can see which statements about capitalism elicited different responses from male and female respondents:

FIGURE 12.19

USA: 18 STATEMENTS ABOUT CAPITALISM—THE
GREATEST DIFFERENCES BY GENDER

Question: "Which of the following statements about
capitalism, if any, would you agree with?"

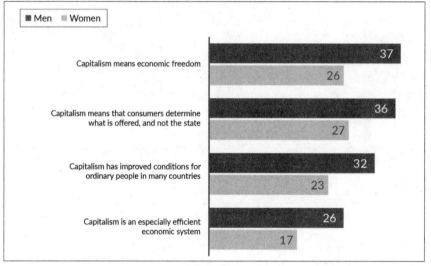

Note: All data are in percentage of respondents
Source: Ipsos MORI survey 20–091774–30

And what about differences based on education? At all levels of education, approval of capitalism dominates. Support for capitalism is admittedly somewhat less pronounced among lower-educated respondents (maximum high school degree, no college), with a coefficient of 1.12, than is the case among higher-educated respondents (1.37). But the differences are not all that great, which is probably related to the fact that there are a significantly greater number of higher-educated respondents in the younger age group who tend to be more critical of capitalism than there are among the pro-capitalist 60-plus age group (Figure 12.20).

FIGURE 12.20

USA: OVERALL COEFFICIENT ON ATTITUDES TOWARD CAPITALISM—ANALYSIS BY EDUCATION

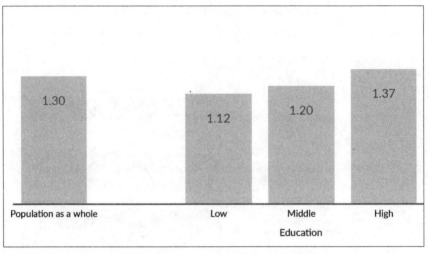

Note: The lower the coefficient, the stronger the anti-capitalist attitude
Source: Ipsos MORI survey 20–091774–30

CONSPIRACY THEORIES AND ATTITUDES TOWARD CAPITALISM

Conspiracy theorists are people who believe that an event or situation—such as a crisis or pandemic—is the result of a secret plan hatched by powerful people. "A conspiracy theory," one definition reads, "is an assumption that individuals or a group of individuals perceived to be powerful are influencing major events in the world, purposefully harming the population while keeping them in the dark about their true goals."[771]

The bogeymen of right-wing conspiracy theorists are super-rich individuals, such as George Soros and the Rothschild family; the bogeymen of left-wing conspiracy theorists are super-rich people, such as the Koch brothers or shadowy, anonymous "lobbyists," who are believed to be pulling the strings behind political developments. Often, however, far-right and far-left conspiracy theorists target the same figures—such as Bill Gates, who attracted massive hostility during the coronavirus crisis. During the 2008 Global Financial Crisis, "greedy bankers" and "financial speculators" were singled out for blame.

In a large-scale empirical study, the social psychologists Roland Imhoff and Martin Bruder found: "Conspiracy mentality can be understood as a generalized political attitude, distinct from established political attitude like right-wing authoritarianism and social dominance orientation."[772]

Conspiracy theorists have strong resentments against powerful social groups, or groups that they perceive to be powerful. The researchers' analysis showed a clear correlation between conspiracy thinking and statements such as:

- "Multinational corporations are to be blamed for most of the world's problems."

- "As a result of their greed, CEOs have lost all their morals."

- "Everybody in the world would be better off if there were fewer international financial speculators."[773]

Conspiracy mentality, as you can see from these statements, is closely related to scapegoating. In an international study in eleven countries that I conducted as part of the project *The Rich in Public Opinion*, it was clear that those with a strong inclination to social envy are far more likely than non-enviers to agree with the statement: "Super-rich people who want more and more power are to blame for many problems in the world, for example, financial crises or humanitarian crises."[774]

Among the questions used in the survey for this book, Ipsos MORI presented all respondents with these two items:

- "If someone were to say: 'In reality, politicians don't decide anything. They are puppets controlled by powerful forces in the background.' Would you agree with that or would you disagree?"

- "And what do you think about the statement: 'A lot of things in politics can only be properly understood if you know that there is a larger plan behind them, something that most people, however, do not know.' Would you agree with that or would you disagree?"

Individuals who agreed with both statements were identified as having a conspiracy mentality.

A factor analysis enabled us to determine which Americans were more pro- or anti-capitalist. We then calculated the average levels of agreement and disagreement of pro- and anti-capitalists with the two conspiracy statements. It turned out that in the United States, decisively anti-capitalist respondents agree somewhat more strongly with the statements quoted above than their decisively pro-capitalist compatriots. Dividing the percentages of Americans who agree with the two statements yields a coefficient of 2.3 for decisively pro-capitalist Americans and a slightly higher coefficient of 2.8 for decisively anti-capitalist Americans (Figure 12.21).

FIGURE 12.21

USA: ANTI-CAPITALIST ATTITUDES AND THE TENDENCY
TO BELIEVE IN CONSPIRACY THEORIES

Conspiracy theory coefficient: Average percentage of respondents
agreeing with the following two statements

"In reality, politicians don't decide anything. They are puppets
controlled by powerful forces in the background"

and

"A lot of things in politics can only be properly understood if you know that there
is a larger plan behind them, something that most people, however, do not know."

divided by the average percentage of respondents disagreeing with both statements.

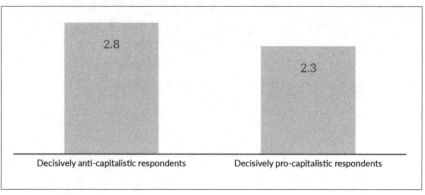

Source: Ipsos MORI survey 20-091774-30

However, the difference between pro- and anti-capitalists in this
respect is significantly smaller in the United States than in all the other
countries we studied—more on this in Chapter 14. Presumably, in
the United States—especially among Trump supporters—there is an
overlap between people who have pro-capitalist attitudes on the one
hand and adhere to conspiracy theories on the other. However, even in
the United States, anti-capitalists have a higher affinity for conspiracy
theories than pro-capitalists.

SUMMARY

The sheer volume of data can be confusing, so it makes sense to summarize everything in a handful of figures, in which the total of 34 responses to the three sets of questions (6 statements on economic freedom, 10 associations with capitalism, 18 statements on capitalism) are condensed. We have calculated coefficients for the three different sets of questions, which show in each case whether pro- or anti-capitalist statements elicit greater agreement.

Overall, we find that positive opinions on capitalism and economic freedom dominate among Americans with a coefficient of 1.30. However, levels of approval are significantly higher if the word "capitalism" is omitted and replaced with a simple description of what capitalism means. Where "capitalism" is not used, the coefficient increases to 1.68—that is, a clear endorsement of economic freedom. Apparently, the word "capitalism" also has a negative connotation in the United States and, as a result, approval is lower when "capitalism" is used—as was the case in sets 2 and 3 of our questions (Figure 12.22).

FIGURE 12.22
USA: COEFFICIENT ON ATTITUDES TOWARD
CAPITALISM—OVERVIEW

Coefficient A:

Average of statements in favor of a liberal economic system divided
by the average of statements in favor of a government-controlled
economic system (without using the term "capitalism").

Coefficient B:

Average of positive associations with the term "capitalism" divided
by the average of negative associations with the term.

Coefficient C:

Average of positive statements about capitalism divided by
the average of negative statements about capitalism.

Combined coefficient for attitudes to capitalism: (A + B + C): 3

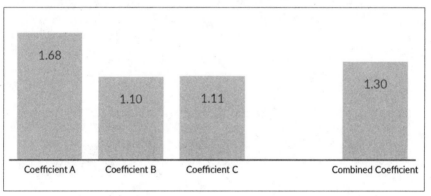

Note: The lower the coefficient, the stronger the anti-capitalist attitude
Source: Ipsos MORI survey 20–091774–30

On the left-right spectrum, the correlation is clear: the more left-wing, the more critical our respondents are of capitalism; the more right-wing, the more pro-capitalist. Americans will not be surprised by this, but this correlation, as we will see in Chapter 14, is not the same in all countries. In many countries, approval of capitalism is highest among the moderate right and declines somewhat as respondents move further to the right.

In the United States overall (i.e., based on a combined analysis of responses to all three sets of questions), far left-wing respondents have a coefficient of 0.63, while moderate left-wingers have a coefficient of 0.89. Thus, among left-wing Americans, whether moderate or on the far left, anti-capitalist attitudes dominate. Respondents who place themselves in the middle of the political spectrum have a coefficient of 1.23, which means they are pro-capitalist. Moderate right-wingers have a coefficient of 2.45, and far right-wing respondents have a coefficient of 2.88 (Figure 12.23)—Americans who class themselves as right-wing are thus strong supporters of capitalism.

FIGURE 12.23

USA: COMBINED COEFFICIENT FOR ATTITUDES TO
CAPITALISM—ANALYSIS BY POLITICAL ORIENTATION

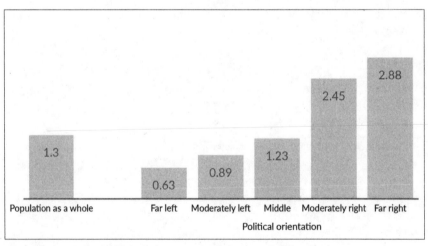

Note: The lower the coefficient, the stronger the anti-capitalist attitude
Source: Ipsos MORI survey 20–091774–30

In addition to political orientation, the age of respondents in the United States plays a crucial role in determining whether they approve or disapprove of capitalism. A combined analysis of all the responses to the three sets of questions reveals that anti-capitalist attitudes predominate among respondents under the age of 30 (0.90). In the age group between 30 and 44, pro- and anti-capitalist attitudes pretty much balance each other out (1.08). Among Americans between the ages of 45 and 59, pro-capitalist attitudes clearly dominate (1.43), and Americans over the age of 60 can be described as outspoken fans of capitalism (2.27). See Figure 12.24 for more details.

FIGURE 12.24

USA: COMBINED COEFFICIENT FOR ATTITUDES
TO CAPITALISM—ANALYSIS BY AGE GROUP

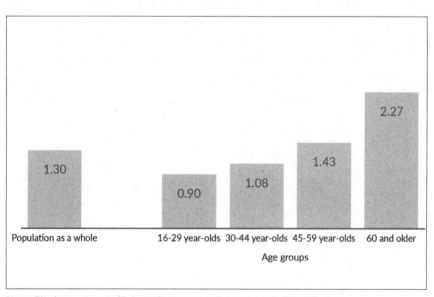

Note: The lower the coefficient, the stronger the anti-capitalist attitude

Source: Ipsos MORI survey 20–091774–30

However, the data also show that this is partly related to the use of the term "capitalism" itself. When respondents are asked substantive questions to determine their attitudes toward economic freedom and whether they are more in favor of a market economy or of strong government intervention in the economy, there is greater approval for the market economy than for strong state intervention in all age groups (even among those under the age of 30).

Approval of capitalism is 51 percent higher in the United States when the word "capitalism" is omitted from the survey items. This is evidenced by the difference between the coefficient for economic freedom (1.68) and the coefficient for those items that included the word "capitalism" (1.11), a difference of 0.57 points, which means that support for the market economy is 51 percent higher when it is described without using the word "capitalism," as depicted in Figure 12.25.

FIGURE 12.25

USA: THE EFFECT OF USING THE WORD "CAPITALISM"

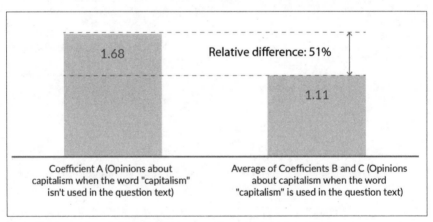

Note: The lower the coefficient, the stronger the anti-capitalist attitude
Source: Ipsos MORI survey 20-091774-30

In the following two chapters, I will present our findings for the surveys in Great Britain and the 19 other surveyed countries.

13

WHAT PEOPLE IN GREAT BRITAIN

THINK OF CAPITALISM

IPSOS MORI SURVEYED a total of 1,096 Britons between the ages of 16 and 75 between July 30 and August 9, 2021, to find out how they feel about capitalism.

ATTITUDES TO ECONOMIC FREEDOM IN GREAT BRITAIN
Unlike in the United States, our British respondents have an ambivalent attitude toward economic freedom. In total, respondents were presented with six statements on economic freedom. Three of these statements had a clear pro-market tendency, for example: "I think private business alone should decide what products to manufacture and what prices to charge for them; the state should not be involved in that." Three statements had a clear pro-government intervention tendency, for example: "We need a lot more state intervention in the economy, since the market fails time and again." Agreement with the three pro-market statements averaged

17.3 percent, while agreement with the pro-government intervention statements averaged 19.7 percent (Figure 13.1).

FIGURE 13.1

GB: SIX STATEMENTS ON A GOOD ECONOMIC SYSTEM

Question: "Below is a list of various things that people have said they consider to be a good economic system. Which of the statements would you say too?"

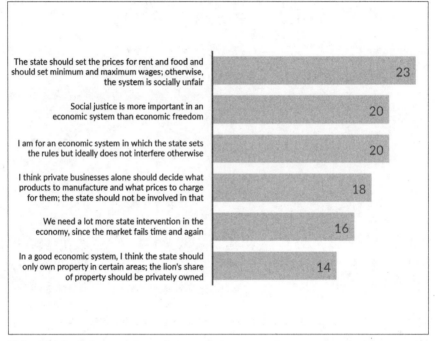

The state should set the prices for rent and food and should set minimum and maximum wages; otherwise, the system is socially unfair — 23

Social justice is more important in an economic system than economic freedom — 20

I am for an economic system in which the state sets the rules but ideally does not interfere otherwise — 20

I think private businesses alone should decide what products to manufacture and what prices to charge for them; the state should not be involved in that — 18

We need a lot more state intervention in the economy, since the market fails time and again — 16

In a good economic system, I think the state should only own property in certain areas; the lion's share of property should be privately owned — 14

Note: All data are in percentage of respondents
Source: Ipsos MORI survey 20–091774–30

In the United States, we saw that there are significant differences between age groups and that older Americans are much more positive about economic freedom than their younger compatriots. In Great Britain, there is little difference: Agreement with the three statements advocating a stronger role for government averages 22.3 percent among those under the age of 30 and 17.3 percent among those over the age of 60; agreement with pro-market statements is 19.7 percent among Britons under the age of 30 and 16 percent among Britons over the age of 60 (Figure 13.2).

FIGURE 13.2

GB: SIX STATEMENTS ON A GOOD ECONOMIC SYSTEM—AVERAGES BY AGE GROUP

Question: "Below is a list of various things that people have said they consider to be a good economic system. Which of the statements would you say too?"

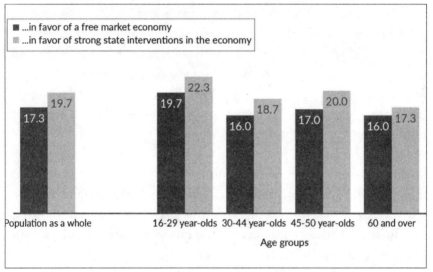

Note: All data are in percentage of respondents
Source: Ipsos MORI survey 20-091774-30

Between age groups, we also see differences in relation to the individual issues raised by the six statements. For example, 30 percent of Britons under the age of 30 think the state should set the prices for rent and food and should set minimum and maximum wages, while only 15 percent of those over the age of 60 agree with such demands. On the other hand, 17 percent of younger Britons say that social justice is more important in an economic system than economic freedom, in contrast to 26 percent of those over the age of 60.

So, in terms of their responses to these six statements about economic freedom, younger and older Britons diverge, although there is no clear tendency—unlike in the United States—for younger people to be more pronounced anti-capitalists than their older compatriots. This can also be seen from the coefficient for pro-market and pro-government intervention statements: 0.88 for Britons under the age of 30 and 0.92 for Britons over the age of 60. Thus, there are hardly any differences between younger and older Britons with regard to their position on economic freedom—unlike in the United States.

As might be expected, low-income earners (household incomes of less than GBP 20,000 per year) are somewhat less pro-market than high-income earners and are somewhat more likely to support government intervention: An average of 15 percent of low-income earners endorse pro-market statements, compared with an average of 20.7 percent of high-income earners (household incomes of more than GBP 55,000 per year) who endorse pro-market statements. And 22 percent of low-income earners favor more government intervention, compared with 19.7 percent of high-income earners. Nevertheless, the differences are not very large. We will see this confirmed later by other questions. In Britain, the differences between income groups in their attitudes toward capitalism are not as great as one might expect.

FIGURE 13.3

GB: SIX STATEMENTS ON A GOOD ECONOMIC
SYSTEM—AVERAGES BY INCOME

Question: "Below is a list of various things that people have said they consider
to be a good economic system. Which of the statements would you say too?"

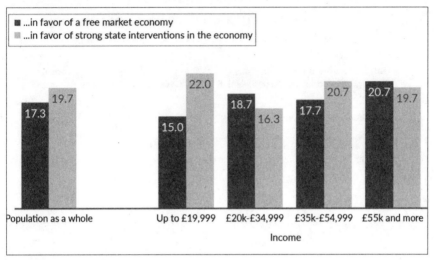

Note: All data are in percentage of respondents
Source: Ipsos MORI survey 20-091774-30

Britons with pronounced left-wing political views are most in favor
of state intervention in the economy (37 percent on average). Only 13
percent of far left-wing Britons support free-market statements. Even
among moderately left-wing Britons, support for state intervention (26.7
percent) is greater than support for a market economy (18.7 percent).
Among Britons who define themselves as political centrists, support for
pro-state and pro-market statements is balanced. In the United States,
the further to the right an American placed themselves on the political
spectrum, the more strongly they supported economic freedom. This is
not the case in Great Britain. Among British respondents, as is the case
in most of our other surveyed countries, the following pattern emerges:

The strongest support for the free-market economy is found in the moderate right spectrum and, while Britons even further to the right are also clearly pro-market, they are not as pro-market as moderate-right Britons (Figure 13.4).

FIGURE 13.4

GB: SIX STATEMENTS ON A GOOD ECONOMIC
SYSTEM—ANALYSIS BY POLITICAL ORIENTATION

Question: "Below is a list of various things that people have said they consider to be a good economic system. Which of the statements would you say too?"

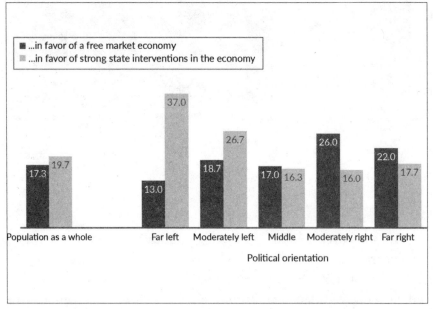

Note: All data are in percentage of respondents
Source: Ipsos MORI survey 20-091774-30

WHAT DO THE BRITISH ASSOCIATE WITH CAPITALISM?

People in Britain tend to associate the term "capitalism" with negative rather than positive things. All of our British respondents were presented with 10 items—five positive and five negative—and asked which they associated with the word "capitalism." An average of 53 percent selected the 5 positive associations. In contrast, negative terms were chosen by an average of 65 percent (Figure 13.5).

FIGURE 13.5

GB: ASSOCIATIONS WITH CAPITALISM

Question: "Please now think about the word 'capitalism.' For each of the following statements, select whether that is something you associate with capitalism."

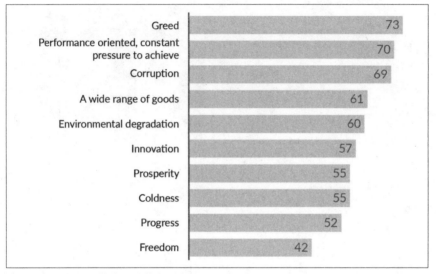

Note: All data are in percentage of respondents
Source: Ipsos MORI survey 20-091774-30

And what role does income play in this association test? Here, too, what we already observed from responses to the questions on economic freedom also holds true: Differences in attitudes toward capitalism between income groups do exist, but they are not as pronounced as one might have expected.

FIGURE 13.6

GB: ASSOCIATION WITH CAPITALISM—ANALYSIS BY INCOME

Question: "Please now think about the word 'capitalism.' For each of the following statements, select whether that is something you associate with capitalism."

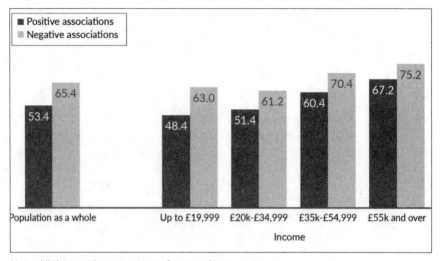

Note: All data are in percentage of respondents
Source: Ipsos MORI survey 20-091774-30

Respondents were asked to rank themselves on a left-right scale. As expected, negative associations with capitalism are strongest on the left. For example, 86 percent of far left-wing Britons associate capitalism with environmental degradation, compared with 56 percent of moderate right-wing Britons. Among far-left Britons, only 33 percent associate capitalism with "freedom," compared with 56 percent of moderate-right Britons. On the far left, 92 percent of Britons think of corruption when they think of capitalism, compared with 56 percent of Britons who are moderately right. Dividing the average percentage of positive associations by the average percentage of negative associations yields a coefficient of 0.58 for respondents with a far left-wing attitude (the lower the number, the more negative the attitude toward capitalism). The coefficient for moderate left-wingers is 0.82, and for those who classify themselves in the political center, the coefficient is 0.84. This means that negative associations with the word "capitalism" predominate not only among left-wing Britons, but also among those in the center. Among moderately right-wing Britons, the coefficient is 1.01, and among those who place themselves on the far right of the political spectrum it is 0.98. In other words, unlike in the United States, in Great Britain, we do not see a clearly pro-capitalist orientation on the right—positive and negative associations with capitalism balance each other out among both the moderate and the far right (Figure 13.7).

FIGURE 13.7

GB: THE ASSOCIATION COEFFICIENT— ANALYSIS BY POLITICAL ORIENTATION

Question: "Please now think about the word 'capitalism.' For each of the following statements, select whether that is something you associate with capitalism."

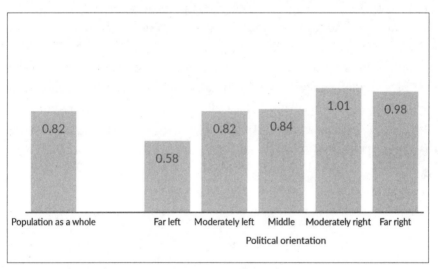

Note: The lower the coefficient, the stronger the anti-capitalist attitude

Source: Ipsos MORI survey 20–091774–30

18 POSITIVE AND NEGATIVE STATEMENTS ABOUT CAPITALISM

Respondents were presented with a total of 18 statements about capitalism, 10 of which were negative and 8 of which were positive. Agreement with the positive statements about capitalism (averaging 14 percent) is much lower than agreement with the negative statements (averaging 29 percent). Dividing the percentage for the positive statements by the percentage for the negative statements gives us a coefficient of 0.49. This is remarkable, since the 18 statements (you can find their exact wording in the Questionnaire on pages 371–375) covered a wide range of topics. In Great Britain, support for the negative statements about capitalism clearly dominates.

The most frequently selected negative statements about capitalism included, for example, that capitalism is dominated by the rich; they set the political agenda. Many Britons also blame capitalism for promoting selfishness and greed (Figure 13.8).

The pro-capitalism statement, which elicited the strongest support (albeit only 20 percent!), is also the most defensive: Capitalism may not be ideal, but it is still better than all other economic systems. Even the statement "capitalism has improved conditions for ordinary people in many countries" received only 14 percent support. The British should know better from their own history—and a look at global developments over the past 40 years shows that this statement is actually indisputable. Nevertheless, it is only supported by a minority of 14 percent (Figure 13.9).

FIGURE 13.8

GB: STATEMENTS ABOUT CAPITALISM—10 NEGATIVE STATEMENTS

Question: "Which of the following statements about
capitalism, if any, would you agree with?"

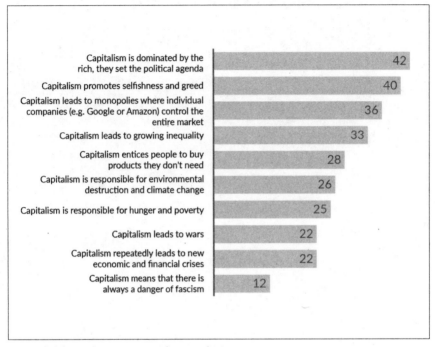

Note: All data are in percentage of respondents
Source: Ipsos MORI survey 20-091774-30

FIGURE 13.9

GB: STATEMENTS ABOUT CAPITALISM—8 POSITIVE STATEMENTS

Question: "Which of the following statements about
capitalism, if any, would you agree with?"

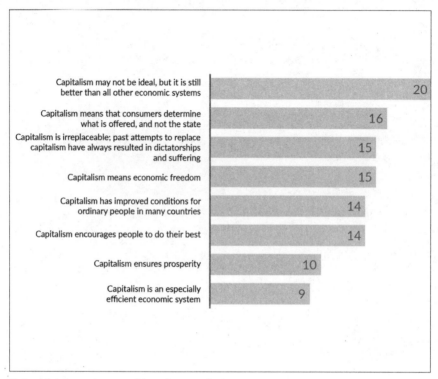

Note: All data are in percentage of respondents
Source: Ipsos MORI survey 20-091774-30

Younger Britons under the age of 30 are indisputably anti-capitalist
with a coefficient of 0.59 (18.7 percent negative and 11.1 percent positive
statements), while among Britons over the age of 60, anti-capitalism is
even more pronounced (0.45). Thus, 24 percent of Britons under the age
of 30 say that capitalism is dominated by the rich, they set the political
agenda, while 51 percent of those over the age of 60 share the same view.

FIGURE 13.10

GB: 18 STATEMENTS ABOUT CAPITALISM—
AVERAGES BY AGE GROUP

Question: "Which of the following statements about capitalism, if any, would you agree with?"

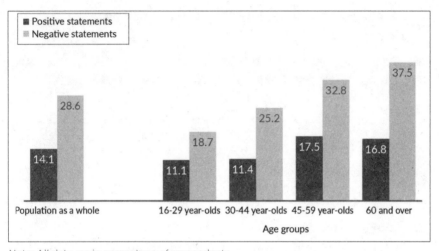

Note: All data are in percentage of respondents
Source: Ipsos MORI survey 20–091774–30

FIGURE 13.11

GB: 18 STATEMENTS ABOUT CAPITALISM—
AGE-GROUP COEFFICIENT

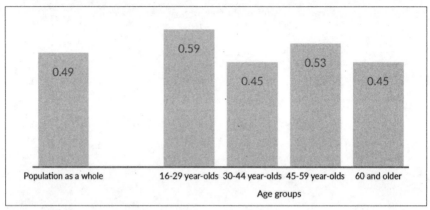

Note: The lower the coefficient, the stronger the anti-capitalist attitude
Source: Ipsos MORI survey 20-091774-30

In terms of income groups, this set of 18 questions again elicits similar responses to those we have already seen to previous questions: In all income groups, agreement with anti-capitalist statements dominates, with somewhat more critical opinions in the lowest income group (less than GBP 20,000) (Figures 13.12 and 13.13). But this set of questions also confirms that income plays a less significant role than one might expect. It is by no means the case that higher earners are pro-capitalist—here, too, support for anti-capitalist statements dominates.

FIGURE 13.12

GB: 18 STATEMENTS ABOUT CAPITALISM—AVERAGES BY INCOME

Question: "Which of the following statements about
capitalism, if any, would you agree with?"

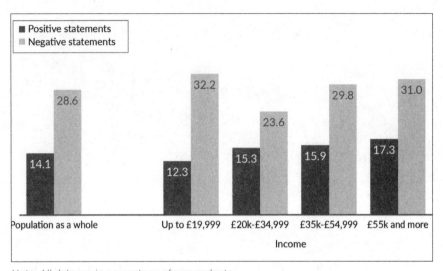

Note: All data are in percentage of respondents
Source: Ipsos MORI survey 20–091774–30

FIGURE 13.13

GB: 18 STATEMENTS ABOUT CAPITALISM—
INCOME-GROUP COEFFICIENT

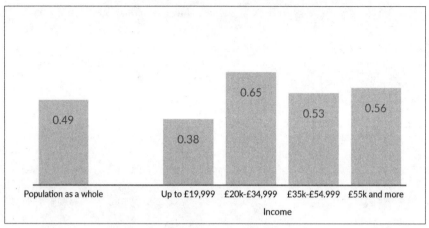

Note: The lower the coefficient, the stronger the anti-capitalist attitude
Source: Ipsos MORI survey 20-091774-30

And what picture emerges when we compare responses to these statements in terms of respondents' classifications on the left-right spectrum? Clear differences emerge in responses to this set of 18 questions: Of Britons on the far left, 63 percent say that capitalism leads to growing inequality, an opinion shared by only 22 percent of far right-wingers. And, while 69 percent of far-left Britons believe that capitalism is dominated by the rich, they set the political agenda, only 28 percent of far right-wing Britons agree (Figure 13.14).

FIGURE 13.14

GB: 18 STATEMENTS ABOUT CAPITALISM— THE LARGEST DIFFERENCES BETWEEN FAR-LEFT AND FAR-RIGHT RESPONDENTS

Question: "Which of the following statements about capitalism, if any, would you agree with?"

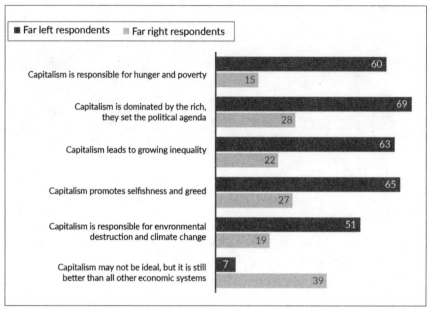

Note: All data are in percentage of respondents
Source: Ipsos MORI survey 20-091774-30

All in all, far left-wing Britons are most anti-capitalist in their responses to these 18 questions with a coefficient of 0.11. They are followed by the moderately left-wing respondents with 0.32. Even among Britons who describe themselves as political centrists, anti-capitalism clearly dominates (0.53). The most pro-capitalist respondents are moderate right-wingers with 1.34 and far right-wingers with 1.32 (remember: in the United States, the coefficient for far right-wingers was 4.0!) (Figures 13.15 and 13.16).

FIGURE 13.15

GB: 18 STATEMENTS ABOUT CAPITALISM—
AVERAGES BY POLITICAL ORIENTATION

Question: "Which of the following statements about
capitalism, if any, would you agree with?"

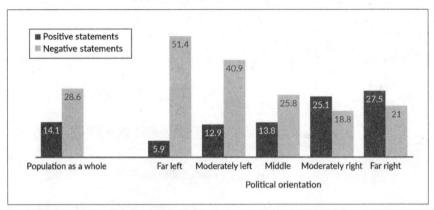

Note: All data are in percentage of respondents
Source: Ipsos MORI survey 20-091774-30

FIGURE 13.16

GB: 18 STATEMENTS ABOUT CAPITALISM—
COEFFICIENT BY POLITICAL ORIENTATION

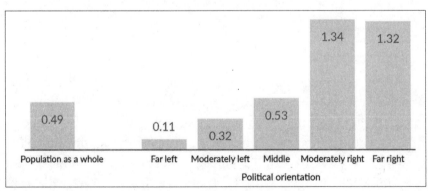

Note: The lower the coefficient, the stronger the anti-capitalist attitude
Source: Ipsos MORI survey 20-091774-30

GENDER AND EDUCATION

Our analysis reveals that women in Great Britain value economic freedom less than men. While pro-government and pro-market statements are evenly balanced among male respondents at 64 percent to 63 percent (0.98), support for pro-state statements clearly outweighs pro-market statements among women at 53 percent to 40 percent (0.75) (Figure 13.17).

FIGURE 13.17

GB: ECONOMIC FREEDOM COEFFICIENT—ANALYSIS BY GENDER

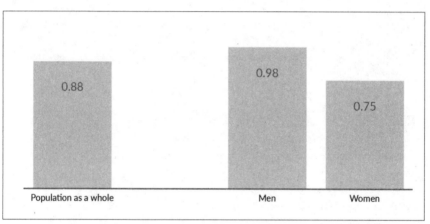

Note: The lower the coefficient, the stronger the anti-capitalist attitude

Source: Ipsos MORI survey 20-091774-30

Analyzing the responses to the capitalism association test in combination with the 18 positive and negative statements on capitalism confirms that men in Great Britain are less anti-capitalist than women (Figure 13.18).

FIGURE 13.18

GB: OVERALL COEFFICIENT ON ATTITUDES TO CAPITALISM—ANALYSIS BY GENDER

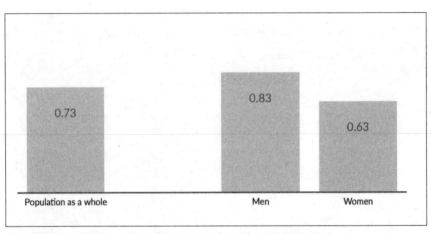

Note: The lower the coefficient, the stronger the anti-capitalist attitude

Source: Ipsos MORI survey 20–091774-30

In Figure 13.19, you can see which statements about capitalism elicited different responses from male and female respondents:

FIGURE 13.19

GB: STATEMENTS ABOUT CAPITALISM—THE GREATEST DIFFERENCES BY GENDER

Question: "Which of the following statements about capitalism, if any, would you agree with?"

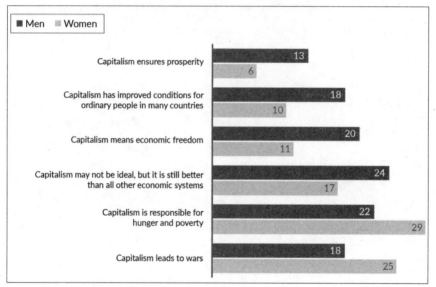

Note: All data are in percentage of respondents

Source: Ipsos MORI survey 20-091774-30

And what about differences based on education levels? In Great Britain, anti-capitalist sentiment dominates at all levels of education. Whether Britons have basic, intermediate or higher education has almost no impact on their feelings toward capitalism (Figure 13.20).

FIGURE 13.20

GB: OVERALL COEFFICIENT ON ATTITUDES TO CAPITALISM—ANALYSIS BY EDUCATION

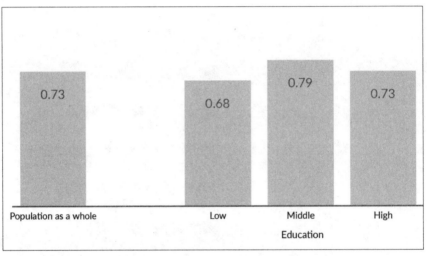

Note: The lower the coefficient, the stronger the anti-capitalist attitude
Source: Ipsos MORI survey 20-091774-30

CONSPIRACY THEORIES AND ATTITUDES TOWARD CAPITALISM

In the previous chapter on the United States, we saw that conspiracy thinkers tend to be more anti-capitalist (or anti-capitalists tend to be more conspiracy-minded).

Our survey also presented the British, for example, with the statement: "Capitalism is dominated by the rich, they set the political agenda." Among respondents with an inclination to conspiracy thinking,

51 percent agreed, compared with only 29 percent of non-conspiracy thinkers. Similarly, 45 percent of conspiracy-thinking Britons believe that capitalism promotes selfishness and greed, compared with 32 percent of Britons not inclined toward conspiracy thinking. And 42 percent of Britons who lean toward conspiracy thinking criticize that capitalism "leads to monopolies where individual companies control the entire market," while only 26 percent of Britons who reject conspiracy thinking say the same.

The same correlation applies in the other direction: respondents with a distinctly anti-capitalist worldview tend to be more conspiracy-minded than pro-capitalists: 49 percent of decisively anti-capitalistic respondents in Great Britain agree that, "In reality, politicians don't decide anything. They are puppets controlled by powerful forces in the background" and only 25 percent disagree. In other words, agreement with this statement outweighs disagreement by 24 percentage points. Among decisively pro-capitalistic respondents, on the other hand, only 26 percent describe politicians as powerless puppets controlled by powerful forces, while 41 percent disagree. Thus, disapproval outweighs approval by only 15 percentage points (Figure 13.21).

This result is all the more remarkable because conspiracy thinking is equally prevalent among right-wing and left-wing Britons: on the 0–10, left-right scale, Britons who are inclined to conspiracy thinking rank themselves on average at 4.79 and Britons who are not inclined to conspiracy thinking at 4.80. When one considers, however, that anti-capitalism is much stronger among left-wing Britons than among right-wing Britons, this confirms how strong the connection is between conspiracy thinking and attitudes toward capitalism in Great Britain.

FIGURE 13.21

GB: "POLITICIANS DON'T DECIDE ANYTHING"

Question: "Do you agree, or disagree, with the following statement:
'In reality, politicians don't decide anything. They are puppets
controlled by powerful forces in the background.'"

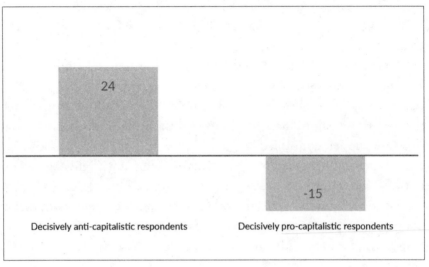

Decisively anti-capitalistic respondents   Decisively pro-capitalistic respondents

Note: Figures show approval minus disapproval in percentage points
Source: Ipsos MORI survey 20–091774–30

A factor analysis enabled us to determine which Britons were more
pro- or anti-capitalist. We then calculated the average levels of agreement
and disagreement of pro- and anti-capitalists with the two conspiracy
statements. It turned out that in Great Britain, decisively anti-capitalist
respondents agree significantly more strongly with the statements
quoted above than their decisively pro-capitalist compatriots. Dividing
the percentages who agree with these two statements results in a coefficient of 1.4 for decisively pro-capitalist Britons, but a significantly higher
coefficient of 2.8 for decisively anti-capitalist Britons (Figure 13.22).

FIGURE 13.22
GB: ·ANTI-CAPITALIST ATTITUDES AND THE TENDENCY
TO BELIEVE IN CONSPIRACY THEORIES

Conspiracy theory coefficient: Average percentage of respondents
agreeing with the following two statements

"In reality, politicians don't decide anything. They are puppets
controlled by powerful forces in the background."

and

"A lot of things in politics can only be properly understood if you know that there
is a larger plan behind them, something that most people, however, do not know."

divided by the average percentage of respondents disagreeing with both statements.

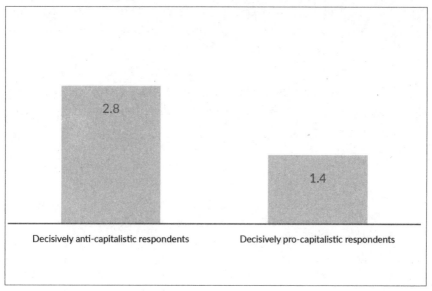

2.8	1.4
Decisively anti-capitalistic respondents	Decisively pro-capitalistic respondents

Source: Ipsos MORI survey 20-091774-30

Thus, there is a clear link between anti-capitalism and conspiracy thinking in Britain, and this link is much stronger in Great Britain than was the case in the United States.

SUMMARY
The sheer volume of data can be confusing, so it makes sense to summarize everything in a handful of figures, in which the total of 34 responses to the three sets of questions (6 statements on economic freedom, 10 associations with capitalism, 18 statements on capitalism) are condensed. We have calculated coefficients for the three different sets of questions, which show in each case whether the pro- or the anti-capitalist statements receive more agreement.

The overall result is that, with a coefficient of 0.73, negative attitudes toward capitalism and economic freedom are dominant in Great Britain.

Indeed, where the word "capitalism" is *not* used (as in the questions on economic freedom), the coefficient is 0.88; where the word "capitalism" *is* used (association test and the 18 statements on capitalism), the coefficient is 0.66 (= (0.82 + 0.49) ÷ 2) (Figure 13.23).

The link between conspiracy thinking and anti-capitalism is clear in Great Britain: Respondents with anti-capitalist attitudes tend to be significantly more inclined to conspiracy thinking than Britons with pro-capitalist attitudes.

FIGURE 13.23
GB: COEFFICIENTS ON ATTITUDES TOWARD
CAPITALISM—OVERVIEW

Coefficient A:

Average of statements in favor of a liberal economic system by the average of statements
in favor of a state-controlled economic system (without using the term "capitalism").

Coefficient B:

Average of positive associations to the term "capitalism" by the
average of negative associations to the term "capitalism."

Coefficient C:

Average of positive statements about capitalism by the
average of negative statements about capitalism.

Combined coefficient: (A + B + C): 3

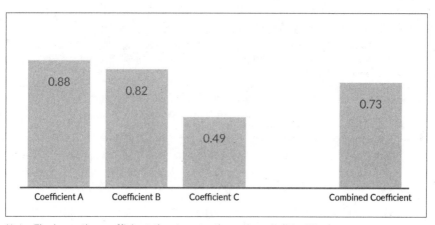

Note: The lower the coefficient, the stronger the anti-capitalist attitude
Source: Ipsos MORI survey 20-091774-30

Approval of capitalism is 33 percent higher in the UK when the word "capitalism" is omitted from the survey items. This is evidenced by the difference between the coefficient for economic freedom (0.88) and the coefficient for items that included the word "capitalism" (0.66), a difference of 0.22 points, or 33 percent, as depicted in Figure 13.24.

FIGURE 13.24

GB: THE EFFECT OF THE TERM "CAPITALISM"

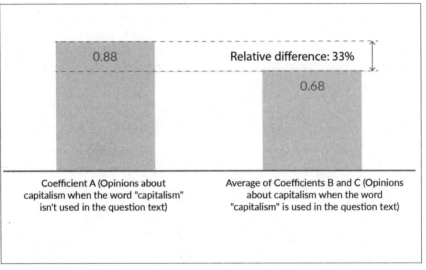

Note: The lower the coefficient, the stronger the anti-capitalist attitude
Source: Ipsos MORI survey 20–091774–30

In the left-right spectrum, the link is also clear: the further to the left a respondent places themselves, the more critical they are of capitalism. Criticism of capitalism is also pronounced among Britons who classify themselves as centrists, whereas Britons who rank themselves as moderately right wing are the most pro-capitalist, followed by those who classify themselves as far right.

In Great Britain as a whole (i.e., taking the answers to all three sets of questions together), the coefficient for far-left respondents is 0.35 and for moderate left respondents it is 0.61. Respondents who place themselves in the political center have a coefficient of 0.80. Those on the moderate right have a coefficient of 1.33 and those on the far right 1.18 (Figure 13.25). Thus, Britons who classify themselves as politically right-wing are supporters of capitalism.

FIGURE 13.25

GB: COMBINED COEFFICIENT FOR ATTITUDES TO CAPITALISM—ANALYSIS BY POLITICAL ORIENTATION

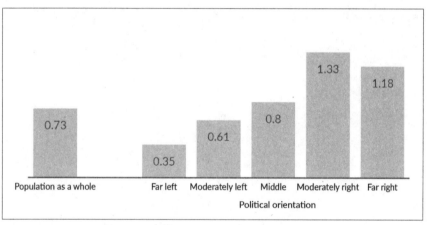

Note: The lower the coefficient, the stronger the anti-capitalist attitude
Source: Ipsos MORI survey 20–091774-30

In contrast, neither age nor education plays a decisive role in how our British respondents feel about capitalism, although it can be said that women are slightly more critical of capitalism than men, and people with low incomes are slightly more critical than higher earners.

In the next chapter, we will explore what respondents in a total of 21 countries think about capitalism.

14

WHAT PEOPLE IN ASIA, EUROPE, SOUTH AMERICA AND THE UNITED STATES THINK OF CAPITALISM

IN THIS CHAPTER, I will analyze the findings of our capitalism survey in 21 countries. I designed the survey together with the Allensbach Institute in Germany and commissioned Ipsos MORI to conduct it around the world. The survey was conducted in the USA and in small, medium and large countries in Europe, South America and Asia. The individual surveys took place between June 2021 and June 2022 in the following countries:

- Argentina

- Austria

- Bosnia and Herzegovina

- Brazil

- Chile

- Czech Republic

- France

- Germany

- Great Britain

- Greece

- Italy

- Japan

- Poland

- Portugal

- Russian Federation

- South Korea

- Spain

- Sweden

- Switzerland

- Turkey

- United States

Representative samples of around 1,000 respondents were surveyed per country. In total, 21,856 respondents took part in the survey. The survey was unique not only in its geographical scope, but also in its depth. In total, each respondent was presented with 34 items on capitalism in three thematic sets. The aim of the survey was to find out what people in different countries think of capitalism and to explore this in relation to differences in political views, age, education, gender and income. In addition, the items were designed to allow us to determine to what extent negative perceptions of capitalism are due to the negative connotation of the word itself and how much is really related to people's rejection of or support for the basic principles of the capitalist economic system.

The following analysis can only *describe* the differences between individual countries, income groups, age groups, etc. To *explain* these differences would require a far more extensive effort as part of a larger project. Historians, sociologists, political scientists, economists and other experts from the 21 countries studied would have to look for explanations in the history, economics and social psychology of each country. In addition, regression analyses would have to be conducted in order to more fully understand the relationships between the variables presented here. All of this is beyond the scope of this chapter. Nevertheless, I hope that this initial overview and systematic exploration of the survey data will inspire other scholars to explore the reasons for the differences between and within the surveyed countries. In this respect, the following should be regarded as a first step in comparative research on popular perceptions of economic freedom, state intervention and capitalism in different countries.

WHAT DO PEOPLE THINK OF ECONOMIC FREEDOM?

As I was preparing the survey, I hypothesized that some people are repelled by the word "capitalism" itself, despite the fact that they essentially hold pro-capitalist opinions. One set of survey questions ("economic freedom") therefore consistently avoided using the word "capitalism." Respondents were presented with a total of six statements, three of which favored economic freedom and market economics. The other three statements advocated restricting economic freedom and a far greater role for the state. The exact wording of the individual survey items can be found in the Questionnaire on pages 371–375.

For example, one statement in the set of questions on "economic freedom" was: "We need a lot more state intervention in the economy, since the market fails time and again." Another read: "I am for an economic system in which the state sets the rules but ideally does not interfere otherwise." For each country, the average percentage agreement with the "pro-economic freedom" statements and the average agreement with the "pro-state" statements were calculated to derive the Coefficient of Economic Freedom, which depicts the attitude toward economic freedom in each surveyed country.

Throughout this chapter, we will keep coming back to this coefficient. A coefficient of exactly 1.0 would mean that there is no clear tendency in the surveyed country and that respondents are balanced between the free-market minded and those more in favor of a strong role for the state in the economy. Thus, all countries with coefficients of between 0.9 and 1.1 have been placed in a "neutral" group (the coefficients are rounded to one decimal place). The four "neutral countries" include Brazil, Switzerland, Great Britain and Germany. Nevertheless, there are still differences within this group. For example, the Brazilians and the Swiss, with coefficients of 1.04 and 1.02 respectively, have somewhat more positive attitudes toward economic freedom than the British (0.88).

A coefficient greater than 1.1 means that people are clearly market-oriented, and a coefficient less than 0.9 means that they rely heavily on state intervention. Overall, positive statements on economic freedom clearly predominate in seven countries. The leader is Poland with a coefficient of 2.40, followed by the USA with 1.68 and the Czech Republic with 1.58. In a total of 10 countries, people are more in favor of state intervention than economic freedom. Bringing up the rear are France, Turkey, Bosnia and Herzegovina and Russia (Figure 14.1).

FIGURE 14.1

ATTITUDES TOWARD ECONOMIC FREEDOM IN 21 COUNTRIES

**Average of statements in favor of a liberal economic system
divided by the average of statements in favor of a state-controlled
economic system (without using the term "capitalism")**

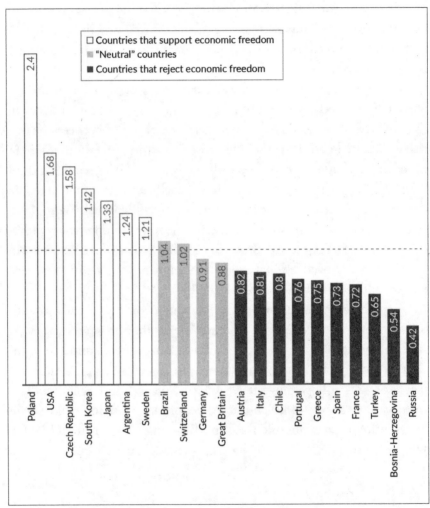

Note: The lower the coefficient, the stronger the anti-capitalist attitude

Sources: Allensbach Institute survey 12038, Ipsos MORI surveys 20-091774-30 and
21-087515-07

WHAT DO PEOPLE THINK ABOUT CAPITALISM IN GENERAL?

While the term "capitalism" was deliberately omitted from the first set of questions, it was explicitly mentioned in the other two sets of questions. In the second set of questions, we wanted to find out what respondents associated with the word "capitalism." This set of questions used a list of 10 terms, namely "prosperity," "innovation," "greed," "coldness," "progress," "corruption," "freedom," "pressure to perform," "a wide range of goods," and "environmental degradation." Again, we determined the average percentage of respondents who associate positive characteristics (e.g., freedom and prosperity) and negative characteristics (e.g., environmental degradation and greed) with the word "capitalism."

In our third set of questions, respondents were presented with a total of 18 positive and negative statements about capitalism. The negative statements included, for example: "Capitalism is responsible for hunger and poverty;" "Capitalism leads to growing inequality;" and "Capitalism entices people to buy products they don't need." The positive statements included, for example, "Capitalism has improved conditions for ordinary people in many countries;" "Capitalism is an especially efficient economic system;" and "Capitalism means that consumers determine what is offered, and not the state." Again, as with the previous sets of questions, we calculated the average percentage of respondents who supported the positive and negative statements and used these figures to calculate a coefficient.

Combining the results from all three sets of questions allowed us to develop an overall picture of what respondents in any given country think of capitalism. We added up the coefficients from all three sets of questions and divided them by three.

Again, this gives us three groups of countries: Since the term "capitalism" has a negative ring for many people, the picture here is somewhat different from our set of "economic freedom" questions—and the group of countries in which anti-capitalist attitudes dominate is larger.

Overall, pro-capitalist attitudes dominate in five countries— Poland, the United States, South Korea, Japan and the Czech Republic.

The "neutral" countries this time are Argentina, Sweden and Brazil. Anti-capitalist attitudes dominate in a majority of surveyed countries (13). Greece, Russia, Bosnia and Herzegovina and Turkey bring up the rear. Surprisingly, Switzerland belongs to this group, albeit only just (Figure 14.2).

FIGURE 14.2

OVERALL COEFFICIENT ON ATTITUDES
TOWARD CAPITALISM IN 21 COUNTRIES

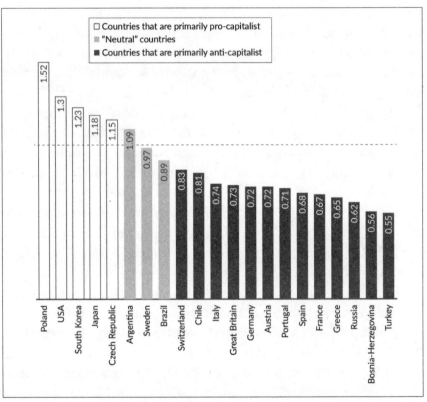

Note: The lower the coefficient, the stronger the anti-capitalist attitude

Sources: Allensbach Institute survey 12038, Ipsos MORI surveys 20-091774-30 and 21-087515-07

WHAT IMPACT DOES USING THE WORD "CAPITALISM" HAVE?
We can see that there are similarities, as well as differences, in the rankings and country groups depicted above. These differences in the "economic freedom" ranking and the "capitalism" ranking can be explained primarily by the fact that, in many countries, the term "capitalism" has a negative connotation. We can assess the scale of this effect by calculating the difference between the coefficients for the two sets of questions in which the word "capitalism" appeared (the 10 characteristics associated with capitalism and the 18 statements about capitalism) and the coefficient on the six questions on economic freedom in which the word "capitalism" was not used.

For instance, approval of capitalism in the United States increases by 51 percent when the word "capitalism" is omitted from the survey item. This is the difference between the coefficient for economic freedom (1.68) and the coefficient for those questions in which the word "capitalism" was mentioned (1.11). The difference here is 0.57 points, which means that approval for a market economy is 51 percent higher when it is described without using the word "capitalism."

You can see that the effect can be very large—as in Poland, the Czech Republic or the United States, for example—but also very small, as in France, Spain or Portugal.

In countries where there is a significant increase in support for the market economy when the word "capitalism" is not used, such as in Poland, the Czech Republic and the United States, we can conclude that people tend to be more repelled by the word itself than by what capitalism actually stands for. Where the effect is small, such as in Spain or France, it is not so much the word that bothers people, but what capitalism actually means. This also applies to Russia, which is an exception because negative attitudes toward the market economy actually *increased* by a substantial 42 percent when the word "capitalism" was *not* used. This shows that the hostility to capitalism in Russia is by no means only related to the word, but above all to what capitalism actually stands for (Figure 14.3).

FIGURE 14.3

PERCENTAGE CHANGE IN APPROVAL OF CAPITALISM WHEN THE WORD "CAPITALISM" IS OMITTED

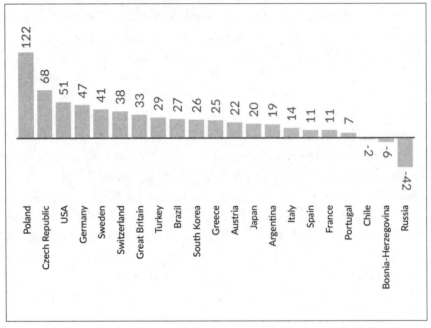

Sources: Allensbach Institute survey12038, Ipsos MORI surveys 20-091774-30 and 21-087515-07

On the one hand, this means that the use or non-use of the term "capitalism" plays a considerable role in connection with people's attitudes toward the evaluation of the issues surveyed here. On the other hand, the questions on economic freedom have made it clear that the rejection of capitalism is by no means only due to the obviously unpopular word. Only in 7 of 21 countries—Poland, the USA, Japan, South Korea, Argentina, Sweden and the Czech Republic—does a positive attitude toward economic freedom clearly predominate.

WHAT ARE THE MOST COMMON POSITIVE AND
NEGATIVE OPINIONS OF CAPITALISM?

One of the most important aims of our survey was not only to determine what people in different countries and sociodemographic groups think about capitalism—i.e., do they tend to be critical or positive toward capitalism—but also to find out which points of criticism toward capitalism dominate and which positive points are particularly valued.

We presented respondents in 21 countries with a list of 18 statements about capitalism—positive and negative. Figure 14.4 shows the frequency with which one of the 18 statements was among the top five statements that respondents in each country agreed with.[775] For example, the statement "Capitalism leads to monopolies" was among the five most frequently selected statements in 16 countries.

The result shows what particularly bothers people about capitalism—and what bothers them less. In all 21 countries, the critical statement that capitalism is dominated by the rich, who determine politics, is among the five most frequently selected statements. In nine countries, namely Austria, Bosnia and Herzegovina, Chile, the Czech Republic, France, Great Britain, Greece, Poland and the United States, this point of criticism is actually the most frequently selected of all statements.

The notion that capitalism promotes inequality is mentioned in the top five statements in 20 out of 21 countries and even ranks first in France (with the same percentage as "Capitalism is dominated by the rich, they set the political agenda"), Italy, Spain, Switzerland, Turkey and Russia.

The critical belief that capitalism promotes selfishness and greed makes it into the top five statements in 20 of the 21 surveyed countries (in Germany and Portugal it ranks first).

In contrast, the accusation that capitalism is responsible for environmental destruction and climate change plays an important role in only 3 out of 21 countries, namely Brazil, where 35 percent of respondents agree with this statement (5th place); Chile, where 32 percent agree (5th place); and Germany, where 48 percent agree (also 5th place) (Figure 14.4).

FIGURE 14.4

NUMBER OF COUNTRIES IN WHICH THE FOLLOWING
STATEMENTS RANKED IN THE "TOP 5" OF 18 STATEMENTS

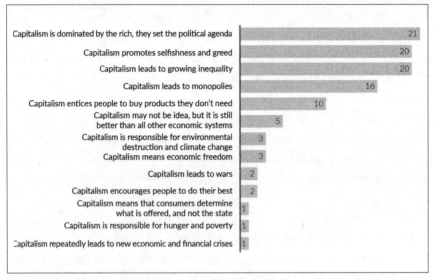

Capitalism is dominated by the rich, they set the political agenda	21
Capitalism promotes selfishness and greed	20
Capitalism leads to growing inequality	20
Capitalism leads to monopolies	16
Capitalism entices people to buy products they don't need	10
Capitalism may not be idea, but it is still better than all other economic systems	5
Capitalism is responsible for environmental destruction and climate change	3
Capitalism means economic freedom	3
Capitalism leads to wars	2
Capitalism encourages people to do their best	2
Capitalism means that consumers determine what is offered, and not the state	1
Capitalism is responsible for hunger and poverty	1
Capitalism repeatedly leads to new economic and financial crises	1

Sources: Allensbach Institute survey 12038, Ipsos MORI surveys 20-091774-30 and
21-087515-07

It is interesting to look at which countries most support the positive
statements about capitalism. In Japan and South Korea, the statement
"Capitalism means economic freedom" achieved the highest level of support of any of the 18 statements. By contrast, this statement only made
it to 10th place in Germany, 8th place in the Czech Republic and 6th
place in Argentina, while in Brazil, France, Spain, Great Britain, Greece,
Italy, Austria, Switzerland, Bosnia and Herzegovina, Turkey, Portugal
and Russia it did not even make it into the top ten. In the United States
and Japan, the statement that capitalism encourages people to do their
best also made it into the top five.

The more descriptive statement that capitalism means economic
freedom ranked among the top five statements in three countries and
the more defensive statement that capitalism may not be ideal, but is

still better than all other economic systems made the top five statements in five countries.

It should give pause for thought that the indisputable statement that capitalism has improved the situation of ordinary people in many countries did not make it into the top five in a single country. In only four countries did this statement rank in 7th, 9th or 10th place, in all the others it was not even among the top ten. In Germany, it elicited agreement from fewer respondents than any other statement on capitalism. Yet there have been so many examples in recent decades—such as China, South Korea and India, along with Poland, the Czech Republic, and the former GDR—confirming that capitalism has improved the situation of ordinary people. If one considers that since the emergence of capitalism the percentage of people around the world who live in extreme poverty has fallen from 90 percent to less than 10 percent today, the degree of misinformation about capitalism becomes clear.

The statement that capitalism is irreplaceable and past attempts to replace capitalism have always resulted in dictatorships and suffering, failed to make the top ten in any of the surveyed countries—with the sole exception of the United States, where it ranked 10th.

"Capitalism means that consumers determine what is offered, and not the state"—the fact that this statement only made it into the top five in Poland and 6th place in the Czech Republic is surely no coincidence, because this is something that many people in the former socialist countries do not yet take for granted (unlike in the West).

WHAT ROLE DOES POLITICAL AFFILIATION PLAY?
We asked all our survey respondents to place themselves on a left-right scale from 0 (far left) to 10 (far right). Those who describe themselves as centrists awarded themselves 5 points accordingly.

Far left: In all the surveyed countries, unsurprisingly, the respondents who describe themselves as being on the far left of the political spectrum (0 to 2 on the scale) are most opposed to capitalism or least pro-capitalist. Nevertheless, there are still some significant differences. In

Japan (0.92) and South Korea (0.97), two countries where respondents generally tend to be more pro-capitalist, even respondents who classify themselves as on the far left of the political spectrum are not vociferously anti-capitalist, but rather neutral. By contrast, in countries where respondents tend to be more generally critical of capitalism, the attitudes of respondents who classify themselves as far left are particularly anti-capitalist (France 0.35, Germany 0.36, Spain 0.36).[776]

Moderate left: The evaluation also varies accordingly for the moderate left (3 to 4 on the scale). In anti-capitalist countries, the moderate left is also severely anti-capitalist (France 0.51, Portugal 0.54, Spain 0.56), while in pro-capitalist countries, the moderate left tends toward a neutral position (South Korea 0.96, the Czech Republic 1.01, Japan 0.92, the United States 0.89).

Centrist: In countries where the majority of the population is anti-capitalist or neutral, centrists also tend to be more anti-capitalist. This is true, for example, of Great Britain, Germany, Greece, Sweden, Portugal, Turkey or France. In the United States, Japan and South Korea, on the other hand, where the population as a whole is pro-capitalist, this also applies to those in the middle of the political spectrum.

Moderate right and far right: Respondents on the right of the political spectrum tend to have a positive perception of capitalism in most of the surveyed countries. However, there are also major differences: In seven countries, namely the United States, Sweden, Argentina, Chile, South Korea, Spain and Switzerland, the correlation holds: the further to the right, the more pro-capitalist. Those who rank themselves in the 8–10 range of the left-right scale, i.e., as being on the far right of the political spectrum, are most strongly in favor of capitalism in some countries (the United States 2.88, Sweden 2.65, Argentina 2.32, Chile 2.01, Spain 2.05, and South Korea 1.80). Among the moderate right (who rank themselves at 6 or 7 on the left-right scale) in the United States, Sweden, Chile and South Korea, support for capitalism is also strong (United States 2.45, Argentina 1.98, Sweden 1.78, Chile 1.46, South Korea 1.43, Spain 1.38), but it is not quite as strong among the moderate right as among the far right (Figure 14.5).

For most countries (10), however, a different correlation holds: In Germany, France, Great Britain, Brazil, Japan, Italy, the Czech Republic, Russia, Bosnia and Herzegovina, Poland[777] and Austria, moderate right-wingers (respondents who rank themselves a 6 or 7 on the left-right scale) have the most positive attitude toward capitalism (or in a few countries, such as Russia and Bosnia and Herzegovina, the least negative attitude), while respondents who are even further to the right (8-10) are less approving of capitalism.

For example, among the moderately right in Brazil, approval of capitalism is 1.58; among the far right, it is lower at 1.44. The same is true in Great Britain, where approval of capitalism is 1.33 among the moderate right and 1.18 among the far right. In Spain, among the moderate right, approval is 1.19; among the far right, it is 0.97. In the Czech Republic, support for capitalism is higher among the moderately right (1.89) than among the far right (1.68), as depicted in Figure 14.6. In Greece, the coefficient was the same (0.91) for respondents who classified themselves as moderate right and far right on the political spectrum and in Turkey and Portugal, too, there were hardly any differences between moderate and far right-wing respondents.[778]

FIGURE 14.5

"THE FURTHER TO THE RIGHT OF THE POLITICAL
SPECTRUM, THE MORE PRO-CAPITALIST" COUNTRIES

Coefficient for overall attitudes toward capitalism

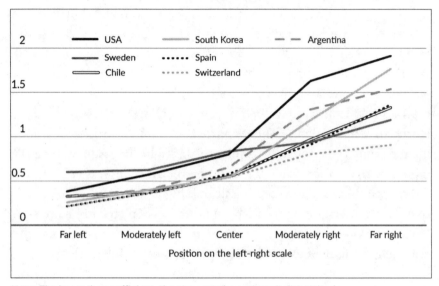

Note: The lower the coefficient, the stronger the anti-capitalist attitude

Source: Ipsos MORI survey 20-091774-30

FIGURE 14.6

COUNTRIES WHERE THE MODERATE
RIGHT IS MOST PRO-CAPITALIST

Coefficient for overall attitudes toward capitalism

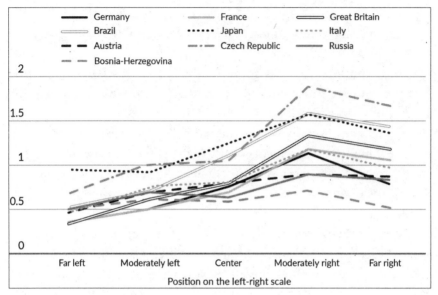

Note: The lower the coefficient, the stronger the anti-capitalist attitude

Sources: Allensbach Institute survey 12038, Ipsos MORI surveys 20-091774-30 and 21-087515-07

WHAT ROLE DOES AGE PLAY?

Do younger people tend to be more critical of capitalism than older people? Or is it the other way around? There are countries where age has hardly any bearing on attitudes toward capitalism. In France, for example, the coefficient is 0.75 for respondents under the age of 30 and 0.71 for respondents over the age of 60. In Switzerland, the coefficient is 0.80 for those under 30 and 0.82 for those over 60. In Greece, the coefficient is 0.71 for respondents under the age of 30 and 0.65 for those over the age of 55. In the Czech Republic, the coefficient is 0.98 for respondents under the age of 30 and 1.06 for those over 55 (although in the Czech Republic, approval of capitalism is higher in the 30–54 age group). There is also no noticeable relationship between age and perceptions of capitalism in Great Britain, Portugal or Italy.

In other countries, however, there is a clear link between age and attitudes toward capitalism. This is clearest in the United States, where respondents over the age of 60 have a very positive attitude toward capitalism (2.27), while younger people are neutral to slightly negative (under the age of 30: 0.90).

And, contrary to what some might claim, this is by no means because younger Americans do not understand the word "capitalism." If anything, the correlation in the United States is even clearer for the set of questions in which the word "capitalism" was not used: Among American respondents over the age of 60, attitudes toward economic freedom are extraordinarily high at 3.72, while among younger Americans under the age of 30, attitudes are neutral to at best slightly positive at 1.13.

In Argentina, Brazil, Chile and Spain, too, younger respondents are more critical of capitalism, although the difference is not as stark as in the United States. In pro-capitalist countries such as South Korea and Japan, younger respondents tend to be neutral and older respondents firmly pro-capitalist.

In Poland, older respondents (1.81) are somewhat more pro-capitalist than their younger counterparts (1.55). In Sweden, France, Great Britain and Austria, younger respondents are—albeit only slightly—more positive about capitalism than their older compatriots. Since the differences are extremely small, however, one should (except perhaps for Sweden) speak of a tie in these countries (Figure 14.7).

FIGURE 14.7

DIFFERENCES IN ATTITUDES TOWARD
CAPITALISM—ANALYSIS BY AGE GROUP

Coefficient for overall attitudes toward capitalism

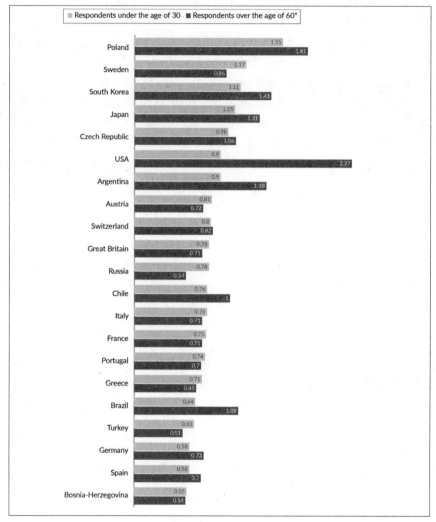

* In Poland, Argentina, Greece, Portugal, Turkey the Czech Republic, Russia and Bosnia and Herzegovina, respondents aged 55 and over

Note: The lower the coefficient, the stronger the anti-capitalist attitude

Sources: Allensbach Institute survey 12038, Ipsos MORI surveys 20-091774-30 and 21-087515-07

WHAT ROLE DOES INCOME PLAY?

Not surprisingly, in *all* countries low-income earners tend to be anti-capitalist or at best neutral, and high-income earners are comparatively more positive (or less negative) about capitalism. But there are also considerable differences between countries: There are countries where the differences between income groups are moderate (such as Great Britain, Turkey and Bosnia and Herzegovina). Switzerland, the United States, South Korea, Poland, Brazil, Italy and Spain, on the other hand, exhibit such greater differences between income groups. These differences are particularly pronounced in Spain and Switzerland, where low earners are vehemently anti-capitalist and high earners are overwhelmingly pro-capitalist (Figure 14.8).

FIGURE 14.8
DIFFERENCES IN ATTITUDES TOWARD
CAPITALISM—ANALYSIS BY INCOME

Coefficient for overall attitudes toward capitalism

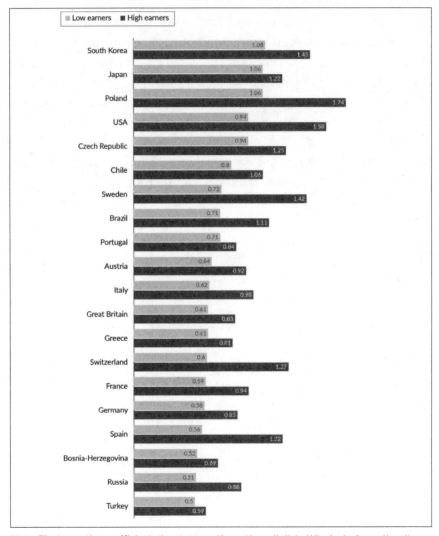

Note: The lower the coefficient, the stronger the anti-capitalist attitude. In Argentina, it was not possible to differentiate by income groups.
Sources: Allensbach Institute survey 12038, Ipsos MORI surveys 20-091774-30 and 21-087515-07

WHAT ROLE DOES GENDER PLAY?

In all countries (except for South Korea and Russia), male respondents are more positive toward capitalism (or less critical of it) than women. But there are differences: In some countries, gender plays a major role in attitudes toward capitalism. In Poland, the Czech Republic, Sweden, Brazil, Argentina, Chile, Portugal and Spain, for example, men have significantly more favorable opinions of capitalism than women. In other countries, however, the differences between men and women are small. In France, for example, women are only marginally more critical of capitalism (0.65) than men (0.71), and the same is true of Turkey (men 0.67 and women 0.64), while in South Korea and Russia there is no difference at all between men and women.

It seems interesting that the differences, though often small, are almost invariably in the same direction—women are less positive toward capitalism than men (Figure 14.9).

FIGURE 14.9
DIFFERENCES IN ATTITUDES TOWARD CAPITALISM BY GENDER

Coefficient for overall attitudes toward capitalism

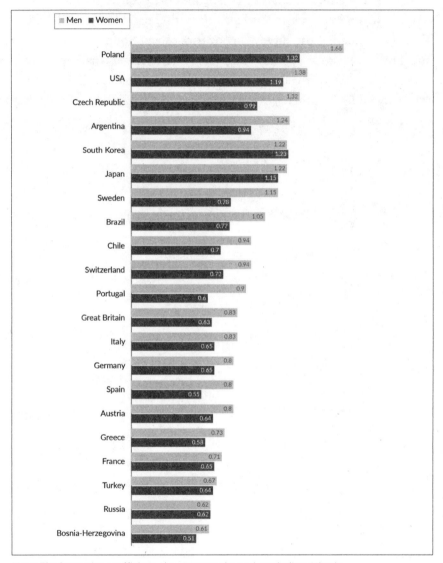

Note: The lower the coefficient, the stronger the anti-capitalist attitude

Sources: Allensbach Institute survey 12038, Ipsos MORI surveys 20-091774-30 and 21-087515-07

WHAT ROLE DOES EDUCATION PLAY?

In 18 of 21 countries, the differences between people with basic and higher education always points in the same direction: people with a higher level of education have a (slightly) more positive or less negative attitude toward capitalism than people with a basic level of education. This is true in all of the surveyed countries except South Korea, Poland and Turkey. In some of these countries (such as Argentina, France, the Czech Republic, Portugal, Brazil and Spain), this tendency is somewhat stronger, while in others (Great Britain, Sweden and Italy) it is very slight (Figure 14.10).

FIGURE 14.10
DIFFERENCES IN ATTITUDES TOWARD
CAPITALISM BY EDUCATION

Coefficient for overall attitudes toward capitalism

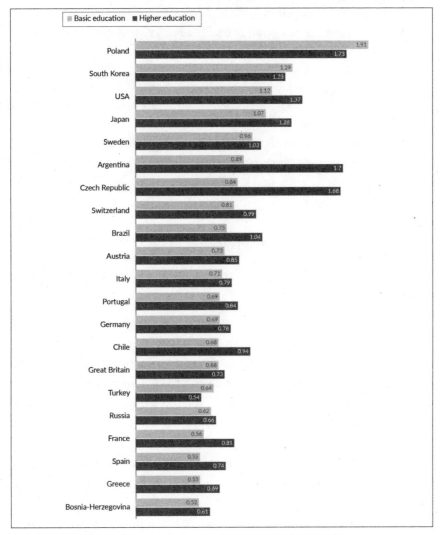

Note: The lower the coefficient, the stronger the anti-capitalist attitude

Sources: Allensbach Institute survey 12038, Ipsos MORI surveys 20-091774-30 and 21-087515-07

THE INFLUENCE OF CONSPIRACY THINKING

Among the statements we presented to the survey's respondents were two that are characteristic of people who tend toward conspiracy thinking. The first was:

> "'In reality, politicians don't decide anything. They are puppets controlled by powerful forces in the background.' Would you agree with that or would you disagree?"

The second was:

> "'A lot of things in politics can only be properly understood if you know that there is a larger plan behind them, something that most people, however, do not know.' Would you agree with that or would you disagree?"

These are two typical statements for people who are prone to conspiracy thinking.

Using factor analysis methods, we constructed—on the basis of responses to 6 of the 18 statements about capitalism—an anti-capitalism scale. The classification of respondents into two groups— "pro-capitalists" and "anti-capitalists" —is based on their responses to the 18 statements about capitalism, in which they were asked to indicate which of the statements they agreed with. Since it would be unnecessarily time-consuming to consider individual responses to all 18 items for this classification, the results of this question were initially subjected to a factor analysis.

A factor analysis is a mathematical-statistical procedure that can be used to determine which answers are frequently selected together by respondents. For example, a factor analysis determines how likely it is that a respondent who says that capitalism leads to increasing inequality also says that capitalism promotes selfishness and profiteering. If it turns out that several statements are selected together particularly frequently, then it is possible to conclude that there are overlaps between these points in terms of their content, i.e., that they are based on a common factor.

In the present case, the analysis revealed three factors: the first encompasses virtually all statements in which capitalism is associated with social injustice. The second factor comprises all the positive statements, and the third the items in which capitalism is associated with tyranny and war.

Three positive and three negative statements about capitalism were selected to form the scale: the two statements statistically most closely associated with the first factor, the three most strongly associated with the second factor, and one that is most strongly associated with the (in total consisting of only three statements and somewhat less significant) third factor.

Specifically, the scale was calculated as follows:

One point was awarded to each respondent who agreed with the following statements:

- Capitalism leads to growing inequality.

- Capitalism promotes selfishness and greed.

- Capitalism means that there is always a danger of fascism.

In addition, one point was awarded to each respondent who did *not* agree with the following statements:

- Capitalism may not be ideal, but it is still better than all other economic systems.

- Capitalism ensures prosperity.

- Capitalism means economic freedom.

This factor analysis allowed us to assign each respondent a score of between 0 and 6 points. Respondents with 5 or 6 points are classed as anti-capitalists and respondents with 0 or 1 point are classed as pro-capitalists.

It turned out that dedicated anti-capitalists agree significantly more strongly with the two conspiracy thinking statements above than dedicated pro-capitalists. This is true for all countries, although in the United States the differences are not so pronounced. For the United States, one can assume that supporters of the Republican party—especially Trump loyalists—are often both pro-capitalist and inclined toward conspiracy theories. In the other countries, differences between pro- and anti-capitalists are much clearer—and remarkably they always point in the same direction. In none of the 21 surveyed countries did we find that pro-capitalists are more likely to be conspiracy theorists than anti-capitalists. This clearly proves the connection between anti-capitalism and conspiracy thinking.

In some countries, such as the Czech Republic, Germany, Switzerland and Sweden, pro-capitalists tend to be particularly dismissive of conspiracy theories. And in Greece, Chile, Poland, Japan, France, Turkey and Russia, anti-capitalists tend to be particularly strong adherents to conspiracy theories (Figures 14.11 and 14.12).

FIGURE 14.11

AGREEMENT AND DISAGREEMENT WITH CONSPIRACY THEORIES

The Conspiracy Theory Coefficient: Average proportion of
respondents who agree with the following two statements:

"In reality, politicians don't decide anything. They are puppets
controlled by powerful forces in the background."

and

"A lot of things in politics can only be properly understood if you know that there
is a larger plan behind them, something that most people, however, do not know."

divided by the average proportion of respondents who
explicitly disagree with the two theses.

	Austria		Poland	
	Dedicated anti-capitalists	Dedicated pro-capitalists	Dedicated anti-capitalists	Dedicated pro-capitalists
A: Average agreement with the two conspiracy statements	57	54	66	48
B: Average disagreement with the two conspiracy statements	20	35	14	25
A : B	2.9	1.5	4.7	1.9

	Italy		Spain	
	Dedicated anti-capitalists	Dedicated pro-capitalists	Dedicated anti-capitalists	Dedicated pro-capitalists
A: Average agreement with the two conspiracy statements	68	49	65	58
B: Average disagreement with the two conspiracy statements	22	39	18	26
A : B	3.1	1.3	3.6	2.2

	South Korea		Great Britain	
	Dedicated anti-capitalists	Dedicated pro-capitalists	Dedicated anti-capitalists	Dedicated pro-capitalists
A: Average agreement with the two conspiracy statements	62	56	58	42
B: Average disagreement with the two conspiracy statements	22	34	21	29
A : B	2.8	1.6	2.8	1.4

	Chile		Brazil	
	Dedicated anti-capitalists	Dedicated pro-capitalists	Dedicated anti-capitalists	Dedicated pro-capitalists
A: Average agreement with the two conspiracy statements	72	58	66	58
B: Average disagreement with the two conspiracy statements	13	24	19	30
A : B	5.5	2.4	3.5	1.9

	Sweden		France	
	Dedicated anti-capitalists	Dedicated pro-capitalists	Dedicated anti-capitalists	Dedicated pro-capitalists
A: Average agreement with the two conspiracy statements	43	32	58	54
B: Average disagreement with the two conspiracy statements	30	50	14	28
A : B	1.4	0.6	4.1	1.9

	USA		Germany	
	Dedicated anti-capitalists	Dedicated pro-capitalists	Dedicated anti-capitalists	Dedicated pro-capitalists
A: Average agreement with the two conspiracy statements	56	57	42	25
B: Average disagreement with the two conspiracy statements	20	25	35	53
A : B	2.8	2.3	1.2	0.5

	Japan		Switzerland	
	Dedicated anti-capitalists	Dedicated pro-capitalists	Dedicated anti-capitalists	Dedicated pro-capitalists
A: Average agreement with the two conspiracy statements	68	44	53	34
B: Average disagreement with the two conspiracy statements	13	18	23	48
A : B	5.2	2.4	2.3	0.7

	Bosnia and Herzegovina		Russia	
	Dedicated anti-capitalists	Dedicated pro-capitalists	Dedicated anti-capitalists	Dedicated pro-capitalists
A: Average agreement with the two conspiracy statements	72	55	77	61
B: Average disagreement with the two conspiracy statements	17	33	11	28
A : B	4.2	1.7	7.0	2.2

	Argentina		Greece	
	Dedicated anti-capitalists	Dedicated pro-capitalists	Dedicated anti-capitalists	Dedicated pro-capitalists
A: Average agreement with the two conspiracy statements	65	54	78	58
B: Average disagreement with the two conspiracy statements	19	30	6	28
A : B	3.4	1.8	13.0	2.1

	Czech Republic		Portugal	
	Dedicated anti-capitalists	Dedicated anti-capitalists	Dedicated anti-capitalists	Dedicated pro-capitalists
A: Average agreement with the two conspiracy statements	76	39	65	45
B: Average disagreement with the two conspiracy statements	11	48	17	33
A : B	6.9	0.8	3.8	1.4

	Turkey	
	Dedicated anti-capitalists	Dedicated pro-capitalists
A: Average agreement with the two conspiracy statements	77	59
B: Average disagreement with the two conspiracy statements	11	25
A : B	7.0	2.4

FIGURE 14.12

ANTI-CAPITALISM AND THE TENDENCY
TO CONSPIRACY THINKING

The Conspiracy Theory Coefficient: Average proportion of
respondents who agree with the following two statements:

**"In reality, politicians don't decide anything. They are puppets
controlled by powerful forces in the background."**

and

**"A lot of things in politics can only be properly understood if you know that there
is a larger plan behind them, something that most people, however, do not know."**

divided by the average proportion of respondents who
explicitly disagree with the two theses.

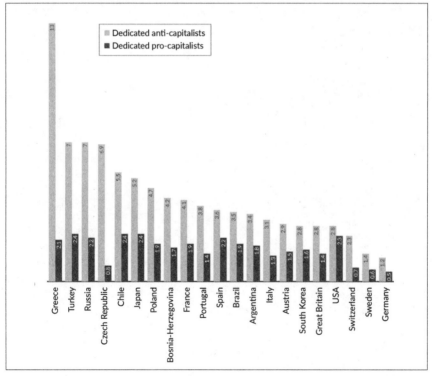

Source: Allensbach Institute survey 12038, Ipsos MORI surveys 20-091774-30 and
21-087515-07

329

ATTITUDES TOWARD CAPITALISM AND THE RICH

For my *The Rich in Public Opinion* research project, I collected data on attitudes toward the rich in 11 countries.[779] In order to compare opinions in different countries, the study developed a Social Envy Coefficient, which allows us to measure the prevalence of social envy in any given country. The study was also designed to find out which personality traits are most frequently attributed to rich people—and whether they tend to be more positive or more negative. These extensive data are then combined to form the Rich Sentiment Index. (Figure 14.13).

FIGURE 14.13

RICH SENTIMENT INDEX (RSI) IN ELEVEN COUNTRIES

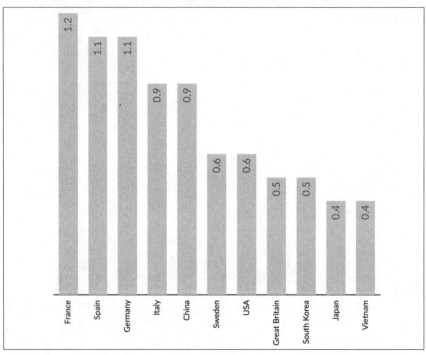

Note: RSI greater than 1: Negative attitudes toward rich people predominate

RSI less than 1: Positive attitudes toward rich people predominate

Sources: Allensbach Institute survey 11085, 8271, Ipsos MORI survey 18-031911-01-02, 19-01009-29, 19-01009-47, 20-091774-05 and 21-041026-01

An RSI greater than 1 indicates a negative perception and a value of less than 1 indicates a positive sentiment toward the rich in any given country. In nine countries we conducted both surveys—that is, the survey on attitudes toward the rich and the survey on attitudes toward capitalism. It can be seen that countries in which the population has a more positive perception of capitalism, attitudes are also more positive toward the rich—for example in the United States, South Korea and Japan. Conversely, in countries where people tend to be more critical of capitalism, they also hold more negative views of the rich—for example in Germany, Spain and France. The only exception is Great Britain, where people are positive about the rich but critical of capitalism.

FIGURE 14.14

THE RELATIONSHIP BETWEEN THE RICH SENTIMENT INDEX (RSI) AND THE COEFFICIENT FOR OVERALL ATTITUDES TOWARD CAPITALISM

For better comparability, the RSI was inverted. The difference between the RSI score and the reference value 1 is subtracted from or added to the reference value. Thus, an RSI of 1.2 becomes a modified RSI of 0.8; an RSI of 0.6 becomes a modified RSI of 1.4.

This ensures that the modified RSI corresponds to the logic of the coefficient for overall attitudes toward capitalism: A value greater than 1 means that positive perceptions of the rich or of capitalism dominate; a value less than 1 indicates that negative perceptions dominate.

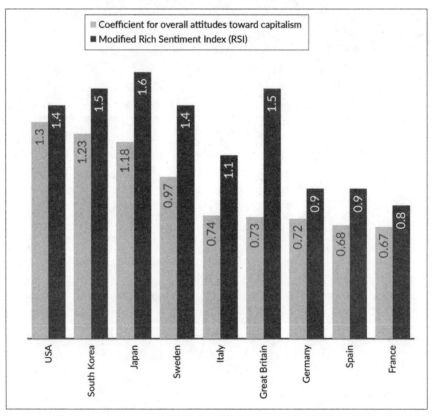

Sources: Allensbach Institute survey11085, Ipsos MORI surveys 18-031911-01-02, 19-01009-29, 19-01009-47, 20-091774-05, 20-09-1774-30 and 21-041026-01

SUMMARY

In only 7 of 21 countries—Poland, the United States, the Czech Republic, Japan, Argentina, South Korea and Sweden—does a positive attitude toward economic freedom clearly prevail. Including the word "capitalism" reduces this to just 5 of 21 countries, namely Poland, the United States, the Czech Republic, Japan and South Korea. In most countries, anti-capitalist sentiment dominates.

What is it exactly that bothers people about capitalism? If you look at the survey's overall conclusions, it is—in this order—primarily the opinion that:

- capitalism is dominated by the rich, they set the political agenda;

- capitalism leads to growing inequality;

- capitalism promotes selfishness and greed;

- capitalism leads to monopolies;

- capitalism entices people to buy products they don't need.

Not surprisingly, anti-capitalism is most pronounced among those on the left of the political spectrum, and the strongest pro-capitalists are to be found on the right of center. But while in some countries the formula is "the more right-wing, the more supportive of capitalism," there are more countries in which moderate right-wingers are somewhat more supportive of capitalism than those on the far right of the political spectrum.

Age has an influence on attitudes toward capitalism in most countries: Younger respondents are slightly more critical of capitalism than older respondents. In most countries, the difference is small. The most significant exception is the United States, where respondents under the age of 30 have a neutral to slightly negative attitude toward capitalism and respondents over the age of 60 are distinctly pro-capitalism.

Not surprisingly—and in all countries—low-income earners tend to be anti-capitalists (or at best neutral), while high-income earners are more positively pro-capitalism (or less negative in their opinions of capitalism). In some countries, however, the differences are very small—this is true, for example, in Great Britain and Turkey. In contrast, the differences between income groups are far larger in Spain, Sweden and Switzerland.

In all countries (except for South Korea and Russia), men are more positive toward capitalism (or at least less critical of it) than women. But there are differences: In some countries, gender plays a major role in attitudes toward capitalism. In Poland, Brazil, Chile, the Czech Republic, Sweden, Portugal and Spain, for example, men are significantly more positive toward capitalism than women. In other countries, however, the differences between male and female respondents are much smaller, and in South Korea men and women are both equally positive about capitalism.

In 18 out of 21 countries, the differences between people with basic and higher levels of education point in the same direction: respondents with a higher level of education are more sympathetic (or at worst, less negative) toward capitalism than their compatriots with a basic education. This is true for all countries except South Korea, Poland and Turkey. The difference is particularly pronounced in Argentina, where respondents with a lower level of education have neutral to slightly negative attitudes toward capitalism and those with a higher level of education have very strong positive attitudes toward capitalism.

In all countries—without exception—we find that anti-capitalists are far more likely to subscribe to conspiracy thinking than pro-capitalists. The analysis clearly demonstrates that there is a strong connection between anti-capitalist attitudes and conspiracy thinking. The conclusiveness of this finding is astonishing: In all of the 21 surveyed countries anti-capitalists are more inclined to conspiracy thinking than pro-capitalists.

CONCLUSION

ANTI-CAPITALISM AS A

POLITICAL RELIGION

IN THE PREVIOUS SECTION OF THIS BOOK, you saw how big the gap is between the facts about capitalism on the one hand and people's opinions on the other. All of these facts confirm that throughout history, capitalism has massively improved the lives of ordinary people in so many countries—in Europe and the United States over the last 200 years and in Asia over the past 50 years. However, we have also seen that the statement "capitalism has improved conditions for ordinary people in many countries" found little agreement in our survey. In Germany, only 15 percent of respondents agreed—less than any other statement about capitalism! In contrast, three times as many (45 percent) said that capitalism is responsible for hunger and poverty—a thesis that, as shown in Chapter 1, does not stand up to any examination of the facts. Our survey also revealed a clear link between conspiracy thinking and anti-capitalism.

Thus, it is clear that anti-capitalism is not grounded in the realm of reason or rationality—it is primarily a rejection based on emotions. The promoters of anti-capitalism are intellectual elites. From Lenin to Hayek, theorists have agreed[780] that anti-capitalism did not have its genesis in the workers' movement, but among intellectuals. If you would like to read a more detailed analysis of why most intellectuals do not like capitalism, this is the subject of Chapter 10 of my book *The Power of Capitalism*.

But to be truly successful, intellectuals' anti-capitalism must resonate with a social sounding board that makes people receptive to it. In earlier forms of society, people often accepted inequality because they saw it as natural or God-given. Characteristic of bourgeois society, according to Marx, is the fact that "the concept of human equality had already acquired the permanence of a fixed popular opinion."[781] While equality was initially regarded only as the equality of people before the law and as equality in human dignity, the view that any inequality must be "structural," and that these structures are worthy of criticism, has increasingly prevailed over the past 200 years. This is true not only in terms of material inequality, but for almost every form of inequality.

Individuals and groups who are not in a supposedly "privileged" situation attribute the contradiction between postulated equality and actual inequality to "structural" and "systemic" causes. Every inequality becomes evidence of injustice within society. Increasingly, the terms "equality" and "justice" are used as synonyms.

This is what makes the religion of anti-capitalism so attractive. I speak of a religion in the sense of the term "political religion," which was first developed by the American political scientist Eric Voegelin in his 1938 book with the same title.[782] A year later, the French sociologist and philosopher Raymond Aron also used the term "religion politique." Following Marx, who had called religion the "*opium* of the people,"[783] he spoke of communism as an "intellectual's religion."[784]

Even Marx's contemporaries were struck by the analogy to religion. In 1868, *The Times* in London wrote of the First International, which

Marx helped initiate: "One has to go back to the time of the birth of Christianity and the rejuvenation of the ancient world by the Germanic nations to find anything analogous to the workers' movement." It aspired to nothing less than the renewal of humanity, "surely the most comprehensive aim to which any institution apart from the Christian Church has ever aspired."[785]

We know from life reports of Marxists that Marxism—for all the scientific pretensions that this theory makes—is rather anchored in the realm of the emotional. Arthur Koestler, who was formerly a communist, begins his contribution to the book *The God That Failed* with the sentences: "A path is not acquired by reasoning. One does not fall in love with a woman, or enter the womb of a church, as a result of logical persuasion. Reason may defend an act of faith—but only after the act has been committed, and the man committed to the act."[786] In the beginning, Koestler reports, he had a "strong dislike of the obviously rich," and he projected his personal problems "onto the structure of society at large."[787]

These, too, are two typical features of anti-capitalism: they satisfy both envy against the rich, which is of course never perceived as envy,[788] and at the same time transform personal failure into a "systemic" or "structural" problem in the sense of the attitude described by psychologists as an *external locus of control.* Unsympathetic envy can thus be rationalized and reinterpreted as a commitment to "social justice."

Based on this interpretation, they turn their own failure into a market failure. In the early 1950s, the American political scientist Gabriel Almond asked 221 former communists from four countries about why they joined the party for his book *The Appeals of Communism.* It turned out that for 52 percent, personal economic difficulties had played a role before they joined. Among Almond's higher echelon respondents, this was true for as many as 67 percent.[789]

But personal problems need by no means be economic problems. Like other authors, the Austrian-American psychoanalyst Wilhelm Reich, who combined Marxism and psychoanalysis, tried to prove that numerous psychological problems, unsatisfied sexuality, neuroses, and so forth, had their ultimate cause in capitalism and "that it is only a thorough turnover of social institutions and ideologies, a turnover that will be dependent upon the outcome of the political struggles of our century, which will create the preconditions for an extensive prophylaxis of neuroses."[790]

The Marxist psychologist Dieter Duhm, who followed this approach, argued in his book *Angst im Kapitalismus* (*Fear in Capitalism*) why fear is the ubiquitous emotional state under capitalism: "It appears in the most diverse guises. In the 'healthy' as fear of what others might think, fear of speaking in front of others, fear of authorities and institutions, fear of or during sexual intercourse, fear of the future or of illness." This fear, he said, is "an indissoluble part not just of our individual lives, but of our society. It belongs to capitalism, not only as its product, but as part of its construction, as a building block without which everything would collapse."[791] Since neurotic anxiety is rooted in capitalism, he argues, it will only disappear if capitalism disappears. In another book, Duhm invokes the "mobilizing power of the psychic appeal"[792] for the struggle against capitalism.

Capitalism, according to this line of reasoning, not only explains all of the evils in the world, but it is also the root of everyone's personal problems and neuroses. Redemption from all evils therefore does not take place in any paradise beyond, but in a society in which private ownership of the means of production is abolished, according to the promise of redemption of the anti-capitalists. Even the struggle against capitalism has an "important therapeutic effect . . . namely the psychological disempowerment of social authorities."[793]

Political religions satisfy human longings and needs that were formerly served by religions. Aron called such doctrines "secular religions . . . that, in the souls of our contemporaries, take the place of the faith that is no more, placing the salvation of mankind in this world, in the more or less distant future, and in the form of a social order yet to be invented."[794]

In classical religions, there is usually a devil figure, who stands as a symbol for the general evil in the world. In the political religion of anti-capitalism, capitalism is the incarnation of evil. It is responsible for all the ills in society and for all personal problems. Capitalism is thus to blame for hunger, poverty, inequality, climate change, pollution, war, alienation, fascism, racism, oppression of women, slavery, colonialism, corruption, crime, anxiety, cultural decay, neurosis and other mental illnesses. Capitalism is even to blame for the non-functioning of socialist systems because economic boycotts led by "US imperialists" are to blame for the fact that people in Cuba or Venezuela, for example, do not have a better life despite socialism.

If there are *too few* goods, capitalism is to blame. The same is true if there are *too many* goods ("the terror of consumption"). And even when I go shopping and can't find the goods I am looking for, capitalism is to blame. The best-selling and award-winning American author Eula Biss is widely celebrated for her novels and begins her book on possession, capitalism, and the value of things, *Having and Being Had* (2020), with this anecdote: "We're on our way home from a furniture store, again. What does it say about capitalism, John asks, that we have money and want to spend it but we can't find anything worth buying? We almost bought something called a credenza, but then John opened the drawers and discovered it wasn't made to last. I think there are limits, I say, to what mass production can produce."[795] Later in the book, the author recounts a conversation with her mother, who asks her if she thinks capitalism is good or bad. "I say I'm tempted to think it's a bad thing but I don't really know what it is."[796]

Such thought patterns and reflexes confirm two things: First, for many people, anti-capitalism is an emotional issue. It is a diffuse feeling of protest against the existing order. Second, there is no evil, neither in society as a whole, nor in someone's personal life, that cannot be blamed on the capitalist "system," even if it is only the fact that they can't find any furniture to buy.

The "underprivileged" are always "victims of circumstances" and never responsible or complicit in their own misery, while the rich are always the "perpetrators" who never deserve their wealth, which they have only ever accumulated as a result of luck or inheritance and/or exploitation.

Capitalism, so the argument goes, is propped up by a small group of super-rich who are portrayed as the real masterminds of world events—I examined the connection between anti-capitalism and conspiracy theories in the previous chapter.

As in many religions, anti-capitalists believe in a great collapse, which will come either in the form of an economic crisis or—today—in the form of a world-destroying ecological catastrophe. Marx's writings and letters are full of "harbingers of the coming collapse."[797] The historian Heiner Schulz has counted a total of more than 3,000 predictions of crises and revolutions in Marx's writings.[798] Anti-capitalists' predictions of the imminent end of capitalism in the 139 years since Karl Marx's death are likely to number in the tens or even hundreds of thousands—and they have been beating the drums again since the 2008 financial crisis and the 2020 corona crisis. "You can now fill binders with reports on the coming collapse," Marx's biographer Jürgen Neffe noted in 2017.[799] And the predictions of doom are by no means limited to die-hard Marxists. At the beginning of 2013, even *Forbes* asked: "Is Capitalism Dying?"[800]

According to the promises of the prophets of a "new," "better" and, above all, "fairer" society, the "apocalypse" or return to barbarism could only be averted by vanquishing capitalism.

But is anti-capitalism really a "political religion" in the sense Eric Voegelin, Raymond Aron, Hans Maier and others used to define the term? The two main arguments against calling anti-capitalism a "political religion" could be that anti-capitalists have no "leader" and no unified party, and that anti-capitalism is not a single, unified worldview.

But therein lies precisely the strength of anti-capitalism: it can take on the most diverse manifestations, Marxism, socialism, environmentalism, but also conservatism, national socialism and fascism. It is compatible with both Christianity (Pope Francis's 2015 social encyclical *Laudato si'* is a flaming indictment of capitalism[801]) and radical Islamism, where it is primarily manifested in the form of anti-Americanism. It can take the form of "scientific socialism" (in the shape of Marxism, for example) as well as that of an emotionally or ethically and morally based "Christian socialism" (as in Catholic social teaching). This adaptability and compatibility with the most diverse, even opposing, worldviews distinguishes anti-capitalism from other political religions and thus makes it attractive, powerful and globally successful.

In its mutability and adaptability to different cultures and creeds, anti-capitalism resembles its antithesis: capitalism. While capitalism is not compatible with as many ideologies as anti-capitalism, it can also take on a wide range of forms, is constantly evolving, and is compatible with different political systems and religions.

However, capitalism is at a disadvantage compared to anti-capitalism because it is not a political religion. Nevertheless, Walter Benjamin, one of the philosophers of the Frankfurt School, claimed exactly this in his unfinished essay "Capitalism as Religion" (which was only published after his death). His essay fails to justify his description of capitalism as a religion, just as it fails to offer even an approximate definition of the term itself. In the first sentence of the essay Benjamin writes: "One can behold in capitalism a religion, that is to say, capitalism essentially serves to satisfy the same worries, anguish, and disquiet formerly answered by so-called religion."[802] This is the only concrete statement in the essay, which is otherwise written in the jargon of nebulous verbiage so typical of Frankfurt School philosophers.

But does capitalism really claim to provide the answers to the same questions as religions? No, capitalism provides an answer as to how people can organize their economic relations in order to "provide sufficient goods and services at reasonable prices"[803] to ensure a good life for as many as possible. If religions tried to give an answer to this question, they would be economic theories. No, capitalism does not give people meaning in life and does not claim to do so. It promises neither the abolition of inequality nor the solution of all earthly problems; it is not utopian and promises no paradise, neither in this world or the next. It is pragmatic and (Benjamin even admits this) definitely not dogmatic.

However, it does not satisfy the needs of people in a secularized world for metaphysical meaning. Therefore, capitalism is not a religion, while its antithesis, anti-capitalism, is.

After every single anti-capitalist experiment over the last 100 years failed without exception, it should be clear that the last thing the world needs is any new socialist experiments. But as the number of years that have passed since the collapse of real-world socialism in the Soviet Union and Eastern Europe increases, socialist thinking has come to enjoy a renaissance. Even Karl Marx is "in" again. In 2013, UNESCO added the *Communist Manifesto* and Volume 1 of *Capital* to its Memory of the World International Register of outstanding documents—no author has made it onto the world organization's list with a comparable text.[804] And the following year, "Marx Rises Again" appeared as a headline in *The New York Times*.[805]

One of the most respected contemporary leftist philosophers, the Slovenian Slavoj Žižek, unabashedly calls for the rehabilitation of the entire line of anti-liberal thinkers of a "closed" society, beginning with Plato.[806] He goes on: "What is needed is a repoliticization of economy: economic life should be controlled and regulated by the free decisions of a community, not run by the blind and chaotic interactions of market forces that are accepted as objective necessity."[807]

In his 2021 book, *A Left That Dares Speak Its Name*, he writes, "What we need today is a Left that dares to speak its name, not a Left that shamefully covers up its core with some cultural fig leaf. And this name is communism."[808] The Left, he argues, should finally abandon the socialist dream of a more equitable and "'just' capitalism" and enact more radical "'communist' measures."[809] As a clearly formulated goal, he proposes that "the opposing class has to be destroyed."[810]

Žižek extols "Lenin's greatness," which lay in the fact that, after the Bolsheviks seized power, he held steadfast to his socialist principles, even though the conditions did not exist for an actual "construction of socialism."[811] According to the theories developed by Marx and Lenin, "socialism" is a necessary transitional stage until the final goal of communism is reached. Žižek suggests reversing this sequence and aiming directly for communism, which should then eventually evolve or regress into socialism. Mao's Great Leap Forward in the late 1950s (which cost 45 million Chinese people their lives, a fact that Žižek omits) presented an opportunity to "bypass socialism and directly enter communism."[812]

In his 2018 book, the Swiss sociologist Jean Ziegler writes: "The capitalist system cannot be reformed gradually and peacefully. We must break the arms of the oligarchs, smash their power."[813] The destruction of capitalism, he claims, must be "complete, radical, so that a new social and economic world order can be established . . . We are animated by the longing for the very Other, for utopia—that is the horizon toward which we must orient our behavior."[814] Ziegler quotes Karl Marx and Che Guevara to show in which direction the journey should proceed. Meanwhile, when asked if he knows anything about what the social and economic system that is to replace capitalism should look like, he replies, "Nothing at all, at least nothing precise."[815] The only thing he does know for sure is what is at the heart of the problem, the root of "monstrous capitalism," namely private property.[816]

Apparently, anti-capitalists never tire of dreaming their dreams. Even as I was writing this book, the leader of an explicitly Marxist-Leninist party was elected president of Peru. A new socialist experiment is beginning. And it is not only in Peru. Many Western countries are also moving toward a planned economy. Of course, they no longer call it a planned economy, preferring to speak instead of the environmental transformation of society, social justice and the fight against climate change.

Marxism and the notion of solving all of the world's problems by eliminating private property were declared dead after the failure of real-world socialism. Nevertheless, just a few decades later, socialism is experiencing a renaissance. In the weeks in which I was writing these lines (September 2021), a referendum was held in Berlin in which a majority (56.4 percent) of residents voted in favor of expropriating large real estate companies and in Graz, Austria, the Austrian Communist Party won the elections.

But anti-capitalism has many guises: it can take on the face of radical environmentalism or the face of the fashionable "woke" movement. It also appears in the omnipotent fantasies of central banks. The recipes, however different they may seem, have one thing in common: the belief that the state should fix any and all problems because politicians and civil servants know better than the market, that is, better than all private participants in the economy. Many contemporary anti-capitalists have stopped talking about the need to abolish capitalism and have started to call for it to be "reigned in," "reformed" or "improved." Capitalism is portrayed as a wild animal ("predatory capitalism") that needs to be "tamed." Intellectuals are constantly thinking up new concepts for "improving" the economic system or limiting its "evils." Intellectuals who believe they can design an economic system on the drawing board are suffering from the same delusion as those who think they can arti-ficially construct a language—but they always insist it needs to happen in service of justice or equality.

Hayek described the idea of "intelligent men coming together for deliberation about how to make the world anew" as a fundamental problem.[817] This kind of "constructivism" or "social rationalism" was the origin of totalitarianism and "all modern socialism."[818] But intellectuals are tireless in constantly dreaming up new variants of socialism.

The most recent example of this is Thomas Piketty. In his highly acclaimed work *Capital in the Twenty-First Century*, he emphasized: "I belong to a generation that came of age listening to news of the collapse of the Communist dictatorships and never felt the slightest affection or nostalgia for those regimes or for the Soviet Union. I was vaccinated for life against the conventional but lazy rhetoric of anticapitalism, some of which simply ignored the historic failure of Communism and much of which turned its back on the intellectual means necessary to push beyond it. I have no interest in denouncing inequality or capitalism per se."[819]

At first glance, this all sounds quite harmless. However, Piketty is a radical anti-capitalist and advocate of socialism, as he demonstrates in his book, *Capital and Ideology*. In a typical constructivist way, he imagines an ideal social and economic system, that he calls "participatory socialism" (to distinguish it from the real-world, actual socialism that has failed miserably in 24 attempts). He is quite right to call his system "socialism," because in essence it is about "transcending the current system of private ownership."[820]

Specifically, Piketty's vision includes the following: Every young adult should receive a large sum of money as a gift from the state at the age of 25, which Piketty calls a "public inheritance for all."[821] This gift would be financed by a progressive tax on private wealth, which would rise to 90 percent on the largest fortunes,[822] and inheritances, which would also be taxed at up to 90 percent.[823] He does not accept the objection that some assets may not generate any current income at all and that the heir could then be forced to sell the inherited assets. On the contrary, according to Piketty, this would have the advantage of "circulating wealth into the hands of more dynamic owners."[824]

Of course, Piketty also proposes a correspondingly high tax on incomes, also rising to a peak of 90 percent.[825] And he would also apply this very same tax rate to dividends, interest, rents, profits, and so on.[826]

In order to "transcend" private ownership, Piketty calls for an approach to regulating stock corporations that, at first glance, would seem to echo Germany's system of codetermination, which gives workers' representatives half the seats on a company's supervisory board. However, according to Piketty, this approach has "limitations," including the fact that shareholders have the casting vote in the event of a tie. If Piketty had his way, he would eliminate this "limitation" by breaking the link between the amount of capital invested in a firm and the shareholder's economic power in the firm: "Investments beyond 10 percent of a firm's capital would obtain voting rights corresponding to one-third of the amount invested."[827] Piketty also calls for an end to the "one share, one vote" model of corporate organization.[828]

Of course, Piketty is clear that asset and property owners would leave such a country in a hurry. "With such a system, the only tax avoidance strategy available to the owners of residential or business property . . . would be to sell the assets and leave the country."[829] To combat this, Piketty suggests, the government would have to introduce an "exit tax" (of, say, 40 percent).[830] In effect, this would erect a fiscal wall to prevent entrepreneurs and other wealthy individuals who have no desire to live under Piketty's "participatory socialism" from turning their backs on the country because they would lose their assets, or a large portion of them. Any country's most important capital, however, is its human capital, that is, the knowledge in the minds of its people. And at a time when entrepreneurs and highly qualified people are part of a global labor market and ties to a country are no longer as strong as they used to be, physical walls will have to be built again at some point to stop people from migrating.

Piketty's proposals prove the point I made earlier: Any attempts to "improve," "correct," or "reform" capitalism that at first seem harmless always end in socialism and bondage. The only difference with traditional socialism is that private property is not nationalized in one fell swoop by order of one party, but the same goal is to be achieved over the course of a few years via taxation and corporate law. After all, the legal title of private property no longer means anything if others decide what to do with it.

I, on the other hand, am convinced that capitalism does not need to be improved by intellectuals; it is constantly self-correcting and improving itself—where it is allowed to. That is why Werner Plumpe's monograph on the history of capitalism has the extremely apt subheading "The Story of an Ongoing Revolution."[831] The essence of capitalism is that it is a learning system. I have developed the idea that in reality there are always only mixed systems, and that *changes in the relative strength of the two components, state and market, in a given system determine whether people's lives improve or get worse.* Accordingly, meaningful change in society is not achieved by turning everything on its head and following some master plan or theory, but—if it seems necessary—by pushing back government in order to give the market more space.

Therefore, the only improvement I have to propose is this: Government should stay out of social and economic affairs more than it does today. This does not mean that government is superfluous or unimportant. But it does mean that today's politicians, political parties and civil servants take themselves far too seriously. And despite this, you don't have to look very far to see that many Western governments are failing to fulfill many of their core responsibilities, as demonstrated by their often-amateurish handling of the coronavirus pandemic. We see the same in many Western countries from decaying infrastructure, failing education systems, and from serious deficits in domestic and foreign security.

The state is often weak precisely where it should be strong—and far too strong where it should be weak, that is, in the economy. Politicians spend much of their time coming up with new ideas for redistribution and state regulation, ignoring the solutions to many of the most urgent problems—such as a rational and efficient immigration policy.

Let us therefore dare to have less government and more capitalism! Not in the sense of a sweeping revolution or sudden upheaval, but as Reagan and Thatcher began—but did not continue—by giving the market much more freedom. More market has always been good for people, whether in China, Vietnam, Poland, South Korea or Sweden. At the same time, there is no room for dogmatism. The utopia of 100 percent pure capitalism is just that—a utopia. And utopian visions of a perfect world have already caused far too much suffering throughout history. More trust in the market instead of blind trust in the state—that is something worth fighting for, because it has been proven to work. And because it is also the more moral system, not only because it reduces poverty and hunger, but above all because it gives people more freedom to dream their own dreams. For this reason alone, capitalism is superior to other systems.

If capitalism really were to come to an end, it would not be because of internal contradictions and systemic weaknesses, but because anti-capitalists were more successful than the supporters of free markets on the ideological front. That anti-capitalists are often more successful than the supporters of the market has many reasons. The people who keep capitalism alive—entrepreneurs, workers and employees—are fully occupied with being productive and creating value. They usually have little time to participate in sociopolitical debates. Unlike intellectuals, the media and politicians, who have far more time for such debates and often have a higher linguistic competence—sometimes, unfortunately, this is their only competence. They do not have to create value because their salaries are mostly funded by the taxpayer.

Entrepreneurs are used to adapting flexibly as conditions evolve. This characteristic is tremendously important in a market economy, and those who fail to master it often pay for their failure with the existence of their company. Opportunism in the sense of permanently and pragmatically adapting to changing conditions, which can be a virtue in business, is more often than not a curse in politics.

The real problem today is not ideologically entrenched anti-capitalists, but the weakness and opportunism of those whose job it should be to stand up for and promote capitalism. At best, they defend capitalism half-heartedly and defensively; often they are quick to retreat from the attacks launched by anti-capitalists, keeping their mouths shut. Many are under the misapprehension that if we could only appease the anti-capitalists to some extent, that would take the wind out of their sails or somehow placate them. The anti-capitalists rightly interpret this retreat as a sign of weakness, feel strengthened, make new demands and intensify their attacks.

Two years ago in London, I had dinner with Madsen Pirie, president of the prestigious Adam Smith Institute. Our conversation turned to the future of capitalism. Pirie was 80 years old at the time—he knew many of the great thinkers and practitioners of capitalism personally, from Friedrich August von Hayek to Margaret Thatcher. At one point, he told me, "Maybe capitalism will ebb away in some countries, but there will always be other countries rediscovering it and becoming successful. And those countries will send a signal out to the rest of the world that no one will be able ignore." I thought of his words as I looked more closely at Vietnam. Like China, it is a country that is ruled by a party that calls itself communist and where there are almost no political freedoms, but where the market economy probably has more adherents than in many Western countries and which has made enormous strides toward economic freedom since the 1980s.

But whether you look at China, Europe or the United States, all over the world there is a battle raging between two concepts—the socialist and the capitalist. It is the struggle between the believers in big government, who are always looking to put new chains of regulation on people, and the forces of freedom, who want to break these chains.

Four decades ago, proponents of capitalism celebrated a number of important intermediate victories—in China, in the United States, in Great Britain, Poland, and even in Sweden. But as the collapse of socialism retreats further and further into the past, the socialist camp is regaining strength and gaining adherents all over the world. The enemies of freedom, who profit from lapses in the collective memory, are on the advance, and capitalism is on the defensive.

The fact that capitalism has survived so far, despite all the predictions of its demise, is no guarantee that it will survive the next decades or centuries. But if capitalism should come to an end, it will not be because it has destroyed itself, but because ever greater problems are created by state intervention, culminating in a crisis of unprecedented proportions. To people whose thinking is framed by anti-capitalist bias, this crisis will be perceived as a crisis of capitalism, and the anti-capitalists, who actually created the crisis by their own actions, will feel vindicated that their prophecies have finally come true. The crisis conjured up by ever new and ever more violent government interventions and the failure of the state will then appear to people as the failure of the market and the failure of capitalism. And that is when it will be most important for voices to rise up and declare: Capitalism is not the problem; it's the solution.

WEIYING ZHANG

MARKET ECONOMY AND

COMMON PROSPERITY

My friend Weiying Zhang is a professor at the National School of Development at Peking University and writes below on capitalism in China. He uses the term "market economy" synonymously with the term "capitalism" (which is also frowned upon in China).

RECENTLY, the Chinese Communist Party launched a campaign for "common prosperity." It strongly emphasizes the reduction of the income gap through a governmental redistribution policy and the so-called "third distribution", which refers to charity and donations.[832] While the benefits of common prosperity are undisputed and the idea of common prosperity is not new in China, a sharp escalation in official rhetoric—combined with a crackdown on excesses in a number of sectors, including the technology and private tuition industries—has generated anxiety among Chinese entrepreneurs and investors.

As a slogan, "the third distribution" is novel, although the initiative has already pressured businesspeople into contributing. Following the official call for "common prosperity," two leading internet companies—Alibaba Holdings and Tencent Holdings—immediately announced contributions of RMB100 billion and RMB50 billion respectively to charitable funds. Other companies have followed suit. Some local governments have even begun asking for charitable donations from the entrepreneurs who plan to make investments in their localities. Entrepreneurs' confidence is being shaken.

Common prosperity is not egalitarianism and does not mean "killing the rich to help the poor," said a senior party official trying to comfort anxious entrepreneurs. Yet the entrepreneurs' concerns are not groundless. Given China's current political, ideological and public opinion climate, downplaying market forces in favour of more government intervention has become the policy norm in the past decade. And this new campaign can be reasonably understood as a further step toward de-marketization in China.

The campaign for common prosperity, I believe, is based on a common distrust of the free market and a widespread misconception of entrepreneurs and profit. As a goal, the pursuit of common prosperity has its own legitimacy. Yet the market economy is the only system through which common prosperity can be achieved. Entrepreneurial profit is essential for markets to work for common prosperity. In my view, attempting to achieve common prosperity through de-marketization and government-dominated redistribution policies, instead of continuing marketization, can only result in the return of common poverty.

The market economy, like a living body, is a complex order that is formed spontaneously. There is no designer.[833] Due to the imperfections of human beings, the actual market economy is always unsatisfactory in one way or another. In reality, there is no "pure" market economy.[834] But human beings are idealistic, and the prospect of utopia is fascinating. When people compare the actual market economy with an idealized utopian society, the problems become obvious though not the advantages. Austrian economist Friedrich Hayek criticized "scientism" or "constructivist rationalism" as thinking based on simple systems (such as physical phenomena), which treated scientific knowledge as the only knowledge. This overestimates the power of reason, claims Hayek— misleading people's understanding of the market.[835] This is especially so when inappropriate intervention by the government or a certain political power disrupts the normal operation of the market economy, making the market economy behave as a morbid market economy. Here, people often assume this is the fault of the market economy itself, which develops into a general anti-market mentality, especially among intellectuals. Indeed, a large number of Western intellectuals—including physicist Albert Einstein, philosopher Bertrand Russell and playwright Bernard Shaw—were critics of the market.

Yet, as economists, we have a responsibility to defend the market economy: to make people correctly understand the market. Unfortunately, mainstream economics does not provide us with a good market theory.[836] The major defect of mainstream economics is the absence of the entrepreneur in the market. And a theory of the market without entrepreneurship cannot be a correct theory of the market.[837]

Mainstream economics assumes that everyone is perfectly rational and knows everything (at least in a sense of probability), and that preferences, resources and technology are all given and known. Under these assumptions, decision-making is equivalent to calculation, which can be done by computer. There is no need for imagination, alertness or judgment. Yet entrepreneurship is useless in such an imaginary market. While Adam Smith changed our thinking from a zero-sum game to a positive sum game a long time ago, mainstream neoclassical economics actually brings us back to zero-sum thinking. When resources and technologies are a given, the "cake" must be a given, and production and distribution can be separated. As a result, even economists like Joseph Stiglitz, a Nobel laureate in economics, cannot really understand the market, and thus become the vanguard of the anti-market.

In this chapter, I attempt to present a short overview of how the market economy generates common prosperity by arguing: (1) the market economy involves cooperation between strangers through which everyone can make the best use of their talents and resources to grow rich; (2) profit is a responsibility system under which everyone earns income only when they create value for others; (3) entrepreneurs are the major drivers of wealth creation; and (4) ordinary people are the biggest beneficiaries of the market economy. In so doing, I present both theoretical arguments and empirical evidence to show that China's future development depends on our faith in the market. If we lose that faith and introduce more and more government intervention, China will only move back toward common poverty.

SEEING THE MIRACLE OF MARKET ECONOMY FROM HISTORY

In order to talk about the contribution of the market economy to mankind we need to look at history. According to research conducted by Bradford DeLong, an economist at the University of California at Berkeley, in human history, from the Paleolithic Age (roughly 2.5 million years ago) to AD 2000 (the period covering 99.4 percent of human history), the world's per capita GDP reached 90 international dollars (this is a measure of wealth by international purchasing power in 1990, around $200 in today's money). By 1750 (another 0.9 percent of human history) the world's per capita GDP had doubled to 180 international dollars. From 1750 to 2000 (i.e., within 0.01 percent of human history), the world's per capita GDP increased 37 times, reaching 6,600 international dollars. In other words, 97 percent of mankind's wealth was created in the past 250 years—that is, in 0.01 percent of the time.[838]

If you draw DeLong's data on a coordinate map, you can see that from 2.5 million years ago to the present, for 99.99 percent of the time, the world's per capita GDP is near to a horizontal line. But in the past 250 years, there has been a sudden almost vertical rise. Whether it is the so-called Western European derivative countries, such as the United States, Canada, Australia or 12 Western European countries themselves, including such countries as the UK, France, Germany or emerging Japan, the vast bulk of economic growth has occurred in the past 200 years. Meanwhile, China's economic growth has mainly occurred in the past 40 years.

The numbers alone cannot explain all the stories. Our ancestors that is, ordinary Chinese people more than 100 years ago, and even Chinese farmers 40 years ago—can consume things that are not much different from the Qin, Han, Sui and Tang Dynasties, and even worse than the Song Dynasty. It is the same in Europe. The ancient Romans could enjoy what an ordinary Englishman could consume in 1800; in fact, the Romans enjoyed more. And what we can consume today is something that people could not imagine 100 years ago, or even 30 years ago.

The improvement of life has greatly extended the life span of people. In 1820, the world's average life expectancy was 26 years, which was about the same as in ancient Rome, but in 2019 it had become 72.6 years (estimated by the United Nations). Now, the average life expectancy in China has reached 77 years. Perhaps the biggest "drawback" of the market economy is that the population as a whole is aging, and people are living longer than ever before.

Yet many young people do not know much about history. They may not even know that China's food coupons were only abolished in 1993. Before the abolition of this rationing system, you needed to have a food coupon in order to buy food from a grain store. You needed an edible oil coupon for edible oil, a cloth coupon for cloth, and so on. Just 40 years ago, the monthly salary of a division-level cadre in China was just over RMB60. At that time, a catty (500 grams) of eggs was more than 60 cents. In other words, a month's salary for a division-level cadre could only buy 100 catties of eggs. Now, the monthly wage of a babysitter in Beijing is about RMB5,500, enough to buy 1,000 catties of eggs. Even if the babysitter ate 10 eggs a day, they couldn't consume that many eggs in two years. When I was in the countryside, the work points earned by farmers for a day's work were worth 20 cents, which was worth half a catty of white flour. Now, in my hometown, a person who is unskilled and only went to elementary or junior high school and works part-time can earn a daily wage of RMB150, enough to buy nearly 50 kilograms of white flour.

Why did this human miracle appear in the past 250 years? In particularly, why did China's own economic miracle appear only in the past 40 years? Have people become smarter or wiser than in the past?

Of course not. Human IQ and wisdom have made little progress since the beginning of recorded history. No matter how smart the Chinese are today, I believe that few can surpass Confucius, Mencius, and Laozi. The same is true in the West. Human intelligence has not changed much in the past few thousand years.

Could it be that the resources have increased? No, that is not the case. The Earth we live on is still the original Earth. Not only have resources not increased, on the contrary, natural resources associated with the land are slowly decreasing. What has changed? The only possible answer is that mankind has developed a new economic system: the market economy. Britain began to engage in the market economy more than 200 years ago, so the economy began to take off more than 200 years ago. China started to move toward a market economy 40 years ago, resulting in China making a huge leap in the past 40 years.

The general belief is that the improvement in living standards comes from technological progress. The question is, what is driving technological progress? Why does technology advance under some systems, but not others? The facts of historical development have proved that only a market economy can significantly promote technological progress and quickly commercialize new technologies to benefit the general public. Ancient society also had some technological inventions, but these inventions rarely created value for consumers and wealth for society, because they were not produced under the pressure of market competition and were difficult to commercialize. What smart people imagine by inspiration may not really meet the needs of consumers.

THE MARKET ECONOMY IS COOPERATION
BETWEEN STRANGERS

So how, and why, does the market economy create such economic miracles? The fundamental reason is that the market economy extends the scale and scope of human cooperation to a level that is not achievable under any other economic system. The market economy is cooperation between strangers. This gives everyone greater opportunities to become rich through specialization, which would be impossible if people only worked within small and familiar groups. Cooperation between strangers needs to be based on trust, which underpins the profit system and ensures common prosperity in the market. The planned economy fails because it cannot provide the necessary information or incentives for cooperation between strangers.

Cooperation can create value, which is a basic principle in economics. Cooperation in a market economy is not simply like a people's commune, where all people work together and do the same work, but cooperation based on division of labour and specialization. Different people do different things and then trade with each other. Division of labour and specialization can maximize everyone's advantages, make the best use of their talents, and promote technological progress. Transactions enable everyone to get what they need. Because no one is willing to trade without benefits, the market economy must be a positive-sum game (in which overall resources are increased), not a zero-sum game (in which one person's gain must mean another's loss).

In traditional society, cooperation is limited to acquaintances and people who are related by blood, such as brothers and sisters, or people in the same village, or in the same church. It is difficult to cultivate cooperation between strangers. And human cooperation today not only transcends blood and kinship, but also transcends regions and national boundaries. It is global. If a company's products are sold, the vast majority of the consumers who buy the products are not known by the producer. Hayek called this the "extended order."[839] It is this large-scale cooperation between strangers that has generated global wealth at an alarming rate.

The key ingredient for achieving cooperation between strangers is, of course, trust. If the buyer does not trust the seller, the former dare not buy the latter's goods, and these goods cannot be sold. Thus, specialization will not help the seller. As a result, everyone would have to produce for themselves, and then return to a self-sufficient, natural economy.

In a market economy, therefore, there is not only an "invisible hand," but also an "invisible eye" watching strangers cooperate.[840] Everyone must behave well and be responsible for their actions. Past criticisms of the market economy are often due to people only knowing the former factor and not seeing the effect of the latter factor—i.e., they believe that the market must be full of fraud. In fact, we have seen that the more developed the market economy is, the more people pay attention to their credit. For an enterprise to succeed in the market, it must establish a good reputation. If a company has a bad reputation and no one trusts it, it will be eliminated.

PROFIT IS TO LET THE BOSS TAKE RESPONSIBILITY

How is trust in the market established? Three concepts are the key to understanding the market economy: enterprise, profit and the entrepreneur.[841]

There are 1.4 billion people in China. If everyone produces their own goods and sells them on the market, who can be trusted? Or, if the trademarks and patents on all commodities on the market were removed, what goods would you dare buy? You might be willing to buy the simplest commodities such as potatoes, rice, and fruit. But would you dare to buy cars, computers, mineral water, and projectors that are difficult to distinguish in terms of quality and function? Surely not! You would be unable to have confidence in 99 percent of the goods on the market.

So how can you proceed? There is a way. China's 1.4 billion people can be divided into 30 groups, such as Henan people, Hebei people, Shandong people, Shaanxi people, Beijing people and so on. After this grouping, although we don't know everyone—we know that this person is Shandongese, the other is Cantonese—we can establish a certain kind of group responsibility. If someone were to cheat us, we would know if it was the Cantonese or Shandongese, at least.

Yet companies are also social groupings. Each company has its own name (trademark). Whoever lied to us, we can sue him, or at the very least not buy from them again. In this way, when production activities appear through enterprises, each enterprise must be responsible for its own products, so that we can build trust. If there is no enterprise, everyone is only engaged in individual production, resulting in little more than subsistence.

How does business enable us to trust each other? The answer is related to ownership allocation and the profit system. For example, an enterprise is composed of 10,000 individuals and, in theory, everyone can become the owner. The annual income of this enterprise is RMB100 million, which is equally divided among the 10,000 employees, and each gets RMB10,000. This sounds fair. But think about it. If something goes wrong, who is responsible? If everyone is required to share the responsibility, in effect, no one is responsible, and the company will have no revenue available for distribution.

In reality, some people bear responsibility for a company's negligence, and others bear strict liability. The person responsible for negligence receives contract income (i.e., salary). If they do not arrive late or leave early, are not absent from work, so not violate the work regulations, and work for a month, they receive one month's salary at the end of the month. They are employees. The other group of people, the managers, take profits and bear strict liability or residual liability.

In simple terms: if others do not discover your mistakes, you are not responsible. You are an employee. If you cannot assign mistakes to others, then all the mistakes are yours. You are a manager. The manager does not have the right to demand sales revenue from consumers by claiming he has not made a mistake, nor can he take his employees to court because he has made a loss. Meanwhile an employee can demand income from the manager as long as he has not made a mistake. If the manager refuses to pay him, he can take the manager or the company to court. This is the difference between a manager and an employee.

Profit is the surplus of enterprise income after deducting costs such as wages. It may be positive or negative and is thus very different from wages and other forms of income, which cannot be negative. Those who take profit must take risks, so it is an incentive mechanism. When any employee makes a mistake, the manager is the first to bear the responsibility. The simplest example: If you own a restaurant and your chef does not keep the kitchen clean and the guests are hospitalized with diarrhea, you are responsible. Therefore, the owner must carefully supervise and regulate the behaviour of the employees, thereby ensuring customers can buy the company's products with confidence.

Furthermore, not only for the employees of the company, but also when the company's suppliers make mistakes, the bosses of the company must take responsibility. For example, if you bought a brand-name computer and a certain part of the computer, such as the screen, chip, or fan, does not function, or the battery exploded, the computer manufacturer, not the supplier of the parts, takes responsibility. In other words, a company uses its own brand to make a promise to its consumers, guaranteeing that if they buy its products it will accept responsibility for any defects. Thus, a market is established that everyone can trust. Cooperation between strangers can proceed in an orderly manner and the continuous increase of social wealth is secured.

Profit is therefore a responsibility and an assessment system. To a large extent, profitability is determined by the owner's capacity to take responsibility for others. The market divides the accounting units through the organizational form of the enterprise and traces the responsibilities of profits, so that everyone is responsible for their actions, and there is trust in the market.

THE RICH IN THE MARKET ECONOMY ARE ELECTED BY CONSUMERS WITH MONEY VOTES

Why do some people become profit-taking entrepreneurs, while others become wage-earning employees? This is determined by the differences in entrepreneurial abilities between people.[842] In a market economy, everyone has the freedom to choose to be an entrepreneur or an employee. There is no discriminatory rule that Person A can be an entrepreneur and Person B can only be an employee. But the result of the competition is that only those with high enough entrepreneurial ability will become entrepreneurs.

Entrepreneurship also means the ability to take responsibility for others. On average, the scale of the profit depends on the entrepreneur's ability. But because the market is full of uncertainty, no matter how capable entrepreneurs are, they may lose money. Behind every successful entrepreneur, there are many failed entrepreneurs. So we should not only see those entrepreneurs who have made a lot of money. We must also see those that have risked and lost everything. If anyone is jealous of an entrepreneur making money, they can choose to become an entrepreneur themselves. One thing they must remember, however, is that if they are not up to it, they could lose everything.

What is the market? The market is a system where others—and not you—have the final say as to whether you have offered the best products or services. What is valuable and what has no value must be evaluated in the market. Buyers have the final say. Therefore, bragging is useless. If anyone does not create value for others, it is impossible to earn income. When two companies compete and we say that a particular one has more advantages, it means that this company adds the most value for consumers (that is, achieves the best balance between quality and price). Competition between enterprises is the competition to create surplus value for consumers.

There is a popular saying that entrepreneurs make money from consumers, making it seem that consumers are being exploited by entrepreneurs. This is wrong. In a competitive market with no privilege, profits can only come from the value created by entrepreneurs *for* consumers, who will not pay RMB10.01 for something worth only RMB10. In fact, the money an entrepreneur makes is only a small part of the wealth they create. Take someone like Bill Gates. No matter how wealthy he is, it is a drop in the bucket compared to the value that Microsoft has created for mankind.

In a market economy, the money an entrepreneur makes is, on average, proportional to the number of customers they serve. An entrepreneur who only provides products and services to a few people cannot make a lot of money. Only entrepreneurs who serve the mass market can make a lot of money.[843] Therefore, the richest entrepreneurs in the market economy are selected by consumers, who essentially vote with their money. Each of us is a consumer. If we are jealous of a certain entrepreneur making too much money, we can only blame ourselves for buying their products. If most consumers no longer use the products provided by Tencent, and no longer use WeChat, QQ, and online games, Mr. Ma Huateng will no longer be rich. And all of us are unwilling to give up using Tencent's products, not because we are stupid or benevolent, but because they bring us greater benefits. We think it worth the money. On the one hand, you willingly buy his products; and on the other hand, you are angry at him for making so much money, which is a contradiction.

ORDINARY PEOPLE ARE THE BIGGEST BENEFICIARIES OF THE MARKET ECONOMY

Who benefits the most from the market economy? Why, ordinary people of course. To give a simple example, Thomas Edison invented the light bulb, which brought convenience to everyone. But the value of light bulbs is much smaller for the rich than the poor, because when there were no light bulbs, the rich could light candles that the poor could not afford.

Another example is TV. Now everyone can watch the songs and plays performed by stars. In the past, only a few wealthy people and palace nobles could enjoy live performances. The same is true for cars. In the past, the rich could take a sedan, while the poor could only walk. But now ordinary people can use a car. The difference between riding an Audi and a Xiali is much smaller than the difference between sitting in a sedan and walking.

This is true for all new products and new technologies. The takeaway provides the greatest convenience to ordinary people, and the WeChat public account allows ordinary people to become self-media people. Yes, some new products are only consumed by the rich at the beginning, and are considered luxury goods. But as the cost falls, they soon become a necessity for most people. The rich are simply paying for the research and development expenses of new products for ordinary people.[844] Therefore, the biggest beneficiaries of the market economy are ordinary people, not the privileged class. At least from the perspective of consumption, the market economy has made people more equal.

How can consumers afford products produced by entrepreneurs? Because when entrepreneurs provide consumers with products in the product market, at the same time they create opportunities for consumers to earn income in the labor market. In a market economy, most people earn most of their income from wages. Wages come from work, and without work, there is no wage. Who created the job? Entrepreneurs! Job opportunities in a society are not given. They are created by entrepreneurs. Without entrepreneurs, most people will have no job opportunities and therefore no income. Furthermore, how much wages workers can earn depends to a large extent on the ability of entrepreneurs, because the workers' productivity is positively related to the ability of entrepreneurs. The value created under entrepreneurs with high ability is greater than that under entrepreneurs with low ability. Therefore, the greater the number of entrepreneurs in a society and the higher their abilities, the higher the wages of workers.

When I say this, of course, it does not mean that workers are fed by entrepreneurs. In a market economy, everyone supports themselves. But job opportunities for workers are indeed created by entrepreneurs. In this regard, China's experience can provide a convincing explanation. In the era of the planned economy, China's urban population was less than 20 percent of the total population. Even with such low urbanization, urban-born people could not find employment opportunities in the cities, and the government had to mobilize 20 million "educated youths" to the countryside. Yet after the opening up of the economy, hundreds of millions of rural people have found work in cities—with companies still sometimes encountering difficulties in recruiting workers from time to time.

Cross-regional data shows that the more entrepreneurs in a region, the greater the number of employees, and the higher employees' average wage. For example, in 2016, the average annual wage of an employee in the private sector positively correlated to the marketization score at the provincial level (the correlation coefficient is +0.71), and, on average, every one-point increase in the marketization score results in a RMB1,826 increase in the average annual wage.[845] The correlation holds consistently. Therefore, the best way to increase the income of workers is to make entrepreneurs freer and more competitive in the market, not the other way around. If entrepreneurs are eliminated, the vast majority of Chinese people will return to absolute poverty.

THE MARKET MAKES INCOME DISTRIBUTION FAIRER

It is understandable that many people are worried about poverty and uneven income distribution in society. However, some people attribute this phenomenon to market-oriented reforms, and some even believe that the result of a market economy must be the widening of the gap between the rich and the poor. This is a misunderstanding.

In the pre-market economy society, whether in the East or the West, the vast majority of people struggled below the survival line. It was a common occurrence that people died of starvation due to famine. The only effective way to solve the poverty problem is a market economy. The freer the economy, the fewer the number of poor people. A study by the World Bank showed that in 2005, among developing countries, the extreme poverty rate of the most market-oriented countries was only 2.7 percent, while the extreme poverty rate of those countries without a free market was 41.5 percent.[846]

China is a very convincing example. According to the World Bank, China's poverty rate fell from 88 percent in 1981 to 0.7 percent in 2015, as measured by the percentage of people living on the equivalent of US$1.90 or less per day by 2011 purchasing-power parity terms.[847] The correlation coefficient between marketization and the poverty rate of the rural population at the provincial level in 2016 is -0.85. On average, whenever a region's marketization score rose by 1 point, the poverty rate of the rural population in that region fell by 1.1 percentage points. Of the 12 regions with a marketization score lower than 8, only two regions have a rural population poverty rate of less than 5 percent; and of 19 regions with a marketization score above 8, only two provinces have a rural poverty rate of more than 5 percent. Among the seven regions with a marketization score exceeding 10, no rural poverty rate exceeds 2 percent. Some 40 years after the reform and opening up of China, the absolute poverty problem in Chinese society has basically been solved.

The market economy can solve the poverty problem more effectively because it provides ordinary people with opportunities to make a fortune. In a non-market economy, such opportunities are only available to a few privileged groups. The urban self-employed in China in the 1980s all came from the lower social groups. People with privileges can serve as soldiers and work in the government or state-owned enterprises, but what about those without privileges and connections? They had to start up their own businesses. They picked up the tatters, set up street stalls, and sold some melon seeds, tea, and clothes. Thus, they became wealthy. This is impossible under a planned economy. By the way, China's garbage disposal and environmental protections have been greatly attributed to people picking up tatters: people that should be greatly rewarded for such endeavours.

Certainly, both government and charitable organizations are important with respect to solving poverty. Yet we must understand that the money for poverty alleviation has been created by entrepreneurs. Governments and charities can transfer wealth from one group of people to another. But it is impossible to create something out of nothing. It is due to entrepreneurs creating the wealth that governments and charities have the money for poverty alleviation. So it is not surprising that international aid funds always flow from market economy countries to non-market economy countries, not the other way around; similarly, China's domestic poverty alleviation funds also flow from regions with a high degree of marketization to regions with a low degree of marketization. If entrepreneurs do not have the incentive to create wealth, the government will have no money to transfer, and people will have to rely increasingly on charity. We must keep this in mind.

Income distribution statistics are misleading since the same income group in statistics can contain different people from year-to-year.[848] When discussing the income gap, people often ignore the vertical flow between rich and poor. A typical example is Piketty,[849] who argues that the rich have become richer and the poor poorer in the past century by assuming no change in the pool of rich and poor. In fact, one of the most significant characteristics of a market economy is that the rich and poor are fluid. As Schumpeter said, in a market economy, the rich club is like a luxury hotel, always full of people, but the names of the guests are always changing.[850] Similarly, the so-called "low-income class," like a budget hotel, are always overcrowded. From time to time, some people move out and new people move in. And the new residents may have been former VIPs used to spending their time in luxury hotels.

According to the Hurun China Rich List, only 30 of the 100 richest people in 2010 remain on the rich-list 10 years later. Among the top 20 in 2010, only three people are still on the top 20 after 10 years, and six people are not even on the 100 people list. A study by Professors Khor and Pencavel from Stanford University found that 50.4 percent of the one-fifth of the Chinese population with the lowest income in 1990 had jumped out of the lowest income group in 1995, and 2.1 percent of them entered the highest income group. Meanwhile, of the richest one-fifth of the population, only 43.9 percent still belonged to the highest income group in 1995, and nearly 5 percent fell into the lowest income group.[851] This shows that the opening up of the economy has greatly improved the vertical mobility of Chinese society. Most of the Chinese entrepreneurs who are now on the rich list were living in relative poverty decades ago, some just one decade ago. It can also be predicted that, as long as China continues to adhere to market-oriented reforms, many of them will no longer be on the list within a few years.

Even if vertical mobility is not considered, and only the Gini coefficient is used to measure income disparity, the common narrative regarding inequalities can be challenged. Taking 2001 as an example, among the 30 provinces, municipalities, and autonomous regions in China, on average, the regions with better-developed markets, with fewer state-run economic sectors and with lower fiscal expenditure as a proportion of GDP, are the regions with the smallest income gap.[852] The same signs of correlations hold consistently.[853] Given that government spending is commonly believed to be an important channel of redistribution from the rich to the poor, it seems surprising that the higher proportion of government spending in GDP brought about the higher income gap.

What this clearly shows is that the less government is involved in economic activities—meaning the more people have freedom to engage in business activities—the fiercer will be competition, resulting in lower profits. Yet if a region has only a few privileged and connected people able to conduct business, or only the most audacious dare to do business, profits will be very high. For example, there are more people in Zhejiang Province involved in business, and there are more wealthy people. Yet levels of profitability are low. But in areas such as Northeast China, where most people are uninvolved in business, those few people that are engaged in business can make a lot of money. Therefore, we see that the more open the market and the less government intervention, the smaller the income gap.

In addition, equality is not only reflected in monetary income, but also other aspects such as freedom, rights, and choices. What freedom did ordinary people have in the past? When I was in the countryside, watermelons and apples produced on farmers' private plots were sold on the black market, and the farmers were considered to be committing the crime of speculation. They were publicly chastised or even locked up. They didn't even have the basic right to be a human being. At that time, the peasants could not afford to eat meat all year round, nor could they buy noodles. But as long as the commune cadres came to the village, everyone rushed to welcome them with white flour and meat. Why? Only by establishing a relationship with them could children hope to join the army or be recruited for public jobs, even though the hope was very small. Therefore, I don't think that reform and opening up have made Chinese society more unequal, but more equal and fairer.

BE WARY OF "ENVY" IN THE GUISE OF "JUSTICE"

In his book *The Birth of Plenty*, the American scholar William Bernstein looked at the rise of the modern West from the perspective of economic, military, and historical systems. He pointed out that there are four preconditions for a flourishing modern society and economy: the first is the property rights system, and the second is science and rationality. Reasonably, the third is presence of capital markets, and the fourth the reduction of transportation costs.

Over the past 40 years of opening up, China's per capita GDP has doubled every 10 years, and everyone's lives have been greatly improved. This is a remarkable achievement. China's ability to do this has a lot to do with the reform of the property rights system, although China's property rights system still needs to be improved. For example, vis-à-vis rural land, the initial contract period for farmers was one year, and farmers were motivated to produce, but none were willing to invest. The government extended the contract period to five years—certainly better than one year but still short of an incentive to implement water conservation projects. The contract period was then extended to 10 years. Yet, still, no one wanted to plant trees. And finally it was extended to 30 years. Even today, the system does not work. If the land cannot be traded, a large number of farmers will be unable to become urban citizens.

China's capital markets grew out of nothing and are constantly developing. State-owned enterprises and state-owned banks may not be able to change much in the short-term, when they are listed domestically and overseas. But in the long-term, they are going in the right direction. The construction of road transportation has greatly reduced transportation costs, and it has also played a very important role in China's economic growth.

China's achievements are largely related to the change of ideas. In the 1980s, with the emergence of self-employed and bonus systems, many in China suffered from "red eye disease," (i.e., envy). Some people could not even accept "distribution according to work." And if "distribution according to work" is not accepted, the economy will not develop, resulting in everyone living in poverty. Through the efforts of economists and other social science workers, "distribution according to work" has gradually been generally accepted. In this way, people have the enthusiasm to work. Later, the idea of capital and other factors of production participating in income distribution was accepted, and entrepreneurial profits were recognized. In this way, the entrepreneurial spirit of the Chinese people was allowed to flourish, establishing China as a country of entrepreneurship, resulting in everyone's life improving.

Regrettably, in terms of ideas, we seem to be backtracking. "Red eye disease" is rooted in human nature. Envy means that, as long as you see that others are better than yourself—such as having higher income than yourself, a smarter mind than yourself, a stronger body or being prettier than yourself—you will feel resentment and think society is unjust. People who are envious do not even care how much they get. Instead, they prefer to be poorer than to see others richer than themselves. What makes them gloat most is to see the rich go bankrupt and celebrities make a fool of themselves. The epistemological basis of envy is zero-sum game thinking, that is, the belief that wealth is a fixed amount.[854] One person's gain means another's loss. Some people become rich only because others become poor. People who indulge in zero-sum thinking are usually keen on concept of class struggle.

If human beings cannot effectively curb "red eye disease," society cannot progress.[855] Therefore, both "red eye disease" and envy are derogatory terms. The Bible regards envy as one of the seven deadly sins. Envy-based acts do not have social legitimacy. In public, people always try to conceal or deny their envy. The trouble is that, thanks to the efforts of some Western leftists, "envy" is now wearing the vest of "fair distribution" and "social justice" and has achieved moral legitimacy. The policy propositions of "fairness" and "justice" are viewed as legitimate, with policies advocating the shifting of people's attention from wealth creation to wealth distribution. This obviously hurts those who hope to get rich by their own efforts, and who are the people the policy advocates claim to be helping.

This brings us back to the issue at the beginning of this article: the responsibility of economists. Why does society need economists? Because the market economy is too fragile and too vulnerable to damage, someone is needed to defend it. The planned economy was designed by a small number of intellectuals and then imposed on society from top to bottom by power, so there are always some powerful people defending it. The market economy is different. It was not designed by intellectuals or by anyone, but spontaneously emerged from bottom to top. This also means that the market economy is like a child without a mother; anyone can beat it and stigmatize it without taking responsibility. People living in the planned economy system who criticize the planned economy inevitably take political and even legal risks, but no matter what system you live in, there is no risk in criticizing the market economy. In fact, countless people have been jailed and even paid the price of their lives for criticizing the planned economy, but no one has ever gotten into any trouble for criticizing the market economy. In this sense, the market economy is really benevolent, and we should really cherish it.

Another problem with the market economy is that, when you have the opportunity to enjoy its benefits, you tend to take them for granted and notice instead its shortcomings. Of course, when you have no opportunity to enjoy its benefits, it has no way to prove its advantages. If you break something yourself, you can blame yourself. If you are excluded and feel powerless, you lack an explanation as to why your situation is so bad.

Chinese people are familiar with comedian Mr. Zhao Benshan's "Selling Crutches." Mr. Fan Wei's leg was not broken, but Zhao Benshan repeatedly said that it was. In the end, Fan Wei himself felt that his leg was really broken, so he couldn't wait to buy Zhao Benshan's crutches. In fact, the problem was not with Fan Wei's legs, but with his brain. Many people are now "selling crutches." What are their "crutches"? Anti-market arguments, with many of the failures of the market economy actually fabricated.

I have only one purpose in saying this: to give everyone a better understanding of what a market economy is and to strengthen our belief in it. What is the most worrying thing about China's future? It is not energy or environmental issues—these are of course very important, but not the most important because technological progress driven by market competition will surely find the answer for us. We do not need to be as pessimistic as Malthus was 200 years ago, or the Club of Rome 50 years ago. China's future development depends on our beliefs. As I argued elsewhere, China's economic successes over the past 40 years are the result of marketization reforms and the rise of entrepreneurship.[856] And China's future growth depends on innovative entrepreneurs.[857] If we strengthen our confidence in the market economy and continue to advance an entrepreneur-friendly institutional environment through market-oriented reform, China will move toward common prosperity. If we lose our faith in the market and introduce more and more government intervention in the name of common prosperity, China will sacrifice the progress it has made and return to poverty. Do not forget that the original intention of the planned economy was to benefit the poor. Yet, as a result, the ranks of the poor swelled, making the destiny of the poor more miserable than ever.

In summary, the market economy is the only road to common prosperity, and the planned economy is a one-way street to common poverty!

This chapter is an updated version of a paper originally published as "Market economy and China's 'common prosperity' campaign," in *Journal of Chinese Economic and Business Studies*, 1–15, DOI: 10.1080/14765284.2021.2004350

THE QUESTIONNAIRE

Q1. Below is a list of various things that people have said they consider to be a good economic system. Which of the statements would you say too?

1. I am for an economic system in which the state sets the rules but ideally does not interfere otherwise

2. The state should set the prices for rent and food and should set minimum and maximum wages; otherwise, the system is socially unfair

3. I think private businesses alone should decide what products to manufacture and what prices to charge for them; the state should not be involved in that

4. We need a lot more state intervention in the economy, since the market fails time and again

5. In a good economic system, I think the state should only own property in certain areas; the lion's share of property should be privately owned

6. Social justice is more important in an economic system than economic freedom

7. None of these

Q2. Please now think about the word **capitalism**. For each of the following statements, select whether that is something you associate with **capitalism**.

1. Prosperity

2. Innovation

3. Greed

4. Coldness

5. Progress

6. Corruption

7. Freedom

8. Performance-oriented, constant pressure to achieve

9. A wide range of goods

10. Environmental degradation

1. Yes—Definitely

2. Yes—Probably

3. No—Probably not

4. No—Definitely not

5. Don't know

Q3. Which of the following statements about capitalism, if any, would you agree with? *Select all that apply*

Capitalism . . .

1. ensures prosperity

2. is responsible for hunger and poverty

3. is an especially efficient economic system

4. leads to growing inequality

5. means that consumers determine what is offered, and not the state

6. is responsible for environmental destruction and climate change

7. means economic freedom

8. repeatedly leads to new economic and financial crises

9. has improved conditions for ordinary people in many countries

10. is dominated by the rich; they set the political agenda

11. encourages people to do their best

12. leads to monopolies where individual companies (e.g., Google or Amazon) control the entire market

13. promotes selfishness and greed

14. may not be ideal, but it is still better than all other economic systems

15. leads to wars

16. is irreplaceable; past attempts to replace capitalism have always resulted in dictatorships and suffering

17. entices people to buy products they don't need

18. means that there is always a danger of fascism

19. None of these

Q4. Political parties are often classified as being to the left, middle-of-the-road, or to the right. How would you describe your own political position?

Please give your answer on a scale of zero to ten where zero means you are far left and ten means you are far right.

0. Far left

1.

2.

3.

4.

5. Middle

6.

7.

8.

9.

10. Far right

11. Don't know

12. Prefer not to say

Q5. Do you agree, or disagree, with the following statement:

In reality, politicians don't decide anything. They are puppets controlled by powerful forces in the background.

1. Agree

2. Disagree

3. Undecided

Q6. Do you agree, or disagree, with the following statement:

A lot of things in politics can only be properly understood if you know that there is a larger plan behind them, something that most people, however, do not know.

1. Agree

2. Disagree

3. Undecided

THE AUTHOR

RAINER ZITELMANN was born in Frankfurt am Main, Germany, in 1957. He studied history and political science from 1978 to 1983 and graduated with distinction. In 1986, he was awarded the title Dr. Phil for his thesis *Hitler. Selbstverständnis eines Revolutionärs* (English: *Hitler's National Socialism*) under the mentorship of Professor Freiherr von Aretin. The study, which was awarded the grade "summa cum laude," received worldwide attention and recognition.

From 1987 to 1992, Zitelmann worked at the Central Institute for Social Science Research at the Free University of Berlin. He then became editor-in-chief of Ullstein-Propyläen publishing house, at that time Germany's third-largest book-publishing group and headed various departments of the leading German daily newspaper *Die Welt*. In 2000, he set up his own business, Dr. ZitelmannPB, GmbH, which has since become the market leader for positioning consulting for real estate companies in Germany. He sold the business in 2016.

In 2016, Zitelmann was awarded his second doctorate, this time in sociology, with his thesis on the psychology of the super-rich, under the mentorship of Professor Wolfgang Lauterbach at the University of Potsdam. His second doctoral dissertation was published in English as *The Wealth Elite* and deals with the psychology of the super-rich.

Zitelmann has written and edited a total of 26 books, which have enjoyed substantial success in a range of languages around the world. He is a much sought-after guest speaker in Asia, the United States, South America and Europe. Over the last few years, he has written articles and given interviews to many of the world's leading media outlets, including *Le Monde*, *Le Point*, *Corriere della Sera*, *Il Giornale*, *Frankfurter Allgemeine Zeitung*, *Die Welt*, *Der Spiegel*, *Neue Zürcher Zeitung*, *The Daily Telegraph*, *The Times*, *Forbes* and numerous media in China, Vietnam, South Korea, Chile, Brazil and Argentina. Readers of this book are especially recommended to read his books *The Power of Capitalism* and *The Rich in Public Opinion*. Detailed information about the life of Rainer Zitelmann can be found at rainer-zitelmann.com.

NOTES

1   The Chinese economist Weiying Zhang, following the tradition of the Austrian School of economics (and in particular Schumpeterian economics), emphasizes the role of entrepreneurship. See Weiying Zhang, *Ideas for China's Future*, and Weiying Zhang, "A Paradigmatic Change."

2   Cf. Kepplinger, *Risikofallen*, 62–63.

3   Fink / Kappner, https://de.irefeurope.org/Diskussionsbeitrage/Artikel/article/Globale-Armut-Positive-Entwicklung-negative-Einschatzung

4   The World Bank defines absolute poverty as an income below the international poverty line of $1.90 (PPP) per day. This is the most severe type of poverty, characterized by severe deprivation of essential items (including and especially food). Measuring poverty in $ (PPP) units takes into account variations in purchasing power in different countries (PPP = Purchasing Power Parity).

5   Cf. Pinker, 87, Rosling, 52, Fink / Kappner, https://de.irefeurope.org/Diskussionsbeitrage/Artikel/article/Globale-Armut-Positive-Entwicklung-negative-Einschatzung and https://www.worldbank.org/en/publication/poverty-and-shared-prosperity

6   Melcher, "Kinderarbeit: Alarmierende Entwicklung laut UN-Studie" in *FAZ*, June 10, 2021. https://www.faz.net/aktuell/wirtschaft/kinderarbeit-alarmierende-entwick-lung-laut-un-studie-17380670.html

7   Norberg, *Progress*, 2.

8   Wagenknecht, 58.

9   Engels, *Condition of the Working Class*, 16.

10   Engels, *Condition of the Working Class*, 16–17.

11   Braudel, 73.

12   Braudel, 74–75.

13   Plumpe, *Das kalte Herz*, 149–150.

14   Braudel, 75.

15   Braudel, 78.

16   Braudel, 78.

17   Braudel, 130.

18   Braudel, 130.

19   Quoted in Braudel, 132.

20   Deaton, 92.

21   McCloskey / Carden, 41.

22   Norberg, *Progress*, 12.

23   Quoted in Braudel, 90–91.

24   Braudel, 91–92.

25   Braudel, 283.

26   Quoted in Braudel, 491.

27   The international dollar is a hypothetical unit of currency that has the same purchasing power parity that the U.S. dollar had in the United States in 1990.

28   Maddison, 70.

29   Maddison, 70.

30   Maddison, 70.

31   Quoted in Lee, 80.

32   Dikötter, *Mao's Great Famine*, 320–321.

33   Chang / Halliday, 533.

34   Deaton, 39.

35   Lee, 159.

36   Zhang, "The China Model," 18–19. Italicized in the original.

37   Zhang, "The China Model," 9–10.

38   Zhang, "The China Model," 10. Italicized in the original.

39   Zhang, "The China Model," 11–12.

40   Zhang, "The China Model," 13.

41   Zhang, "The China Model," 14.

42   Zhang, *Ideas for China's Future*, 229.

43   Zhang, *The Logic*, 158.

44   DiLorenzo, 95–96.

45   Wemheuer, 17–18, 59.

46   Wemheuer, 17.

47   Wemheuer, 235.

48   https://www.bpb.de/nachschlagen/zahlen-und-fakten/globalisierung/52693/
      unterernaehrung

49   Norberg, *Progress*, 25–26.

50   Miller / Kim / Roberts, *Index of Economic Freedom 2021*, 22.

51   Oxford Poverty & Human Development Initiative, *Global MPI 2021*: http://hdr.
      undp.org/en/2021-MPI

52   Miller / Kim / Roberts, *Index of Economic Freedom 2021*, 25.

53   Cf. Zitelmann, *The Power of Capitalism*, Chapter 2.

54   Moyo, 8.

55   Moyo, 55.

56   Moyo, 67.

57   Norberg, *Global Capitalism*, 199.

58   UNICEF "Kinderarbeit weltweit: Die 7 wichtigsten Fragen und
      Antworten": https://www.unicef.de/informieren/aktuelles/blog/
      kinderarbeit-fragen-und-antworten/166982

59   More, *Utopia*, 79–80.

60   Andreä, Johann Valentin, 171.

61   Sachweh, 45.

62   Sachweh, 235.

63   Sachweh, 68.

64   Innovation should not be confused with invention here. Innovations are creative
      novelties for which there is actual demand. Inventions can be "creative" and "great"
      but without commercial success because consumers do not find them attractive at
      the time they occur or because the inventor does not market them well.

65   Schumpeter, "Unternehmerfunktion und Arbeiterinteresse," 229. Italicized in the original.

66   Quoted in Jungbluth, *Oetkers*, 62.

67   Zitelmann, *The Rich in Public Opinion*, 307.

68   Zitelmann, *The Rich in Public Opinion*, 157.

69   Cowen, 54–55.

70   Cowen, 55.

71   Sowell, *Intellectuals and Society*, 50–51. Italicized in the original.

72   Watkins / Brook, *Equal is Unfair*, 10. Italicized in the original.

73   Marx, *Critique of the Gotha Programme*, 20.

74   Marx, *Critique of the Gotha Programme*, 11.

75   Marx, *Critique of the Gotha Programme*, 21.

76   Kelley / Evans, 7.

77   Kelley / Evans, 3.

78   Kelley / Evans, 15. Italicized in the original.

79   Kelley / Evans, 14.

80   Foster, 184. Italicized in the original.

81   Sullivan, quoted in Foster, 184.

82   Neuhäuser, 107, footnote 1.

83   Neuhäuser, 32.

84   Scheidel, 227.

85   Neuhäuser, 145.

86   Neuhäuser, 146.

87   Neuhäuser, 147.

88   Neuhäuser, 147.

89   Deaton, 78.

90   Deaton, 82.

91   Deaton, 83.

92   Deaton, 89.

93   Lindert / Williamson, 198.

94   http://www.sozialpolitik-aktuell.de/files/sozialpolitik-aktuell/_Politikfelder/ Finanzierung/Datensammlung/PDF-Dateien/abbII1a.pdf

95   Piketty, *Capital in the Twenty-First Century*, 16.

96   Cf. the contributions in Delsol / Lecaussin / Martin.

97   Cf. Palmer, xv.

98   Ponciano, https://www.forbes.com/sites/jonathanponciano/2020/09/08/
        self-made-score/?sh=6a41b14d41e4

99   Edwards / Bourne, 10.

100   Arnott / Bernstein / Wu, 2.

101   Piketty, *Capital in the Twenty-First Century*, 438.

102   Pinker, 104–105.

103   Delsol, 8.

104   All figures from Edwards / Bourne, 3.

105   Edwards / Bourne, 5.

106   Sowell, *Intellectuals and Society*, 36.

107   Sowell, *Intellectuals and Society*, 36.

108   Knight / McCreddie, 49, 51.

109   Knight / McCreddie, 55.

110   Knight / McCreddie, 46.

111   Scheidel, 405.

112   Scheidel, 409.

113   Scheidel, 414.

114   Niemietz, "Mythos vom Globalisierungsverlierer," 155.

115   Edwards / Bourne, 16–17.

116   Pinker, 117.

117   Watkins / Brook, *Equal is Unfair*, 40.

118   Tillessen, 46.

119   Tillessen, 47.

120   Tillessen, 56.

121   Tillessen, 30.

122   Federal Government of the Federal Republic of Germany, *6. Armuts- und
        Reichtumsbericht der Deutschen Bundesregierung (2021), Kurzfassung*, XVI. https://
        www.armuts-und-reichtumsbericht.de/SharedDocs/Downloads/Berichte/entwurf-
        sechster-armuts-reichttumsbericht-kurzfassung.pdf?__blob=publicationFile&v=2

123   https://schoolinreviews.com/
        pisa-results-published-in-dec-2019-which-countries-score-the-highest-and-why/

124   https://observer.com/2019/07/best-countries-start-business-economic-freedom/

125   Scheidel, 9.

126   Scheidel, 22.

127   Zitelmann, "Zur Argumentationsstrategie" (1977), 28.

128   Klein, 51.

129   Klein, 75.

130   Klein, 6.

131   Klein, 6–7.

132   Klein, 7.

133   Klein, 9.

134   Klein, 82.

135   Klein, 19.

136   Klein, 34.

137   Klein, 34.

138   Klein, 55.

139   Klein, 79.

140   Klein, 81.

141   Klein, 81.

142   Klein, 81.

143   Klein, 81.

144   Klein, 80.

145   Klein, 19.

146   Klein, 49.

147   Wendling / Emerson, et al., *EPI*, 2020, 1.

148   Wendling / Emerson, et al., *EPI*, 2020, 10.

149   Weede, "Wirtschaftliche Freiheit," 448.

150   Miller / Kim / Roberts, *Index of Economic Freedom 2021*, 26.

151   Méndez.

152   Méndez.

153   Mavragani / Nikolaou / Tsagarakis.

154   Mavragani / Nikolaou / Tsagarakis, 8.

155   Antweiler / Copeland / Taylor, 41.

156   Mavragani / Nikolaou / Tsagarakis, 1.

157   Medvedev, *The Ecologist*, 20, 1, Jan/Feb, 1990, 24.

158   Feshbach / Friendly, Jr., 1.

159   Higginbotham, 12.

160   Higginbotham, 20.

161   Higginbotham, 20.

162   Higginbotham, 20.

163   Higginbotham, 271.

164   Higginbotham, 272.

165   Higginbotham, 44.

166   Higginbotham, 74.

167   Higginbotham, 325.

168   Higginbotham, 324.

169   Higginbotham, 327–328.

170   Higginbotham, 478, note to page 321.

171   Beleites, 152.

172   Pinker, 143.

173   Zitelmann, *The Power of Capitalism*, Chapter 1.

174   Dikötter, *Mao's Great Famine*, 57.

175   Dikötter, *Mao's Great Famine*, 61.

176   Chang / Halliday, 566.

177   Pinker, 143.

178   Fink / Kurz, "Umweltdesaster DDR": https://www.insm-oekonomenblog.
       de/22661-bitteres-aus-bitterfeld-das-umweltdesaster-der-ddr-und-seine-lehren/

179   Report from the Federal Foundation for Coming to Terms with the
       GDR's Past: https://deutsche-einheit-1990.de/ministerien/muner/
       verschmutzung/#:~:text=Insgesamt%20sind%20viele%20Fl%C3%BCsse%20
       und,Siedlungsabf%C3%A4lle%20auf%20%E2%80%9Ewilden%E2%80%9C%20
       M%C3%BClldeponien.

180   Report from the Federal Foundation for Coming to Terms with the
       GDR's Past: https://deutsche-einheit-1990.de/ministerien/muner/
       verschmutzung/#:~:text=Insgesamt%20sind%20viele%20Fl%C3%BCsse%20
       und,Siedlungsabf%C3%A4lle%20auf%20%E2%80%9Ewilden%E2%80%9C%20
       M%C3%BClldeponien.

181   Beleites, 163.

182   Knabe, *Klimakiller DDR*.

183   Fink / Kurz, "Umweltdesaster DDR": https://www.insm-oekonomenblog.
       de/22661-bitteres-aus-bitterfeld-das-umweltdesaster-der-ddr-und-seine-lehren/.

184   Fink / Kurz, "Umweltdesaster DDR": https://www.insm-oekonomenblog.
       de/22661-bitteres-aus-bitterfeld-das-umweltdesaster-der-ddr-und-seine-lehren/.

185   Fink / Kurz, "Umweltdesaster DDR": https://www.insm-oekonomenblog.
       de/22661-bitteres-aus-bitterfeld-das-umweltdesaster-der-ddr-und-seine-lehren/.

186 Fink / Kurz, "Umweltdesaster DDR": https://www.insm-oekonomenblog. de/22661-bitteres-aus-bitterfeld-das-umweltdesaster-der-ddr-und-seine-lehren/.

187 Knabe, *Klimakiller DDR*.

188 Knabe, *Klimakiller DDR*.

189 Knabe, *Klimakiller DDR*.

190 Williams, "Environmentalists are Dead Wrong."

191 Follett, "7 Enviro Predictions."

192 McAfee, 59.

193 McAfee, 80.

194 Cf. Kreutzer / Land.

195 Hayek, *The Road to Serfdom*, 36.

196 *Wall Street Journal*, "World's Dumbest Energy Policy": https://www.wsj.com/ articles/worlds-dumbest-energy-policy-11548807424.

197 Gates, 87. Deaths per Terawatt hour (TWh). The figures provided here cover the entire process of generating energy, from extracting fuels to turning them into electricity, as well as the environmental problems they cause, such as air pollution.

198 Graw, 184–185.

199 Gates, 85.

200 Gates, 190.

201 Ruprecht / Lüdecke, 58. 15,895 deaths have been confirmed, and 2,539 people are still missing, Cf. Graw, *Die Grünen*, 180.

202 Shellenberger, 152 et seq.

203 Rupprecht / Lüdecke, 46 et seq., 126.

204 Kerry Emanuel, quoted in Shellenberger, 155.

205 Shellenberger, 164 et seq.

206 Weimer, "Sogar Bill Gates . . ."

207 Gates, 87.

208 Neubauer, *Ökofimmel*.

209 Polleit, *Antikapitalist*, 48.

210 Polleit, *Antikapitalist*, 48.

211 Polleit, *Antikapitalist*, 49. Italicized in the original.

212 Polleit, *Antikapitalist*, 49 et seq.

213 Marx, *Capital*, Volume I, 763.

214 Marx, *Grundrisse*, 748.

215 Marx, *Grundrisse*, 748.

216   Marx, *Grundrisse*, 749.

217   Rosdolsky, 382.

218   Zitelmann, "Left-Wing Intellectuals," https://www.forbes.com/sites/rainerzitel-
       mann/2020/03/30/left-wing-intellectuals-are-thrilled-corona-and-dreams-of-the-end-
       of-capitalism/?sh=130c65d57420.

219   Davies, "The Last Global Crisis."

220   Schumpeter, *Theory*, 218.

221   Schumpeter, *Theory*, 219.

222   Schumpeter, *Theory*, 220–221.

223   Schumpeter, *Theory*, 223.

224   Schumpeter, *Theory*, 218.

225   Schumpeter, *Capitalism*, 82.

226   Schumpeter, *Capitalism*, 83. Italicized in the original.

227   Schumpeter, *Capitalism*, 84.

228   Schumpeter, quoted in Hagemann, 444.

229   Sombart, *Der moderne*, III.2., 585.

230   Sombart, *Der moderne*, III.2., 586.

231   Schumpeter, quoted in Hagemann, 444. Hagemann does, however, go on to write
       that Schumpeter partially relativized this thesis in response to the Great Depression.

232   DiLorenzo, 156 et seq.

233   DiLorenzo, 181.

234   DiLorenzo, 183.

235   Voegeli, 47.

236   White, quoted in Tempelman, 5.

237   Krugman, quoted in Ravier / Lewin, 57.

238   Greenspan, 233. Greenspan's thesis is preposterous. The homeownership rate is not
       an indicator of prosperity, as Greenspan then and many policymakers to this day
       believe or claim. The homeownership rate is almost consistently much higher in poor
       countries than in rich countries. Affluent Switzerland has one of the world's lowest
       homeownership rates, at 41 percent, which compares with 88 percent in Nepal and
       96 percent in Romania, for example.

239   Norberg, *Financial Fiasco*, 30.

240   Woods, *Meltdown*, 15.

241   Norberg, *Financial Fiasco*, 33.

242   Norberg, *Financial Fiasco*, 41.

243 Norberg, *Financial Fiasco*, 42.

244 Brook / Watkins, 53.

245 Brook / Watkins, 54–55.

246 Norberg, *Financial Fiasco*, 132.

247 Collier / Kay, 14.

248 Collier / Kay, 69.

249 Bookstaber, 257.

250 Zitelmann, *The Power of Capitalism*, 146.

251 Baader, *Geldsozialismus*, 94.

252 Consider, for example, the two oil crises of the 1970s, both of which were triggered by the then-powerful Organization of the Petroleum Exporting Countries (OPEC). The price of oil, adjusted for inflation, rose by about 1,000 percent in less than ten years as a result of these policies, precipitating severe recessions in many countries, including developing countries, and causing a sharp increase in unemployment and inflation.

253 Ziegler, 45.

254 Ziegler, 56.

255 Ziegler, 119.

256 Ziegler, 97–98.

257 Krugman, "Oligarchy."

258 Stiglitz, xix.

259 Chomsky, *Requiem*, 140.

260 Walter, Marg, 19.

261 Walter / Marg, 129.

262 Walter / Marg, 130.

263 Walter / Marg, 130.

264 Boldt, "Top-Manager Reitzle."

265 Page / Gilens, *Democracy*, 100.

266 Page / Gilens, *Democracy*, 101.

267 Page / Gilens, *Democracy*, 104.

268 Edwards / Bourne, 22.

269 https://www.n-tv.de/politik/Wahlkampf-kostet-Bloomberg-eine-Milliarde-article21727861.html.

270   Kamarck, "If money can't buy you votes," https://www.brookings.edu/blog/fixgov/2020/03/05/if-money-cant-buy-you-votes-what-can-it-buy-lessons-from-michael-bloombergs-2020-run/

271   Edwards / Bourne, 25.

272   Page / Gilens, *Democracy*, 98.

273   Page / Gilens, *Democracy*, 96.

274   Smith, B.A. "The Power of Money."

275   Bartels, 98, table on page 100.

276   Page / Bartels / Seawright, "Democracy and the Policy Preferences of Wealthy Americans": https://faculty.wcas.northwestern.edu/~jnd260/cab/CAB2012%20-%20Page1.pdf.

277   Page / Bartels / Seawright, "Democracy and the Policy Preferences of Wealthy Americans," 53. Admittedly, it is difficult to conduct studies that involve the very wealthy. I conducted a study of 45 wealthy Germans, all of whom had net assets worth more than €10 million—most were worth between €30 million and €1 billion. But my study was a qualitative study rather than a quantitative one. Cf. Zitelmann, *The Wealth Elite*.

278   Page / Bartels / Seawright, 68.

279   Page / Bartels / Seawright, 54.

280   York, "Does Rising . . . ?," unnumbered.

281   York, "Does Rising . . . ?," unnumbered.

282   Edwards / Bourne, 24.

283   Gilens, *Affluence*, 57, 53.

284   Gilens, *Affluence*, 121.

285   Gilens, *Affluence*, 117.

286   Niskanen / Moore, unnumbered.

287   Niskanen / Moore, unnumbered.

288   Stiglitz, 92.

289   Gilens, *Affluence*, 238.

290   *Frankfurter Allgemeine Zeitung*, "Doppelt so viele Unternehmer," https://www.faz.net/aktuell/wirtschaft/deutlich-mehr-unternehmer-im-bundestag-15225816.html.

291   https://www.welt.de/wirtschaft/article234058756/Bundestagswahl-Das-sind-die-Berufe-der-neuen-Abgeordneten.html.

292   Page / Gilens, 106.

293   Page / Gilens, 106.

294   Transparency International, *Corruption Perceptions Index 2020*, https://www.transparency.org/en/cpi/2020/index/nzl, https://www.transparency.org/en/cpi/2020/index/rus, https://infographics.economist.com/2016/Cronyism_index/.

295   Meltzer, 13.

296   Transparency International, *Corruption Perceptions Index (CPI) 2020*: https://www.transparency.org/en/cpi/2020/index/nzl and Miller / Kim / Roberts, *2021 Index of Economic Freedom.*

297   Mises, *Socialism*, 344.

298   Mises, *Socialism*, 351.

299   Lenin, *Imperialism*, 23.

300   Lenin, *Imperialism*, 28.

301   Smith, *Wealth*, 119.

302   McKenzie / Lee, 5.

303   Lenin, *Imperialism*, 23.

304   Lenin, *Imperialism*, 36.

305   Lenin, *Imperialism*, 37.

306   Lenin, *Imperialism*, 40.

307   Plumpe, *Das kalte Herz*, 233.

308   Plumpe, *Das kalte Herz*, 626.

309   Schumpeter, *Capitalism*, 99.

310   Schumpeter, *Capitalism*, 99.

311   Schumpeter, *Capitalism*, 99.

312   Schumpeter, *Capitalism*, 100.

313   Schumpeter, *Capitalism*, 102.

314   McKenzie / Lee, 23. Italicized in the original.

315   McKenzie / Lee, xxi. Italicized in the original.

316   McKenzie / Lee, xx.

317   McKenzie / Lee, xix.

318   Schumpeter, *Capitalism*, 83. Italicized in the original.

319   Marx, *Capital Volume III*, 644.

320   McKenzie / Lee, 222. Italicized in the original.

321   Pettinger, "Advantages and Disadvantages of Monopolies."

322   McKenzie / Lee, 51–52.

323   Petit, 121 et seq.

324   Cowen, 102–103.

325   Petit, 130–131.

326   Petit, 116.

327   Petit, 53 et seq.

328   Stone, *Amazon Unbound*.

329   Petit, 257.

330   Auer / Petit, 112.

331   Auer / Petit, 117.

332   Auer / Petit, 119.

333   Auer / Petit, 119.

334   Friedman, *Capitalism*, 104.

335   Cowen, 84.

336   Bourne, "Is This Time Different?" https://www.cato.org/sites/cato.org/
       files/2019–09/Is%20This%20Time%20Different%3F.pdf

337   Bourne, "Is This Time Different?," 7.

338   Bourne, "Is This Time Different?," 8.

339   Bourne, "Is This Time Different?," 9.

340   Bourne, "Is This Time Different?," 15.

341   Heuer, "Die Einfalt der Vervielfältiger."

342   https://de.statista.com/statistik/daten/studie/181577/umfrage/
       marktanteile-der-hersteller-von-druckern-weltweit-seit-2009/.

343   Bourne, "Is This Time Different?," 9.

344   Liebowitz / Margolis, 267.

345   Gassmann, "Ewige Allmacht."

346   Friedman, *Capitalism*, 31.

347   Cowen, 84.

348   Quoted in Meissner, 23.

349   Quoted in Meissner, 24.

350   Quoted in Meissner, 31.

351   Quoted in Meissner, 91.

352   Meissner, 49.

353   DiLorenzo, 153.

354   Rhonheimer, "Ludwig Erhards Konzept," 101.

355   Kirzner, *Competition and Entrepreneurship*, 22–23.

356   Rand, *America's Persecuted Minority*, 52–53. Italicized in the original.

357   Rand, *America's Persecuted Minority*, 55. Italicized in the original.

358   Rand, *America's Persecuted Minority*, 57.

359   Zhang, *Ideas for China's Future*, 54.

360   Zhang, *Ideas for China's future*, 55.

361   Erhard, 174 et seq. Other instances cited by Rhonheimer, "Ludwig Erhards Konzept," 91 et seq.

362   DiLorenzo, 154. Italicized in the original.

363   Cowen, 89.

364   Cowen, 95.

365   Cowen, 115.

366   Simon, 22–23.

367   Net return on sales is operating income (before tax) divided by revenues (excluding sales tax).

368   Simon, 41.

369   Simon, 1.

370   Simon, 88–89.

371   Simon, 88.

372   Simon, 88.

373   Simon, v.

374   Collier / Kay, 7.

375   Collier / Kay, 14.

376   Collier, *The Future of Capitalism*, 92.

377   Collier, *The Future of Capitalism*, 92. Italicized in the original.

378   Collier, *The Future of Capitalism*, 93.

379   Collier, *The Future of Capitalism*, 93–94.

380   Rand, *The Virtue of Selfishness*, 5. Italicized in the original.

381   Backhaus, 11.

382   Hitler, speech from November 13, 1930, quoted in Zitelmann, *Hitler's National Socialism*, 301

383   Arendt, 79.

384   Arendt, 79.

385   Smith, A., 71.

386   Mises, *Socialism*, 357.

387   Sowell, *Intellectuals and Society*, 67–68. Italicized in the original.

388   Simon, *True Profit*, 69.

389   For more details, cf. Zitelmann, *The Wealth Elite*, Chapter 12, 232–242.

390   Cf. also Courtois et al., *The Black Book of Communism.*

391   Plumpe, *Das kalte Herz,* 640.

392   Charles / Ritz, 108–109.

393   Sloterdijk, 44.

394   Sloterdijk, 44.

395   Schwarzenegger, quoted in Andrews, 66.

396   Schwarzenegger, quoted in Lommel, 25.

397   Pope Francis, encyclical Laudato si', paragraph 203.

398   Pope Francis, encyclical Laudato si', paragraph 193.

399   Ziegler, 60–61.

400   Ziegler, 62.

401   Ziegler, 64.

402   Scruton, 47.

403   Marcuse, 12. Italicized in the original.

404   Marcuse, 23.

405   Quoted in Hecken, 127.

406   Pasolini, "A Challenge to Television Network Executives" in *Corriere della Sera,* December 9, 1973.

407   Pasolini, "Don't Be Afraid to Have a Heart" in *Corriere della Sera,* March 10, 1975.

408   Pasolini, "Open Letter to Italo Calvino: From Pasolini—What I Feel Nostalgic About" in *Paese Sera,* July 8, 1974.

409   Plumpe, *Das kalte Herz,* 78.

410   Plumpe, *Das kalte Herz,* 79.

411   Plumpe, *Das kalte Herz,* 213–214.

412   Plumpe, *Das kalte Herz,* 214.

413   Carey, 93.

414   Carey, 94.

415   Carey, 105.

416   Carey, 106.

417   Briesen, 12 et seq.

418   König, *Konsumgesellschaft,* 272.

419   Korn, quoted in Hecken, 37.

420   Korn, quoted in Hecken, 50.

421   Korn, quoted in Hecken, 49.

422   Lundberg, 70–71.

423   Lundberg, 68.

424   Galbraith, 1.

425   Lawson.

426   Lawson.

427   Hecken, 215.

428   Bourdieu and Wacquant, quoted in Hartmann, *The Sociology of Elites*, 115.

429   Bourdieu, 513 et seq.

430   Ludwig Erhard, quoted in Hecken, 113.

431   Tillessen, 43.

432   Tillessen, 30.

433   Tillessen, 56.

434   Tillessen, 57.

435   Tillessen, 40.

436   Tillessen, 40.

437   Tillessen, 25.

438   Tillessen, 34.

439   Tillessen, 34.

440   Tillessen, 36.

441   Tillessen, 61.

442   Tillessen, 61.

443   Tillessen, 70.

444   Tillessen, 86.

445   Tillessen, 186.

446   Tillessen, 183.

447   Hecken, 148.

448   Hecken, 221.

449   Trentmann, 4.

450   Trentmann, 8.

451   Schoeck, *Envy*, 260.

452   Trentmann, 678.

453   Trentmann, 680.

454   Trentmann, 686.

455   Ziegler, 62. Italicized in the original.

456   Ziegler, 63. Italicized in the original.

457   Ziegler, 64.

458   Chomsky, *Requiem*, 125–126. Italicized in the original.

459   Chomsky, *Reqiuem*, 127.

460   Heller, 18.

461   Kürschner, 5.

462   Heller, 12.

463   Samland, 13–18.

464   Schultz, quoted in Ries / Ries, 129.

465   Shapiro / Hitsch / Tuchman, 3.

466   Koch, "Wirkt Werbung überhaupt nicht?"

467   Schoeck, *Ungleichheit*, 176.

468   https://en.wikipedia.org/wiki/Obsolescence.

469   https://en.wikipedia.org/wiki/Planned_obsolescence

470   Cf. Prakash et al.: https://www.umweltbundesamt.de/publikationen/
      einfluss-der-nutzungsdauer-von-produkten-auf-ihre-1

471   König, *Wegwerfgesellschaft*, 119.

472   König, *Wegwerfgesellschaft*, 118–119.

473   Snow, *Ford*, 299.

474   König, *Wegwerfgesellschaft*, 119.

475   Quoted in König, *Wegwerfgesellschaft*, 121.

476   Easterlin, "Does Economic Growth Improve the Human Lot?"; Regarding a pre-
      sentation of the research and the controversy surrounding Easterlin., Cf. Weimann /
      Knabe / Schön, 17 et seq.

477   Cf. Kahneman / Deaton, "High Income Improves"

478   Cf. Killingsworth: https://www.pnas.org/content/118/4/e2016976118

479   Pinker, 157.

480   Pinker, 157.

481   Rosling, 114.

482   Gartzke, "Capitalist Peace," 168. Footnote 10 with several references.

483   Weede, "Frieden durch Kapitalismus," 67.

484   Weede, "Frieden durch Kapitalismus," 68.

485   Gartzke, "Capitalist Peace," 180.

486   Gartzke, "Capitalist Peace," 180.

487   Gartzke / Hewitt, 129.

488   Gartzke / Hewitt, 138.

489   Cobden, 71.

490   Gartzke, "Capitalist Peace," 170.

491   Weede, "The Expansion," 821. Italicized in the original.

492   Cf. Schneider / Gleditsch / Petter, 3 et seq., which distinguishes between four main arguments.

493   Weede, "The Expansion," 824.

494   Weede, "The Expansion," 823.

495   Weede, "The Capitalist Peace and the Rise of China," 159.

496   Jäger / Beckmann, 9–146.

497   Quoted in Ferguson, *The Pity of War*, 31.

498   Lenin, *Imperialism*, 9–10.

499   Plumpe, "Logik des modernen Krieges," 327.

500   Plumpe, "Logik des modernen Krieges," 328.

501   Plumpe, "Logik des modernen Krieges," 332. Italicized in the original.

502   Plumpe, "Logik des modernen Krieges," 343.

503   Ferguson, *The Pity of War*, 32.

504   Steed, quoted in Ferguson, *The Pity of War*, 32.

505   Ferguson, *The Pity of War*, 33.

506   Ferguson, *The Pity of War*, 438.

507   Gartzke, "The Capitalist Peace," 171.

508   Figures last revised in 2015, accessed on May 25, 2021: http://commons.ch/deutsch/wp-content/uploads/Top-15-L%C3%A4nder-nach-Gesamtwert-aller-ihrer-Rohstoffvorkommen.pdf

509   Figures to 2019, accessed on May 25, 2021: https://data.worldbank.org/

510   Figures to 2019, accessed on May 25, 2021: https://data.worldbank.org/

511   Accessed on May 25, 2021: https://www.tradinghours.com/markets/sgx

512   Accessed on May 25, 2021: https://www.tradinghours.com/markets/moex

513   Miller / Kim / Roberts, Heritage Foundation *Index of Economic Freedom 2021*.

514   Figures to 2019, accessed on May 25, 2021: https://data.worldbank.org/

515   Figures to 2019, accessed on May 25, 2021: https://data.worldbank.org/

516   Collier, *The Bottom Billion*, 38 et seq.

517   Cf. Zitelmann, "Zur Begründung des 'Lebensraum'-Motivs in Hitlers Weltanschauung."

518   Cf. Bukharin, 94, Luxemburg, 430.

519   Quoted in Zitelmann, *Hitler's National Socialism*, 372–373.

520   Quoted in Zitelmann, *Hitler's National Socialism*, 375.

521   Quoted in Zitelmann, *Hitler's National Socialism*, 346.

522   Quoted in Zitelmann, *Hitler's National Socialism*, 301.

523   Quoted in Zitelmann, *Hitler's National Socialism*, 301. Italicized in the original.

524   Zitelmann, *Hitler's National Socialism*, 301. Italicized in the original.

525   Cf. Zitelmann, *Hitler's National Socialism*, 513–514.

526   Quoted in Zitelmann, *Hitler's National Socialism*, 303.

527   Piketty, *Capital in the Twenty-First Century*, 498.

528   Piketty, *Capital in the Twenty-First Century*, 498.

529   Piketty, *Capital in the Twenty-First Century*, 499.

530   Piketty, *Capital in the Twenty-First Century*, 499–500.

531   Piketty, *Capital in the Twenty-First Century*, 500.

532   Piketty, *Capital in the Twenty-First Century*, 504–505.

533   Piketty, *Capital in the Twenty-First Century*, 507; Scheidel, 195.

534   Piketty, *Capital in the Twenty-First Century*, 507.

535   Banken, 390.

536   Scheidel, 136.

537   Scheidel, 115.

538   Scheidel, 115.

539   Scheidel, 119.

540   Scheidel, 119.

541   Scheidel, 6.

542   Scheidel, 134.

543   Scheidel, 133.

544   Scheidel, 154.

545   Scheidel, 165.

546   Bierling, 107.

547   https://www.amazon.de/Spiegel-Nr-2003–13–01–2003-Blut/dp/B00RI3V8QC

548   https://en.wikipedia.org/wiki/Fahrenheit_9/11

549   Chomsky, interviewed by Christopher Cramer: https://www.pressenza.com/2018/05/noam-chomsky-discusses-iraq/

550   Bierling, 109.

551   Bierling, 110.

552   Bierling, 109.

553   Bierling, 110.

554   Mueller, 180.

555   Mueller, 172.

556   Mueller, 172.

557   Plumpe, *Das kalte Herz*, 171.

558   Plumpe, *Das kalte Herz*, 171.

559   Horkheimer, "The Jews and Europe," 78.

560   Dimitrov, quoted in McDermott, 131.

561   Hitler, quoted in Zitelmann, *Hitler's National Socialism*, 336. ("Cutting coupons" refers to collecting interest payments on government and corporate bonds. At that time, this required the presentation of a paper coupon to a bank, which was cut off the bond certificate).

562   Hitler, August 7, 1920, quoted in Zitelmann, *Hitler's National Socialism*, 311.

563   Hitler, August 25, 1920, quoted in Zitelmann, *Hitler's National Socialism*, 312.

564   Quoted in Zitelmann, *Hitler's National Socialism*, 311.

565   Turner, *German Big Business*, 127.

566   Turner, *German Big Business*, 66.

567   Turner, *German Big Business*, 127.

568   Turner, *German Big Business*, 135.

569   Pollock, 442.

570   For many years, Reusch was chairman of the board of the Gutehoffnungshütte conglomerate, a major coal-and-steel company based in the Ruhr region.

571   Turner, *Big German Business*, 98.

572   Turner, *Big German Business*, 181.

573   Zitelmann, *Hitler's National Socialism*, 425–428.

574   Turner, *Big German Business*, 342.

575   Turner, "Emil Kirdorf and the Nazi Party," 324–344.

576   Turner, "Big Business and the Rise of Hitler," 64.

577   Turner, "Big Business and the Rise of Hitler," 66.

578   Falter, 74.

579   Falter, 29.

580   Turner, *Big German Business*, 118.

581   Turner, *Big German Business*, 253.

582   Turner, "Big Business and the Rise of Hitler," 63.

583   Turner, *Big German Business*, 254.

584 Franz von Papen was Hitler's immediate predecessor as chancellor in 1933. Von Papen was a member of the "Center," a Catholic party, until 1932, and thereafter served as an independent.

585 Turner, *Big German Business*, 345.

586 Falter, 81.

587 Falter, 76.

588 Falter, 187.

589 Aly, 16.

590 Quoted in Aly, 16.

591 Aly, 30.

592 Aly, 52.

593 Aly, 51.

594 Aly, 60–63. (The real state inflation tax was a tax on the gross rent, not on rental profit.)

595 Aly, 65.

596 Aly, 62.

597 Aly, 65.

598 Banken, 347 et seq.

599 Banken, 424.

600 Banken, 439.

601 Banken, 426.

602 Hitler, quoted in Zitelmann, *Hitler's National Socialism*, 323. Italicized in the original.

603 Hitler, September 14, 1936, quoted in Zitelmann, *Hitler's National Socialism*, 208.

604 Cf. Zitelmann, *Hitler's National Socialism*, 325.

605 Pollock, 441.

606 Pollock, 444.

607 Pollock, 453.

608 Barkai, 203.

609 Petzina, 162.

610 Petzina, 159 et seq.

611 Aly, 6.

612 Aly, 4.

613 Aly, 323.

614 Götz, 56.

615   Schmiechen-Ackermann, 36.

616   Cf. the quotes in Chapter 9 of this book (War).

617   Hitler, August 26, 1942, quoted in Zitelmann, *Hitler's National Socialism*, 513.

618   Hitler, July 22, 1942, quoted in Zitelmann, *Hitler's National Socialism*, 302.

619   Hitler, March 24, 1942, Cf. Zitelmann, *Hitler's National Socialism*, 329.

620   Quoted in Zitelmann, *Hitler's National Socialism*, 332.

621   Quoted in Zitelmann, *Hitler's National Socialism*, 332–333.

622   Hayek, *Constitution*, 112.

623   Hayek, *Constitution*, 118.

624   The Gospel of John, New International Version, 18:36

625   Schroeder, "The Dismal Fate."

626   Henri Barbusse, quoted in Hollander, 132.

627   Shaw, 112.

628   Alfred Kerr, quoted in Ryklin, 74.

629   Ryklin, 139.

630   Quoted in Easton, "Labour's manifesto."

631   Lenin, "How to Organize Competition?" in *Selected Works Vol. II*, 259–260.

632   Lenin, "How to Organize Competition?" in *Selected Works Vol. II*, 262.

633   Baberowski, *Scorched Earth*, 39.

634   Baberowski, *Scorched Earth*, 36.

635   Baberowski, *Scorched Earth*, 36.

636   Wemheuer, 45.

637   Lenin, "The Famine," in *Selected Works Vol. II*, 345.

638   Koenen, 805.

639   Koenen, 805.

640   Quoted in Courtois, 8.

641   Quoted in Werth, 107.

642   Quoted in Werth, 105.

643   Quoted in Werth, 105.

644   Quoted in Werth, 102.

645   Quoted in Werth, 75–76.

646   Wemheuer, 45.

647   Koenen, 813.

648   Werth, 114.

649   Koenen, 814.

650 Lenin, "The New Economic Policy and the Tasks of the Political Education Departments" in V. I. Lenin *Collected Works, Vol. 33*, 63.

651 Lenin, "The New Economic Policy and the Tasks of the Political Education Departments" in V. I. Lenin *Collected Works, Vol. 33*, 63–64.

652 Lenin, "The New Economic Policy and the Tasks of the Political Education Departments" in V. I. Lenin *Collected Works, Vol. 33*, 64.

653 Baberowski, *Scorched Earth*, 68.

654 Altrichter, 53–54.

655 Werth, 123, Wemheuer, 59.

656 Altrichter, 54.

657 Stalin, "The Seventh Enlarged Plenum of the E.C.C.I." in Stalin, *Works, Vol. 9*, 37.

658 Baberowski, *Scorched Earth*, 78.

659 Baberowski, *Scorched Earth*, 76.

660 Commission of the Central Committee of the Communist Party of the Soviet Union, *History of the Communist Party of the Soviet Union (Bolsheviks)*, 305. Italicized in the original.

661 Stalin, quoted in *History of the Communist Party of the Soviet Union (Bolsheviks)*, 305.

662 Stalin, "Political Report of the Central Committee to the Sixteenth Congress of the C.P.S.U.(B.)," Stalin *Works, Vol. 12*, 297.

663 Stalin, "Political Report of the Central Committee to the Sixteenth Congress of the C.P.S.U.(B.)," Stalin, *Works, Vol. 12*, 344.

664 Baberowski, *Scorched Earth*, 149. Italicized in the original.

665 Wemheuer, 67.

666 Wemheuer, 69.

667 Werth, 162.

668 *History of the Communist Party of the Soviet Union (Bolsheviks)*, 307. Italicized in the original.

669 *History of the Communist Party of the Soviet Union (Bolsheviks)*, 308.

670 Duranty, quoted in Hollander, *From Benito*, 124.

671 Waldo Frank, quoted in Niemietz, *Socialism*, 69.

672 Altrichter, 84.

673 Werth, 167, 155.

674 Werth, 204.

675 Werth, 206.

676 Werth, 213.

677   Baberowski, *Der Rote Terror*, 116.

678   Baberowski, *Scorched Earth*, 98.

679   Stalin, "Political Report of the Central Committee to the Sixteenth Congress of the
      C.P.S.U.(B.)," Stalin, *Works, Vol. 12*, 317.

680   Altrichter, 88.

681   Dikötter, *Cultural Revolution*, 5.

682   Dikötter, *Cultural Revolution*, 5.

683   Dikötter, *Cultural Revolution*, 9–10.

684   Dikötter, *Cultural Revolution*, 19.

685   Dikötter, *Cultural Revolution*, 22.

686   Dikötter, *Cultural Revolution*, 24.

687   Dikötter, *Cultural Revolution*, xi.

688   Dikötter, *Cultural Revolution*, 62.

689   Dikötter, *Cultural Revolution*, 73.

690   Dikötter, *Cultural Revolution*, 75.

691   Dikötter, *Cultural Revolution*, 75.

692   Dikötter, *Cultural Revolution*, 78.

693   Dikötter, *Cultural Revolution*, 87, 92.

694   Dikötter, *Cultural Revolution*, 92.

695   Chang / Halliday, 403.

696   Chang / Halliday, 405.

697   Chang / Halliday, 405–406.

698   Chang / Halliday, 407.

699   Chang / Halliday, 408.

700   Dikötter, *Cultural Revolution*, 100.

701   Dikötter, *Cultural Revolution*, 96.

702   Mao, *Quotations*, 11–12.

703   Dikötter, *Cultural Revolution*, 119.

704   Dikötter, *Cultural Revolution*, 164.

705   Dikötter, *Cultural Revolution*, 174.

706   Dikötter, *Cultural Revolution*, 176.

707   Dikötter, *Cultural Revolution*, 176.

708   Dikötter, *Cultural Revolution*, 278.

709   Dikötter, *Cultural Revolution*, 274.

710   Dikötter, *Cultural Revolution*, 225.

1NOTES

711   Dikötter, *Cultural Revolution*, 277.

712   Dikötter, *Cultural Revolution*, 284.

713   Zhang, *Ideas for China's Future*, 142.

714   Zhang, *Ideas for China's Future*, 143.

715   Zhang, *Ideas for China's Future*, 144.

716   Simone de Beauvoir, quoted in Niemietz, *Socialism*, 106.

717   Jean-Paul Sartre, quoted in Niemietz, *Socialism*, 108.

718   Cf. Sobanet.

719   For figures on the victims of the Khmer Rouge, cf. Bultmann, *Kambodscha,* 160–161.

720   Bultmann, *Kambodscha*, 95.

721   Bultmann, *Kambodscha*, 72.

722   Bultmann, *Kambodscha*, 72 et seq.

723   Bultmann, *Kambodscha*, 88.

724   Quoted in Chandler et al., 107.

725   Bultmann, *Kambodscha*, 92.

726   Bultmann, *Kambodscha*, 138.

727   Bultmann, *Kambodscha*, 138.

728   Bultmann, *Kambodscha*, 97.

729   Bultmann, *Kambodscha*, 99.

730   Margolin, "Cambodia," 585.

731   Margolin, "Cambodia," 597.

732   Margolin, "Cambodia," 628.

733   Quoted in Bultmann, *Kambodscha*, 137.

734   Quoted in Bultmann, *Kambodscha*, 120.

735   Bultmann, *Kambodscha*, 121.

736   Bultmann, *Kambodscha*, 148.

737   Bultmann, *Kambodscha*, 141.

738   Bultmann, *Kambodscha*, 8.

739   Bultmann, *Kambodscha*, 144.

740   Bultmann, *Kambodscha*, 126.

741   Stuart-Fox, quoted in Bultmann, *Inside Cambodian Insurgency*, 98.

742   Margolin, "Cambodia," 627.

743   Margolin, "Cambodia," 616.

744   Cf. numerous statements from Chomsky in Hollander, *From Benito*, 201.

402

745   Žižek, quoted in Gray, *The Violent Visions*, https://www.nybooks.com/
      articles/2012/07/12/violent-visions-slavoj-zizek/.

746   Žižek, quoted in Hollander, *From Benito*, 29.

747   Hollander, *From Benito*, 30.

748   Quoted in Gallegos, 80.

749   Quoted in Clark, 60.

750   Proclamation by the Central Committee of the German Communist Party, June 11,
      1945: https://ghdi.ghi-dc.org/docpage.cfm?docpage_id=3252&language=english.

751   Engels, in Karl Marx and Frederick Engels, *Selected Works, Vol. III*, 147. Italicized in
      the original.

752   Engels, "Socialism: Utopian and Scientific," in Karl Marx and Frederick Engels,
      Selected Works, Vol. III, 151.

753   Lenin, "State and Revolution," 456.

754   Marx, in Karl Marx and Frederick Engels, *Selected Works. Vol. III*, 26. Italicized in
      the original.

755   Lenin, "State and Revolution," 464. Italicized in the original.

756   *Documents of the 22nd Congress of the Communist Party of the Soviet Union*, October
      1961, 319.

757   *Documents of the 22nd Congress of the Communist Party of the Soviet Union*, October
      1961, 512. Italicized in the original.

758   *Documents of the 22nd Congress of the Communist Party of the Soviet Union*, October
      1961, 537. Italicized in the original.

759   *Documents of the 22nd Congress of the Communist Party of the Soviet Union*, October
      1961, 542.

760   *Documents of the 22nd Congress of the Communist Party of the Soviet Union*, October
      1961, 539.

761   *Documents of the 22nd Congress of the Communist Party of the Soviet Union*, October
      1961, 540.

762   Marx, in Karl Marx and Frederick Engels, *Selected Works, Vol. III*, 19.

763   https://de.statista.com/themen/5811/kalter-krieg/#dossierSummary__chapter2

764   https://www.jec.senate.gov/reports/97th%20Congress/Consumption%20in%20
      the%20USSR%20-%20An%20International%20Comparison%20(1058).pdf.

765   Aslund, *Russia's Crony Capitalism*.

766   In 2020.

767   Marx, *A Contribution*, 20–21.

768   Niemietz, *Socialism*, 48–49.

769   Niemietz, *Socialism*, 47.

770   *Edelman Trust Barometer 2020*.

771   Nocun / Lamberty, 18.

772   Imhoff / Bruder.

773   Imhoff / Bruder.

774   Zitelmann, *The Rich in Public Opinion*.

775   This comparison of statement rankings, i.e., how often a statement made it into the top 5 or whether it was the most frequent, second most frequent, etc., provides a more meaningful comparison than simply comparing percentages between individual countries. For example, in Great Britain, the percentage of respondents who declined to offer an opinion or selected "none of these" is generally very high in many surveys (for this item: 27 percent); in some countries (France, Sweden, Japan), it is 11 to 14 percent, whereas in Germany it is only 2 percent, and in South Korea, 5 percent. This makes any comparison of the percentages with which respondents agreed with the individual statements somewhat problematic.

776   One outlier is Poland, where those on the far left of the political spectrum (1.30) and those on the moderate left (a very high 1.91) are both pro-capitalist. We initially suspected that this was an error in the data. Upon reexamination, we confirmed there was no error.

777   For Poland, please see the preceding footnote.

778   The differences in the three countries, Greece, Turkey and Portugal, were so small to nonexistent that they have been omitted from the two graphs 14.5 and 14.6.

779   For more detail, cf. Zitelmann, "Attitudes to wealth in seven countries: The Social Envy Coefficient and the Rich Sentiment Index": https://onlinelibrary.wiley.com/doi/10.1111/ecaf.12468

780   Hayek, *Intellectuals*, 9, Lenin, "What is to be Done?", 347 et seq.

781   Marx, *Capital. Volume I*, 152.

782   Voegelin, *The Political Religions*.

783   Marx, "Toward a Critique of Hegel's Philosophy of Right." Italicized in the original.

784   Aron, *The Opium of the Intellectuals*, 318.

785   *The Times*, quoted in Braunthal, 135.

786   Koestler, 15.

787   Koestler, 18.

788   Koestler even argued that envy did not play a role in his strong dislike of the rich.

789   Almond, 201.

790   Reich, xxv.

791   Duhm, *Angst*, 8.

792   Duhm, *Warenstruktur*, 19.

793   Duhm, *Angst*, 151.

794   Aron, quoted in Rabbinbach, 114.

795   Biss, 3.

796   Biss, 43.

797   Neffe, *Marx*, 354.

798   Cf. Neffe, *Marx*, 354.

799   Neffe, *Marx*, 464.

800   Greenwald, "Is Capitalism Dying?"

801   For a critical perspective, cf. Rhonheimer, *Politik für den Menschen*, 225 et seq.

802   Benjamin, 259.

803   Plumpe, *Das kalte Herz*, 640.

804   Neffe, *Marx*, 19.

805   Douthat, "Marx rises again," in *The New York Times*, April 19, 2014.

806   Žižek, "The Will Not to Know," https://thephilosophicalsalon.com/the-will-not-to-know/.

807   Žižek, "The Will Not to Know," https://thephilosophicalsalon.com/the-will-not-to-know/.

808   Žižek, *A Left that Dares*, 6.

809   Žižek, *A Left that Dares*, 15.

810   Žižek, *A Left that Dares*, 12.

811   Žižek, *A Left that Dares*, 5.

812   Žižek, *A Left that Dares*, 14.

813   Ziegler, 121.

814   Ziegler, 116.

815   Ziegler, 126.

816   Ziegler, 36.

817   Hayek, *Constitution*, 113.

818   Hayek, "Kinds of Rationalism," 85.

819   Piketty, *Capital in the Twenty-First Century*, 31.

820   Piketty, *Capital and Ideology*, 989.

821   Piketty, *Capital and Ideology*, 983.

822   Piketty, *Capital and Ideology*, 982.

823   Piketty, *Capital and Ideology*, 985.

824   Piketty, *Capital and Ideology*, 977, footnote 17.

825   Piketty, *Capital and Ideology*, 982.

826   Piketty, *Capital and Ideology*, 988.

827   Piketty, *Capital and Ideology*, 974.

828   Piketty, *Capital and Ideology*, 975.

829   Piketty, *Capital and Ideology*, 994.

830   Piketty, *Capital and Ideology*, 994. A milder form of exit tax already exists in
      Germany and many other Western countries. In Germany, it is primarily regulated
      in Section 6 of the Foreign Tax Act (AStG).

831   Plumpe, *Das kalte Herz*, 2019.

832   For the Western media reports on this campaign, see e.g.
      https://www.thetimes.co.uk/article/xi-promises-third-distribution-of-wealth-in-
      billionaire-crackdown-c9xxl5hsc; https://www.reuters.com/world/china/
      what-is-chinas-common-prosperity-drive-why-does-it-matter-2021-09-02/

833   Cf. Hayek, *The Fatal Conceit*.

834   Zitelmann, *The Power of Capitalism*, vi-vii.

835   Cf. Hayek, *The Fatal Conceit*.

836   Cf. Zhang, "A paradigmatic change."

837   Cf. Kirzner.

838   Cf. Beinhocker, 9-10.

839   Cf. Hayek, *The Fatal Conceit*.

840   Klein, 2.

841   Zhang, *The Logic of the Market*, 9–12.

842   Cf. Zhang, *The Origin of the Capitalist Firm*.

843   Cf. Mises, *The Anti-Capitalistic Mentality*, Chapter 1.

844   Hayek, *The Constitution of Liberty*, 917–98.

845   The marketization scores for both nation-level and provincial level are compiled by
      Beijing National Institute of Economic Research. The development of private sector
      is one of the five components of the index and is strongly correlated with the other
      four components (including government-market relation, development of product
      market, development of factor market, and development of intermediary organiza-
      tions and legal environment). The marketization score in 2016 ranges between 1.29

(the lowest) and 15.98 (the highest), which is the most recent data available. See Wang et al (2017) for technical definitions and calculation of the marketization score.

846   Zitelmann, *The Power of Capitalism*, 129.

847   "Poverty headcount ratio at $1.90 a day (2011 PPP) (% of population) | Data": *data. worldbank.org*. Retrieved June 1, 2019.

848   Cf. Sowell, *Intellectuals and Society*, Chapter 3 and *Discrimination and Disparities*, Chapter 4.

849   Cf. Piketty, *Capital in the Twenty-First Century*.

850   Schumpeter, *Theory of Economic Development*, 156

851   Cf. Khor / Pencavel.

852   Cf. Zhang, *The Logic of the Market*, Chapter 13.

853   Marketization is related to economic freedom. The literature on the relationship between economic freedom and inequality across countries has found mixed results. Bennett and Nikolaev (2017) find that the results of previous studies are sensitive to the choice of country sample, time period and/or inequality measure used. The detailed discussion of this literature is beyond the theme of the current paper.

854   Cf. Rubin, "Folk Economics" and Zitelmann, *The Rich in Public Opinion*, Chapter 5.

855   Cf. Schoeck, Chapter 5.

856   Zhang, "The China model view is factually false."

857   Zhang, "China's future growth depends on innovation entrepreneurs."

BIBLIOGRAPHY

Almond, Gabriel A. *The Appeals of Communism*. Princeton: Princeton University Press, 1954.

Altrichter, Helmut. *Kleine Geschichte der Sowjetunion 1917–1991*. Munich: Verlag C.H. Beck, 3rd Edition, 2007.

Aly, Götz. *Hitler's Beneficiaries. Plunder, Racial War, and the Nazi Welfare State*, New York: Metropolitan Books, 2006.

Andreä, Johann Valentin. "Christianopolis. An Ideal State of the Seventeenth Century" in Held, Felix Emil (translator), *Johann Valentin Andreae's Christianopolis. An Ideal State of the Seventeenth Century*. Illinois: University of Illinois, 1914.

Andrews, Nigel. *True Myths: The Life and Times of Arnold Schwarzenegger*. New York: Bloomsbury, 2003.

Antweiler, Werner, Brian R. Copeland, and M. Scott Taylor. "Is Free Trade Good for the Environment?" Working Paper 6707. Cambridge: National Bureau of Economic Research, August 1998. https://www.jstor.org/stable/2677817

Arendt, Hannah. *On Revolution*. London: Penguin Books, 1977.

Arnott, Robert, William Bernstein, and Lillian Wu. "The Rich Get Poorer: The Myth of Dynastic Wealth." *Cato Journal, Vol. 35, No. 3, Fall 2015.*

Aron, Raymond. *Opium for Intellectuals*. New York: W.W. Norton & Company, Inc., 1962.

Aslund, Anders. *Russia's Crony Capitalism. The Path from Market Economy to Kleptocracy.* New Haven and London: Yale University Press, 2019.

Auer, Dirk, and Nicolas Petit. "Two Systems of Belief About Monopoly: The Press vs. Antitrust." *Cato Journal Vol. 39, No. 1 (Winter 2019)*, 99–132. https://www.cato.org/sites/cato.org/files/serials/files/cato-journal/2019/2/cj-v39n1–7.pdf.

Ausubel, Jesse H. "The Return of Nature. How Technology Liberates the Environment." *The Breakthrough Journal,* May 12, 2015. https://thebreakthrough.org/journal/issue-5/the-return-of-nature.

Baader, Roland. *Geld, Gold und Gottspieler. Am Vorabend der nächsten Wirtschaftskrise.* Gräfelfing: Resch Verlag, 2004.

Baader, Roland. *Geldsozialismus. Die wirklichen Ursachen der neuen globalen Depression.* Gräfelfing: Resch Verlag, 2010.

Baberowski, Jörg. *Der rote Terror. Die Geschichte des Stalinismus, Third Edition.* Frankfurt am Main: Fischer Taschenbuch, 2014.

Baberowski, Jörg. *Scorched Earth: Stalin's Reign of Terror.* Stanford: Yale University Press, 2016.

Backhaus, Julien. *Ego. Gewinner sind gute Egoisten.* Munich: Finanzbuch Verlag, 2020.

Banken, Ralf. *Hitlers Steuerstaat. Die Steuerpolitik im Dritten Reich.* Berlin and Boston: De Gruyter, 2018.

Barkai, Avraham. *Nazi Economics: Ideology, Theory, and Policy.* New Haven: Yale University Press, 1990.

Bartels, Larry M. *Unequal Democracy. The Political Economy of the New Gilded Age, Second Edition.* Princeton and Oxford: Russel Sage Foundation New York, Princeton University Press, 2016.

Beinhocker, William Oliver. *The Origin of Wealth: Evolution, Complexity and Radical Remaking of Economics*. Boston: Harvard Business School Press, 2006.

Beleites, Michael. *Dicke Luft: Zwischen Ruß und Revolte. Die unabhängige Umweltbewegung in der DDR*. Leipzig: Evangelische Verlagsanstalt, 2016.

Benjamin, Walter. "Capitalism as Religion." In *The Frankfurt School on Religion. Key Writings by the Major Thinkers*. Edited by Eduardo Mendieta. New York and London: Routledge, 2005, 259–262.

Bernstein, William J., and Grover Gardner. *The Birth of Plenty (Vol. 165)*. New York: McGraw-Hill, 2004.

Bierling, Stephan. *Geschichte des Irakkrieges. Der Sturz Saddams und Amerikas Albtraum im Mittleren Osten*, Verlag C.H. Beck, Munich, 2010.

Biss, Eula. *Having and Being Had*. New York: Riverhead Books, 2020.

Boldt, Klaus. "Top-Manager Reitzle wirft Bundesregierung bei Corona-Politik Versagen vor." *Die Welt*, April 3, 2021. https://www.welt.de/wirtschaft/article229695277/Corona-Politik-Wolfgang-Reitzle-uebt-scharfe-Kritik-an-Bundesregierung.html

Bookstaber, Richard. *A Demon of Our Own Design: Markets, Hedge Funds, and the Perils of Financial Innovation*. Hoboken: John Wiley & Sons, Inc., 2007.

Bourdieu, Pierre. *Distinction: A Social Critique of the Judgement of Taste*. Abingdon: Routledge, 2010.

Bourne, Ryan. "Is This Time Different? Schumpeter, the Tech Giants, and Monopoly Fatalism." *Cato Institute, Policy Analysis, June 17, 2019, No. 872.*

Braudel, Fernand. *Civilization and Capitalism, 15th–18th Century, Vol. I: The Structures of Everyday Life.* London: William Collins Sons & Co Ltd, 1985.

Braunthal, Julius. *History of the International. Volume 1: 1864–1914.* New York: Frederick A. Praeger Publishers, 1967.

Brecht, Bertolt. "Alfabet" (1934) in *The Collected Poems of Bertolt Brecht, translated by David Constantine and Tom Kuhn.* New York: Liveright, 2018.

Briesen, Detlef. *Warenhaus, Massenkonsum und Sozialmoral. Zur Geschichte der Konsumkritik im 20. Jahrhundert.* Frankfurt: Campus Verlag, 2001.

Brook, Yaron, and Don Watkins. *Free Market Revolution. How Ayn Rand's Ideas Can End Big Government.* Santa Ana: Ayn Rand Institute, Palgrave Macmillan, 2012.

Bukharin, Nikolai. *Imperialism and World Economy.* London: Martin Lawrence Limited, 1929.

Bultmann, Daniel. *Inside Cambodian Insurgency. A Sociological Perspective on Civil Wars and Conflict.* London and New York: Taylor & Francis, 2016.

Bultmann, Daniel. *Kambodscha unter den Roten Khmer. Die Erschaffung des perfekten Sozialisten.* Paderborn: Brill | Schöningh, 2017.

Campanella, Tommaso. *The City of the Sun* in *Ideal Commonwealths: Comprising More's Utopia, Bacon's New Atlantis, Campanella's City of the Sun, and Harrington's Oceans.* New York: The Colonial Press, 1901.

Carey, John. *The Intellectuals and the Masses. Pride and Prejudice Among the Literary Intelligentsia, 1880–1939.* New York: St. Martin's Press, 1993.

Chandler, David P. et.al. *Pol Pot Plans the Future: Confidential Leadership Documents from Democratic Kampuchea, 1976–1977.* New Haven: Yale University South East Asia Studies, 1988.

Chang, Jung, and Jon Halliday. *Mao: The Unknown Story.* London: Jonathan Cape, 2005.

Charles, Ray, and David Ritz. *Brother Ray. Ray Charles' Own Story.* Cambridge: Da Capo Press, 2004.

Chomsky, Noam. *Requiem for the American Dream. The 10 Principles of Concentration of Wealth & Power.* New York: Seven Stories Press, 2015.

Chomsky, Noam. Interviewed by Christopher Cramer for *Pressenza International Press Agency*, May 1, 2018. https://www.pressenza.com/2018/05/noam-chomsky-discusses-iraq/.

Clark, A.C. *The Revolutionary Has No Clothes. Hugo Chávez's Bolivarian Farce.* New York and London: Encounter Books, 2009.

Cobden, Richard. "On the Total and Immediate Repeal of the Corn Laws." *The National Review, Volume X, September to February 1887–8.* London: 1888.

Collier, Paul. *The Bottom Billion: Why the Poorest Countries Are Failing and What Can Be Done about It.* Oxford: Oxford University Press, 2007.

Collier, Paul. *The Future of Capitalism: Facing the New Anxieties.* New York: Penguin, 2019.

Collier, Paul, and John Kay. *Greed Is Dead: Politics After Individualism.* London: Allan Lane, 2020.

Commission of the Central Committee of the Communist Party of the Soviet Union. *History of the Communist Party of the Soviet Union (Bolsheviks): Short Course.* Moscow: Foreign Languages Publishing House, 1945.

Courtois, Stéphane, Nicolas Werth, Jean-Louis Panné, Andrzej Paczkowski, Karel Bartosek, and Jean-Louis Margolin. *The Black Book of Communism. Crimes, Terror, Repression.* Cambridge: Harvard University Press, 1999.

Cowen, Tyler. *Big Business. A Love Letter to an American Anti-Hero.* New York: St. Martin's Press, 2019.

Davies, William. "The Last Global Crisis didn't Change the World. But This One Could." *The Guardian*, March 24, 2020. https://www.theguardian.com/commentisfree/2020/mar/24/coronavirus-crisis-change-world-financial-global-capitalism

Deaton, Angus. *The Great Escape. Health, Wealth, and the Origins of Inequality.* Princeton and Oxford: Princeton University Press, 2013.

Delsol, Jean-Philippe, Nicolas Lecaussin, and Emmanuel Martin (eds.). *Anti-Piketty: Capital for the 21st Century.* Washington: Cato Institute, 2017.

Delsol, Jean-Philippe. "The Great Process of Equalization of Conditions." In Delsol, Jean-Philippe, Nicolas Lecaussin, and Emmanuel Martin (eds.). *Anti-Piketty: Capital for the 21st Century.* Washington: Cato Institute, 2017, 5–18.

Dikötter, Frank. *Mao's Great Famine: The History of China's Most Devastating Catastrophe, 1958–62.* London and New York: Bloomsbury, 2010.

Dikötter, Frank. *The Cultural Revolution. A People's History. 1962–1976.* London, Oxford, New Delhi and Sydney: Bloomsbury Press, 2017.

DiLorenzo, Thomas J. *How Capitalism Saved America. The Untold History of Our Country, from the Pilgrims to the Present.* New York: Crown Forum, 2004.

Dimitrov, Georgi. "The Fascist Offensive and the Tasks of the Communist International in the Struggle of the Working Class against Fascism." Main report delivered at the Seventh World Congress of the Communist International on August 2, 1935. https://www.marxists.org/reference/archive/dimitrov/works/1935/08_02.htm.

Documents of the 22nd Congress of the Communist Party of the Soviet Union, October 17–31, 1961. Moscow: Foreign Language Publishing House, 1961.

Douthat, Ross. "Marx Rises Again." In *The New York Times*, April 19, 2014.

Duhm, Dieter, *Angst im Kapitalismus. Zweiter Versuch der gesellschaftlichen Begründung zwischenmenschlicher Angst in der kapitalistischen Warengesellschaft.* Lampertheim: Verlag Kübler KG, 11th Edition, 1975.

Duhm, Dieter. *Warenstruktur und zerstörte Zwischenmenschlichkeit. Zur politökonomischen Begründung der psychischen Situation des Individuums im Kapitalismus.* Cologne: Verlag Rolf Horst, 1975.

Easterlin, Richard A., "Does economic growth improve the human lot? Some empirical evidence." In David, Paul A., and Melvin Reder (eds.). *Nations and Households in Economic Growth.* Palo Alto: Stanford University Press, 1974, 90–125.

Easton, George. "Labour's manifesto is more Keynesian than Marxist." In *The New Statesman*, June 2015.

Edelman. *Edelman Trust Barometer 2020.* https://www.edelman.com/trust/2020-trust-barometer.

Edwards, Chris, and Ryan Bourne. "Exploring Wealth Inequality." *Cato Institute Policy Analysis, November 5, 2019, No. 881.* https://www.cato.org/sites/cato.org/files/2020–01/pa-881-updated-2.pdf

Engels, Frederick. *The Condition of the Working Class in England 1820–1895*. Oxford: Oxford University Press, 1999.

Engels, Frederick. "Socialism: Utopian and Scientific." In Marx, Karl and Frederick Engels. *Selected Works, Vol. III*. Moscow: Progress Publishers, 1970, 115–151.

Erhard, Ludwig. *Wohlstand für Alle*, 8th Edition. Düsseldorf: Econ Verlag, 1964.

Falter, Jürgen W. *Hitlers Parteigenossen. Die Mitglieder der NSDAP 1919–1945*. Frankfurt and New York: Campus Verlag, 2020.

Federal Government of the Federal Republic of Germany (Bundesregierung der Bundesrepublik Deutschland). *Lebenslagen in Deutschland. Der Sechste Armuts- und Reichtumsbericht der Bundesregierung, Kurzfassung*. May 2021.

Federal Foundation for Coming to Terms with the GDR's Past (Bundesstiftung Aufarbeitung), Bericht 1990: https://deutsche-einheit-1990.de/ministerien/muner/verschmutzung/.

Ferguson, Niall. *The Pity of War. Explaining World War I*. New York: Basic Books, 1999.

Feshbach, Murry, and Alfred Friendly Jr. *Ecocide in the USSR. Health and Nature Under Siege*. New York: Basic Books, 1992.

Fink, Alexander, and Kalle Kappner. "Globale Armut: Positive Entwicklung, negative Einschätzung." In de.irefeuropa.org. https://de.irefeurope.org/Diskussionsbeitrage/Artikel/article/Globale-Armut-Positive-Entwicklung-negative-Einschatzung.

Fink, Alexander, Alexander Mengden, and Fabian Kurz. "Umweltdesaster DDR: Bitteres aus Bitterfeld." *IREF*, August 16, 2019. https://de.irefeurope.org/Diskussionsbeitrage/Artikel/article/Umweltdesaster-DDR-Bitteres-aus-Bitterfeld.

Follett, Andrew. "7 Enviro Predictions From Earth Day 1970 That Were Just Dead Wrong." April 22, 2016. https://daily-caller.com/2016/04/22/7-enviro-predictions-from-earth-day-1970-that-were-just-dead-wrong/

Foster, George M. "The Anatomy of Envy: A Study in Symbolic Behavior." In *The University of Chicago Press Journals, Vol. 13, No. 2,* April 1972, 165–202.

Frankfurter Allgemeine Zeitung. "Doppelt so viele Unternehmer im neuen Bundestag." September 30, 2017. https://www.faz.net/aktuell/wirtschaft/deutlich-mehr-unternehmer-im-bundestag-15225816.html

Friedman, Milton. *Capitalism and Freedom.* Chicago: The University of Chicago Press, 1962.

Galbraith, John Kenneth. *The Affluent Society. Fortieth Anniversary Edition.* Boston: Houghton Mifflin Company, 1998.

Gallegos, Raúl. *Crude Nation. How Oil Riches Ruined Venezuela.* Dulles: Potomac Books, University of Nebraska Press, 2016.

Gartzke, Erik. "The Capitalist Peace." *American Journal of Political Science, Vol. 51, No. 1,* January 2007, 166–191. https://www.jstor.org/stable/4122913.

Gartzke, Erik, and Joseph Hewitt. "International Crises and the Capitalist Peace." *International Interactions, 36:2,* May 18, 2010, 115—45. https://www.tandfonline.com/doi/full/10.1080/03050621003784846.

Gassmann, Michael. "Ewige Allmacht? Plötzlich wankt Amazons Monopol." In *Die Welt,* February 6, 2021. https://www.welt.de/wirtschaft/plus225775833/D2C-Trend-Amazon-muss-um-sein-Monopol-fuerchten.html.

Gates, Bill. *How to Avoid a Climate Disaster. The Solutions We Have and the Breakthroughs We Need.* London: Allen Lane, 2021.

Gilens, Martin. *Affluence & Influence. Economic Inequality and Political Power in America.* New York, Princeton and Oxford: Russell Sage Foundation, Princeton University Press, 2012.

Götz, Norbert. "Die nationalsozialistische Volksgemeinschaft im synchronen und diachronen Vergleich." In Detlef Schmiechen-Ackermann (ed.). *"Volksgemeinschaft": Mythos, wirkungsmächtige soziale Verheißung oder soziale Realität im „Dritten Reich"? Zwischenbilanz einer kontroversen Debatte.* Paderborn: Ferdinand Schöningh Verlag, 2012, 55–68.

Graw, Ansgar. *Die Grünen an der Macht. Eine kritische Bilanz.* Munich: Finanzbuch Verlag, 2020.

Gray, John. "The Violent Visions of Slavoj Žižek." In *New York Review of Books,* July 12, 2012, 23. https://www.nybooks.com/articles/2012/07/12/violent-visions-slavoj-zizek/.

Greenspan, Alan. *The Age of Turbulence. Adventures in a New World.* New York: Penguin Books, 2007.

Greenwald, Igor. "Is Capitalism Dying?" in Forbes.com, January 7, 2013. https://www.forbes.com/sites/igorgreenwald/2013/01/07/is-capitalism-dying/?sh=4fe3cc432820.

Hagemann, Harald. "Schumpeter und die Weltwirtschaftskrise: Die Vorzüge schlechter Zeiten oder eine pathologische Depression?" In Frambach, Hans, Norbert Koubek, Heinz D. Kurz, and Reinhard Pfriem. *Schöpferische Zerstörung und der Wandel des Unternehmertums. Zur Aktualität von Joseph A. Schumpeter.* Marburg: Metropolis Verlag, 2019, 433–454.

Hartmann, Michael. *The Sociology of Elites.* New York: Routledge, 2006.

Hayek, F. A., and W. W. Bartley III (ed.). *The Fatal Conceit: The Errors of Socialism*. London: Routledge, 1988.

Hayek, Friedrich August von. *The Road to Serfdom*. Chicago: University of Chicago Press, 1944.

Hayek, Friedrich August von. "Kinds of Rationalism." In Hayek, Friedrich August von. *Studies in Philosophy, Politics, and Economics*. Chicago: The University Press of Chicago, 1967.

Hayek, Friedrich August von. *The Constitution of Liberty, The Definitive Edition*. London: The University of Chicago Press, 2011.

Hecken, Thomas. *Das Versagen der Intellektuellen. Eine Verteidigung des Konsums gegen seine deutschen Verächter*. Bielefeld: transcript Verlag, 2010.

Heller, Eva. *Wie Werbung wirkt: Theorien und Tatsachen*. Frankfurt: Fischer Taschenbuch Verlag, 1996.

Heuer, Steffan. "Die Einfalt der Vervielfältiger." *brand eins, Heft 2/2001*. https://www.brandeins.de/magazine/brand-eins-wirtschaftsmagazin/2001/organisation/die-einfalt-der-vervielfaeltiger.

Higginbotham, Adam. *Midnight in Chernobyl. The Untold Story of the World's Greatest Nuclear Disaster*. London: Corgi Books, 2019.

Hollander, Paul. *From Benito Mussolini to Hugo Chávez. Intellectuals and a Century of Political Hero Worship*. Cambridge: Cambridge University Press, 2016.

Horkheimer, Max. "The Jews and Europe." In Bronner, Steven Eric, and Douglas MacKay Kellner (eds.). *Critical Theory and Society: A Reader*. New York: Routledge, 1989.

Imhoff, Roland, and Martin Bruder. "Speaking (Un-)Truth to Power: Conspiracy Mentality as A Generalised Political Attitude." *European Journal of Personality 28(1)*, January 2014, 25–43.

Jäger, Thomas, and Rasmus Beckmann (eds.). *Handbuch Kriegstheorien.* Wiesbaden: VS Verlag für Sozialwissenschaften, Springer Fachmedien, 2011.

Jungbluth, Rüdiger. *Die Oetkers. Geschäfte und Geheimnisse der bekanntesten Wirtschaftsdynastie Deutschlands.* Frankfurt and New York: Bastei Lübbe Verlag, 2004.

Kahneman, Daniel, and Angus Deaton. "High income improves evaluation of life but not emotional well-being." *Proceedings of the National Academy of Sciences 107 (2010)*, 16489–16493.

Kamarck, Elaine. "If money can't buy you votes, what can it buy? Lessons from Michael Bloomberg's 2020 run." *Brookings,* March 5, 2020. https://www.brookings.edu/blog/fixgov/2020/03/05/if-money-cant-buy-you-votes-what-can-it-buy-lessons-from-michael-bloombergs-2020-.

Kelley, Jonathan, and M.D.R. Evans. "Societal inequality and individual subjective well-being: Results from 68 societies and over 200.000 individuals, 1981–2008." *Social Science Research 62 (2016)*, 1–23. https://pubmed.ncbi.nlm.nih.gov/28126092/.

Kepplinger, Hans Mathias. *Risikofallen und wie man sie vermeidet.* Cologne: Herbert von Halem Verlag, 2021.

Khor, N., and J. Pencavel, J. "Income mobility of individuals in China and the United States." *Economics of Transition, 14 (3)*, 2006, 417–458.

Killingsworth, Matthew, A. "Experienced well-being rises with income, even above $75,000 per year." *PNAS Vol. 118 No. 4 e2016976118,* January 26, 2021. https://doi.org/10.1073/pnas.2016976118

Kirzner, Israel M. *Competition and Entrepreneurship.* London and Chicago: The University of Chicago Press, 1973.

Klein, Naomi. *This Changes Everything: Capitalism vs. the Climate.* New York: Simon & Schuster, 2019.

Knabe, Hubertus. "Klimakiller DDR." September 19, 2019. https://hubertus-knabe.de/klimakiller-ddr/

Knight, Damien, and Harry McCreddie. "Understanding the 'facts' about top pay." In Shackleton, J.R. (ed.), *Top Dogs & Fat Cats. The Debate on High Pay.* London: Institute of Economic Affairs, 2019, 40–56.

Koch, Thomas. "Wirkt Werbung überhaupt nicht? Oder nur falsch?" *Wirtschaftswoche*, March 2, 2021. https://www.wiwo.de/unternehmen/dienstleister/werbesprech-wirkt-werbung-ueberhaupt-nicht-oder-nur-falsch/26962092.html.

Koenen, Gerd. *Die Farbe Rot. Ursprünge und Geschichte des Kommunismus.* Munich: Beck Verlag, 2017.

König, Wolfgang. *Kleine Geschichte der Konsumgesellschaft. Konsum als Lebensform der Moderne.* Stuttgart: Franz Steiner Verlag, 2008.

König, Wolfgang. *Geschichte der Wegwerfgesellschaft. Die Kehrseite des Konsums.* Stuttgart: Franz Steiner Verlag, 2019.

Koestler, Arthur. In Crossmann, Richard (ed.), *The God That Failed. Six Studies in Communism.* New York: Harper Collins, 1950.

Kreutzer, Ralf T., and Karl-Heinz Land. *Dematerialisierung. Die Neuverteilung der Welt in Zeiten des digitalen Darwinismus.* Cologne: Future Vision Press, 2015.

Krugman, Paul. "Oligarchy, American Style." *The New York Times*, November 3, 2011. https://www.nytimes.com/2011/11/04/opinion/oligarchy-american-style.html.

Kürschner, Jens. *Unterschwellige Werbung als Priming-Instrument. Eine Untersuchung.* Norderstedt: Grin Verlag, Books on Demand, 2012.

Lawson, Neal. "Do we want to shop or to be free? We'd better choose fast." *The Guardian*, August 2, 2009. https://www.theguardian.com/commentisfree/2009/aug/02/consumerism-society-shopping.

Lee, Felix. *Macht und Moderne. Chinas großer Reformer Deng Xiaoping. Die Biographie*. Berlin: Rotbuch Verlag, 2014.

Lenin, Vladimir Ilyich. *Imperialism, The Highest Stage of Capitalism*. Moscow: Foreign Languages Publishing House, 1950.

Lenin, Vladimir Ilyich. "How to Organize Competition?" In *Selected Works Vol. II*. Moscow: Foreign Language Publishing House, 1947, 256–263.

Lenin, Vladimir Ilyich. "The Famine (A Letter to the Workers of Petrograd)." In *Selected Works Vol. II*. Moscow: Foreign Language Publishing House, 1947, 345–351.

Lenin, Vladimir Ilyich. "What Is to Be Done?" In Lenin, Vladimir Ilyich. *Collected Works, Volume 5*. Moscow: Foreign Languages Publishing House, 1961, 347–531.

Lenin, Vladimir Ilyich. "The State and Revolution. The Marxist Theory of the State & the Tasks of the Proletariat in the Revolution." In Lenin, Vladimir Ilyich. *Collected Works, Volume 25, June–September 1917*, Moscow: Progress Publishers, 1964, 381–492.

Lenin, Vladimir Ilyich. "The New Economic Policy and the Tasks of the Political Education Departments." In *V. I. Lenin Collected Works, Vol. 33, August 1921—March 1923, 2nd English Edition*. Moscow: Progress Publishers, 1965, 60–79.

Liebowitz, Stan J., and Stephen E. Margolis. *Winners, Losers & Microsoft. Competition and Antitrust in High Technology*. Oakland: The Independent Institute, 1999.

Lindert, Peter H., and Jeffrey G Williamson. "English Workers' Living Standards During the Industrial Revolution: A New Look." In Mokyr, Joel (ed.), *The Economics of the Industrial Revolution*. New York: Routledge, 2011, 177–205.

Lommel, Cookie. *Schwarzenegger. A Man with a Plan*. Munich and Zürich: Heyne Verlag, 2004.

Lundberg, Ferdinand. *The Rich and the Super-Rich. A Study in the Power of Money Today*. New York: Lyle Stuart, 1968.

Luxemburg, Rosa. *Gesammelte Werke, Vol. 5: Ökonomische Schriften*. Berlin: Karl Dietz Verlag, 1975.

Maddison, Angus. *Contours of the World Economy 1–2030 AD, Essays in Macro-Economic History*. New York: Oxford University Press, 2007.

Maier, Hans. *Politische Religionen. Die totalitären Regime und das Christentum*. Freiburg, Basel and Vienna: Herder Verlag, 1995.

Maier, Hans (ed.). *Totalitarismus und Politische Religionen. Band III: Deutungsgeschichte und Theorie*. Paderborn: Schöningh Verlag, 2003.

Mao Zedong. *Quotations from Chairman Mao Zedong*. Peking: Foreign Languages Press, 1972.

Marcuse, Herbert. *One-Dimensional Man: Studies in the Ideology of Advanced Industrial Society*. Boston: Beacon Press, 1964.

Margolin, Jean-Louis. "Cambodia: The Country of Disconcerting Crimes" in Courtois, Stéphane, Nicolas Werth, Jean-Louis Panné, Andrzej Paczkowski, Karel Bartosek, and Jean-Louis Margolin. *The Black Book of Communism: Crimes, Terror, Repression*. Cambridge: Harvard University Press, 1999, 577–635.

Marx, Karl. *A Contribution to the Critique of Political Economy*. Moscow: Progress Publishers, 1970.

Marx, Karl. "Critique of the Gotha Programme." In Marx, Karl, and Frederick Engels. *Selected Works in Three Volumes. Vol. III*. Moscow: Progress Publishers, 1973, 9–30

Marx, Karl. *Grundrisse. Foundations of the Critique of Political Economy*. Harmondsworth: Penguin Books, 1973.

Marx, Karl. *Capital. Volume I: A Critique of Political Economy (Penguin Classics)*. London: Penguin Books, 1976.

Marx, Karl. *Capital. Volume III*. Moscow: Progress Publishers, 1965.

Marx, Karl. "Toward a Critique of Hegel's Philosophy of Right." In Lawrence, Hugh (ed.). *Karl Marx Selected Writings*. Indianapolis: Hackett Publishing Company, Inc., 1994, 27–39.

Marx, Karl, and Frederick Engels. *Selected Works in Three Volumes. Vol. III*. Moscow: Progress Publishers, 1973.

Mavragani, Amaryllis, Ioannis E. Nikolaou, and Konstantino P. Tsagarakis. "Open Economy, Institutional Quality, and Environmental Performance: A Macroeconomic Approach." *Sustainability 2016, 8, 601*, 1–13.

McAfee, Andrew. *The Surprising Story of How We Learned to Prosper Using Fewer Resources—and What Happens Next*. New York: Scribner, 2019.

McCloskey, Deirdre Nansen, and Art Carden. *Leave Me Alone and I'll Make You Rich. How the Bourgeois Deal Enriched the World*. London and Chicago: The University of Chicago Press, 2020.

McDermott, Kevin, and Jeremy Agnew. *The Comintern: A History of International Communism from Lenin to Stalin*. London: Macmillan Press, 1996.

McKenzie, Richard B., and Dwight R. Lee. *In Defense of Monopoly. How Market Power Fosters Creative Production*. Ann Arbor: The University of Michigan Press, 2008.

Medvedev, Zhores A. "Environmental Destruction of the Soviet Union." *The Ecologist, Vol. 20, No. 1*, January/February 1990.

Meissner, Gerd. *SAP—Die heimliche Software-Macht. Wie ein mittelständisches Unternehmen den Weltmarkt erobert*. Hamburg: Hoffmann und Campe, 1997.

Melcher, Jacqueline. "Kinderarbeit: Alarmierende Entwicklung laut UN-Studie." *FAZ*, June 10, 2021: https://www.faz.net/aktuell/wirtschaft/kinderarbeit-alarmierende-entwicklung-laut-un-studie-17380670.html.

Meltzer, Allan H. *Why Capitalism?* New York: Oxford University Press, NY, 2012.

Méndez, Daniel Fernández. "The Real Relationship Between Capitalism and the Environment." December 1, 2018: https://mises.org/ko/wire/real-relationship-between-capitalism-and-environment

Miller, Terry, Anthony B. Kim, and James M. Roberts. *2021 Index of Economic Freedom*. Washington: The Heritage Foundation, 2021.

Mises, Ludwig von. *Socialism: An Economic and Sociological Analysis*. Indianapolis: Liberty Fund, 1981.

Mises, Ludwig von. *The Anti-Capitalistic Mentality*. Indianapolis: Liberty Fund, 1972.

More, Thomas. *The Utopia of Thomas More*. New York: The MacMillan Company, 1912.

Moyo, Dambisa. *Dead Aid: Why Aid Is Not Working and How There Is A Better Way For Africa*. New York: Farrar, Straus and Giroux, 2009.

Mueller, John. "Capitalism, Peace, and the Historical Movement of Ideas." *International Interactions, 36*, 2010, 169–184.

Neffe, Jürgen. *Marx. Der Unvollendete*. Munich: C. Bertelsmann, 3rd Edition, 2017.

Neubauer, Alexander. *Ökofimmel. Wie wir versuchen, die Welt zu retten—und was wir damit anrichten*. Berlin: Deutsche Verlags Anstalt, 2012.

Neuhäuser, Christian. *Reichtum als moralisches Problem*. Berlin: Suhrkamp Verlag, 2018.

Niemietz, Kristian. "Der Mythos vom Globalisierungsverlierer. Armut im Westen." In Hoffmann, Christian, and Pierre Bessard (eds.). *Das Ende der Armut. Chancen einer globalen Marktwirtschaft*. Zürich: Liberales Institut Zürich, 2012, 141–159.

Niemietz, Kristian. *Socialism. The Failed Idea That Never Dies*. London: Institute of Economic Affairs, 2019.

Niskanen, William A., and Stephan Moore. "Supply-Side Tax Cuts and the Truth about the Reagan Economic Record." *Cato Policy Analysis*, October 22, 1996.

Nocun, Katharina, and Pia Lamberty. *Fake Facts. Wie Verschwörungstheorien unser Denken bestimmen*. Cologne: Bastei Lübbe, 2020.

Norberg, Johan. *In Defense of Global Capitalism*. Washington: CATO Institute, 2003.

Norberg, Johan. *Financial Fiasco. How America's Infatuation with Homeownership and Easy Money Created the Economic Crisis*. Washington: CATO Institute, 2009.

Norberg, Johan. *Progress: Ten Reasons to Look Forward to the Future*. London: Oneworld Publications, 2017.

Ogilvy, David. *Confessions of an Advertising Man*. London: Atheneum, 1963.

Oxford Poverty & Human Development Initiative, Global MPI 2021. http://hdr. undp.org/en/2021-MPI.

Page, Benjamin I., and Martin Gilens. *Democracy in America? What Has Gone Wrong and What We Can Do About It*. Chicago and London: The University of Chicago Press, 2017.

Page, Benjamin I., Larry M. Bartels, and Jason Seawright. "Democracy and the Policy Preferences of Wealthy Americans." *Cambridge University Press Perspectives on Politics, March 2013, Vol. 11, No. 1*. https://www.cambridge.org/core/journals/perspectives-on-politics/article/abs/democracy-and-the-policy-preferences-of-wealthy-americans/B783EEF6785FEE093198ABED8D2C3D61.

Palmer, Tom G. "Foreword." In Delsol, Jean-Philippe, Nicolas Lecaussin, and Emmanuel Martin (eds.). *Anti-Piketty: Capital for the 21st Century*. Washington: Cato Institute, 2017, xi–xvi.

Pasolini, Pier Paolo. "A Challenge to Television Network Executives." In *Corriere della Sera*, December 9, 1973.

Pasolini, Pier Paolo. "Open Letter to Italo Calvino: From Pasolini— What I Feel Nostalgic About." In *Paese Sera*, July 8, 1974.

Pasolini, Pier Paolo. "Don't Be Afraid to Have a Heart." In *Corriere della Sera*, March 10, 1975.

Petit, Nicolas. *Big Tech and The Digital Economy. The Moligopoly Scenario*. Oxford: Oxford University Press, 2020.

Pettinger, Tejvan. "Advantages and Disadvantages of Monopolies." *Economics Help*, October 4, 2020. https://www.economicshelp.org/blog/265/economics/are-monopolies-always-bad/.

Petzina, Dieter. *Autarkiepolitik im Dritten Reich. Der nationalsozialistische Vierjahresplan*. Stuttgart: dva, 1968.

Piketty, Thomas. *Capital in the Twenty-First Century*. Cambridge: The Belknap Press of Harvard University Press, 2014.

Piketty, Thomas. *Capital and Ideology*. Cambridge: The Belknap Press of Harvard University Press, 2020.

Pinker, Steven. *Enlightenment Now. The Case for Reason, Science, Humanism, and Progress*. New York: Viking, 2018.

Plumpe, Werner. *Das kalte Herz. Kapitalismus: Die Geschichte einer andauernden Revolution*. Berlin: Rowohlt Verlag, 2019.

Plumpe, Werner. "Die Logik des modernen Krieges und die Unternehmen: Überlegungen zum Ersten Weltkrieg." In *Jahrbuch für Wirtschaftsgeschichte 2015; 56 (2)*, 325–357.

Polleit, Thorsten. *Der Antikapitalist. Ein Weltverbesserer, der keiner ist*. Munich: Finanzbuch Verlag, 2020.

Pollock, Frederick. "Is National Socialism a New Order?" *Zeitschrift für Sozialforschung 9.3* (1941), 440–455.

Ponciano, Jonathan. "The Forbes 400 Self-Made Score: From Silver Spooners to Bootstrappers." *Forbes.com*, September 8, 2020. https://www.forbes.com/sites/jonathanponciano/2020/09/08/self-made-score/?sh=6a41b14d41e4.

Pope Francis. "Encyclical Letter Laudato Si' of the Holy Father Francis on Care for Our Common Home." 2015. https://www.vatican.va/content/francesco/en/encyclicals/documents/papa-francesco_20150524_enciclica-laudato-si.html.

Prakash, Siddharth, Günther Dehoust, Martin Gsell, Tobias Schleicher, and Rainer Stamminger. *Einfluss der Nutzungsdauer von Produkten auf ihre Umweltwirkung: Schaffung einer Informationsgrundlage und Entwicklung von Strategien gegen 'Obsoleszenz.'* Dessau-Roßlau: Umweltbundesamt, 2016. https://www.umweltbundesamt.de/publikationen/einfluss-der-nutzungsdauer-von-produkten-auf-ihre-1.

Rand, Ayn. *The Virtue of Selfishness. A New Concept of Egoism.* New York: Signet, 1964.

Rand, Ayn. "America's Persecuted Minority." In *Capitalism: The Unknown Ideal (50th Anniversary Edition). With Additional Articles by Nathaniel Branden, Alan Greenspan, and Robert Hessen.* New York: New American Library, 1967, 40–62

Ravier, Adrian, and Peter Lewin. "The Subprime Crisis." *Quarterly Journal of Austrian Economics, Vol. 15, No. 1,* 2012, 45–74.

Reich, Wilhelm. *Character Analysis. Third Enlarged Edition.* New York: Pocket Books, 1976.

Rhonheimer, Martin. "Ludwig Erhards Konzept der sozialen Marktwirtschaft und seine wettbewerbstheoretischen Grundlagen." *Zeitschrift für Marktwirtschaft und Ethik 5* (2), 2017, 83–106.

Rhonheimer, Martin. "Politik für den Menschen braucht weder 'christlich' noch 'sozial' zu sein." In Rausch, Bettina, and Simon Varga. *Christlich-soziale Signaturen. Grundlagen einer politischen Debatte.* Vienna: edition noir, 2020, 215–246.

Ries, Al, and Laura Ries. *The Fall of Advertising and the Rise of PR.* New York: HarperCollins, 2002.

Rosdolsky, Roman. *The Making of Marx's Capital.* London: Pluto Press, 1977.

Rosling, Hans, with Anna Rosling and Ola Rosling Rönnlund. *Factfulness: Ten Reasons We're Wrong About the World—And Why Things Are Better Than You Think.* London: Sceptre, 2018.

Rubin, Paul. "Folk Economics." *Southern Journal of Economics 70 (1),* 2003, 157–171.

Ruprecht, Götz, and Horst-Joachim Lüdecke. *Kernenergie. Der Weg in die Zukunft.* Jena: TvR Medienverlag, 2018.

Ryklin, Michail. *Kommunismus als Religion. Die Intellektuellen und die Oktoberrevolution.* Frankfurt and Leipzig: Verlag der Weltreligionen im Insel Verlag, 2008.

Sachweh, Patrick. *Deutungsmuster sozialer Ungleichheit. Wahrnehmung und Legitimation gesellschaftlicher Privilegierung und Benachteiligung,* also submitted as a doctoral dissertation at the University of Bremen 2009, Frankfurt and New York: Campus Verlag, 2009.

Samland, Bernd M. *Übersetzt du noch oder verstehst du schon? Werbe-Englisch für Anfänger.* Freiburg: Herder Verlag, 2011.

Scheidel, Walter. *The Great Leveler: Violence and the History of Inequality from the Stone Age to the Twenty-First Century.* Princeton: Princeton University Press, 2018.

Schmiechen-Ackermann, Detlef (ed.). *"Volksgemeinschaft": Mythos, wirkungsmächtige soziale Verheißung oder soziale Realität im "Dritten Reich"? Zwischenbilanz einer kontroversen Debatte.* Paderborn: Ferdinand Schöningh Verlag, 2012.

Schneider, Gerald, and Nils Petter Gleditsch (eds.). *Assessing the Capitalist Peace.* London and New York: Routledge, 2015.

Schoeck, Helmut. *Envy: A Theory of Social Behaviour.* Indianapolis: Liberty Fund, 1966.

Schoeck, Helmut. *Das Recht auf Ungleichheit.* Frankfurt and Berlin: Herbig, 3rd Expanded Edition, 1990.

Schroeder, Gertrude. "The Dismal Fate of Soviet-Type Economies: Mises was Right." *Cato Journal, Vol. 11, No. 1,* 1991, 13–25.

Schumpeter, Joseph. *The Theory of Economic Development.* Cambridge: Harvard University Press, 1949.

Schumpeter, Joseph. *Capitalism, Socialism and Democracy.* London and New York: Routledge, 2003.

Schumpeter, Joseph. "Unternehmerfunktion und Arbeiterinteresse." In Herzog, Lisa, and Axel Honneth (eds.). *Schumpeter, Joseph, Schriften zur Ökonomie und Soziologie*. Berlin: Suhrkamp Verlag, 2016, 222–240.

Scruton, Roger. *Fools, Frauds and Firebrands. Thinkers of the New Left*. London: Bloomsbury Continuum, 2019.

Shackleton, J.R. (ed.). *Top Dogs & Fat Cats. The Debate on High Pay*. London: Institute of Economic Affairs, 2019.

Shapiro, Bradley T., Günter J. Hitsch, and Anna E. Tuchmann. "TV Advertising Effectiveness and Profitability: Generalizable Results from 288 Brands." *Econometrica. Journal of the Econometric Society, Vol. 89, Issue 4*, July 2021, 1855–1879.

Shaw, George Bernard. *The Rationalization of Russia*. Bloomington: Indiana University Press, 1964.

Shellenberger, Michael. *Apocalypse Never. Why Environmental Alarmism Hurts Us All*. New York: Harper Collins, 2020.

Simon, Hermann. *True Profit! No Company Ever Went Broke Turning a Profit*. Bonn: Copernicus, 2021.

Sloterdijk, Peter. *You Must Change Your Life: On Anthropotechnics*. Cambridge: Polity Press, 2013.

Smith, Adam. *Wealth of Nations* (1776). In Smith, Adam. *The Wisdom of Adam Smith*. Indianapolis: Liberty Press, 1976.

Smith, Bradley A. "The Power of Money is Overrated." *The New York Times*, February 29, 2016. https://www.nytimes.com/roomfordebate/2016/02/25/does-money-really-matter-in-politics/the-power-of-politcal-money-is-overrated

Snow, Richard. *I Invented the Modern Age. The Rise of Henry Ford*. New York: Scribner, Reprint Edition, 2013.

Sobanet, Andrew. *Generation Stalin. French Writers, the Fatherland, and the Cult of Personality.* Bloomington: Indiana University Press, 2018.

Sombart, Werner. *Der moderne Kapitalismus. Band III. Das Wirtschaftsleben im Zeitalter des Hochkapitalismus, Zweiter Halbband.* Berlin: Duncker & Humblot, 1969.

Sowell, Thomas. *Intellectuals and Society. Revised and Enlarged Edition.* New York: Basic Books, 2011.

Sowell, Thomas. *Discrimination and Disparities.* New York: Basic Books, NY, 2019.

Stalin, Joseph V. "The Seventh Enlarged Plenum of the E.C.C.I." In Stalin, Joseph. *Works, Vol. 9, December 1926–July 1927.* Moscow: Foreign Languages Publishing House, 1954.

Stalin, Joseph V. "Political Report of the Central Committee to the Sixteenth Congress of the C.P.S.U.(B.) June 27, 1930." In Stalin, Joseph. *Works, Vol. 12, April 1929–June 1930.* Moscow: Foreign Languages Publishing House, 1954, 242–268.

Stiglitz, Joseph. *The Great Divide. Unequal Societies and What We Can Do About Them.* New York: W.W. Norton & Company, 2015.

Stone, Brad. *Amazon Unbound. Jeff Bezos and the Invention of a Global Empire.* New York: Simon & Schuster, 2021.

The Economist. "Our crony-capitalism index: Planet Plutocrat." *The Economist,* March 15, 2014. https://www.economist.com/international/2014/03/15/planet-plutocrat.

Tempelman, Jerry H. "Austrian Business Cycle Theory and the Global Financial Crisis: Confessions of a Mainstream Economist." *Quarterly Journal of Austrian Economics, Vol. 13, No. 1,* 2010, 3–15.

Tillessen, Carl. *Konsum. Warum wir kaufen, was wir nicht brauchen.* Hamburg: Harper Collins, 2020.

Transparency International. *Corruption Perceptions Index 2020.* https://www.transparency.org/en/cpi/2020/index/nzl.

Trentmann, Frank. *Empire of Things: How We Became a World of Consumers, from the Fifteenth Century to the Twenty-First.* London: Penguin, 2017.

Turner Jr., Henry Ashby. "Emil Kirdorf and the Nazi Party." *Central European History Vol. 1 (December 1, 1968),* 324–344.

Turner Jr., Henry Ashby. "Big Business and the Rise of Hitler." *The American Historical Review Vol. 75 No. 1 (October 1969),* 56–70.

Turner Jr., Henry Ashby. *German Big Business and the Rise of Hitler.* Oxford and New York: Oxford University Press, 1985.

UNICEF. "Kinderarbeit: Die 7 wichtigsten Fragen und Antworten." https://www.unicef.de/informieren/aktuelles/blog/kinderarbeit-fragen-und-antworten/166982.

Voegeli, William. *Never Enough: America's Limitless Welfare State.* New York: Encounter Books, 2010.

Voegelin, Eric. *The Political Religions* In Voegelin, Eric. *Modernity Without Restraint: The Political Religions, The New Science of Politics, and Science, Politics, and Gnosticism (Collected Works of Eric Voegelin, Volume 5).* Columbia and London: University of Missouri Press, 1999.

Wagenknecht, Sahra. *Die Selbstgerechten: Mein Gegenprogramm—für Gemeinsinn und Zusammenhalt.* Frankfurt: Campus Verlag, 2021.

Wall Street Journal. "World's Dumbest Energy Policy. After giving up nuclear power Germany now wants to abandon coal." *Wall Street Journal,* January 29, 2019. https://www.wsj.com/articles/worlds-dumbest-energy-policy-11548807424.

Walter, Franz, and Stine Marg (eds.). *Sprachlose Elite? Wie Unternehmer Politik und Gesellschaft sehen*. Reinbek bei Hamburg: BP-Gesellschaftsstudie, Rowohlt Verlag, 2015.

Wang, Xiaolu, Fan Gang, and Yu Jingwen. *Marketization Index of China's Provinces (Zhongguo fensheng shichanghua zhishu baogao)*. Beijing: Social Sciences, 2017.

Watkins, Don, and Yaron Brook. *Equal is Unfair. America's Misguided Fight Against Income Inequality*. New York: St. Martin's Press, 2016.

Weede, Erich. "Frieden durch Kapitalismus. Eine Ergänzung und Alternative zum demokratischen Frieden." *Internationale Politik IP*, July 2005, 65–73.

Weede, Erich. "Wirtschaftliche Freiheit. Hintergrundbedingungen, Auswirkungen und Gefährdungen." *Wirtschaftspolitische Blätter 3–4*, 2014, 443–455.

Weede, Erich. "The Capitalist Peace and the Rise of China: Establishing Global Harmony by Economic Interdependence." In Schneider, Gerald and Nils Petter Gleditsch (eds.). *Assessing the Capitalist Peace*. London and New York: Routledge, 2015, 158–165.

Weede, Erich. "The Expansion of Economic Freedom and the Capitalist Peace." In Thompson, William R. (ed.). *Oxford Encyclopedia for Empirical International Relations Theory*, 2018, 820–836. https://www.pollux-fid.de/r/cr-10.1093/acrefore/9780190228637.013.276.

Weimann, Joachim, Andreas Knabe, and Ronnie Schön. *Geld macht doch glücklich. Wo die ökonomische Glücksforschung irrt*. Stuttgart: Schäffer Poeschel Verlag, 2012.

Weimer, Wolfram. "Sogar Bill Gates setzt darauf: Warum Kernenergie wieder angesagt ist." *Focus.de*, July 23, 2021. https://www.focus.de/finanzen/nur-in-deutschland-gibt-es-kein-comeback-verblueffend-die-kernenergie-erlebt-ein-globales-comeback_id_13519732.html.

Wemheuer, Felix. *Der große Hunger. Hungersnöte unter Stalin und Mao*. Berlin: Rotbuch Verlag, 2012.

Wendling, Z.A., J.W. Emerson, A. de Sherbinin, D. C. Esty, et al. *Environmental Performance Index 2020. Global metrics for the environment: Ranking country performance on sustainability issues*. New Haven: Yale Center for Environmental Law & Policy, Yale University, 2020.

Werth, Nicolas. "A State against Its People: Violence, Repression, and Terror in the Soviet Union." In Courtois, Stéphane, Nicolas Werth, Jean-Louis Panné, Andrzej Paczkowski, Karel Bartosek, and Jean-Louis Margolin. *The Black Book of Communism. Crimes, Terror, Repression*. Cambridge: Harvard University Press, 1999, 33–268.

Williams, Walter E. "Environmentalists Are Dead Wrong." April 26, 2017. https://www.creators.com/read/walter-williams/04/17/environmentalists-are-dead-wrong.

Woods Jr., Thomas E. *Meltdown. A Free-Market Look at Why the Stock Market Collapsed, the Economy Tanked, and Government Bailouts Will Make Things Worse*. Washington: Regnery Publishing, 2009.

York, John. "Does Rising Income Inequality Threaten Democracy?" *Poverty and Inequality Report*. The Heritage Foundation, June 30, 2017. https://www.heritage.org/poverty-and-inequality/report/does-rising-income-inequality-threaten-democracy.

Zhang, Weiying. *The Logic of the Market. An Insider's View of Chinese Economic Reform*. Washington: Cato Institute, 2015.

Zhang, Weiying. "China's future growth depends on innovation entrepreneurs." *Journal of Chinese Economic and Business Studies, 15 (1)*, 2017, 19–40.

Zhang, Weiying. *The Origin of the Capitalist Firm: An Entrepreneurial/Contractual Theory of the Firm*. Singapore: Springer Nature, 2018.

Zhang, Weiying. "The China model view is factually false." *Journal of Chinese Economic and Business Studies 2019*. https://www.tandfonline.com/doi/abs/10.1080/14765284.2019.1663696.

Zhang, Weiying. *Ideas for China's Future*. Singapore: Palgrave Macmillan, 2020.

Zhang, Weiying. "A paradigmatic change is needed for understanding the real market." *China Economic Review Vol. 66 (C)*, 2021. https://www.researchgate.net/publication/349085342_A_paradigmatic_change_is_needed_for_understanding_the_real_market.

Zhang, Weiying. "Market economy and China's 'common prosperity' campaign." *Journal of Chinese Economic and Business Studies,* 2021, 1–15.

Ziegler, Jean. *Was ist so schlimm am Kapitalismus? Antworten auf die Fragen meiner Enkelin*. Munich: C. Bertelsmann, 2018.

Zitelmann, Rainer. "Zur Argumentationsstrategie linker Umweltpolitik." In *3 Aufsätze von einem Insider, der keine Lust mehr an dem Verein hat*. N.P., 1977. https://www.rainer-zitelmann.de/jahr-1977/.

Zitelmann, Rainer. "Zur Begründung des 'Lebensraum'-Motivs in Hitlers Weltanschauung." In Zitelmann, Rainer. *Hitler. Selbstverständnis eines Revolutionärs*. Reinbeck: Lau Verlag, 5th Expanded Edition, 2017, 557–576.

Zitelmann, Rainer. *The Wealth Elite. A Groundbreaking Study of the Psychology of the Super Rich*. London: LiD Publishing Limited, 2018.

Zitelmann, Rainer. *The Power of Capitalism*. London: LiD Publishing Limited, 2019.

Zitelmann, Rainer. "Left-Wing Intellectuals Are Thrilled: Corona And Dreams of the End of Capitalism." *Forbes.com*, March 30, 2020. https://www.forbes.com/sites/rainerzitelmann/2020/03/30/left-wing-intellectuals-are-thrilled-corona-and-dreams-of-the-end-of-capitalism/?sh=130c65d57420.

Zitelmann, Rainer. *The Rich in Public Opinion: What We Think About When We Think About Wealth*. Washington: Cato Institute, 2020.

Zitelmann, Rainer. *Hitler's National Socialism*. Oxford: Management Books 2000, 2022.

Žižek, Slavoj. *A Left that Dares Speak Its Name: 34 Untimely Interventions*. London: Polity Press, 2020.

Žižek, Slavoj. "The Will Not to Know." August 24, 2020. https://thephilosophicalsalon.com/the-will-not-to-know/.

INDEX OF PERSONS